American Magic and Dread

Penn Studies in Contemporary American Fiction

Emory Elliott, Series Editor

A complete list of books in the series is available from the publisher.

American Magic and Dread

Don DeLillo's Dialogue with Culture

Mark Osteen

PENN

University of Pennsylvania Press

Philadelphia

10 9 8 7 6 5 4 3 2 1

Published by
University of Pennsylvania Press
Philadelphia, Pennsylvania 19104-4011

Library of Congress Cataloging-in-Publication Data
Osteen, Mark.
American magic and dread : Don DeLillo's dialogue with culture / Mark Osteen.
p.   cm. — (Penn studies in contemporary American fiction)
Includes bibliographical references and index.
ISBN 0-8122-3551-7 (alk. paper)
1. DeLillo, Don—Criticism and interpretation.   2. Postmodernism (Literature)—
United States.   3. Culture in literature.   I. Title.   II. Series.
PS3554.E4425   Z76   2000
813'.54—dc21

                                                                00-024546

Contents

Introduction

Early in Don DeLillo's novel *White Noise*, Murray Jay Siskind, an eccentric colleague of protagonist Jack Gladney, enthusiastically announces his wish to immerse himself in "American magic and dread" (*WN* 19). Siskind's project involves reading such periodicals as *Ufologist Today* and *American Transvestite*, studying the television listings, and taking fact-finding trips to the supermarket and the shopping mall. Although DeLillo's attitude is a good deal more complex than Siskind's, he shares his character's fascination with these phenomena. Indeed, this study argues that DeLillo's work undertakes a dialogue with American cultural institutions and their discourses that dramatizes the dialectical relationship between, as well as the myriad shapes, meanings, and consequences of, American magic and dread. In DeLillo's work, the bombardment of consciousness by cinematic and consumer images; the fetishization of secrecy, violence, and celebrity; the fragmentation of the grand narratives of history, heroism, and high culture all combine to induce a paralyzing dread. His characters respond by seeking forms of magic—quasi-religious rituals, pseudodivine authorities, miraculous transformations—that they hope will help them rediscover sacredness and community.

In his fiction and in interviews, DeLillo emphasizes the power of language to shape identity and society. His fiction manifests that power: with his unsurpassed ear for dialogue, talent for aphorism, and astonishing ability to imitate the discourses of different cultural milieux, he stands as perhaps the most gifted stylist in American letters today. My subtitle is therefore meant to suggest the discursive and dramatic properties of DeLillo's work: a playwright as well as a novelist, he writes fictions that borrow from Renaissance masques, classical satires, Platonic dialogues and contemporary theater. If at times his alienated, narcissistic characters seem little more than voices exchanging witty miniature essays, their talk seldom yields genuine communication. Thus the major structural tropes in his fiction are figures of broken exchange and failed reciprocity: the cinematic cross-cut, the incomplete return, the unanswered question. Moreover, his protagonists repeatedly confront structures whose monolithic authority is represented by monologic discourse: the characters' alienation is manifest in linguistic tyrannies. Yet their elaborate strategies to evade or subvert those authorities usually lead only to exploitation by other, equally impacable forces, ideologies, or discourses.

Although unapologetically contemporary, DeLillo's work is much more intertextually embedded than has previously been recognized, quoting figures as diverse as Pythagoras, Saint Augustine, Georg Cantor, Lewis Carroll, Walter Benjamin, Sergei Eisenstein, Ernest Becker, Herman Kahn, Jean-Luc Godard, and Susan Sontag. Hence his dialogue with contemporary culture operates partly as a conversation with the high cultural icons and practices of the past; it is also a dialogue with history. But despite its manifold generic and intertextual sources, DeLillo's work repeatedly addresses a set of related themes: the tension between American individualism and the pull of public life; the prevalence of spectacle—movies, advertising, televised disasters, terrorist violence—and the consequent decay of historical consciousness; the complicity of late capitalist society with antisocial phenomena such as murder, war, pornography; the unfulfilled yearning for transcendence.

Dissecting the relationships between consumerism and religion, between individuals and collectives, DeLillo's work explores the myriad magical antidotes to postmodern dread. Recognizing that consumerism offers communion without real community, his characters seek solace in purgative rituals. DeLillo demonstrates how the pursuit of such perfect structures paves the way to fascism, and how the desire for purification may become just another image or commodity. But if the characters' magical remedies fail, their quests still provide glimpses of a potentially redemptive realm. Thus while DeLillo repeatedly critiques fetishistic oversimplifications, he sympathizes with his characters' inchoate mysticism, as his typically mysterious, even magical endings suggest. In short, DeLillo's work catalogues the varieties of American religious experience, repeatedly asking the question posed at the beginning of *Mao II*: "When the Old God leaves the world, what happens to all the unexpended faith?" (*M* 7).

But for me the most bracing feature of DeLillo's work is that he satirizes postmodern cultural forms not from some privileged position outside the culture, but from within those very forms. His works brilliantly mimic the argots of the same cultural forms—violent thrillers and conspiracy theories, pop music, advertising, science fiction, military tactics, film and television—that he anatomizes. Because of this strategy, DeLillo has been read both as a denouncer and as a defender of postmodern culture. I argue that neither description adequately fits. Instead, I show that his dialogue with contemporary cultural institutions respects their power but criticizes their dangerous consequences. Indeed, by adopting these discourses, DeLillo is able to concentrate his cultural critique more forcefully upon their dehumanizing potential.

Just as DeLillo borrows his narrative forms from the idioms of his chosen subject, so each chapter of this study draws its methodology from the discourses and institutions depicted in the text. My opening chapter thus assesses the influence of film on DeLillo's early fiction, particularly addressing his relationship with French *nouvelle vague* filmmaker Jean-Luc Godard. I suggest that DeLillo's early fictions employ cinematic allusions and techniques to reveal the harmful effects of cinematic representation on subjectivity. The early stories preview both the concerns of his later fiction and the frightening late twentieth-century world that those works depict. *Americana* more thoroughly introduces one of DeLillo's chief concerns— the power of images—through its fractured Bildungsroman narrative, in which protagonist David Bell withdraws from his glamorous TV job to liberate himself from his movie-fed self-image by making an autobiographical film. But the film, a pastiche of techniques adapted from his father's archive of television commercials and his own cinematic education, instead teaches him a "lesson in the effect of echoes": that perfect originality, or even an identity outside of the domain of images, is impossible—and perhaps undesirable. The early fiction thus depicts the multiply framed nature of postmodern subjectivity, while also posing a crucial question to radical writers and filmmakers: how can your work avoid becoming just another commodity?

My second chapter interprets his next two novels as essays in what Bell calls "the nature of diminishing existence" (*A* 277). In each, the protagonist pursues ascetic simplifications that end (or rather do not end) by enveloping him further in the oppressive institutions from which he has tried to escape. In *End Zone*, college football player Gary Harkness's obsession with nuclear holocaust epitomizes his quest for an "end zone" that nullifies all complexities of meaning. In this novel DeLillo traces our fascination with nuclear holocaust tales to an ascetic desire for violent purification; our fictions manifest a deep attraction to terminality. Revealing the religious and linguistic mutations that underlie the lure of apocalypse, DeLillo criticizes both the dreadful ideology of national security and the magical fictions that exploit it. In *Great Jones Street*, rock star Bucky Wunderlick abandons his group in mid-tour to seek a "moral form to master commerce": a pathway out of commodification and celebrity. But Bucky discovers (like *Mao II*'s Bill Gray) that even silence can be marketed to a ravenous public desperate for mythic figures. In both novels, DeLillo's formal innovations suggest his rejection of the characters' solutions: both texts employ unconventional plots that downplay narrative movement, thereby resisting consumption and the satisfaction of conventional closure.

A Menippean satire of Joycean complexity, *Ratner's Star*, treated in Chapter 3, traverses a wildly eccentric orbit apparently far removed from DeLillo's other fictions. Here he blends an imaginative history of mathematics with a symbiotic rewriting of Lewis Carroll's *Alice* books to produce a disturbing parable of the hazards of scientific arrogance. Through his intertextual dialogue with Carroll, DeLillo depicts the faith in mathematics as a dream that ineluctably leads to the looking-glass world of uncertainty and self-reflexivity that is twentieth-century hard science. Responding fearfully to this uncertainty, DeLillo's scientists resort to magic, seeking the age-old chimera of a purified scientific language. But instead they find an infinite regress of self-reference whose paradoxes are embodied in the novel's palindromic structure, and especially in its recurrent trope of the boomerang, which comes not only to represent human history and the shape of the cosmos, but also to imply that the power of science, like that of any other fiction, depends on our belief in it.

The next chapter pairs DeLillo's two most penetrating assessments of obsession. In the guise of a movie thriller, *Running Dog* mounts a complex consideration of the enduring appeal of fascism, of the power of film to mold subjectivity, and of the convergence of film and fascism in pornographic representation. In this postmodern grail-quest tale, the sacred icon is instead an unholy grail that symbolizes its pursuers' consumption by greed. Investigating the fascinations of fascism and exposing how such fascinations become commodities, *Running Dog* reveals the collusion of surveillance technologies and capitalism in the marketing of violent obsession. *The Names* blends domestic drama, quest tale and expatriate novel into a profound meditation on language as it traces protagonist James Axton's emerging awareness of his complicity with systems of terror. Adapting

Axton's son Tap's "counter-language," Ob, as his hidden structural principle, DeLillo charts Axton's development through a series of "ob" words. Hence Axton begins the novel as a self-deluded dilettante who denies domestic and political obligations and objectifies "Orientals." But his dreadful encounter with a murderous language cult obliterates his smug neutrality. Finally, after reading Tap's fictional rendering of the ritual of tongue-speaking, Axton achieves a new apprehension of language as a currency that counteracts the lethal literality of the Names cult. Dread gives way to magic: obliteration yields to oblation in the practice of glossolalia, which is presented as a gift that restores community and relieves the pressures of history.

In Chapter 5, "The Theology of Secrets," I suggest how the protagonists of *Players* and *Libra* invent secret lives as fantasies of subversion, only to find those secrets reappropriated by the institutions they meant to oppose. In *Players*, numbed urbanites Lyle and Pammy Wynant pursue separate forms of terrorism: Lyle gets involved with a violent cadre that aims to destroy "the idea of money"; Pammy becomes the third party in a destructive gay male relationship. DeLillo details how secrecy counteracts dread by forming a shield against the prying of institutions and the depersonalization of the postmodern economy. The protagonists' self-scripted narratives conclude, however, by reducing them to fungible counters in an elaborate game of hide-and-seek. Extending these themes, *Libra* investigates the "theology of secrets" (*L* 442) as a form of authorship, offering at once a plausible conspiracy theory about the assassination of President Kennedy and a critique of such conspiracy theories. The novel's divided plot lines — a sympathetic portrayal of Lee Oswald that converges with an account of rogue CIA agents scripting a story in which Oswald performs — embody the deep ruptures that DeLillo diagnoses not only in Oswald, but in the American soul. Oswald, the disaffected nobody, emerges as an American everyman; if the CIA is "the best organized church in the Christian world" (*L* 260), Oswald is its patsy and its prophet.

White Noise, DeLillo's mordant satire of consumerism, television, and the post-nuclear family, explores the places where Americans seek "peace of mind in a profit-oriented context" (*WN* 87), echoing the "panasonic" discourses of popular culture to deconstruct the dialectical relationship between magic and dread. An American book of the dead, the novel "channels" the discourses of popular culture both to dissect the religion of consumerism and to discover what DeLillo calls the "radiance in dailiness" ("Outsider" 63). Through Jack Gladney's haunted voice, DeLillo implies that the waves and radiation of mass culture may have made us materially richer but have stolen our spiritual property. Yet the novel's deadpan denouement suggests that if the waning of orthodox faith has left only tabloid tales of resurrection and the mantras of marketing, such "spells" may be necessary, consoling responses to a centerless world. In Chapter 6 I imitate DeLillo's method, punctuating analytical passages with phrases drawn from the novel's lists of brand names and litanies of electronic voices, in order to suggest that any effective analysis of the novel must acknowledge — along with DeLillo — its own imbrication in the discourses that it critiques.

Following upon *White Noise*'s comedy and *Libra*'s historical ambition, *Mao II*, discussed in Chapter 7, appears at first to be a more polished treatment of *Great Jones Street*'s themes. But the novel is important less for its themes than for the directness with which it addresses DeLillo's stance as an oppositional writer through the figure of novelist Bill Gray. After years of withdrawal from public life Gray has begun to realize, like Bucky Wunderlick, that his very reclusiveness only makes him more ripe for exploitation by the society of the spectacle. Gray declares — and at first DeLillo seems to espouse his declaration — that the words moving masses today are not narratives of isolated artists, but dramas staged by terrorists and fanatics who harness the power of images. *Mao II* dramatizes how Gray's Romantic authorship has been supplanted by what I call spectacular authorship, which counters the Western mythos of individualism as effectively as Andy Warhol's silkscreens exploded the narratives of Western art. Gray's anonymous death seems to forecast a bleak future for art and individualism, but this forecast is brightened, I argue, by novel's more genuine model of authorship: not the maker of sentences but the maker of photographs, Brita Nilsson, who shapes the culture as much as she is shaped by it. In the right hands, the novel implies, the camera can be as effective a weapon as the gun.

DeLillo's latest novel, *Underworld*, a monumental chronicle of American life since the 1950s, explores in unprecedented detail the myriad relationships between the two most hazardous consequences of the Cold War, weapons and waste. Beginning from the famed 1951 Dodgers-Giants playoff game and then looping backward from the 1990s, *Underworld* traces the dissolution of the American community into isolated monads of fear and estrangement. In Chapter 8 I argue that as *Underworld* shuttles back and forth from public figures and famous events to unknown, private lives, it embodies in form and content how "everything is connected" (*U* 825). Numerous motifs thread their way through the text, weaving a cohesive narrative from its multiple strands and demonstrating the collusion of weapons and waste. Two brothers, Matt and Nick Shay, exemplify the alienation and terror wrought by these twin forces (and their shadow, the ideology of containment), as well as the longing for wholeness, harmony, and radiance those forces steal and distort. Again DeLillo imitates the discourses that he records, using a montage-like arrangement of fragments to document the psychic and cultural fission, the material and spiritual waste, of militarism and capitalism. Yet DeLillo finds seeds of regeneration in the work of real and fictional underground artists such as Lenny Bruce, Klara Sax, and Sergei Eisenstein, who salvage the waste and weapons of the Cold War and transform them into signs of redemption. Imitating them, *Underworld* reconstructs out of the fragments of the Cold War a counterhistory that resists and undermines the technologies of war and capitalism.

This last movement propels *Underworld* past the bleak denouement of *Mao II*. DeLillo presents art as the soundest magic against dread, the truest source of radiance and community. Albeit tentatively and ambiguously, *Underworld* suggests that artists may achieve an accommodation with culture that is also act of resistance. By accepting the writer's inevitable involvement in postmodern culture while fiercely challenging all forms of institutional power, *Underworld*, most powerfully of all DeLillo's work, provides a model for contemporary artists and critics of all stripes.

Chapter 1
Children of Godard
and Coca-Cola

Cinema and Consumerism in the Early Fiction

In an interview with Tom LeClair, Don DeLillo was asked the "great bar-mitzvah question"—to name some writers who had influenced him. He eventually listed novels by Joyce, Nabokov, Faulkner, and Lowry, but he first cited not a novelist but a filmmaker: "Probably the movies of Jean-Luc Godard had a more immediate effect on my early work than anything I'd ever read" (Interview with LeClair 25). While writing his first novel, *Americana*, DeLillo kept in mind "the strong image, the short ambiguous scene, the dream sense of some movies, the artificiality, the arbitrary choices of some directors, the cutting and editing. The power of images" (Interview with LeClair 25). Indeed, the influence of film on the plot, narrative structures, and themes of DeLillo's early work is enormous. These early fictions provide DeLillo's initial analysis of American magic and dread, one that illustrates how both conditions are reflected and shaped by cinema.

DeLillo's early fiction depicts a disturbing collusion between cinema —even in its least mainstream form—and consumer practices and products. In his early stories, characters look to film images for the icons and ideals that will permit them to rise above their alienation, but these images merely model for them the very aimlessness and fear from which they have sought to escape. In *Americana* DeLillo provides multiple frames for his protagonist's quest for stable identity and perfect originality; but the presence of these frames (the most powerful of which is film history), eventually exposes this quest as a chimera, and originality as merely the echo of an echo. Film is revealed not as a magical solution, but as a mirror that reflects the distortions of personal and national history.

DeLillo's debts to various cinematic figures and techniques are apparent throughout his work, as later chapters of this study demonstrate. The specific influence of Godard first appears in three uncollected early short stories, "Coming Sun. Mon. Tues.," "Baghdad Towers West," and "The Uniforms," which both demonstrate DeLillo's debt to avant-garde cinema and function as previews for DeLillo's later work, introducing situations, characters, and scenes that he later reuses. Presaging DeLillo's novels, they also forecast the coming attractions and dangers of postmodern culture that DeLillo anatomizes so brilliantly in his novels: the effacement of historical consciousness; dehumanization by institutions and technology; the power of images to mold subjectivity and blur the differences between reality and representations; the totalizing effects of consumer capitalism; the yearning for magical antidotes to overwhelming dread.

COMING ATTRACTIONS: PREVIEWS AND PRETEXTS IN THE EARLY SHORT FICTION

The title of "Coming Sun. Mon. Tues." imitates a marquee advertising coming attractions, as if the story were the plot outline of an upcoming movie. And indeed, with its vague characterizations and detached point of view, the story resembles nothing so much as a film scenario or "treatment." The title is followed by excerpts from an imaginary review by "The Times," calling it a *social document* about the *bitterness and urgency of today's rebellious youth* ("Coming" 391). Published in the "Briefer Comment" section of *Kenyon Review*, the story possesses an essayistic quality that typifies much of DeLillo's work, in which hyperarticulate characters exchange mini-essays in tersely elegant prose. The essaylike format of this early story also echoes the practices of Godard, who has called himself "an essayist, producing essays in novel form or novels in essay form: only instead of writing, I film them" (Godard 171). One of those cinematic essays was the sociological study-cum-romantic comedy *Masculin féminin*, which was released at about the same time as DeLillo's story, and which traces the fortunes of Paul, a polltaker and lukewarm Marxist, as he tries to woo Madeleine, a budding pop singer. Along with its light comedy, Godard's film intersperses political placards and descriptions of the action, incongruent episodes of violence, self-reflexive comments on filmmaking, and remarks on the nature of observation. DeLillo's epigraph functions similarly both as a preview or summary of the narrative and as Godardian self-commentary, inviting us to measure our responses against its description:

will it be "*evocative and bittersweet*" and "*somewhat controversial*" as the "review" promises? Like Godard, DeLillo foregrounds the collaboration between auteur and audience in making meaning.

The plot of the story is quite complicated, considering its brevity. It depicts a stereotypical youthful couple doing youthful things—window shopping, drinking wine, being Bohemian. When the girl gets pregnant, they visit an "abortionist" who tells them to "come back next Tuesday" ("Coming" 392). The boy tries halfheartedly to get a job and fails; the couple attend parties in which everyone speaks the revolutionary cant of the day. He steals a car, they fight, and she goes home to her stereotypical parents. The boy visits a bar where he sees his father with a woman who is not his mother; the boy is sent to jail (apparently for car theft, but we aren't sure). Finally the couple reunite and decide to have the baby. My sketchy outline may seem unfair to the story, but the text does little more to flesh out the action or characters, who are viewed as through a telephoto lens. The story eschews character development for a studied neutrality; connects plot elements simply by "then"; remains vague about setting ("it is Greenwich Village or the West Side. . . . or it is Soho or it is Montmartre" ["Coming" 391]), perhaps to create an allegorical universality or perhaps to reflect the vagueness of its protagonists' aspirations. Although told in a single paragraph, the story abruptly and inexplicably shifts from scene to scene, as if to render the protagonists' disjointed sense of time and causality.[1]

Some of the story's events—the car theft, the girl's pregnancy—seem to have been borrowed from Godard's *Breathless*. Like Jean-Paul Belmondo's Michel in that film, DeLillo's boy constantly looks at himself in the mirror ("Coming" 392, 394): like Michel's, his rebellion is the prescripted defiance of movie tough guys. The boy's cinematic models are clearly exhibited when he "stands in front of a movie theater looking at a poster of Jean Paul Belmondo" ("Coming" 393), mimicking the scene in *Breathless* when Belmondo gazes at a poster of Humphrey Bogart in *The Harder They Fall*. DeLillo reuses this scene in *Americana*, when novice filmmaker David Bell looks "at the poster of Belmondo looking at the poster of purposeful Bogart" (*A* 287).[2] Like Bell, the boy in the earlier story is an image "made in the image and likeness of images" (*A* 130), able to see himself only when reflected from a screen or piece of glass. At the end of the story the couple look at themselves in distorted funhouse mirrors ("Coming" 394), illustrating the infinite regress of images that has shaped —or misshaped—their identities. DeLillo's distancing devices place the characters in a neverland where all events occur as if in a dream. Likewise, Godard typically cuts out connectives and explanations in order to speak in a "purer present tense," as Susan Sontag puts it ("Godard" 257). DeLillo's Godardian strategies suggest that the future for these young people will be an eternal present of instant gratification and consumer fulfillment in which psychological density has been supplanted by endless mirror images.

DeLillo's 1968 story "Baghdad Towers West" seems less cinematic than the other two stories I am considering, although its predictions about postmodern culture and its previews of DeLillo's future work are just as striking. The story concerns a middle-aged man who rents an apartment in a building called Baghdad Towers West from three young women, each of whom is seeking success in a field of pop culture. A place without history, Baghdad Towers promises "a new kind of mystery, electronic and ultra-modern, in which the angel of death pushes a vacuum cleaner and all the werewolves are schnauzers" ("Baghdad" 198–99). The sterile setting prefigures DeLillo's use of architecture as a symbol of postmodern alienation in *Players*, where the World Trade Center and the protagonists' boxlike apartment suggest their self-enclosure. The situation of the story is a virtual replay of a scene in *Masculin féminin* in which Paul temporarily stays in the apartment that Madeleine shares with two other young women. Paul is conducting a survey about the condition of French youth; much of the film consists of "interviews" in which the respondent is framed by a stationary camera as another character asks questions from offscreen. In "Baghdad Towers West" the three women similarly speak to the narrator "as if [he] were interviewing them for a profile in Look magazine" (200). Caroline: "I sculpt. . . . I am committed to junk. Give me sparkplugs, Maytag washers, jet engines, the teeth of combs. Today all beauty is apocalyptic and it demands new forms for its expression. . . . Doom is my medium" (200).[3] Robin: "I want to model. . . . I want to wear long vicious boots. . . . I want to be high fashion" (200). Melinda Bird: "I want to act. . . . All my life I've wanted to act. . . . I like to walk up and down Broadway and look at the lights and at the fabulous people" ("Baghdad" 201). In one of his best-known placards in *Masculin féminin*, Godard dubs his characters "children of Marx and Coca-Cola" for their uneasy allegiance both to leftist politics and to pop-cultural images. The women in DeLillo's story have a similarly mixed genealogy: over their beds, they have pinned photos of "Bogie, Marilyn, Ringo, Ike, Lurleen, Stokely, Marlon, Ravi and Papa" ("Baghdad" 196–97).

While the women's responses all seem prescribed from contemporary pop culture, the narrator's identity is drawn from classic Hollywood features. As he first gazes up at the building, a film clip unreels in his mind: "But I knew I was not the young Jimmy Stewart ('I'll lick you yet New York') fresh from the midwest, not the urbane Cary Grant about to trade quips with Rosalind Russell [in *His Girl Friday*]. . . . I was, in fact, nobody" ("Baghdad" 198). His sorties into "the midst of the Pepsi Generation" (204) send him to a club called Moloch, where "the spectators seated at tables watched the dancers watching the spectators watching the dancers" ("Baghdad" 203): as in "Coming Sun. Mon. Tues.," culture has become a Baudrillardian precession of simulacra, a "generation by models of a real without origin or reality: a hyperreal" (Baudrillard "Simulacra" 166). The narrator thus feels that he is constantly performing; even when ensconced safely in bed he imagines "the eerie kind of background music used in old Hitchcock films [such as *Spellbound*] to indicate that Gregory Peck is going nuts" ("Baghdad" 207).

Slowly withdrawing into sleep, the narrator hopes to find "something new, which was myself, or at least the beginnings of myself" ("Baghdad" 205). His dreams are dictated by the beds: in Caroline's bed he has apocalyptic dreams; in Robin's he dreams of striking poses as flashbulbs explode and "Michelangelo Antonioni emerges from the darkness and kisses my hand" ("Baghdad" 205); in Melinda Bird's he finds himself on stage in "some cynically modern version of Peter Pan" ("Baghdad" 207). The narrator's quest for purity prefigures those of several later DeLillo protagonists, including Bucky Wunderlick, the disenchanted rock star of *Great Jones Street*, Glen Selvy, the soldier without a cause of *Running Dog*, and Shaver Stevens, the disgruntled hockey player in DeLillo's pseudonymous novel *Amazons*. His love of sleep also echoes *Masculin féminin*. In one scene Paul, suffering over his unrequited passion for Madeleine, pleads with sleep to "free me a moment from myself." DeLillo's narrator seeks a similar retreat from self-awareness, a haven safe from images and observation. Sleep seems less a natural function than a magical trance state, a spell to ward off despair.

But after being rebuffed for clumsily attempting to grope one of the women, the narrator plunges even deeper, finally—paradoxically—asking the security guards to put him "on permanent security"—to maintain vigilance over the apartment even when he is there. His fantasy of security replicates the postmodern panopticon described in *Running Dog* (analyzed in chapter 4), in which "Everybody's on camera" all the time (*RD* 150). The result of this ubiquitous camera eye is not security, however, but an insecurity so total that even slumber becomes a performance. The narrator's tranquility thus soon gives way to an undefined dread that presages the nebulous anxiety of later protagonists, such as *White Noise*'s Jack Gladney: "From bed to bed I went, searching for applause . . . for the Barrymores, Balenciaga, the odd sad hope of fulfillment. But what I found was sheer terror. I would wake up sweating, or screaming, and yet I could not remember a single dream" ("Baghdad" 216). Even earlier, his serenity was accompanied by an urge to "set the whole thing on fire" ("Baghdad" 211), to bring about the very apocalyptic ending that he most fears.

In this story DeLillo envisions the future as belonging neither to the paralyzed narrator nor to the young women, none of whom end up attaining their dreams, but to people like Ulysses, the dispirited fourth-grader who sets only easily achievable goals ("If I try to achieve a goal that's simply beyond my abilities, I'm bound to be disappointed"), and whose epic journey consists of riding the elevators autistically from floor to floor ("Baghdad" 208–9). Just as in *Players* elevators are represented as "places" (*P* 24) that connote the emptiness of their inhabitants, so Ulysses's elevator replicates the narrator's "empty box within an empty box" ("Baghdad" 208), a domain safe from the urban nightmare reported on the narrator's radio: "From my seat in the helicopter I can see it all, the entire metropolitan area, through the poisonous smoke and fog. It is a scene of unbelievable terror and madness" ("Baghdad" 210).

This vision of an automotive apocalypse parallels another Godard film, *Weekend*, with its famous seven-minute tracking shot of a colossal traffic jam and its terrifying vision of an amoral, cannibalistic near future. In this film, Godard presents the out-of-control automobile as the embodiment of rampant consumerism. Thus the corruption of Corinne and Rolande Duran, the repellent protagonists of the film, is displayed as much by Rolande's callous disregard for traffic laws as by their plan to murder her parents for their money. After a wild drive, they crash; as the cars burn, Corinne screams, apparently in pain. But in fact she is only lamenting the loss of her Hermès handbag. They later encounter actors playing Rousseau and Emily Brontë, the latter of whom they nonchalantly burn. But no matter; as Rolande says, "they're only imaginary characters. We're little more than that ourselves." These postmodernist touches are not merely gimmicks; they dramatize Godard's message that the bourgeoisie live an imaginary life built upon the unacknowledged exploitation of workers and third world countries. If the Durands' "freedom is violence"—merely the "highest stage of barbarism"—the rest of their journey transports them back from "advanced savagery to primitive barbarism": they are hijacked, stripped of their car, and kidnapped by a brutal gang of roving, cannibalistic—and cinematically literate—revolutionaries, whose radio codenames are drawn from classic cinema (in one scene "Battleship Potemkin" calls to "The Searchers") and whose slogan is "the horror of the bourgeoisie can only be overcome by more horror," which they are happy to provide. At the end of the film Corinne blithely consumes a stew made of English tourists and, perhaps, some parts of her husband as well. The implication, of course,

13
Cinema and
Consumerism
in the Early
Fiction

is that she has always been a cannibal, that her meal merely literalizes the violent consumerism that has always defined her class. The terrorists thus enable the Durands to act out their savagery more honestly. For Godard, then, the bourgeoisie are themselves terrorists. But so is he: Godard conceives of his films as terrorist acts—as what Robert Stam terms a series of "guerrilla raids" (259)—not only upon capitalism and bourgeois culture, but also upon cinematic conventions such as linear plot, character development, and structural and visual continuity.

DeLillo's "The Uniforms" is essentially a gloss on *Weekend*, as he admits in an appendix to a reprint of the story: "I consider this piece of work a movie as much as anything else. . . . [It] is an attempt to hammer and nail my own frame around somebody else's movie. The movie in question is 'Weekend,' made of course by the mock-illustrious Jean-Luc Godard" (Appendix 532–33). Some of his borrowings are obvious: in one scene DeLillo's terrorists eat a pig ("Uniforms" 452), in imitation of the pig slaughtering scene in *Weekend*; in another, they stop a car and ask the occupants if they'd rather eat bananas picked by oppressed workers or sleep in a bed full of tarantulas. The man who chooses the bananas is murdered ("Uniforms" 452–53). This inquisition reenacts a scene in *Weekend* in which the autoless Corinne and Rolande are asked by passing motorists if they'd rather be "screwed by Mao or Johnson." When Rolande answers "Johnson," the car drives off without them. As the question about bananas indicates, the politics of DeLillo's revolutionaries are merely a pretext for murder and rape. Hence, after they kill the occupants of a tank and cut off their genitals, they rationalize that "the tank was full of products made by Dow Chemical" ("Uniforms" 453).[4]

But the story is not just a rehash of Godard's outrageous movie. For one thing, DeLillo omits most of the cars and concentrates on the terrorists. His story is even more plotless than *Weekend*, lacking even the auto journey to give it shape. And while the deadpan depiction of acts of violence mirrors Godard's film, the perpetrators are even more clearly movie-mad: at the beginning, one terrorist edits film clips of their previous attack; another is nicknamed Breathless ("Uniforms" 451); yet another experiences repeated flashbacks of a "soft-focus childhood" in which he sees himself running in slow motion ("Uniforms" 453). Likewise, their debates about the meaning of history are really arguments about historical films: they don't care about the righteousness of the atomic bombing of Hiroshima, but only about whether Alain Resnais "faked the film-clips of the bomb victims in [*Hiroshima Mon Amour*]" ("Uniforms" 455). The past is just a film; wars and war movies are the same thing. Thus their knowledge of the American Revolution and Civil War is derived solely from "the films of John Ford and John Huston," who have shown that "tight dusty uniforms are most acceptable to the devouring eye of history and the camera" ("Uniforms" 454). In short, their politics is a combination of fashion statement and film criticism: "the revolutionary uniform must be tight and spare. . . . We have thrown off the shackles of black-and-white revisionism. We will shoot in color because color is the color of childhood fantasy" ("Uniforms" 454). It follows that one of their final actions (presaging the prologue of *Players*) is to slaughter a group of golfing "middle class white Protestants," apparently because they have ugly clothes ("Uniforms" 456; cf. *P* 7).

Ironically, after perpetrating all these horrific acts, the terrorists go window-shopping ("Uniforms" 454). DeLillo's point is perhaps too obvious: these "revolutionaries" are wedded to the capitalism they claim to want to destroy. Not only do they carefully filch their victims' "Gucci wallets," "Tiffany cigarette cases" and "Patek-Philippe wristwatches" ("Uniforms" 455), but DeLillo's descriptions of the revolutionaries focus almost entirely on their clothes—their "uniforms"—which are carefully assembled for the most striking effect. Thus one wears a fez, a Mau Mau shirt, a safari jacket, granny glasses, and track shoes; another wears a motorcycle helmet, jump boots, a cowhide vest, and bandoliers. Just as history is pastiche, so radicalism equals the ability to arrange a fashionably outrageous ensemble. The story dramatizes DeLillo's recognition that, as Steven Connor argues, in postmodern culture "images, styles, and representations are not the promotional accessories to economic products; they are the products themselves" (46). But DeLillo reverses Godard's association between terrorism and consumerism: whereas for Godard the bourgeoisie are terrorists, for DeLillo the terrorists are bourgeois consumers.

DeLillo's prescient vision of terrorist manipulation of the media anticipates the themes of *Mao II* as well as the media savvy of real-life terrorists. But the relationship between the media and violence works both ways: the bombardment of consciousness by images is itself a form of violence. DeLillo has described "contemporary violence as a kind of sardonic response to the promise of consumer fulfillment" ("Outsider" 57). In this case, unlike that of *Libra*'s Oswald, it's not that the murderers are alienated from the glorious paradise they see advertised on TV; rather, it's that violence has become just another way to embody the right brand image. Moreover, it's not that the terrorists are inauthentic; it's that the collaboration of cinema and consumerism has blurred the distinction between commitment and celebrity, between reality and representations, as suggested when DeLillo's revolutionaries see "a film crew shooting a television commercial for a movie about television" ("Uniforms" 455). If these terrorists' crimes are movie crimes, they are no less real for all that. As Baudrillard has observed, "all hold ups, hijacks and the like are now as it were simulation hold ups, in the sense that they are inscribed in advance in the decoding and orchestration rituals of the media, anticipated in their mode of presentation and possible consequences" ("Simulacra" 179). "The Uniforms" depicts this collapse of distinction as a terrorism of representation that implicates us all.

At the end of "The Uniforms," we learn that a "Godard film was playing at the local cinema" (459). DeLillo seems to be claiming that Godard's vaunted revolution against bourgeois film conventions is itself just fashion; the story also implies that Godard's deadpan depiction of violence mistakenly conflates political and aesthetic radicalism and thereby desensitizes viewers to actual violence. As Godard has admitted, "The more one indulges in spectacle . . . the more one becomes immersed in what one is trying to destroy" (Stam 182). But then how does DeLillo's story, with its neutral portrayal of equally atrocious crimes, escape the same complicity? At the end of the appendix to his story, DeLillo writes, "Thousands of short stories and novels have been made into movies. I simply tried to reverse the process. . . . I submit this mode of work as a legitimate challenge to writers of radical intent" (533). His challenge is most obviously a charge to write "cinematic" stories that dispense with conventions such as plot, psychology, and closure. But he is also asking whether "radical" techniques necessarily promote radical politics. How, in other words, can one honestly portray revolution or violence without glorifying it? DeLillo leaves these questions unanswered; indeed he raises them again as part of the self-critical dialogue with postmodern culture that continues throughout his work. Nevertheless, by placing a cinematic frame around the story, he at least acknowledges the potential complicity of his own radical art in the alliance of consumerism and violence, in the collaboration of magic and dread.

All three of these stories examine the relationship between subjectivity and cinema, between image and identity, between real and reel, prompting disturbing questions about what lies ahead in the post-postmodern future. The apocalypse of *Weekend*? The aimless anomie of "Coming Sun. Mon. Tues"? The catatonic oblivion of "Baghdad Towers West"? In exploring the collusion between cinema and consumerism, DeLillo questions the possibility of any truly radical filmmaking aesthetic. And by hammering new frames around these pretextual films, DeLillo presents advertisements for the future that turn the camera back upon novelists and imagemakers, as if to ask, "to what degree is our art just another consumer product?"

"A LESSON IN THE EFFECT OF ECHOES":
INTERVIEW AND INTERTEXT IN *AMERICANA*

David Bell, the protagonist and narrator of *Americana*, displays the same schizophrenia about cinema and consumer culture exhibited in Godard's films and DeLillo's earlier fiction. He also continues the pattern of withdrawal, begun by the narrator of "Baghdad Towers West," that typifies many of DeLillo's later characters. Abandoning his high-profile career at a television network, Bell hopes to discover an authentic origin, a core identity, a genuine passion. From the outset, however, Bell's desires are contradictory: he wants both to discover and to destroy his past. In fact, his greatest problem may be his awareness that his identity is not only composed of the psychological patterns bequeathed him by his parents, but is also burdened by the immense weight of the cultural images, texts, and discourses that have influenced him. Hoping to liberate himself, Bell examines his past, revises it by making it into a movie, and then writes about it in the text we are reading.

Of course, Bell's memoir lies within a long and illustrious literary history that goes back at least to Saint Augustine (who is quoted by Ted Warburton, the network's mad memowriter). Similarly, in writing Bell's fictional life, first novelist Don DeLillo contributes to one of the novel's most distinguished subgenres: the *Kunstlerroman*. Like other *Kunstlerroman* heroes, Bell composes a work of art—an autobiographical film—that demonstrates both his talent and his limitations; but his work is "a lesson in the effect of echoes" (*A* 58), a pastiche of the styles and techniques of previous filmmakers—particularly Godard—that reveals nothing so much as the impossibility of complete artistic originality. DeLillo suggests that Bell's quest for originality and a true self beneath the images that have constructed him is futile, partly because it is based upon outmoded notions of originality and identity no longer recuperable in postmodern America. Instead, Bell's quest demonstrates the inescapability of and interrelationship between cinematic and commercial images, and the profound way that they form—and fragment—postmodern subjectivity. The novel, with its interpolated and multiply framed film, becomes a kind of self-interview, as David Bell's dialogue with himself dramatizes DeLillo's dialogue with postmodern culture.

At his job with the TV network, Bell feels alienated, hopeless, with "no echo for grief" (*A* 29). The network strikes him as a series of "test patterns and shadows" (*A* 270) of previous images that are themselves unoriginal. At times he imagines he is living in one of those "dull morality tales about power plays and timid adulteries" (*A* 20), such as *Patterns* or *The*

Man in the Gray Flannel Suit (both 1956), in vogue in the 1950s. The memo anonymously sent by Ted Warburton, the network's "tribal conscience" (*A* 62), describes David's condition: "And never can a man be more disastrously in death than when death itself shall be deathless" (*A* 21). Warburton glosses this passage from Saint Augustine's *City of God* (Book 13, Chapter 22, 421) to mean that living is nothing but a process of dying; yet once one dies, he or she goes on dying forever, so that death is never "finished" (*A* 100–101). For David it signifies that his life at the network is an unending death, providing only the "immortality" embodied in his fear that "all of us at the network existed only on videotape. Our words and actions seemed to have a disturbingly elapsed quality. . . . And there was the feeling that somebody's deadly pinky might nudge a button and we would all be erased forever" (*A* 23). Yet David's oppression by inherited images is accompanied by a movie-fed narcissism: a man who resembles "a number of Hollywood stars known for their interchangeability" (*A* 93), Bell revels in his image, constantly looking at himself in the mirror and boasting of his handsomeness. As Tom LeClair notes, David is thus torn between his desire to participate in "the Bell system" (*A* 41) of mass communication and a desire to flee from it (*Loop* 32). He escapes, ostensibly to make a documentary about the Navajos, with a surrogate family, the most important of whom is Sully, an avant-garde sculptress who stands in for David's demented (and now deceased) mother.

Part 2 of the novel interrupts the linear narrative for a flashback in which David recalls his adolescence and family life. Within the tale of his belatedness emerges a mini-*Bildungsroman* that follows most *Bildungsroman* conventions: the early life in a provincial town (Old Holly), constraints by family and education, movement to the city, a series of love affairs.[5] This section is multiply framed: framed intertextually by the *Bildungsroman/Kunstlerroman* tradition and by the "echoes" from movies that have helped to create his identity, it also functions as a tale-within-a tale, and hence it is also intratextually framed by the narrative of Bell's later life that surrounds it, and eventually by the frame around the entire novel, which David, alone on an island, narrates in 1999.[6] These multiple echoes, or frames within frames, themselves suggest the quixotic nature of David's quest to be free from the past.

Unlike earlier *Bildungsroman* protagonists, David's education is not literary but cinematic,[7] and his identity has been shaped most dramatically by those "American pyramids" (*A* 12) Burt Lancaster and Kirk Douglas. As Sergeant Warden in *From Here to Eternity*, Lancaster is a "crescendo of male perfection"; through him David discovers the "true power of the image" (*A* 13, 12). Warden is an unreachable ideal, "the icon of a new religion" at once private and mass-produced. Perfectly synthesizing the roles of friend, big brother and father, Lancaster/Warden substitutes for David's less satisfactory real father, fifty-five-year-old ad executive Clinton Bell. Clinton also echoes a number of popular 1950s figures, particularly Tom Rath, the protagonist of *The Man in the Gray Flannel Suit*. Like Rath, Clinton has three children (two girls and a younger boy), strives to balance the demands of corporate and domestic life, and is haunted by his violent actions in World War II. But unlike Rath, Clinton conceives of his family as ad images mirroring those in his basement archive of videotaped TV commercials, which he reruns repeatedly to "find the common threads and nuances" in those that have achieved "high test ratings" (*A* 84). These mass-cultural artifacts, replacing the personal mementos and home movies preserved by other middle-class males, are his Americana. Habitué of the Playboy Club and avid consumer of Jaguars and expensive cologne (*A* 152), Clinton boasts that he is successful because he has the "right brand image" (*A* 85); having created himself from TV commercials and best-sellers, Clinton has become commodified. Hence, when David films the commercial that is his life, he also tries to trade his father in for a better brand.

In his early years, David believes devoutly in the American dream of the good life, which encompasses "all those things which all people are said to want, materials and objects and the shadows they cast." He buys "the institutional messages, the psalms and placards, the pictures, the words. Better living through chemistry. The Sears, Roebuck catalog. Aunt Jemima. All the impulses of all the media were fed into the circuitry of my dreams. One thinks of echoes. One thinks of an image made in the image and likeness of images. It was that complex" (*A* 130). As the allusion to Genesis 1:26 suggests, cinematic and commercial images are David's sacred texts. But unlike the Divine Word, these intertextual discourses are mass-produced copies, designed and consumed anonymously. David's dreams thus again exemplify Baudrillard's domain of the simulacrum, in which signs follow "an uninterrupted circuit without reference or circumference" (Baudrillard, "Simulacra" 170). Marx's commodity fetishism here reaches its ultimate stage, as social relationships yield to relationships not between commodities but between images. Consumer capitalism has engendered new economies of meaning and identity, in which experience, as John Johnston notes, "can only appear to be 'always already' framed, multiply mediated, and available only through sets of competing and often contradictory images and representations" ("Post-cinematic" 97). As Baudrillard writes, the problem is that "illusion is no longer possible, because the real is no longer possible" ("Simulacra" 177): originality and unitary identity become impossible because representations refer back only to other representations.

Paradoxically, David aims to use cinematic representation to delve beneath the representations that have formed him; he hopes that by re-presenting himself to himself, he may find the source of his pathology, the glue for his identity, and thereby transcend his oppression by the past.

Thus, very early in David's journey (which halts in a town called Ft. Curtis), he conceives the idea for a "messy autobiographical-type film . . . a long unmanageable movie full of fragments of everything that's part of my life," which may "explain the darkness, if only to myself" (*A* 205–6). The psychological "darkness" issues from his mother, Ann. Molested by the family physician and then stricken with cancer, she shared the story of her molestation with the adolescent David, inciting unresolved Oedipal feelings in him. At David's "coming out" party, he sees her spitting on the ice cubes; later that night, David breathlessly anticipates an Oedipal encounter with Ann, only to be interrupted by the sound of his father's feet on the stairs (*A* 197). With her patrician Virginia heritage, Ann represents a high cultural legacy at odds with Clinton's commercialized world. Thus her haunting presence comes to David filtered through echoes from his "sacred scroll" at college (*A* 145), Joyce's *Ulysses*, rewritten with David as Stephen Dedalus.[8] The conflict between Ann and Clinton thus engenders several conflicts in David—object of Oedipal desire vs. obstacle to that desire; the literary vs. the cinematic, high culture vs. popular culture, Godard vs. Coca-Cola—producing the fragmented psyche that David attempts to suture with his film.

Like his entire story, David's film is multiply framed. First, it is framed intratextually within the novel so that we "see" it only through Bell, who, as narrator, interprets it in advance (LeClair, *Loop* 43). Second, because it is presented after we have learned about David's early life, it stands as both artwork and symptom, forcing us to read "through" the cinematic text to apprehend its sources. The film even contains its own intratextual frame: its first sequence, in which fledgling actor Austin Wakely plays fledgling filmmaker David Bell with his back to a full-length mirror, facing the camera (*A* 241). The length he choses for the framing episode—20 seconds, a "popular commercial length" (*A* 241)—betrays his father's influence, as well as his own self-conception as a commodity. The film is also framed intertextually by numerous films and filmmakers; this "signature" scene is also an intertextual mirror, reflecting both the autobiographical intention of the film and the derivativeness that David describes to his friend Ken Wild:

It's a sort of first-person thing but without me in it in any physical sense, except fleetingly, . . . my mirror image at any rate. . . . It'll be part dream, part fiction, part movies. . . . By that I mean certain juxtapositions of movies with reality, certain images that have stayed with me, certain influences too. . . . Ghosts and shadows everywhere in terms of technique. Bresson. Miklós Jancsó. Ozu. Shirley Clarke. The interview technique. The monologue. The anti-movie. The single camera position. The expressionless actor. The shot extended to its ultimate limit in time. (*A* 263)

Bell hopes that by incorporating these cinematic "ghosts and shadows" he can banish them and the psychic echoes that resound in his consciousness. For him (and for DeLillo, whose novel frames David's film), intertextuality here approaches a Barthesian infinite regress in which even the self who approaches a text is "already a plurality of other texts, of infinite, or more precisely, lost codes" (*S/Z* 10).[9] Bell hopes to create what Derrida calls an "iterable" text (315): one simultaneously derivative and original, a tissue of citations that is thereby one of a kind. That paradoxical condition is further implied when David prepares actress Carol Deming for segment 5 by mentioning Bergman's *Persona*, a film that movingly examines identity and "the nature of diminishing existence" (*A* 277)—a phrase that David uses to describe his life (and which, I show in the next chapter, applies to DeLillo's next two protagonists as well)—through the blending and exchange of two female protagonists. David is attempting to execute a similar feat: to split himself into interviewer and interviewee, to undertake a dialogue with himself that will yield a unitary subject. But despite these dizzying multiple frames, David's citation of influences shows a yearning to recover "lost" codes and points us toward the techniques and traumas that have inspired his film.

The film consists mostly of interviews with actors playing figures from Bell's life. Facing the camera directly, they respond to questions from off-screen. In most ways it is a very uncinematic movie and seems to bear little resemblance to the work of French filmmaker Robert Bresson. But Bresson is an acknowledged influence on Godard, especially in his use of "expressionless" acting (D. A. Cook 542); in addition, Bresson's nearly dialogue-free narratives proceed with minimal camera movement ("the single camera position") to suggest the social conditions entrapping the characters. Like Bresson, Hungarian filmmaker Miklós Jancsó employs a very static camera, while experimenting with "the shot extended to its ultimate limit in time." (*Winter Wind* [*Sirokko*, 1969], for example, consists of only thirteen shots [D. A. Cook 705].) Like Bresson and Jancsó, Japanese filmmaker Yasujiro Ozu mastered the long take and the static camera, which he usually placed about three feet high—the vantage point of a person sitting on a tatami mat. Instead of using alternating over-the-shoulder shots, as do American directors, Ozu often had his actors directly face the camera, which thereby assumes the addressee's point of view. The technique places the viewer within the scene to share the characters' intimacies. Most famously, Ozu exploited the value of empty space: often when actors leave a room, his camera does not follow them, but remains trained on the vacant room for several seconds.[10] Thus though these classicist filmmakers' work seems antithetical to David's gabfest, the ghosts of their techniques animate his movie, joining the spirits of his own past in spectral company. Bell's appropriation of these anti-Hollywood techniques suggests that he wants to produce a film that resists the primacy of Image and to create one that, to paraphrase Bresson, is not a spectacle but a style.

The "interview technique" and the "monologue" recall the work of another avant-garde filmmaker, Shirley Clarke, and particularly her influential film *The Connection* (1961), which depicts junkies awaiting their connection while being filmed by a documentary crew, to whom the characters speak directly.[11] Like Bell, she uses intratextual framing to comment on the impossibility of objectivity and the blurry line between acting and behaving. For example, in *The Connection* the director of the film-within-the-film claims to want to make "an honest human document," but constantly exhorts the actors to produce some "action"—to behave unlike their "normal" selves. Ultimately, the director's quest for total authenticity overwhelms his desire for objectivity, and he allows himself to be injected with heroin. But Clarke implies that the real drugs are cinematic images, which we crave as a way of ensuring ourselves that we exist. Near the end of *The Connection* we glimpse the cameraman, reflected in a window, shooting the scene we are watching, an image that David replicates near the end of his own film when he appears "reflected in a mirror as I hold the camera" (*A* 347). For both Bell and Clarke, film is not a window but a mirror; objectivity is impossible not only because of one's emotional involvement in what one films, but also because the medium ineluctably alters both observer and observed.

All of these echoes are quieter, however, than the one David admits when he calls himself a "child of Godard and Coca-Cola" (*A* 269), a witty transmutation of Godard's famous description of his characters in *Masculin féminin* as "children of Marx and Coca-Cola." [12] As I noted in the first part of this chapter, DeLillo is himself a "child of Godard." In *Americana* one of the principal Godardian strategies is what Richard Roud calls the "analogical" plot (93): the inclusion of seemingly irrelevant digressions that function as commentary or collage. As its title suggests, *Americana* also resembles a collage-like assortment of photos or postcards, and incorporates diverse literary and cinematic sources and models. Throughout his oeuvre DeLillo also resembles Godard in his deconstructions of popular genres.[13]

Bell's film also seeks a Godardian spontaneity, exemplifying Godard's view that the best films are those "in which the character conducts a dialectical search, experimenting and discovering his theme and structure as he goes along" (Giannetti 27). The film thus fits Godard's description of one of his early films as "a secret diary . . . or the monologue of someone trying to justify himself before an almost accusing camera, as one does before a lawyer or psychiatrist" (Godard, "Marginal Notes" 179).

Segment 5 contains such a monologue, as Carol Deming, playing David's sister Mary, admits that her life with a mobster has been modeled after Godard's *Breathless* (*A* 277). David, too, borrows from that film. In one scene from *Breathless*, Jean Seberg's Patricia and Jean-Paul Belmondo's Michel read an excerpt from William Faulkner's *Wild Palms* that presents the choice between grief and nothingness. Michel chooses the latter, as would Carol/Mary, who says she "needed death in order to believe I was living" (*A* 279). Likewise, Godard's Patricia could be speaking for Mary when she says, "I don't know if I'm unhappy because I'm not free, or not free because I'm unhappy." David's scene is thus again multiply framed: not only is Carol playing Mary, but, David's film implies, Mary was imitating Jean Seberg as Patricia, who herself assumes various roles in *Breathless*, including interviewer and thief's moll. Later, in segment 11, David's fellow traveler Bobby Brand and Carol improvise their dialogue so that Carol's "real" life shades into her performance as Mary (*A* 306). Jean Seberg's tragic story merges with that of Patricia, whose affair with Michel turns out to be just another "act"; Mary's existence becomes a gloss on Patricia's, and Carol's performance as Mary amounts to playing herself. David's projection of his sister's life thus demonstrates not just that Godard's film (itself a pastiche of 1940s Hollywood B pictures) has influenced Mary, Carol, and other women who have watched it, but that behavior and identity are "always already" framed.

Also prefiguring *Americana* in both plot and theme is Godard's 1965 film *Pierrot le fou*, whose schizoid protagonist, Ferdinand, flees from his deadening bourgeois existence for an experiment in spontaneity and violence with a woman named Marianne. The stultification of his previous life is dramatized in a cocktail party scene (resembling the early scenes in *Americana)* in which the characters' conversations consist entirely of commercials for such products as Olds Rocket 88 and Odorono deodorant. Asked about his previous life, Ferdinand answers, "I was in television." His adventure, like Bell's, is self-consciously patterned after the films of B-movie director Samuel Fuller, who appears in a cameo, talking portentously about film.[14] The psychological purpose of David's film is concisely expressed in another scene in *Pierrot*, when Ferdinand and Marianne watch an earlier Godard film, *Le grand escroc*, in which Jean Seberg says, "[W]e are carefully looking for . . . that moment when the imaginary character has given way to the real one . . . if there ever was a real one."

Bell's film, however, most clearly resembles *Masculin féminin*, which is subtitled "A film in 15 precise acts," the same number of segments that David films during the time of the novel, and which uses the "interview technique" virtually all the way through its running time. For Godard's characters, as for Bell, nothing exists prior to mechanical reproduction: even Paul's declarations of love are spoken not to Madeleine but to a recording machine. More significantly, Godard dramatizes the conflict between "Marx and Coca-Cola" in a variety of ways. In one scene, Robert, one male protagonist, reads the instructions for becoming a perfect "revolutionary machine," while his interlocutor, Catherine, washes dishes, a box of Tide detergent prominently displayed in the background. The scene prompts us to wonder not only whether the revolution requires males to help with the dishes but also whether becoming a "revolutionary machine" is truly preferable to—or even different from—being a consuming machine. As with the revolutionaries in "The Uniforms," the politics of Godard's characters seem mostly a matter of fashion. So thoroughly molded are they by seemingly opposed ideologies that they are not even aware of any contradiction between them.

So much for Godard. But what about Coca-Cola? Segment 4 of David's film dramatizes his views on consumerism through multiple frames. The camera records eight minutes of a TV game show, including the commercials, while Ft. Curtis resident Glen Yost (as Clinton Bell) is interviewed from off-camera. He describes television as an "electronic form of packaging" in which the image is the most important product (*A* 270). TV and advertising are symbiotically related: both make the viewer "want to change the way he lives" by appealing to the "universal third person," which advertising has discovered, and which it exploits "to express the possibilities open to the consumer. To consume in America is not to buy, it is to dream. Advertising is the suggestion that the dream of entering the third person singular might possibly be fulfilled" (*A* 270).[15] This universal third person is not a real person, however, just as the chief products of postmodern society are not commodities; rather, as Guy Debord has famously argued (*Society* 16), both are images.

Glen/Clinton's formulation echoes Fredric Jameson's discussion of what he calls "seriality," the characteristic condition of consumer society, in which "the uniqueness of my own experience is undermined by a secret anonymity, a statistical quality. Somehow I feel I am no longer central, that I am merely doing just what everybody else is doing. . . . [But] *everybody else* feels exactly the same way" (76, emphasis in original). The result is an endless circuit in which everyone projects onto everyone else "an optical illusion of centrality as 'public opinion' " (77). Through such means, the argument continues, the discourses of consumer capitalism have so thoroughly colonized the self that each individual conceives of him/herself primarily (if not only) as a consumer. All states of mind, relationships and processes are transformed either into needs for products or commodities, or into the results of consuming. Nothing is immune to consumption; nothing is prior to the image. But while advertising discovered this person, it didn't invent him: in fact, says Glen/Clinton, he "came over on the *Mayflower*" (*A* 271). That is, advertising is not just a form of Americana; America is itself no more than an advertisement.

In *Americana* advertising is presented as a prototypical form of American magic. But whether advertising really operates in so sinister and totalizing a way is debatable. Certainly successful commercials aim to incite desires and illustrate ways to fulfill them, while preying most upon those with limited access to other information and opportunities: children, the poor, the ignorant. And yet, as Judith Williamson has argued, even the most unsubtle ads leave gaps for the viewer or reader to fill with personal images, thereby inviting participation in the economy of meaning created by advertising's "currency of signs" (14, 20). Indeed, Yost/Clinton notes that consuming dreamers realize the limitations of their dreams. Recognizing these limits, advertising has learned to exploit the "anti-image": the slice-of-life commercial that brings movie-fueled desires back down to earth and hence counteracts the image (*A* 272). This conflict is also reflected in David's psyche and film: while modeling himself after Burt and Kirk—bigger-than-life images—he nonetheless makes a film based on the styles of Ozu, Bresson, Clarke—epitomes of the "anti-image." Godard's films encapsulate the conflict: although he once defined the cinema as "research in the form of spectacle" ("Marginal Notes" 181), his films aim to explode our passive acceptance of spectacle by constantly upsetting our expectations about plot, form, and character. What does DeLillo think? He remains elusive. His use of multiples frames in the "Clinton" sequence permits David to editorialize only through an actor pretending to be his father; DeLillo's voice is thus audible only as a series of echoes, forcing us to question the source and veracity of the argument, as well as our own complicity with the conditions described. DeLillo thus uses Clinton's monologue to generate dialogues between himself and his readers, himself and his narrator, his narrator and his alter egos: here is another lesson in the effect of echoes.

The collision and collusion between image and anti-image, between high culture and consumer culture, is forcefully dramatized by David's repeated appropriation of a scene from Akira Kurosawa's 1952 film, *Ikiru* ("To Live"). *Ikiru* concerns an aging bureaucrat named Watanabe, whose life embodies "the nature of diminishing existence." Watanabe's vitality has been crushed by years of toil in the Citizens Section of the city government; when he learns that he has stomach cancer, he is forced to examine that stultifying life. Rather than simply running away, as David does, Watanabe uses his position to help a group of local women turn a swampy field into a playground. In a moving scene near the end of the film, Watanabe is viewed sitting on a swing amid falling snow, softly singing to himself a sad song from childhood. David adapts this scene for the seventh segment of his film, in which Sully, filmed swinging on a snowless playground, substitutes for Watanabe and for David's cancer-ridden mother (*A* 290). The scene constitutes David's attempt to generate the kind of retrospective epiphany that Watanabe undergoes. Here again Bell attempts to transform intertextual echoes into original sounds.[16] Its effect, however, remains ambiguous, as Sully's presence weakens "what was for [David] an all too overarching moment" (*A* 290).

   Ikiru reappears in unexpected places. In segment 4, Clinton/Yost tells of a mouthwash commercial he once made in which a triumphant race-car driver gets the girl by using the right oral hygiene product. But the client turned it down because in the background of the celebrating crowd was an aged Asian man who violated the ad's atmosphere of "health, happiness, freshness, mouth-appeal" (*A* 274). The anti-image intruded on the image. The old man—it is Watanabe—migrated from David's trove of images from classic cinema. The old man's unlikely presence brings to light what the ad is trying to suppress: that postwar prosperity was built on the (Japanese) ruins and suffering of war; that the fear of death lurks behind ads for personal care products. The appearance of Watanabe also explains why David has decided to abandon the network: he identifies himself with the old man and fears his own living death.

   The same fragment of *Ikiru* reappears in segment 8, in which Yost/Clinton narrates "his" (actually a blend of Clinton's and Yost's) experiences in the Bataan Death March. Just outside Orani he and the other prisoners experienced a collective vision of a Japanese officer who appeared to be an old man swinging, singing a song, and blessing them (*A* 296)—Watanabe again. In one sense, Watanabe here represents Ann (who also died from cancer) and the peaceful family life Clinton has lost forever. In another sense, the old man is Clinton himself, crushed by the war and enduring a death-in-life similar to Watanabe's. Thus when, in the final image of this sequence, Clinton recalls burying a Filipino prisoner alive, we recognize it as a symbol of his own voluntary self-interment ("he's buried alive but still breathing"—*A* 285) as well as of David's Oedipal wish to kill him. *Ikiru* has mutated into a primal scene in which the son is haunted by the mother-as-Watanabe and wants to replace the father-as-Watanabe. David's fixation on the old man demonstrates that he is trying simultaneously to bury and to unearth his parents, both to assemble and to disassemble the montage of the past. Near the end of the Bataan sequence Clinton/Yost blames his country for treasuring "the sacrifice of its sons, making slogans out of their death and selling war bonds with it or soap for all we knew" (*A* 297). The implication is that twentieth-century war is simply consumerism carried on by other means—and vice versa. Thus the insertion of Watanabe—emblem of the "anti-image"—in these sequences signifies David's wish to create a cinematic form that would escape the cycle of consumption, a set of images that would exist, paradoxically, outside of the regime of "inauthentic" images: true images that would do for him what the playground does for Watanabe.[17]

With these goals in mind, David interviews "himself" in segments 6, 10, and 12. First "David" interrogates David's project, recalling how he once filmed an aged black couple at a demonstration, believing that he was celebrating their dignity. Now he realizes that he was patronizing them and cheapening their suffering (*A* 286): as Paul recognizes at the end of *Masculin féminin*, the "observation of behavior . . . insidiously substitutes an attempt to form value judgments" that may not even reflect the observer's real point of view. In these framing segments David confronts, like Paul, what Giannetti calls the "twin dangers of subjectivity and objectivity" (Giannetti 47)—or, more accurately, the collapse of the distinction between them. Both 6 and 12 also function as temporal mirrors in which "David" (Austin) addresses the future David: "Hello to myself in the remote future, watching this in fear and darkness. . . . I hope you've finally become part of your time, David" (*A* 286). In 12, however, Austin/David just stands silently against a wall, ready to answer questions that the 1999 David (who narrates the novel) might pose. But the older David has no questions; what remains is a silence of twenty seconds—the length of a commercial.

Not only does this mute tableau suggest that the younger David has no answers for the older one; it also mocks David's exploration of the past. Indeed, while these moments highlight the consistency of identity over time, they also illustrate that Bell's existence has been "twenty-eight years in the movies," a pastiche of Fellini's *La strada*, the dance of death in Bergman's *The Seventh Seal*, Albert Finney falling down the stairs in Karel Reisz's *Saturday Night and Sunday Morning*, "Burt Lancaster toweling his chest . . . Bell looking at the poster of Belmondo looking at the poster of purposeful Bogart. . . . Watanabe, singing to his unseen infancy," and Shane riding toward the mountains (*A* 287).[18] Not simply "images of unchanging male power," as LeClair claims (*Loop* 54), these framed frames are also figures of abandonment, alienation and death. They reconfirm that David's identity, like that of Belmondo's Michel, remains a performance, an image made in the "image and likeness of images," a copy of a copy.

The final segment of David's film restages the confrontation with his mother in Part 2, with Sully as Ann Bell and Bud Yost as David. Even as he films it, he realizes that his portrayal will be an anticlimactic version of the remembered anticlimax. He perceives that the Yosts' loving family possesses a quality that he has never known and that his film cannot capture. Watching in the dim light, he wonders if he will ever screen the sequence and, if so, why "this mute soliloquy of woman and boy should mean anything more, even to me, than what it so clearly was, face of one and head of the other, and I wondered of this commercial whether it would sell the product" (*A* 317). His "very own commercial, a life in the life" (*A* 317) was designed to recreate the typified and simplified lives offered by advertising (Schudson 215), in which problems are solved easily by consuming, but instead has enmeshed him in the past. Placing himself into the third person has been a paradoxical attempt to make his past more real by filming it; he has strived to be "objective." But the transformation of experience into film images has merely reframed them. Still "listening for a sound behind" him (*A* 318), David has heard only the echo of his own recording instruments. Yet he continues filming, as if "to obliterate the memory by mocking it, . . . spilling seed into the uncaptured light" (*A* 317); the masturbatory image implies that the light and sounds of the past can neither be captured nor banished: to abolish the echoes is to silence the singer as well. Not only is "actual" experience unrepresentable, but his film has magnified his limitations: like his father, he can make only commercials. Ironically, in striving to liberate himself from consumption, he has repackaged himself into commodity, commercial and self-consumer all at once. Moving from real to reel, he has "consumed" himself but left the sought-after essence unreached, unconsumed.

After David's Oedipal wish is granted through sexual intercourse with Sully, he again confronts disappointment when he learns that she permitted it only out of pity. Thus at the end of Part 3 he leaves Ft. Curtis to seek out "the final extreme"—an erasure of self somewhere beyond representation. Part 4 returns us to the narrative frame, as the older, islanded David meditates on his experiences from the future. "Little of myself seems to be left" (*A* 345), he writes, as if his film and his book have used up his stock of images. The text has sought to create meaning, while the film is an "exercise in diametrics which attempts to unmake meaning" (*A* 347); their conjunction has produced only an "ultimate schizogram"—a conflicted message that mirrors David's psychic fission. Even worse, David soon grasps that his quest has been "merely a literary venture, an attempt to find pattern and motive, to make of something wild a squeamish thesis on the essence of the nation's soul" (*A* 349). He understands that the pursuit of pure origins is itself a clichéd movie image, a piece of Americana available for consumption.

Traveling across the arid U.S. southwest, David pursues his dream of purity in an automobile—that potent symbol of twentieth-century consumer technology so celebrated and condemned in Godard's films. On an auto test track in Texas he experiences the same "montage of speed, guns, torture, rape, orgy and consumer packaging" (*A* 33) from which he had tried to escape (LeClair, *Loop* 46), albeit in a cruder and perhaps more honest form; like the characters in *Weekend*, he moves from advanced savagery to primitive barbarism. His pursuit of magic has yielded only transmutations of dread. This grotesque scene and David's near rape by a traveling homosexual near the end of the novel are narrated without inflection or comment, a technique that, LeClair argues, proves the limitations of David's insights: he does not perceive (although DeLillo does) that he is merely replicating the corporate behavior from which he has fled (LeClair, *Loop* 48). But I think he does: that's why he runs from it. Nonetheless, David has nowhere to go. It may be that only the older David, alone on his island, understands the full horror of these "archetypes of the dismal mystery, sons and daughters of the archetypes" (*A* 377). Still, a problem remains: as a character says in *Pierrot le fou*, "once one knows what one wants, where to go, what one is, everything still remains a mystery." Thus the older David's solution—withdrawal—seems as unsatisfactory as the younger David's resigned return to the Hollywood movie in which he was living. If even the older David has not learned the lessons of echoes, then his constant reviewing of his footage and the memoir we are reading are merely sterile exercises in narcissistic nostalgia.

But the older David does seem to have realized that subjectivity is not a product but a process growing out of a constant surplus of signification and narrative, and that those most abject or "dark" aspects of the self—also sources of treasured moments of illumination—may elude representation (Docherty 185). That is, the narrator Bell may recognize that he cannot master even the images of himself that his own work musters. Instead of adhering to such outmoded notions of control and identity, he may become truly "part of his time" by accepting heterogeneity, belatedness, lack of control—his "postness." He might even accept his schizoid psyche as a survival tool in a schizoid world, and learn to tolerate the neces-

29
Cinema and
Consumerism
in the Early
Fiction

sity for endless self-dialogue and interview. If he can relinquish control of self-representation, then perhaps he can "unmake" the meanings he has inherited, and thus understand that "objectivity" is as chimerical as univocal truth. If so, David may in a different respect become the "ultimate schizogram" (A 347): a message that paradoxically represents the impossibility of full comprehension.

The structure of *Americana* presents another set of formal, thematic, self-reflexive challenges to radical writers. Itself a kind of schizogram, it presents a series of shifting frames and redoubled echoes that relates consumerism to a revolution in economies of identity while also offering a radical model for characterization in which contradictions need not, cannot, be resolved. It interrogates the possibility of authentic political or artistic activity in a world consumed by cinematic and capitalist representations, asking whether the desire for authenticity, revolution, and purity inevitably becomes a consumer product. The novel's conclusion, in which David returns to New York, presumably to take up his previous life, also rejects conventional notions of plot structure. In undermining his narrative of apocalypse—that unveiling movement from "mystification to enlightenment and revelation" (Docherty 184)—DeLillo may be suggesting how novels (and perhaps films) can avoid becoming mere merchandise. Finally, *Americana* demonstrates how the irretrievability of authentic origins also encompasses the impossibility of ends—whether of plots, of quests, or of self-creation. If so, DeLillo's unveiling of the truth that David—and we, too—can never stop hearing echoes may be the most important lesson of all.

Chapter 2
The Nature of
Diminishing Existence

Davcontent avid Bell describes Bergman's *Persona* as an "unparalleled" study of "the nature of diminishing existence" (*A* 277). DeLillo's next two novels, *End Zone* and *Great Jones Street*, chart similar deliberate movements toward silence and oblivion. Each protagonist employs pseudo-ascetic strategies in an attempt to pare away complexities of choice and rediscover transcendence. Gary Harkness, in *End Zone*, seeks a language and landscape of simplicity in the jargon and strategy of nuclear deterrence. *Great Jones Street*'s rock star Bucky Wunderlick tries to escape from the marketplace that has transformed him into a product. Both quests fail: Gary's encounter with the "simplicities" of a nuclear war voids possibilities of meaning; Bucky's withdrawal becomes another commodity or marketing tool. In both novels DeLillo demonstrates how the characters' magical solutions merely reproduce the terror and anomie that originally drove them away. Rather than discovering a purer existence, each one becomes a victim or unwilling votary of technology or capitalism, two twentieth-century idols that DeLillo examines repeatedly. But although DeLillo criticizes the fascistic elements in each character's willed diminishment, he understands their desperate desire to lose themselves and thereby find some vestige of the sacred in a world from which God too has withdrawn.

In *The Genealogy of Morals* Nietzsche writes that the ascetic "treats life as a maze in which we must retrace our steps to the point at which we entered or as an error which only a resolute act can correct, and he further *insists* that we conduct our lives conformably to his ideal" (Nietzsche 253; emphasis in original). Many of DeLillo's novels portray characters who seek primal simplicity through strategies of ascetic self-denial. For example, *Great Jones Street*'s Bucky Wunderlick withdraws from the noise of rock-'n'-roll stardom to a small, silent room in New York City's urban desert; *Running Dog*'s Glen Selvy seeks simplification in a mechanizing routine that ultimately compels him to commit ritual suicide. *White Noise* demonstrates that ascetics are also driven by their principles of attenuation towards an obsession with ends, as narrator Jack Gladney tries to control his fear of death by mastering discourses of authority and becoming a killer. Indeed, each of these characters pursues an origin that is also an end: each narrows himself to discover either a life governed by rules that obviate the need for thought or an end to life itself. Each narrator strives to reduce competing impulses and discourses into a single-line story that moves inexorably toward perfect, violent closure. But none of them find the solution to their malaise or the source of the maze; rather than helping them cope with their fears, asceticism deflects their life-preserving impulses into a pursuit of apocalypse. These novels critique the American ascetic ideal as a ineffectual magic solution to varieties of dread.[1]

DeLillo, who once called himself a "failed ascetic" ("A Talk" 26), has stated that obsession is useful to writers because it involves "centering and narrowing down, an intense convergence. An obsessed person is an automatic piece of fiction. He has a purity of movement, an integrity. . . . Obsession . . . seems . . . close to the natural condition of a novelist at work on a book" (Interview with LeClair 29). Obsession focuses consciousness upon a single goal, and an obsessive, like a novelist, creates a plot that travels in a straight line towards terminality: as Gladney states, "all plots tend to move deathward" (*WN* 26). But if DeLillo's obsession with obsessives implies some sympathy for their quests, his novels resist the terminality they so desperately seek: they almost invariably end by not ending, sometimes circling back to their beginnings, sometimes offering ambiguous epilogues that cast doubt on their apocalyptic denouements, and sometimes trailing off indeterminately.[2] DeLillo's critique is thus not only directed at American asceticism and its attraction to apocalypse; he also links these phenomena to a universal desire for fictional closure. In depicting his characters' failed pursuits of apocalypse, DeLillo deconstructs the impulse toward apocalyptic endings both as a tendency in human consciousness and as a trait of our narratives.

End Zone's narrator, college football player Gary Harkness, retreats in confusion to a tiny college on the Texas desert, where he flirts with self-annihilation through a fixation with nuclear holocaust. Gary desires an "end zone" in which complexities of meaning and choice are voided, an existence that approaches emptiness. In this text DeLillo traces the source of our cultural fascination with nuclear apocalypse to an ascetic desire for "diminished existence" through violent cleansing, for a purification that conquers the dread of death, paradoxically, by bringing it about. *End Zone* charts ways that we turn nuclear apocalypse into a mythic fiction that satisfies our deep need for fictional closure. However, *End Zone* is finally against the end. By revealing the religious and linguistic mutations that underlie the lure of apocalypse, the novel criticizes both the ideology of atomic weapons and the conventional fiction that exploits it. Moreover, by resisting his readers' desire for novelistic closure DeLillo uses his own fiction as an antidote for that apocalyptic disease.

Americana introduces the relationship between asceticism and apocalypse when Sully quotes a Sioux medicine man named Black Knife, who maintains that America is a

nation of ascetics. . . . We have been redesigning our landscape all these years to cut out unneeded objects such as trees, mountains and all those buildings which do not make practical use of every inch of space. The ascetic hates waste. . . . What we really want to do . . . is to destroy the forests, white saltbox houses . . . antebellum mansions. . . . It's what we are. . . . We feel a private thrill, admit it, at the sight of beauty in flames. We wish to blast all the fine old things to oblivion and replace them with tasteless identical structures. Boxes of cancer cells. Neat gray chambers for meditation and the reading of advertisements. Imagine the fantastic prairie motels we could build if we would give in completely to the demons of our true nature. (*A* 118)

We want to simplify the landscape by building perfect architectural and mental structures in which we all become indistinguishable. This is the ascetic dream: to destroy everything and start over, but now to make everyone perfect, that is, identical. And the new image of our "ascetic scheme," according to Bell, is "the low motel, neat and clean at ground zero" (*A* 210).

Deserts and motels: one prefigures the landscape after a nuclear war, and the other reflects the terminal condition of the American ascetic spirit. Again and again DeLillo's ascetics end their tales in one or both of these terminal sites. The desert is harsh, unforgiving—and clean. As a character in *The Names* expresses it, "the desert is a solution. Simple, inevitable. It's like a mathematical solution applied to the affairs of the planet" (*N* 294).

Motels represent for DeLillo an almost irresistible urge to create sterile spaces, to destroy history by demolishing its architectural symbols. Often DeLillo's motels are found in the desert, and thus do not interrupt its terminal geography so much as interiorize it. The blandness of motel rooms betrays the spiritlessness at the heart of this ascetic ideal: we want to create deserts, and then fill them with rooms that reflect a graver emptiness. For DeLillo deserts and motels are fictional end zones, places where plots end.[3] Not surprisingly, then, Gary Harkness contemplates nuclear war during long walks into the desert, and plays his nuclear war game in a motel room at the edge of that desert. In Black Knife's statement, DeLillo shows that the urge to destroy so as to achieve individuality and solitude actually annihilates both. The ascetic quest for purity is merely part of that consumer fantasy of indistinguishability described in *Americana* as the "universal third person" (*A* 270); instead of individuality, we become identical commodities—motel rooms. Rather than filling our lives, these terminal delusions diminish them.

Like *Americana* before it and *Great Jones Street* after it, *End Zone* dramatizes how the ascetic ideal is already appropriated by consumerism, and how the desert is always filled with motels of the mind. In *End Zone* DeLillo shows that these tendencies also underlie our cultural fascination with nuclear annihilation.[4] As its title suggests, *End Zone* is about "extreme places and extreme states of mind" ("Outsider" 57). The extreme place is again the southwestern Texas desert, the location of Logos College, where Gary Harkness has landed, after several failures, to play college football. An empty landscape is made to be filled, and the characters in this novel fill it with games of all kinds, the most obvious one being football. The Logos coach, Emmett Creed, demands that his players lead "a simple life" and provides a comforting routine that creates "order out of chaos" (*EZ* 5, 10). Gary, who came to Logos because he "wanted to disappear" (*EZ* 26), responds to these exhortations of self-discipline because they resonate with his desire for self-annihilation and remind him of his own father, who lives according to such hearty directives as "When the going gets tough, the tough get going." Gary embraces "simplicity, repetition, solitude, starkness, discipline upon discipline," believing that "the small fanatical monk who clung to my liver would thrive on such ascetic scraps" (*EZ* 30). Coach Creed, master plotter, is another ascetic, a "landlocked Ahab . . . unfolding his life toward a single moment," who straitens experience into a linear narrative with the goal line at the end (*EZ* 54). Like Bell, Bucky, and Selvy, Gary seeks an origin that is also an "end zone" where language is lean and life is narrowed into "the straightest of lines . . . uncomplicated by history, enigma, holocaust or dream" (*EZ* 4).

The words of Creed and of Gary's father "hark back," as another character puts it, to ancient ways; they represent those primal origins to which the ascetic wishes to return. Their discourse is authoritative, in Mikhail Bakhtin's sense, because it is felt to be "located in a distanced zone," presenting itself as the "word of the fathers." Such authoritative discourse "permits no play with the context framing it, no play with its borders, no gradual and flexible transitions," and demands "unconditional allegiance" (Bakhtin, "Discourse" 342–43). It is fused with authority, so that "when Coach says we hit, we hit" (*EZ* 35). This discourse is a monologue; it is the Logos, the Word of God. The football team thus operates according to the same principle of indistinguishability that governs motel construction and mass production, and the coach's goal is to turn the team into goal-bound ascetics like himself. Late in the novel, after the season has ended with a loss and team solidarity has begun to evaporate, Creed calls Gary into his office and, mixing punishment and honor, makes him co-captain. He tells him that football is an "interlocking of a number of systems" in which the individual is a small element; when the systems interlock, "there's a satisfaction to the game that can't be duplicated. There's a harmony." Sacrificing oneself for the team is a mode of asceticism that paradoxically enables self-knowledge through self-annihilation: "We need more self-sacrifice, more discipline. . . . We need to renounce everything that turns us from the knowledge of ourselves. . . . Loneliness is strength. . . . [Nothing] makes more sense than self-denial. It's the only way to attain moral perfection. . . . Purify the will. Learn humility. Restrict the sense life" (*EZ* 199–201). Creed has already converted Taft Robinson, the African-American running back introduced on the first page of the novel, with these advertisements for the ascetic's terminal geography.

Creed's aim, which Gary alternately embraces and repudiates, is to produce a life in which self-awareness is overwhelmed by routine. He aims to generate what Robert Jay Lifton would call a "totalistic environment," one that ostensibly "contains the key to absolute virtue" and that "mobilizes the vast human potential for guilt and shame in its imperative of eliminating all 'taints' and 'poisons' in a demand for purity." It also loads language in ways that "eliminate ambiguity about even the most complex human problems and reduces them to definitive-sounding, thought-terminating images" (Lifton 298). Obviously such asceticism is only a step away from fascism, from "final solutions" that resolve "problems" through mass atrocity. Thus Creed's prize ascetic, Taft Robinson, gains a mixture of pleasure and horror in reading about "the ovens, the showers, the experiments, the teeth, the lampshades, the soap" (*EZ* 240). Likewise, Gary becomes obsessed with that other final solution: nuclear war.

35
The Nature of
Diminishing
Existence

Nietzsche points out that the prevalence of the ascetic ideal testifies at once to modern mankind's desperate attempts to affirm life and to our "persistent morbidity . . . [our] *taedium vitae*, exhaustion, the longing for 'the end' " (Nietzsche 256). In *End Zone* the authorities' asceticism fuses the survival instinct with the impulse toward "the end" by prompting players to invent games that create seemingly perfect structures that impel them in the direction of end zones. One of these is "Bang, You're Dead," which the football players play in the dormitory. The rules are simple: you follow the order to die. Here words function as weapons; language is simplified into imperatives and existence attenuated into a brief plot in which one lives, is shot, and dies beautifully. Another such structure is the football game played in a blizzard near the end of the novel. Slowly eliminating rules and play possibilities (no passing, no deception), the players reduce the game to the plodding of identical white players toward the goal line. They find comfort in bodily contact and the warmth generated by violence, and the bitter cold is both mortifying and satisfying in this winter desert. Both games simplify even Creed's asceticism, combining deathward motion with a yearning for the primitive.

Gary's terminal desires are manifested more directly in his fixation with nuclear holocaust, which commences when he reads a book on nuclear war and, half-ashamed, finds that he likes it: "I liked dwelling on the destruction of great cities. . . . Pleasure in the contemplation of millions dying and dead. I became fascinated by words and phrases like thermal hurricane, overkill, circular error probability . . . stark deterrence, dose-rate contours, kill-ratio, spasm war. Pleasure in these words" (*EZ* 20–21). He begins to take circular walks into the desert and back while contemplating nuclear destruction, trying to punish himself until he ceases enjoying it. But instead "pleasure nourished itself on the black bones of revulsion and dread" (*EZ* 43). In chapter 16 he discusses this morbid fascination with an Army officer, Major Staley, in a desert motel "barely distinguishable from the land around it." Staley explains that "there's a kind of theology at work here. The bombs are a kind of god. . . . We begin to capitulate to the overwhelming presence. It's so powerful. . . . We say let the god have his way. . . . Let it happen, whatever he ordains" (*EZ* 80). The notion of The Bomb as God may at first seem implausible. But *End Zone* demonstrates through Gary's obsessions that our society's ambivalent mixture of attraction and terror regarding nuclear weapons does resemble religious feeling. Ira Chernus has persuasively analyzed this nuclear theology, suggesting that our cultural fascination with nuclear weapons grows from a distortion of religious impulses. Nuclear weapons, he argues, inspire both awe and dread, and remain mysteriously fascinating both because of their complex technology and because of their seemingly limitless force. The numinousness of nuclear weapons—their mystery and power—induces us to identify with their destructive force, and finally to try to merge with that power by invoking them to rain down upon us (Chernus 12–19).

Tom LeClair has paired the theology of The Bomb with Creed's discourse, viewing them as similar versions of logocentrism, a re-inscription of theological values based upon what Derrida denounces as a "metaphysics of presence," which claims to supply final meanings and answers and bring an end to play (LeClair, *Loop* 65). But a key element in the attraction for nuclear weapons is their capacity to bring total destruction. Thus they can be "present" in our minds only when not used—when absent physically—because when truly "present"—that is, when used—they could cause an ultimate absence, the end of civilization and perhaps even the extinction of humanity. This sinister deity, then, resembles the God described by Nick Shay in "The Cloud of Unknowing" section of *Underworld*, whom we cherish precisely for His "negation" (*U* 295). The Bomb eludes the metaphysics of presence because it generates logical contradictions: it is the one weapon whose value depends upon its never being used. That all-out nuclear war could extinguish mankind is arguable, but the symbolic force of these weapons is unmistakable: they represent a negation, an ultimate simplicity, an end zone, for which we often yearn. As DeLillo's later story, "Human Moments in World War III," puts it, war can be "a form of longing" (576).

In *The Fate of the Earth* Jonathan Schell shows convincingly that a full-scale nuclear conflict would result in a "gross simplification of the landscape" into a "republic of insects and grass" (65).[5] Gary's obsession with nuclear holocaust reflects the ascetic urge to bring about this simplification, to view holocaust as a path to purification that leads to regeneration. In its ultimate expression, asceticism grows into what Spencer Weart calls a "Samson complex" (228): a longing for an apocalypse that will annihilate the human species in an attempt to cleanse it of evil; a desire to purify the world by destroying it. A nuclear war would satisfy the ascetic's unbearable desire for violent termination, providing the human narrative with a closure as complete as it is possible to conceive: the simplification of nothingness. Gary sees in the stark desert landscape a reflection of his own fascination with the results of nuclear war—this is his end zone. Late in the novel, Gary's roommate, Anatole Bloomberg, concludes similarly that "an individual's capacity for violence is closely linked with his ascetic tendencies." He goes on to assert mockingly that in "our silence and our terror we may steer our technology toward the metaphysical, toward the creation of some unimaginable weapon able to pierce spiritual barriers, to maim or kill whatever dark presence envelopes the world" (*EZ* 215). Lifton associates such views with what he calls "nuclearism": the religion of nuclear weapons, which regards them as "a solution to death anxiety and a way of restoring the lost sense of immortality," and which generates an ideology in which " 'grace' and even 'salvation'—the mastery of death and evil—are achieved through the power of a new technological deity." At the heart of nuclearism is the ascetic ideal of The Bomb's "purifying function" (69, 79).[6] Here, then, lies another paradox in our theological relationship with The Bomb: according to the logic of deterrence, in which having nuclear weapons prevents others from using them on us, they become the means of our deliverance from their own "dark presence." They can magically efface themselves and the dread that lurks in their shadow. The Bomb thus seems to save us from Itself. Moreover, as Anatole suggests, if we use nuclear weapons, we will never have to fear them again. The Bomb, then, generates a paradoxical nucleus in which magic and dread are inextricably fused.

White Noise extends these themes through the Gladney family's fascination with televised disasters. If in *End Zone* apocalypse is a game, in *White Noise* it is a TV show. And when the family is confronted with a real disaster—a toxic cloud that stands in for a mushroom cloud—they betray the same mixture of fear and fascination that Gary Harkness shows: the cloud is "a terrible thing to see," but it is also "spectacular, part of the grandness of a sweeping event." Their fear is "accompanied by a sense of awe that bordered on the religious" (*WN* 127). Like Gary, they want both to flee from mass death and to embrace it. Their attitude prompts Jack to wonder whether the "point of Armageddon" is to create a condition of "no ambiguity, no more doubt"; he worries that "if enough people want it to happen," it will happen (*WN* 137). His colleague, Murray Jay Siskind, exploits this wish in his college course on car crash films, telling his students that such movies break "away from complicated human passions to show us something elemental, something fiery and loud and head-on. It's a conservative wish-fulfillment, a yearning for naivete. . . . We want to reverse the flow of experience, of worldliness and its possibilities." Through such experiences we may "improve, prosper, perfect ourselves" (*WN* 218). Viewing disasters allows us to blend the longing for a return to innocence with the yearning to reach an end zone. This same desire, DeLillo implies in both novels, also underlies our need for fictional closure. We crave a cataclysmic end that ties up all complications into a consumable package and lets us fantasize about starting over.

Such renditions of nuclear apocalypse and weapons present them as symbols, as a "Big Bang" recapitulating the primal explosion of the Creation, as a magical device that solves all problems at once by blowing them to oblivion. This mythic response ignores the realities of the effects of nuclear weapons, which of course would be much closer to chaos than to order. After the devastating blast and heat would follow the horrors of radiation sickness, epidemic, and famine. But for those actually sending the missiles, a nuclear war might very well seem clean since they would be protected from its horrible effects.[7] Similarly, nuclear strategists have presented nuclear war as a game in order to wall themselves off from its realities. The jargon from which Gary Harkness gains so much guilty pleasure exemplifies this practice. He explains to Staley that "there's no way to express thirty million dead. No words. So certain men are recruited to reinvent the language. [The words] don't explain, they don't clarify, they don't express. They're painkillers. Everything becomes abstract" (*EZ* 85). Gary argues that the jargon of nuclear strategists protects them—and, they hope, us—from recognizing the enormity of what their words represent. The language of nuclear strategy is founded upon paradox: the words are designed not to signify but to resist signification, to shield users from responsibility for planning and carrying out mass destruction. Just as the weapons themselves would radically simplify geography, so the jargon simplifies language by emptying it of referentiality and proceeding toward meaninglessness. The result is a kind of linguistic end zone, or verbal ground zero. Here again nuclear holocaust engenders a metaphysics not of presence, but of absence.

The global ecology after an all-out nuclear war—the predominant threat in 1972, if not today—would be drastically reduced. Indeed, such a war could extinguish the human race. Schell implies that such a result, which paradoxically kills death because no more people would be left to die, would therefore cause the death of meaning itself: since no more human beings would be left to ascribe significance to experience, meaning would be annihilated along with the people who produce it (Schell 128–29). In this sense, the jargon of nuclear war does accurately signify the results of using nuclear weapons: both jargon and weapons murder meaning. Hence the voiding of complexity and meaning potentially caused by nuclear war is perfectly represented by the sterile language of nuclear strategy.

One of Gary's teammates is taking a course on "the untellable"; nuclear war is often referred to as "the unthinkable." *End Zone* implies a theological and linguistic relationship between the two. To grasp the "unthinkable," nuclear strategists invent words and phrases that have significance only within the parameters of their game theories. The jargon attains the status of a secret language, acquiring a cultlike authority appropriate for a religious ritual. Like Creed's commands, the jargon of nuclear strategy presents itself as authoritative discourse, sharply demarcated from the real horrors it tries not to specify. Like Creed's discourse, it generates a totalistic environment that annihilates complexity and operates within an illusory framework of absolute morality—us against them. Gary's attempts to master nuclear holocaust by mastering the discourse of its priesthood thus seems logical. Strategic jargon tries to make nuclear war "untellable" by detaching words from real-world contexts, blocking us from confronting the horrors of nuclear war, and therefore stopping us from doing anything to prevent it. But ultimately nuclear holocaust is "untellable" not only because such vast destruction boggles the mind, and not only because we create psychic defenses to avoid thinking about it, but because we must translate it into language that is always insufficient to represent a condition in which meaning is necessarily absent because all users of language are dead. By killing meaning, nuclear holocaust casts its shadow over language itself.

In Part 2 of *End Zone* DeLillo provides a terse but involving description of the big football game between Logos and its archrival Centrex (theology vs. technology). Since we are not players, the signals become an impenetrable argot comparable to the jargon of nuclear strategy. In giving his play-by-play account, the narrator vows to "unbox the lexicon" of football for all eyes to see, and thereby disclose its "cryptic ticking mechanism" (*EZ* 113). This tactic implies that, as in "Bang, You're Dead," words themselves are the primary weapons; football jargon, like that of nuclear strategy, is a destructive implement that "cleanses" the landscape of complexity and choice. DeLillo has stated that the characters in *End Zone* are "pieces of jargon. They engage in wars of jargon with each other" (Interview with LeClair 21). In the penultimate chapter of the novel, Gary and Staley play a nuclear war game using its jargon in Staley's desert motel room. Most of the terms and even the crisis scenario that initiates the game come directly from Herman Kahn's book *On Escalation*, which uses an "escalation ladder" to predict how a crisis might move up the rungs into nuclear war (Kahn 37–50). Kahn is one of those men recruited to reinvent the language, having coined many of those terms that fascinate Gary, such as "stark deterrence" and "super-ready status." The game also adheres quite closely to Kahn's escalation ladder, moving inexorably from "ostensible crisis" to "spasm response" (*EZ* 221–25; cf Kahn 42–50). Like Kahn, Staley denies that nuclear war will necessarily be all-out or "insensate." He tells Gary that future wars will be so "humane" that we will "practically have a referee and a timekeeper," as in a football game (*EZ* 82). But clearly those who think in terms of "scenarios" already see nuclear war as a game. Under the pretext of "thinking about the unthinkable" (the title of one of Kahn's earlier books), strategists such as Kahn and Staley actually prevent our thinking about nuclear holocaust by camouflaging it with pseudo-objective terminology. The habit of thinking in jargon encourages them to conceive of war as a perfect, rule-bound structure, occurring within white lines that demarcate the thinkable from the unthinkable. This, then, is how jargon itself is a weapon: the violence it does to meaning, and the simplifications it effects on morality and responsibility, harden the mind to accept, even welcome, apocalypse.

In this way the ascetic desire for purity mushrooms into a form of fascism that permits atrocity. Imagining nuclear holocaust as a game makes it more likely to occur; once framed, it seems more manageable and desirable. Nuclear war becomes merely another fiction with a preconceived end. Indeed, Kahn's book is a kind of prolegomena to any future nuclear war fiction, a sketch of an ideal novel that ends in a satisfying spasm of violence. Like Kahn's scenarios, Gary's and Staley's war game begins with Gary overwhelmed by his many options; as it proceeds, however, the choices become increasingly limited as the war follows its inexorable logic, and it ends, like Kahn's scenario, with all-out war. Of course, nuclear war is not a game: a real nuclear war could have no winner, because it would destroy the means by which such things could be decided. In the novel, the end of the game is punctuated by a ringing phone, a symbol of the outside intruding upon the insular world of the game. But real nuclear war ultimately eludes any framework we can give it, whether linguistic or ludic. Its meaning is truly the voiding of meaning: an ultimate simplicity. *End Zone* shows how the conventional strategic mentality prepares us for its coming by fostering the notion that nuclear holocaust is a game or plot with a satisfyingly apocalyptic conclusion.

Gary seems to understand that the jargon itself is somehow to blame, because earlier in his desert walk he thinks that by contemplating the destruction of humankind we will be forced to "reinvent the language" constructively. During a walk into the desert he encounters a mound of "simple shit, nothing more . . . perhaps the one thing that did not betray its definition" (*EZ* 88). Seeing defecation as a "terminal act" because of the "nullity in the very word," Gary experiments with synonyms, then again is led to imagine millions killed in another terminal act, an atomic war.[8] He then decides that "In some form of void, freed from consciousness, the mind remakes itself. What we must know must be learned from blanked-out pages. To begin to reword the overflowing world. . . . To re-recite the alphabet" (*EZ* 89). Perhaps by restoring the lost simplicity of language one can avoid the dangerous abstractions of nuclear theorists. But the rest of the novel makes it clear that this is merely another of Gary's mystifications: the desire to blank out and then rewrite those empty pages is scatologically inspired expression of the eschatological impulse—the "Samson complex"—that makes nuclear holocaust attractive and shit seem evocative. Gary continues to hunger for closure that will lead to renewal; yet at the end of the novel, he fasts so fanatically that he finally has to be fed through tubes. Thus the meaning of his fast remains ambiguous. Earlier Creed showed him a painting of Saint Teresa of Avila, reminding him that she ate her food out of a human skull (*EZ* 202). Creed urges Gary to purify himself similarly, to emulate a Sioux warrior through disciplines like fasting and solitude (*EZ* 200). It is not certain whether Gary's final fast demonstrates his intention to follow Creed's advice, or a repudiation of his unity with the team and hence a rejection of his responsibilities as captain and hence of Creed's asceticism. To make sense of this conclusion we must first analyze the novel's recurrent motif of consuming.

Three-hundred-pound lineman Anatole Bloomberg also practices modes of self-discipline. At first Gary "reveres" Anatole's weight. To weigh three hundred pounds seems to him "a worthwhile goal for prospective saints and flagellants. The new asceticism. All the visionary possibilities of the fast. . . . To expand and wallow . . . . Somehow it was the opposite of death" (*EZ* 49). Anatole's comic "asceticism" seems life-affirming. Then he goes on a diet, but gives it up because "What I had considered self-control was really self-indulgence. To make me pretty" (*EZ* 76). His words complicate the significance of Gary's final fast: is it self-indulgence or self-mortification? Or are they the same? The connection between nuclear weapons and consumption may seem distant, but DeLillo implies a fundamental relationship between them through the symbolic weight of another character, Gary's girlfriend Myna Corbett. She too is obese, and although she has a pretty face, she rejects the "responsibilities of beauty" (*EZ* 66). Nevertheless Myna spends a great deal of time arranging striking combinations of clothing to wear. Gary is first attracted to her when he sees her wearing an orange dress appliqued with a picture of a mushroom cloud, and later tells her that she resembles "an explosion over the desert" (*EZ* 41, 68). His attraction to Myna is thus coupled with his fascination with nuclear holocaust. At one point she and Gary make love in the library, and Myna now appears to him as the "knowable word, the fleshmade sigh and syllable"; she seems "cloud-bosomed, ultimate" (*EZ* 218). In the person of Myna, Gary not only loves The Bomb; he wants to have sex with it. He finds in her flesh a relief from his mentors' jargon and his rites of attenuation.

Myna further tangles the relationship between self-mortification and self-indulgence when she returns from vacation many pounds lighter. Although she had seemed to be a nonconformist, she claims that she had been "satisfied just consuming everything that came along." Her clothes fetish "made my life a whole big thing of consumption, consuming, consume" (*EZ* 227–28). Now, she claims, she can discover who she really is underneath the fat. She asserts that her obesity represented consumerism, but by losing weight and accepting the responsibilities of beauty, she may be placing herself more solidly into the consumer fantasy of emaciated female beauty. Even self-discipline, in other words, may be self-indulgence, or an outgrowth of the American consumer mythology of self-improvement. She believes that she is now facing the responsibilities of beauty, but the reader may wish to ask whose beauty it is.

We can now clarify the relationship between consumption and nu-clear weapons. Franco Fornari has argued that the nuclear arms race is a form of potlatch, a ceremony in certain pretechnological societies in which prestige is established by extravagant gift giving. According to this argu-ment, the arms race represents "a cycle of prodigality-challenge in which each of the adversaries, by wasting an enormous amount of wealth on armaments, hopes to intimidate the other and prove his own superiority" (Fornari 19). Yet many, perhaps most, people in the United States do not see expenditures on nuclear arms as waste but as a necessary deterrent to nuclear attack. We establish prestige through threat, not through prodi-gality. Myna's conversion from rituals of consumption to rituals of attri-tion implies a more plausible interpretation of the relationship between nuclear weapons and consumer economics. *End Zone* suggests, through the complex relationship among eating, asceticism, and apocalypse, that The Bomb has been incorporated into late capitalist mythology: it is the ultimate consumer item. We spend huge sums on nuclear weapons, not to use them, but merely to *possess* them as symbols of power and wealth, as consummate emblems of "Better Living Through Chemistry" (*U* 499). Nuclear weapons offer themselves as the answer to our sense of dissat-isfaction, bringing fulfillment with a Big Bang. But we cannot consume them; they are commodities utterly without use-value, because to use them is to annihilate them and the global economy in which they have value. *End Zone* reveals how the ascetic impulse and its accompanying hunger for apocalyptic endings emerge from the promptings of consumer culture, where nuclear weapons might bring instant relief from the headaches of morality and politics. Myna, first a consumer and then a dieter, and Gary, an ascetic and finally a faster, thus represent the two strains of our relation-ship with nuclear weapons: on the one hand we want to consume them and have them consume us; on the other hand we see them as a means of salvation, a colossal cleanser.

We might now read Gary's final hunger strike as his response to Myna's new self; yet his motives remain indeterminate. He may be trying to pare himself down further, to face his responsibilities, or his fast may be his final act of desperation, the last step toward suicide as closure, the end zone for his internal scrimmage. Indeed, the novel's inconclusive conclusion conforms perfectly to the unmistakable sense of anticlimax in its final section. One reason for this impression is that DeLillo places that staple of sports fiction, the Big Game, not at the end of the novel but in the middle, and then in Part 3 depicts the team's disintegration and Gary's further explorations. (In this regard, it resembles a nuclear disaster novel: Part 1 builds to a confrontation, the middle section details the "war," and Part 3 describes the aftermath.) An even more radical departure is that the Logos team loses the game, although one could argue that losing is perfectly in keeping with Creed's creed of self-mortification: what better method of self-discipline could be imagined than losing the Big Game? Most significant is that DeLillo resists his characters' desire for linearity and violent closure, and denies it to us as well. *End Zone* deconstructs conventional plot structure. In an aside at the beginning of the description of the game, DeLillo's narrator addresses the exemplary spectator, listing what readers look for in sports fiction and what spectators want in football games. The exemplary spectator understands that "sport is a benign illusion . . . that order is possible." Both reader and spectator need "details" of "statistics, patterns, mysteries, numbers, idioms, symbols"; both spectators and readers want the saving illusion of a perfect structure that reduces the complexity of real life to the simplicity of goal-driven behavior (*EZ* 112). In short, as DeLillo has stated elsewhere, *End Zone* dramatizes how "fiction itself is a sort of game" (Interview with LeClair 21).

But DeLillo changes the rules. In conventional genre fiction, which *End Zone* pretends at first to be, we are impelled by the Author, the masterplotter and God of the text, towards closure. He eliminates, like Creed, unnecessary details, giving us all we need to know. Appropriately, given the novel's food motif, the narrator describes his play-by-play as "a form of sustenance" (*EZ* 112). But the author denies us that sustenance of a conclusion that ties up the text into a neat, consumable package. Just as Gary fasts at the end, so must the reader who seek the easy consumption promised by conventional fiction. Instead, readers are forced to nourish themselves, like Gary, "on the black bones of revulsion and dread," and on a plot that wallows in atrocity and resists climax, closure, and character development. Paradoxically, while sustaining a critique of asceticism, the novel forces an asceticism of reading upon its audience. Despite the novel's zany wit and humor, the reader of *End Zone* might be said to resemble Saint Teresa, taking morbid nourishment from a human skull.

According to the categories defined by Marianna Torgovnick, *End Zone* offers a "confrontational" conclusion that flouts generic conventions and forces readers to question their expectations about closure (Torgovnick 18). *End Zone*'s end is genuinely strange, even in this age of open endings. The novel seems simply to trickle off, leaving the reader to hunt for the missing pages. It does not play the game of conventional fiction. In *White Noise* Gladney asserts that "We edge nearer death every time we plot. It is like a contract that we must sign" (*WN* 26). DeLillo breaks that contract, demonstrating that this desire to move deathward is behind the desire to read, invent, or inhabit apocalyptic fictions.[9] *End Zone* implicitly critiques fictions that pander to our apocalyptic yearnings by promulgating the myth of a world that can be remade from the ashes, those that portray nuclear war as an antidote to the tedium of everyday life. *End Zone* does not end in apocalypse, but instead exposes the intimate connection between the need for fictional closure and the desire for the end of the world. The novel concludes—or fails to conclude—on Gary's description of his enigmatic hunger strike: "In the end they had to carry me to the infirmary and feed me through plastic tubes" (*EZ* 242). He may be moving deathward, or he may be defying death by trying to wrest control of his life from Creed. This ending does not simplify; it multiplies questions. We may feel some-how cheated: by replacing the asceticism of apocalypse with an asceticism of reading, the novel forces readers to confront their own desire for violent closure. The end of *End Zone* is also self-critical in that DeLillo turns his irony upon himself: he too has displayed his fascination with nuclear holocaust by writing novels about it. The anti-apocalyptic ending of *End Zone* thus simultaneously critiques conventional plot and speaks against "the end" as conveyed and consumed in our apocalyptic fictions. Just as it repudiates conventional closure, *End Zone* repudiates nuclear apocalypse.

But like nuclear holocaust, *End Zone* finally escapes its ludic frame. In presenting fiction as a kind of endgame, *End Zone* self-consciously illuminates the tendency of fiction to proceed towards end zones, to satisfy the consumer mentality that craves apocalypse as a solution to personal or political dilemmas. We cannot read it as a running back races toward the goal line; instead DeLillo locates us within an indeterminate terminal land-scape that frustrates our wish to find the end zone. Just as the jargon of nuclear holocaust is a bomb, so fiction that exploits such apocalyptic yearn-ings is a destructive weapon, yielding to our desire for self-annihilation, our ascetic and consumerist urges toward the simplification of experience. In its refusal to provide closure, *End Zone* defuses the bomb hidden in most end-ings and thus begins the operations necessary to defuse nuclear weapons as well.

Near the conclusion of *End Zone*, Gary Harkness visits Taft Robinson's sparsely furnished room and learns that, like him, Taft believes in "static forms of beauty." Robinson plays the radio to hear the rests that punctuate the noise: "it becomes almost a spiritual exercise. Silence, words, silence, silence, silence" (*EZ* 240). Bucky Wunderlick, the narrator-protagonist of DeLillo's next novel, *Great Jones Street*, abandons his rock group in mid-tour for a small apartment in New York City, seeking the same silence and purity that Harkness finds in the Texas desert. As Opel Hampson, Wunderlick's girlfriend, tells him, "Great Jones, Bond Street, the Bowery. These places are deserts, too" (*GJS* 90). Like Gary, Bucky longs for a self-annihilation, or at least a life at "the edge of every void" (*GJS* 1). *Great Jones Street* offers another study in "the nature of diminishing existence," anatomizing Bucky's pseudo-ascetic quest as an attempt to rediscover the transcendence he once found in music. On the last tour, his audience had merely mimed the screams the group used to receive; deprived of its echoes, the group's music became meaningless. Now Bucky moves further into silence. His fans, who seemed to have been propelling him ever closer to suicide, expect him to "return with a new language for them to speak or they'd seek a divine silence attendant to my own" (*GJS* 3). Like Harkness, Wunderlick is "interested in endings" and wants to terminate his legendary existence as a pop icon and cultural myth. Thus he begins where many of DeLillo's ascetic protagonists eventually reside: "in endland" (*GJS* 3–4), a terminal landscape, devoid of noise and complexity. For Bucky, Great Jones Street lies at the crossroad between public sacrifice and private self-immolation.

Wunderlick's spiritual exile is part of a long tradition in American culture, perhaps best exemplified by Thoreau's *Walden*. In "Economy," Thoreau describes his enterprise as determining "what are the true necessaries and means of life" (Thoreau 50). He argues that one must economize by simplifying one's life.[10] *Great Jones Street* reexamines such Thoreauvian economies in the light of the late capitalist economy of commodity consumption. Like Thoreau, Bucky withdraws and simplifies his existence in an attempt to discover a richer internal economy; he wants to remove himself from the circulation of commodities to conjure up more authentic forms of value. He seeks more authentic forms of language and being in silence and immobility, and in them hopes to find "a moral form to master commerce" (*GJS* 70). But ironically, his withdrawal, like that of Bill Gray in DeLillo's later novel, *Mao II*, merely enhances his celebrity. At the novel's opening (written after the action has been completed), Wunderlick notes that "fame requires every kind of excess" (*GJS* 1). In contrast to Thoreau's, Bucky's economy of silence comes to be seen as just another form of excess. As his silence and even his suicidal impulses are appropriated by a commodity culture hungry for violence, he becomes the victim of his own and his audience's craving for sacrifices. In this economy, even purity becomes a product. Thus if Bucky ultimately does "master commerce," he does so not by subduing it (indeed, one of his key realizations is that the market is inescapable) but by letting it consume him so that he can be reborn in a new language, a new guise.

In the first part of the novel (chapters 1–11), Bucky's retreat brings him close to the silent immobility he seeks. His barren room allows him to test "the depths of silence. Or one's willingness to be silent. Or one's fear of this willingness" (*GJS* 25). But his career has been devolving from activism to inwardness to meaninglessness all along: his last album, entitled *Pee-Pee-Maw-Maw*, celebrated economy in such lyrics as "Blank mumble blat / Babble song, babble song . . . / The beast is loose / Least is best" (*GJS* 118). Bucky is echoing DeLillo, who once commented, "Babbling can be frustrated speech or it can be a purer form, an alternate speech" (Interview with LeClair 24). In terms of his artistic trajectory, then, Bucky's movement toward babbling and silence merely amounts to "traveling a straight line to the end of an idea" (*GJS* 248)—Thoreauvian purity. He contemplates his silent phone as a reflection of his desired condition, believing that "the fact that it will not speak enables us to see it in a new way, as an object rather than an instrument. . . . The phone has made a descent into total dumbness, and so becomes beautiful" (*GJS* 31). Lacking both use-value and exchange-value, the dead phone achieves perfection. Bucky likewise seeks objecthood as a means of recovering a "pure" identity outside the series of images he has presented to the public, which has swallowed and regurgitated them in half-digested form. Bucky hopes that this Thoreauvian economy will remove him from the market economy symbolized by his manager Globke, whose obsessions are vividly figured when Bucky interrupts him fishing a dime out of his toilet. Globke is constantly "propelled, ballistically, to and from distant points of commerce" (*GJS* 11); his inveterate traveling contrasts with Bucky's newfound immobility. At first granting Bucky his whim—he is, after all, a valuable commodity—Globke's obsession with "product" ("You were failing to deliver product"—*GJS* 186) spurs him eventually to force Bucky's return.

Globke urges him to give in to the "great circulatory process," to capitalize on his withdrawal and build his legend. Wunderlick considers yielding "to the seductions of the void, taking a generation with me into blank climates. . . . I'd be the epoch's barren hero, a man who knew the surest way to minimize" (*GJS* 67–68). But he soon discovers that his withdrawal only leaves a void to be filled by others; rather than increasing his control over his image, he further relinquishes control to the media's circulating rumors and to buyers and sellers of various stripes. The longer he is silent, the more the rumors about his whereabouts multiply, so that the real Bucky is replaced by mythic facsimiles. His celebrity has become a thing apart from him, managed either by the recording industry or by his own public, who interpret even withdrawal and suicide as a message, a call to form a mass movement. No longer master of his own production, Bucky nonetheless continues to reproduce and circulate in the form of simulacra. He has come, like the talk-show host Delfina in *Valparaiso*, to "live in a box in a state of endless replication" (*Valparaiso* 94). An androgynous boy named Hanes, who later steals the illicit word-inhibiting drug around which the plot revolves, tells Bucky that "you're dead when we want you dead. Then you land and do a make-believe concert. We put you on and take you off. . . . Things don't get better just because they get more simple" (*GJS* 43). The reverberation of Bucky's sound has grown louder than the originating music; like David Bell, Bucky is learning "a lesson in the effect of echoes" (*A* 58). He has become an echo of himself.

Bucky's condition strikingly resembles Jean Baudrillard's description of the postmodern condition. For Baudrillard, consumerism is not an "indeterminate marginal sector" of postmodern life, but rather "a complete system of values" ("Consumer Society" 49). Origins and essences are lost or disseminated; in their place are only simulacra, "models of a real without origin or reality: a hypperreal" ("Simulations" 166). Thus early in the novel Bucky tells a reporter from Running Dog News Service that he has no fabled house in the mountains but only "the facsimile of a house"; Transparanoia, the conglomerate that Globke has formed around Bucky's products, really "markets facsimiles. Everybody under contract has his or her facsimile" (*GJS* 24). For Baudrillard, death is the sole condition that eludes the hyperreal; hence "all bound energies aim for their own demise" ("Symbolic Exchange" 123): "all plots tend to move deathward" (*WN* 26). Logically, then, the end zone of Wunderlick's straight line is death: perhaps death will free him from simulacra. The proliferating rumors about his death and the market's exploitation of those rumors imply, however, that even death may become hyperreal. It scarcely matters whether the "real" Bucky dies, so long as the legend lives on.

An urban guerrilla collective called Happy Valley Farm Commune, along with several other groups, pursues the word-blocking drug (referred to as "the product") through its agents. Appropriating the Thoreauvian economy of solitude and simplicity, the commune wants to use Bucky's image to return "the idea of privacy to the idea of American life" (*GJS* 193). Opel tells him that

they think you exemplify some old idea of men alone with the land. You stepped out of your legend to pursue personal freedom. . . . The return of the private man, according to them, is the only way to destroy the notion of mass man. Mass man ruined our freedoms for us. Turning inward will get them back. Revolutionary solitude. Turn inward one and all. (*GJS* 60)

Happy Valley Farm Commune represents the terrorism of fame, which refashions its gods into consumable objects. Paradoxically, they want to give privacy mass appeal, to transform ascetic inwardness into a collective movement and thereby restore an idea that has never really been lost. Of course, consumerism, as Baudrillard observes, always transforms collective satisfactions into private ones, by collectively assigning "consumers a place in relation to a code, without . . . giving rise to any collective solidarity" ("Consumer Society" 55).

Happy Valley exemplifies how commodity culture turns political awareness into private pleasures, how it transforms first-person consciousness into that "universal third person" (*A* 270) discussed in chapter 1 by appropriating even the symbols of individual rebellion. Happy Valley both produces and exploits this condition of seriality, in which each consumer, as I noted earlier, is simultaneously totally alone and indistinguishable from all others. Through the commune's machinations and the circulation of his own fame, Bucky has become little more than a point or nexus at which the lines of competing plots—each one based on the obsessive pursuit of products—intersect. His self-purification, his pursuit of the end of an idea, has become a form of serial reproduction that only exemplifies and accelerates the goal-driven behavior of commercial interests toward commodities. A third person even to himself, Bucky is just another consumer product (LeClair, *Loop* 96; DeCurtis 140); as such, he can consume himself.

Opel personifies Bucky's parasitic relationship with his audience, but she also tries to warn him about the consequences of the path he is taking. Their relationship is defined by the shifting poles of mobility and stasis. Following the group on tour, Opel has become the quintessential traveler. Her goals are "to keep moving. To forget everything. To *be* the sound. . . . She wanted to exist as music does, nowhere, beyond the maps of language" (*GJS* 12; emphasis in original). Upon her return in chapter 8, she informs Bucky that she too has become involved in the bidding for "the product" (the drug), wheeling and dealing for Happy Valley. But in *Great Jones Street*, she seeks immobility as an antidote to traveling, a word that comes to represent buying and selling of any kind: a traveler is a salesperson who loses all shadings of self and becomes an instrument of commerce, a container for products—"luggage" (*GJS* 91). Paradoxically, traveling, not stasis, is the route to commodification: one circulates in the consumer economy and thereby becomes a thing. To counteract this narrowing, she stays with Bucky, hoping to attain a purer "thingness," to resist commodification through utter inertness. Together they seek in objecthood "a moral form to master commerce" and repel the circulation that submits commodities to exchanges (*GJS* 70). Ironically, Opel's presence reawakens Bucky:

> Opel had stolen my immobility. I had been motionless as salt. People had swirled around me and I had plotted changes in the weather, gradations of light and silence. I had centered myself, learning of the existence of an interior motion, a shift in levels from isolation to solitude to wordlessness to immobility. When Opel occupied that center I became the thing that swirled. (*GJS* 85–86)

He tells Opel that when he first left the group, "suicide was nearer to me than my big toe. . . . I really think it was expected of me. . . . I want to return but in a different way. New extremities. It's like a passage from suicide to murder" (*GJS* 86). She warns him about "that little touch of the antichrist" in him and advises him that "evil is movement toward void and that's where we both agree you're heading" (*GJS* 88). Her advice to repudiate traveling may be sound, but, as we have seen, Bucky's immobility only encourages others to exploit him. While he remains still, his reputation circulates, encouraging his audience to perceive him as a sacrificial victim. Opel prevents his sacrifice by dying; substituting herself for him, she achieves the immobility she had sought. Consequently, Bucky attempts to draw back from the void, recognizing that self-annihilation will not repudiate the excesses of fame, but only exemplify them. He now contemplates returning, and Opel provides him with a means: a parcel containing the Mountain Tapes, raw recordings he made in a frenzy of inspiration but has never released. Hanes brings the tapes and exchanges them for the package with the word-blocking drug. This event is central in more than one sense: not only does it take place midway through chapter 13, in the exact center of the novel, but in exchanging the two items—tapes and drug—for each other the novel identifies them, implying that Bucky's tapes are also a drug that blocks his expression by making him prey to the mercenary machinations of others. The identification of the two products constitutes another lesson in the effect of echoes: Wunderlick is irrevocably implicated in the circulation of simulacra.

Bucky's upstairs neighbor, hack writer Eddie Fenig ("pfenig" means penny), embodies the market slavery that Bucky attempts to resist. Whereas

Bucky is terse, passive, and vague, Fenig is hyperactive, logorrheic, a language-secreting insect who generates millions of words and keeps them all in a massive trunk. Like Opel, he is identified by his luggage, which contains his products. Some writers are men of letters; Fenig is "a man of numbers" (GJS 51), defining his labor not by quality but by sheer quantity. He paces back and forth in his room, desperately seeking an entry into the market, his movement a microcosmic version of the other characters' commercial "traveling." He does not fear failing to write, only failing to sell, and attempts various mordantly funny strategies to appeal to the market, ranging from pornography for children to financial writing for millionaires, and finally to "terminal fantasies" written for the denizens of urban deserts like Great Jones Street (GJS 221). He poses the question with which DeLillo's protagonists so often grapple: "Why are terminal events so pleasing, I wonder?" (GJS 223). This novel's answer is that they satisfy the consumerist desire to destroy our gods and thereby satisfy the desire for simplification through destruction displayed in End Zone. In Fenig's work, the furthest expression of the "idea of privacy" turns out to be elimination of private citizens; the ultimate purification is the emptiness toward which Bucky— also a terminal fantasy of his public—has been drawn. Fenig epitomizes the way that commodity culture obliterates the distinction between art and commerce, between private rituals and public forms.

He also knows what Bucky discovers only gradually: once an artist discovers an audience, he can sell it anything. But Fenig doesn't sell, and his desperate descriptions of the magical, dreadful market illustrate his frustrated, circular motion:

the market is a strange thing, almost a living organism. It changes, it palpitates, it grows, it excretes. It sucks things in and spews them up. It's a living wheel that turns and crackles. . . . It loves and kills. . . . The big wheel spins and gyrates and makes firecracker noises, going faster and faster and throwing off anybody who can't hold on. . . . The market is phenomenal, bright as a hundred cities, turning and turning, and there are little figures everywhere trying to hold on with one hand but they're getting thrown off into the surrounding night, the silence, the emptiness, the darkness, the basin, the crater, the pit. (GJS 27, 141)

One of those little figures trying to leap onto the racing merry-go-round, Fenig worships the market that spews him up. He is willing to remake himself in its image. In submitting to the power of the simulacrum that Bucky resists, Fenig measures his value strictly by the serial productions he has sold. Indeed, Fenig is only a simulacrum of a writer, and Bucky imagines that in Fenig's closet are "four more Fenigs, laced, hooded, neatly creased" (GJS 223).

But Fenig's lurid description of the market is more than a lively metaphor for the power of commerce and the circulation of commodities. Fenig's wheel is transformed into a spinning disk that signifies Wunderlick's awareness of his own commodified identity. This figure emerges most clearly in the "Superslick Mind Contracting Media Kit" that separates the first two parts of the novel. This section contains interviews and articles and, most importantly, song lyrics from Bucky's first three albums, which show how his career has progressed (or regressed) from political commentary to self-obsession. The lyrics of "Diamond Stylus," the title track from his second album, graphically present the image of a spinning disk. In it the singer speaks alternately as the vinyl record and the phonograph stylus: "It scratched out lines on my face / Test pressing time. . . . Turning into burning thing / Circling into wordtime . . . . Re-volve / Is the time I have to live / Ma-trix / Is the mother-cut" (*GJS* 112). The spinning market ("it's a living wheel . . . turning and turning") has merged with the performer and his product, the record. As the stylus, Bucky has now completed his inward journey around the grooves, only to be stuck at the center, repeating the same meaningless noises over and over. Now he wants to abandon the disk completely, or perhaps become its central hole; as such he would not so much speak as enable the speech of the other mechanisms. But the stylus can be picked up again, and placed at the beginning; likewise, Bucky allows himself to be manipulated into "circling into wordtime," restarting his repetitive circulation in the marketplace, and bouncing back into his box of endless replication. In figuring himself as a vinyl record, the singer illustrates his own condition as mass-produced object undergoing "test pressing." The figures of stylus and record, then, capture Bucky's condition as simulacrum and echo, his entrapment in a circulating economy that he no longer operates. Later in the novel, Globke's wife speaks on the phone to Bucky about "the stillness at the center of a thing in motion," as Bucky listens to his own voice "revolving at thirty-three and a third" (*GJS* 166). This wheel—the record as spinning market—is what Bucky has become. The figures of stylus and record lie at the center of the "media kit" interlude; thus the song marks both Bucky's first recognition of his condition as commodity and his first repudiation of that condition. But Bucky still sees no alternative to sacrifice, to becoming a "burning thing."

The spinning record also functions as a self-reflexive image of the novel's own structural economy. The passive and nearly immobile Wunderlick resides at the center of the market's (and the novel's) circulation, the void around which the quest for the two mysterious products revolves. As a result, the first two-thirds of the novel contain almost no linear action; instead, a rotating set of characters visits Wunderlick in his apartment, vying either for the drug or for the Mountain Tapes. The still point of this turning world, Bucky is the central hole that permits the record to play. His economy of movement becomes the novel's. This static, circular quality accounts, I think, both for the novel's difficulty and for its critical neglect in DeLillo's increasingly acclaimed oeuvre.[11] Like Bucky, DeLillo economizes, turning his novel into a rotating set of dialogues. *Great Jones Street* imitates Bucky's lyrics as it "circles into wordtime," mimicking the circular journey of a phonograph stylus toward the center where Bucky stays. Its plot bears some resemblance to that of *Running Dog*, in which a top-secret funding organization called Radial Matrix sends agents to find a reputedly pornographic film of Hitler: like *Great Jones Street*, *Running Dog* revolves around a competition to own and control a product. Indeed, "Diamond Stylus" implies that *Great Jones Street* is also a "radial matrix": an interlocking set of grooved circulations and returns. At first linear, then static, it is ultimately circular, because the book we are reading marks Bucky's final return.

Great Jones Street depicts a group of grotesque, stylized performances by a series of nearly indistinguishable characters identified by little more than their voices. It is a theater in which Bucky has evolved from performer to spectator; since his audience now seems to have more power than he, perhaps he can regain power by becoming a spectator himself.[12] More specifically, the novel resembles a masque, that theatrical form popularized in the English Renaissance and characterized by an extravagant procession of masked figures designed for royal entertainment (Meagher 33). The royal personage here is, of course, Bucky Wunderlick, who, as in Renaissance masques, is requested at the end to join (or rejoin) the performance. The masque is less a drama than a series of tableaux, and *Great Jones Street*'s chapters function similarly, as setpieces with rotating but repeated characters: Globke, Azarian (Bucky's bandmate), Hanes, Fenig, a set of journalists, a former rock star named Watney, Bohack (apparent leader of Happy Valley), and one Dr. Pepper, a figure who appears twice in disguise (as a brush salesman and as a "professor of latent history") before entering as Pepper (which may also be a disguise). The characters in Renaissance masques were usually allegorical representations of qualities such as Fame, Suspicion, and Virtue. Likewise, the characters in this novel are variations on the theme of commerce: some (Hanes, Skippy, Dr. Pepper) are named after consumer products; others (Fenig) symbolize the pursuit of money; still others (Watney) generate facsimiles of themselves that suggest their own two-dimensionality.[13] The party that occupies chapter 10, populated by zany minor characters, most of whom never reappear, functions as the antimasque, the "foil to the masque proper" (Holman 32–33), that is also a condensed version of the entire novel. If the characters' interchangeability makes a first reading of the novel rather dizzying, that indistinguishability is precisely the point: obsessively pursuing products and seeking to impress pop royalty, they have become human simulacra. Indeed, I want to argue later that this static, circular structural economy constitutes DeLillo's own method of "mastering commerce," of resisting having his novel read merely as a rock 'n' roll story, a plot-driven pop novel about drugs—in short, as a consumer product.

In Part 2 the characters' circulating quests for the two products accelerate. This section introduces Dr. Pepper and Watney, the two characters who best exemplify commerce in the novel. Like Bucky, Pepper exists in a shadow world where rumors of his existence precede and supersede his physical presence. He is a shapechanger, a composite figure who seems to have been "put together from a strip of silent film, frame by frame," a simulacrum who exists for the sole purpose of buying and selling (*GJS* 170). Pepper is the "alternative monarch" required by the masque, a Proteus figure whose mimetic skill "enables him to adapt to every character" (Fletcher 19–20). Like Opel, he defines himself as a traveler, and his travels have made him a transient in his own identity. Claiming to deal in what he calls "pure products" (*GJS* 175), Pepper alludes ironically to William Carlos Williams's poem "To Elsie," which begins, "The pure products of America / go crazy" (W. C. Williams 28). Pepper's use of the phrase shows what the consumer economy does to the "purity" sought by Thoreau and his spiritual kin: "purity" becomes a product as marketable as any other (as does craziness, for that matter), one as exploitable as the "young slatterns" in Williams's poem. Pepper hopes to end his career in drug dealing with a legendary feat: securing the secret word-inhibiting drug. Unlike the other dealers in the novel, however, this alternative king has the power to impose silence upon Bucky.

The cynical Watney has never believed in music as expression, but has known all along that it is just an act. Formerly a merchant of musical "product," he's now "a buyer who sometimes sells" drugs (*GJS* 154). Like Opel, he is an inveterate traveler defined by the "luggage" he leaves with Bucky when he departs: a suitcase containing bubblegum cards embossed with his own picture. Watney traffics in facsimiles of fulfillment. Some of his bubblegum cards also contain LSD, as if to suggest that fame is also a facsimile-producing drug. Watney's drug dealing again reveals the connection between the two products: Bucky's music is a drug that deflects rebellion into consumption, and the word-stealing drug is, as LeClair observes, a "symbol of extreme consumer narcosis" that is also reflected in the hypnosis that Bucky has observed on the faces of his audience (*Loop* 100). But despite their appearance as magicians, both Watney and Pepper really deal in dread. Their hunger for ownership is a craving for power, and they acquire that most valuable commodity through acts of violence, using fear as their medium of exchange. DeLillo thus suggests that the real product of these "underground" merchants is the same "numbed terror" that characterizes the slatterns in Williams's poem, the same fear that drives Bucky's bandmate Azarian eventually to his death (see *GJS* 32, 123), the same dread that motivates Happy Valley to try to silence Bucky for good.

The central event of the novel's second section is not a commercial transaction, however, but an epiphanic moment of resistance to commerce. It occurs when Bucky encounters an immobile version of himself in his neighbor Mrs. Micklewhite's malformed, mute son, whose haunting cries obtrude from below occasionally to remind Bucky of "the beauty and horror of wordless things" (*GJS* 52). The Micklewhite boy represents Bucky's own inchoate reborn self, and his wordlessness constitutes the "pure" form of expression that Bucky has been seeking. The boy seems to Bucky to resemble "some impossible mutation, bird to brown worm . . . and I began to feel that I myself was the other point of the progression" (*GJS* 161). He is fascinated by the boy because he embodies "what we'd always feared, ourselves in radical divestment," and is "drawn into what I felt was his ascendancy, the helpless strength of his entrapment in tepid flesh, in the reductions of being" (*GJS* 161). Recognizing the boy's "embryonic beauty," Bucky touches this incarnation of his own impulse toward wordless immobility. Symbolizing Bucky's own half-formed attempts to remake himself, the Micklewhite boy's authentic expression of suffering is the antithesis of the echo chamber of fame into which Bucky has been sucked. Whereas Wunderlick's very silence has become a product, the Micklewhite boy's cries reach a human depth unplumbed by any sound Bucky has ever made. Indeed, the Micklewhite boy is the one person in the novel who does not respond at all to Bucky's fame; he is utterly self-absorbed, trapped in his helpless body. He has managed to achieve what Bucky has futilely sought in withdrawal: escape from commodification. His dead father tried to put him in a freak show, but failed. "Who'd buy him?" his mother asks (*GJS* 134). In this figure, then, Wunderlick sees a reflection of both what he is and what he can never be, a truly unmoving emblem of his own rebirth, forever half finished. The Micklewhite boy signifies both Bucky's desired regression to infantilism and his attempt to discover in wordlessness a moral form to master commerce.

Bucky's own starkly primitive expressions of suffering—those mysterious Mountain Tapes—introduce part 3 of the novel. The songs, "genuinely infantile" (*GJS* 148), resemble those on the first solo album of John Lennon, as well as the fabled "Basement Tapes" of Bob Dylan, both of whom Bucky resembles in other ways. Lennon's tragic fate also illustrates

Wunderlick's likely end: destruction by his own fans. Indeed, the tapes articulate his growing sense that he must sacrifice himself: "Maiden words to learn / Being young restores the god / That eats itself. . . . Strip by strip / I pick the skin from off my face / Becoming god. . . . / Better than the feast that ends / When they pick us from their teeth" (*GJS* 203–4). Gradually venturing outside of his room, Wunderlick seems to have resigned himself to returning and submitting himself to the terminal fantasies of his audience. "They want your sound. They want your words. They want your arms and legs and unmentionables," says Globke (*GJS* 144), who himself wants the Mountain Tapes so badly that he steals them during one of Bucky's outings. The audience craves product, he says. "They're yowling for their food. Feed me, feed me" (*GJS* 186). Nothing is too distasteful for him so long as it creates or extends the life of products. Bucky at first agrees to go along with Globke's scheme for his return—an entire tour based on "guest appearances" designed to exploit Bucky's withdrawal and enhance his mystique—because the plan fulfills the sacrificial yearnings Bucky voiced on the Mountain Tapes. But his submission proves that, despite the authenticity of the tapes, he no longer owns himself. Thus, while Bucky can release the tapes, he still does not know how to release himself from his imprisonment in the house of fame.

Ironically, it is the mercenary Watney who emerges as the unlikely source of Bucky's illumination. He observes shrewdly that even in death Bucky will have no true power:

You have the illusion of power. . . . Nothing truly moves to your sound. Nothing is shaken or bent. You're a bloody artist you are. Less than four ounces on the meat scale. . . . You're above ground not under. The true underground is the place where power flows. . . . The corporations. The military. The banks. This is the underground network. . . . Your audience is not the relevant audience. It doesn't make anything. It doesn't sell to others. Your life consumes itself. Chomp. (*GJS* 231–32)

It turns out that the drug (the pursuit of which Watney abandons) was invented by the true underground power—"U.S. Guv"—probably to silence radicals. Thus Watney is right: the overt and the covert powers are the same; the largest drug dealer is the same entity that supposedly fights the distribution of underground drugs. Watney also suggests that rock music works almost as well as the drug by deflecting political dissent into self-consuming noise and echo. Bucky's fans have been ingesting this drug all along—and so has he.

Thus Wunderlick seems driven to consume himself. His sacrificial longings dramatize his recognition that "fame requires every kind of excess." Moreover, Bucky's need to sacrifice himself amounts to recognition of his own valuelessness. Georges Bataille's writings on sacrifice and waste are particularly pertinent here. For Bataille excess—the surplus taken from the mass of useful wealth, the waste, the unusable—is a primary fact of political economy. Bucky has become this "accursed share": the scapegoat or hero whose violent death both consecrates the victim and preserves the community (Bataille 58–59).[14] He is ready to become the gift to the gods of celebrity: Bucky tells Watney, "I'm tired of my body. I want to be a dream, their dream. I want to flow right through them" (*GJS* 231). Watney responds with admiration at the "genius of [his] excess" (*GJS* 231). It is now clear that Bucky's Thoreauvian economy of simplicity has been only another manifestation of fame's economy of excess. Bucky recognizes that his sacrificial death will allow him the greatest possible intimacy with his fans; he will be one of them, "Ceremonial flesh injected with cursed preservatives. Eating myself: lessons in the effects of auto-cannibalism" (*GJS* 185). Bucky can now gain use-value and enhance his exchange-value best by dying.

Enter Bohack, the apparent leader of Happy Valley Farm Commune, who aims to enforce the commune's vision of Bucky's exchange-value through just such a sacrifice. Now that he has become their "group-image," these "acolytes of [his] silence" must coerce him into remaining that way or lose their power and identity (*GJS* 194). At once eschewing and typifying the consumer economy, Happy Valley Farm Commune, simply a more openly terroristic component of his ravenous public, dictates how Bucky will "use" himself: he must commit the "perfect suicide," which occurs "when people know you're dead on one level but refuse to accept it on a deeper level. . . . It's what you owe us. . . . We patterned our whole lives after your example. What happens? . . . You decide to step back into the legend. No good, Bucky" (*GJS* 243). The Bucky Wunderlick industry no longer needs him. To implement their concept of "privacy," of "Reducing yourself to minimums" (*GJS* 194), they will use the excesses of "mindless violence" ("the only truly philosophical violence" [*GJS* 191]). Such violence, as DeLillo has stated elsewhere, is a "sardonic response to the promise of consumer fulfillment in America" ("Outsider" 57). Thus if violent death is in one sense the culmination of Wunderlick's linear trajectory toward the void, it is also the logical outcome of his entrapment on that spinning wheel, the consumer economy. According to Bataille, the way a society uses its excess defines it; the "use" that Wunderlick's society makes of him reveals that the cult of celebrity, the consumer economy, and even rock 'n' roll itself are driven as much by the need to destroy as by the need to acquire. In this sense, Bucky's withdrawal is as much a product of the economy of fame and commerce as is his desired return; both must lead to destruction.

Suicide is what everyone (including himself) has been expecting, but when faced with the prospect, Wunderlick demurs, claiming that he's "not innocent enough" (*GJS* 243–44). In any case, suicide would only augment his legend. So Bohack offers him the second-best solution: silence. To ensure it the group burns the Mountain Tapes and then injects him with the word-inhibiting drug. In allowing himself to be injected, Bucky has indeed traveled a straight line to the end of the ascetic idea of purification and rebirth, that Thoreauvian economy which, paradoxically, is a necessary part of the "excess" economy of fame. But he no longer owns the idea. Instead it is owned by Happy Valley, whose real leader, a man named Chess who also may be Dr. Pepper, finally surfaces to lecture Bucky on the true nature of privacy. The possibility that Chess (formerly a theatrical producer [*GJS* 253]) may be Pepper casts the entire quest for the product into a different light. If Chess is Pepper, then the entire pursuit of the product has actually been a circle—Chess's circle, Chess's masque, a Chess game with Bucky as mated king—and Bucky's pursuit of silence only a "straight line intersecting the circle" (*GJS* 254). The entire plot, in short, would have been an elaborate plan to mislead Bucky in order to carry out Happy Valley's scheme; the wheel of commerce would not have been circulating at all, but would only have appeared to be moving while actually standing still. Although the novel leaves this possibility indeterminate, in any case Bucky accepts injection with the drug, voicing his acquiescence with his last words: "Pee-pee-maw-maw" (*GJS* 244).

The product-driven plot of *Great Jones Street* closes with Bucky Wunderlick entering the linguistic void toward which he has been plunging from the beginning. In that sense the plot has traversed a straight line from withdrawal to silence to wordlessness. Bucky enjoys his infantile state, envisioning himself as a kind of living chant. In the final chapter he walks through the city, listening to recitations of the kind of "elemental lists" that Gary Harkness contemplates as the path to true purity (*EZ* 89; cf *GJS* 259, 260, 262). Yet the conclusion remains ambiguous: such pseudo-ascetic rituals, saints, and lists are dangerous, as *End Zone* has shown us. Nor is Bucky merely a spectator; paradoxically, in not speaking he briefly reassumes center stage. Thus, if he attains the wordless condition of the Micklewhite boy, he does not resist the consumer system by doing so: wordlessness itself has become his "act." Rumor now generates a saintly Bucky performing good deeds for the inhabitants of the urban desert. In yet another spin of the disk, he is denied even this dubious purity when the drug's effects wear off. And his first word is "mouth": even the rebirth of language exhibits postmodern self-reflexivity (*GJS* 264). Thus, while in one sense Bucky's muteness is a triumph—he has finally managed to wrest control of his sound and won a kind of freedom—in another sense, he is doubly defeated: the commune has denied him control over both his withdrawal and his return, and the comforting wordlessness in which he hides eventually seeps away as well.

In traveling straight to the end, he has also returned to the womb: the line is also a circle. The novel's plot likewise combines the linear movement of obsession with a cyclic turn to primal simplicity, blending the ascetic's competing impulses toward death and rebirth. But in one final spin of the disk, the book itself ultimately becomes Bucky's path back to public life, and so he finally may defeat the circulation of his simulacra, ironically, by creating another self in words, one, we are asked to believe, that constitutes the "real" Bucky. Yet this victory may also a defeat. Because the book we are reading is also a consumer product (either in our world or in Bucky's fictional universe), Bucky's escape and return, his final performances, are part of the same circulating economy that he has tried to elude. If one makes products, the novel suggests, one is also made by them; in that sense a written record can no more "master commerce" than can a vinyl one.

Great Jones Street is DeLillo's first demonstration of the limits of the Joycean principles of "silence, exile [and] cunning" (Interview with LeClair 20) that are even more thoroughly deconstructed in *Mao II*, as I argue later. Indeed, *Great Jones Street* implicitly critiques DeLillo's own withdrawal from the public eye by implying that to resist fame is only to allow it to escape one's own management, to allow facsimiles to replace one's "true" self. But DeLillo realizes what Bucky learns only belatedly: that "the artist sits still, finally, because the materials he deals with begin to shape his life, instead of being shaped, and in stillness he seeks a form of self-defense, one that ends with putrefaction, or stillness caught in time lapse" (*GJS* 126). Bucky's recognition that stillness leads to putrefaction suggests a demand for action. Whereas Wunderlick has already defined himself in terms of the consumer economy—whatever he does in the future will be affiliated with it and appropriated by it—DeLillo has never courted popularity. Instead, he continues to maintain that the artist must stand outside society, "independent of affiliation and independent of influence. . . . There are so many temptations for American writers to become part of the system . . . that now, more than ever, we have to resist" ("Seven Seconds" 390). DeLillo's early and later writing remains politically charged and self-critical because it dramatizes how aesthetic and ascetic withdrawal may easily be transformed into apologies for violence, consumer numbness, and exploitation.

Great Jones Street finally involves itself in a paradox: in being consumed, it participates in the consumer economy in which books are marketed; yet it must be read in order for its critique of that economy to register. Hence, the most important way that *Great Jones Street* enacts DeLillo's vow to resist becoming part of the system is through its own structure, which provides, in its static and circular structural economy, an antidote to the goal-bound, commodity-obsessed behavior of its characters. As we have seen, until the last few chapters the novel embodies Bucky's quest for thingness: its static plot brings it very near to inertness. Although it finally moves toward a provisional closure, it shares with *End Zone* a deconstruction of linear plots and a resistance to conventional characterization that repudiate the system that transforms fiction into a consumer product and the writer into a celebrity. The novel resists its own consumption.[15] Moreover, in analyzing the relationship between artist and audience, it implicates its readers in its criticism of consumerism. That is, the novel's economies of form create difficulties that encourage readers to work harder; we cannot passively ingest its words but must actively engage with them, or risk finding ourselves mocked as we read. Once again DeLillo's analysis of the relationship between consumerism and "high" art forces both him and his readers into a dialogue with cultural forms that is potent precisely because it confronts those forms from the inside: first offering itself as a rock 'n' roll book, *Great Jones Street* quickly frustrates the reader's desire to find in it the transient pleasures of the genre. The degree to which *Great Jones Street* resists passive consumption, then, is also the degree to which it defeats the sterilizing pursuit of commodities that it critically depicts. In place of linear plot and narcotizing commodities, it offers a different economy: a commerce between text and reader that leaves the value of both enhanced not by consumption, but by labor. In that sense, it is DeLillo's novel, whose structural economy both encompasses Bucky's return and transcends it, that becomes the "moral form" that may enable both its readers and its author to master commerce.

Chapter 3
Boomerang

Ratner's Star Through the Looking Glass

Despite Don DeLillo's opinion that *Ratner's Star* is the best of his early novels (Interview with LeClair 27), it has the been the least understood of all his works. As DeLillo admits, *Ratner's Star* seems to revolve in distant "orbit around the other books" he has written ("Art of Fiction" 289). Certainly its cartoonish characters, static structure, and arcane subject matter make it difficult to comprehend and even more difficult to like. Like Johannes Kepler's *Somnium*, one of the internal models for *Ratner's Star* (*RS* 57), the novel's "speculative meditations on the 'unsolvable knot' of science and mysticism" (*RS* 306) blend (not always successfully) numerous aims and genres. *Ratner's Star* is a Menippean satire, an allegorical history of mathematics, a biography of 14-year-old math prodigy Billy Twillig, a disquisition on bats, a work of science fiction, a rewriting of Lewis Carroll's Alice books. Beneath all, it is a dream-text that dramatizes the powerful, unforeseen effects of the underworlds that exist beneath our daytime reality.

The novel breaks into two distinct parts. The first part, "Adventures," consists of twelve discrete episodes set in Field Experiment Number One (FENO), a cycloid-shaped think tank located somewhere in Asia, which depict Billy Twillig's gradual decryption of a message issuing (apparently) from outer space. This section fits DeLillo's characterization of the novel as "naked structure" (Interview with LeClair 27), and its chapter headings — "Expansion," "Dichotomy," "Convergence," etc. — resemble a self-reflexive outline of a generic novel. Static and crowded with bizarre characters, "Adventures" takes the form of a hypertrophic children's book in which various scary creatures confront a youthful protagonist; its episodic structure mimics the form ("and then, . . . and then, . . . and then") of the stories small children tell.[1]

The dramatistic quality of DeLillo's early novels is exaggerated in "Adventures," in which Billy engages in a series of dialogues with characters representing specific scientific specialties. But few of these dialogues yield understanding; instead the characters use speech for competition (Timur Nūt), exploitation ("Troxl," Cheops Feeley), catechism (Armand Verbene, S.J.), or pontification (Endor, Ratner). *Ratner's Star* subsumes these failures of communication into its larger one: the inability to decipher the "message" from the "Ratnerians" and the shocking discovery of its real source. Subjecting these failed dialogues to the dialogical force of natural history, the novel unmasks the characters' monologic claims to authority as "false, hypocritical, greedy, limited, narrowly rationalistic, indequate to reality" (Bakhtin, "Discourse" 311–12). Billy himself is the chief dialogical presence in the novel, and his mixture of innocence, terror, genius, and awe permits DeLillo to interrogate the role of science as sacerdotal authority.

The second part, "Reflections," seems to be a different book, in which DeLillo adopts a Woolfian free indirect discourse that seamlessly moves from mind to mind. As he has noted, the two parts are mirror images: 1 versus –1, linear versus circulating, "Discrete [versus] continuous. Day, night. Left brain, right brain. But they also link together. The second part bends back to the first" (Interview with LeClair 28). Taking DeLillo's cue, I want to argue that *Ratner's Star* coheres structurally and thematically, first, by tracking the developing sensibility of Billy Twillig, and second, through its covert history of mathematics, which DeLillo presents as a narrative of madness, creativity, pride, and self-deception — as an underground or secret history like those later portrayed in *Libra* and *Underworld*.[2] But it coheres most forcefully through the repetition of the "stellated twilligon" or boomerang figure, which represents a myriad of themes and structures, including Billy's *Bildung*, the distance to and from Ratner's Star, the shape of the cosmos, and the path of human history. As its name indicates, the "stellated twilligon" is Billy's mathematical discovery, and it embodies his desire to become a "star" by combining self-reflection and astronomical vision. An example of the "recursive symmetries" analyzed by practitioners of chaos theory (Hayles, "Introduction" 10), the boomerang — which is thrown away only to return to its source — betokens both the "naked structure" of the novel and the failure of any human creation to achieve perfect objectivity. Most importantly, then, the figure represents *Ratner's Star*'s self-reflexive examination of self-reflexivity. Itself structured as a mirror or boomerang, the novel depicts a looking-glass world that humans constantly mistake for a window.

By dramatizing how human enterprises inevitably reflect human failings and limitations, *Ratner's Star* attains a deeper thematic coherence with DeLillo's other works: it exposes science as a form of magic designed to quell our terror of mortality. Mathematics, DeLillo suggests, is a makeshift bridge built over a pool of dread. Exploring the relationships between secular knowledge and sacred intuition, between logic and primal fear, *Ratner's Star* embodies how all representations—whether scientific or literary—depend upon our belief in them. Ultimately, then, it interrogates even its own design as a "piece of mathematics" (Interview with LeClair 27), challenging readers to make it cohere and yet undermining such system-building impulses. In its ambition to encompass all forms of human endeavor, *Ratner's Star* becomes a profound meditation on the inextricable relationships among science, fiction, and faith that implies that though our ostensibly perfect structures always bear the taint of fallibility, we desperately need them to provide the illusion of control and to answer our fear of death.

KHALIX IN NUMBERLAND

Nourished from Below

Ratner's Star is the most heavily intertextual of DeLillo's early novels, and its "unconscious" or underground stream of history is fed especially by the work and lives of mathematicians such as Pythagoras, René Descartes, Leonhard Euler, and Georg Cantor. The second tributary of its underground history (as John Johnston has briefly noted ["Generic" 267]) is more literary: *Ratner's Star* possesses all fourteen features of classical Menippean satire.[3] Typical of the genre, its characters are mouthpieces for the author's critique of "a learning . . . insufficient to explain or control the irrational and the human world" (Relihan x). Subversive, heteroglossic, and trangressive (Bakhtin, *Problems* 133), Menippean satire is also self-parodic, ridiculing "the author who has dared to write in such an unorthodox way" while denying "the possibility of expressing truth in words" (Relihan 10, 11).

Two English Menippean satires are particularly salient. The first is Part 3 of *Gulliver's Travels*, where the "projectors" of Balnibarbi, ignoring the poverty surrounding them, contrive such ridiculous projects as reducing excrement to food (excrement is significant in *Ratner's Star*) and attempting to replace nouns with the objects to which they refer (Swift

163, 175).[4] The latter enterprise is mirrored in Robert Hopper Softly's Logicon project, which seeks to create a language cleansed of anything but self-reference. The second and more important pretexts are the Alice books of Lewis Carroll (Charles Lutwidge Dodgson), an Oxford logician and mathematician almost as eccentric as DeLillo's scientists. These intertextual links, which are much more pervasive and significant than DeLillo or his critics have acknowledged, form an indispensable substratum for the novel.[5] Indeed, DeLillo's and Carroll's texts exemplify what David Cowart calls "literary symbiosis": a relationship in which a later text rewrites a precursor in a manner that places them in a mutually illuminating dialogue (Cowart, *Symbiosis* 10–11). Through these intertextual dialogues, *Ratner's Star* depicts history as a subterranean stream that unexpectedly flows into the daylight world.

Reversing *Alice in Wonderland*, *Ratner's Star* commences with ascent rather than descent, as Billy boards a plane for FENO. This verifiable reality — "*khalix, calculus*" (that is, stones) — seems as "real as the number one" (*RS* 3).[6] But from the beginning the narrative is beset by uncertainty: "pulsing in dust and fumes," the "somnolent horizon" reveals "a fiction whose limits were determined by one's perspective, not unlike those imaginary quantities (the square root of minus-one, for instance) that lead to fresh dimensions" (*RS* 3). *Ratner's Star*'s universe is the uncertain cosmos of twentieth-century science and epistemology; yet the "reproductive" dust depicted here and at the novel's conclusion (438) offers a sign of renewal.

Billy's psyche and science in general are "nourished from below" by primal terrors springing from "the plane of obsession, the starkest tract of awareness" (*RS* 4); the magic of Billy's mathematics is fueled by dread. This underworld emerges most strongly in the childhood memories that punctuate chapters 1, 2, 4, 7, and 11 (a sequence that hides the integral series — 1, 2, 3, 4; see *RS* 69). This "substratum" is both psychic and geographic: Billy's father worked in the subways, and when the boy was seven years old took him for a visit there, just for the "sheer scary fun of it" (*RS* 5: like "Reflections," "Adventures" opens with Billy taking "a scary ride" underground). Afterward Billy consoles himself with the thought that "there is at least one prime number between a given number and its double" (*RS* 5). Mathematics is both personal nourishment and the sustenance of history, and appears in this chapter in its earliest historical role as a mixture of practical skills (rope stretchers surveying unplotted land [*RS* 10]), "directions for knowing all dark things" ([*RS* 12] [7]), and abstract poetry (the definition of "cosine" [*RS* 7]). Offering beauty, austerity, permanence, universality, and precision, mathematics makes sense of a chaotic, menacing world (*RS* 13).

The White Rabbit for Billy's journey is his mentor, Robert Hopper Softly, who appears in "Adventures" primarily through his manuscript, which depicts math as a dialectical combat between fear and knowledge. But when Billy reminds himself that "there is always a danger linked to the science of probing the substratum" (*RS* 18), it is not clear whether the danger issues from the superstition that science combats, or from the belief in the objectivity of scientific truth. Thus Softly's manuscript warns that "although the true excavation is just beginning, it's not too early to prepare ourselves for some startling reversals" (*RS* 8). Indeed, Billy's mother's habitual response to her husband's self-delusions—"keep believing it, shit-for-brains"—satirically comments on the way that mathematics constructs a coherent but fragile worldview out of agreed-upon fictions. The phrase also offers a salutary caution to the reader, who is invited both to suspend disbelief, and to observe him- or herself believing, and thereby avoid the characters' delusions.

Flow and Grow

The next three chapters introduce Billy to the labyrinthine design and bizarre characters of FENO, while tracing the history of mathematics from the ancient Greeks through the early Renaissance. Throughout these chapters, Billy confronts the same troubling question posed by the Caterpillar in chapter 5 of *Alice's Adventures in Wonderland* (*AW*): "Who are you?" (Carroll 67). Just as in *Through the Looking Glass* (*TLG*), where Alice encounters Humpty Dumpty's belligerent questions about her name (Carroll 263) and the White Knight's logical conundrums about the name of his poem (Carroll 306–7), so at the beginning of chapter 2, "Flow," Billy considers the gap between identity and name. Whereas numbers are "never more nor less than what was meant" (*RS* 26), to bear a name "is both terrible and necessary. The child . . . comes eventually to see that an escape from verbal designation is never complete, never more than a delay in meeting one's substitute, that alphabetic shadow abstracted from its physical source" (*RS* 19). Late to talk and mistrustful of language, Billy has seen his name undergo many metamorphoses. A votary of the "star system" and hopeful of Billy's potential celebrity, his mother, Faye, shortened his surname from Terwilliger to "Twillig"—a name with a "twinkle" in it, perfect for a "superstar" (*RS* 25). But if one's parents can amputate one's name so cavalierly, they might do the same to one's person; no wonder he imagines that they are plotting to dispose of him (*RS* 28).

"Flow" also corresponds to the frighteningly transient world of the second chapter of *AW*, where all is in flux—especially Alice's size—and she

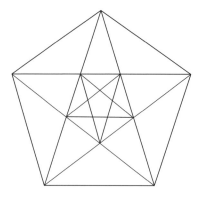

Figure 1. The Pythagorean mystic pentagram.

nearly drowns in the flow of her own tears (Carroll 35–44). At fourteen, on the brink of puberty, Billy feels alienated from his changing body: like Alice, he is "a radical accelerate" of "unique dimensions" (*RS* 20) who is alternately elevated and diminished, praised and pushed around. Tiny at birth, Billy later thought of himself as "something that would never be altered" (*RS* 74), but he has always feared shrinking (a potential represented at FENO by microminiaturization expert Byron Dyne [20]).[8] Nor is there dimensional security at FENO, which, like Wonderland, is a Heraclitean universe in which "all things flow" (*RS* 31; see Wheelwright 44). This liquidity is acknowledged by that "wizened child of Thales and Heraclitus" (*RS* 22), the celebrated mathematician and mystic Henrik Endor, and embodied by the mysteriously spreading liquid shadows that permeate FENO and presage the eclipse that ends the novel (*RS* 20).[9]

The convergence of mathematics and mysticism is best represented here by Pythagoras, whom DeLillo has called the "guiding spirit" of the book (Interview with LeClair 27). His influence is palpable throughout "Flow": the characters congregate in groups like the secret societies Pythagoras established in Crotona (the name of Billy's home street in the Bronx); they stay in the Gnomonics Complex, where rooms are separated by an L-shaped partition modeled after the L-shaped ruler (gnomon) with which Pythagoreans showed relationships between numbers (Wheelwright 203); Endor wears a badge bearing the "mystic pentagram" (Hollingdale 21) by which Pythagoreans declared their membership in the society (Figure 1).

The Pythagoreans combined a highly developed understanding of geometry with a set of sophisticated spiritual practices and beliefs. One of these was the doctrine of metempsychosis or transmigration of souls, which

Figure 2. The Pythagorean holy *tetraktys*.

is metaphorically displayed throughout *Ratner's Star*: in its intertextual relations to previous texts; in its reincarnation of figures from the history of science; and in its speculative philosophy of history, in which things turn inside out and repeat themselves as on a giant wheel. For the Pythagoreans, as for the Egyptians, each number possessed a specific mystical significance. The most sacred were 4 and 10, which were combined in the holy *tetraktys* (*RS* 37)—a triangular configuration of 10 pebbles on a base of 4 that symbolized perfection (Figure 2). Likewise, the Pythagorean cosmos was mathematically harmonious. They made it so partly by postulating the existence of a tenth heavenly body called "counter-earth," which they believed revolved around the Central Fire directly opposite our planet and thereby created balance in the cosmos (Burch 280, 284–86; I show the importance of this theory in "The Value-Dark Dimension" section of this chapter). But as Pythagoreanism developed, its followers eventually had to confront "the terror of the irrational," the dreadful "screech and claw of the inexpressible," when they discovered irrational numbers in the "ratio of diagonal to side of square" (*RS* 22), which can be expressed only as $\sqrt{2}$ and cannot be turned into a fraction or even a repeating decimal (approximately 1.4142): the exact number can never be determined. This discovery jolted the Pythagorean cosmos: if the ratio of a diagonal and side of a square is only imperfectly measurable, then lines are infinitely divisible. And if so, then "the little points of which the Pythagoreans built their universe do not exist," or are purely mathematical (Gorman 137).

Since this discovery undermined their founding principles, the Pythagoreans wisely kept it a secret. But because of this secrecy and Pythagoras's reputation as a wizard, mobs eventually attacked his school and burned its buildings. Softly's manuscript describes what their demise left behind: "A sense of order in nature. The notion of mathematical proof. The word 'mathematics' itself" (*RS* 44), as well as an ambivalent attitude toward science. Their legacy lies behind the attempt of Cyril Kyriakos's group in *Ratner's Star* to define the word "science": does it include faith healing, ceremonial chants, herb concoctions? Kyriakos suspects that what actually needs adjusting is our "view of the very distant past," which continues to live "in the midst of our supercivilized urban centers" (*RS* 36), a premise that Billy can verify. No study of science, concludes Cyril, is "complete without a reference to terror," ever the wellspring of scientific inquiry (*RS* 36). Billy's squeamishness about "shitpiss" ("number one or number two"—*RS* 24) and Cyril's baby (*RS* 36) betrays a similar fear of death as well as an unquestioning belief in reason that is as unbalanced as Cyril's one-armed body.

Chapter 3, "Shape," traces this relationship between science and superstition into the early Renaissance, while also mimicking Chapter III of *AW*, which depicts various strange animals and a "long tale" shaped as a long mouse's tail. In this chapter the aptly named U.F.O. Schwarz explains to Billy why he is here: to decipher a radio "message" consisting of 101 pulses in groups of 14, 28, and 57 issuing from an apparent extraterrestrial civilization near Ratner's Star. Schwarz, with his densely packed fat body, represents the positivistic faith of early Renaissance science—"there is no reality more independent of our perception and more true to itself than mathematical reality" (*RS* 48)—that spurred Copernicus and Kepler to their historic investigations of the planetary orbits. Blind astral engineer Olin Nyquist also reminds Billy that "it wasn't so very long ago that the universe was regarded solely in geometric terms. Circles, squares, equilateral triangles" (*RS* 49),[10] and proposes a variety of other possible shapes for the universe, including a double helix, a Möbius strip, and a "whale's tail" (*RS* 49). But while Nyquist acknowledges the mysteries discovered by quantum mechanics and chaos theory (*RS* 49, 51), he clings to the faith in finding "a totally harmonious picture of the world system" (*RS* 49).

But Billy's most significant encounters in "Shape" are with women who blend mysticism with maternal and erotic attraction, and who exemplify the inextricability of the otherworldly and the down-to-earth. Rahda Hamadryad, an "untouchable," introduces the theme of animal communication in her experimental rats—despised terrestrial beings whose name spells "star" in reverse—who ironically communicate more clearly than the celestial "Ratnerians." She foreshadows the "startling reversals" at novel's end, when bats swarm from caverns to warn of the eclipse and the evagination of history. Then Kepler's ghostly presence is ratified when Billy meets Viverrine Gentian, an elderly, witchlike Christian Scientist who explicates Kepler's *Somnium* (*Dream*) and quotes a passage about witches and lunar eclipses (*RS* 57).[11] Surrounded by "musical dust" (*RS* 58), Viverrine presages the potentially regenerative connection between science and mysticism that irrupts with the dust at the end of DeLillo's novel. The chapter ends with Billy taking comfort in Kepler's discovery of the "pristine ellipse" in "the shadow cast by the armillary sphere" (*RS* 59).

In chapter 4 of *AW*, Alice visits the White Rabbit's house, drinks from a bottle, and grows so large that her limbs protrude from the building. Later she eats a cake that shrinks her so much that she's threatened by a puppy. Her expansion, like Billy's, exaggerates the changes she will undergo in puberty (see Carroll 59). During these metamorphoses, Alice chats with herself, "taking first one side, then the other, and making quite a conversation of it" (Carroll 59), as Billy does here. Chapter 4 of *Ratner's Star*, "Expansion," in which Billy learns that Space Brain, the computer at the center of FENO, is spreading "beyond its own hardware" (*RS* 61), pairs these metamorphoses with a consideration of René Descartes's contributions to mathematics and philosophy, and especially his landmark discussion of the mind-body problem.

Space Brain, programmed by Shirl Trumpy, represents the Cartesian "self-designed" contemplative mind; its expansion has mutated *cogito, ergo sum* into "OGRE" (*RS* 68). If Shirl and Space Brain represent the mind, Soma Tobias, the architect of FENO's cycloid-shaped building, symbolizes body (*soma* is Greek for "body"); despite their shared initials, Soma and Shirl never meet. Having chosen the cycloid form for its "magical properties" (*RS* 78), Soma is obsessed with the bodily suffering that seems to accompany mathematical genius: she mentions Pascal, the philosopher and mathematical prodigy who was instrumental in the development of geometry and who, late in life, racked by insomnia and a throbbing toothache, did important work on the cycloid to keep his mind off his pain.[12] Full of preconceptions about genius, Soma is astonished that, unlike the frail Descartes, Billy doesn't spend his days in bed.

Between mind and body comes the narcoleptic LoQuadro, an expert in "bi-levelism," who lectures Billy on "the true nature of expansion" (*RS* 65). In the seventeenth century, he declares, it was believed that science would eventually unlock all the keys to knowledge and integrate disparate fields. But LoQuadro also notes the mystery and indeterminacy in numbers, and the unexpected symmetries (embodied in such phenomena as fractals) that keep "turning up in the most unexpected places" (*RS* 67). Thus, accepting the impossibility of true integration, bi-levelism yields to sophistry: they can talk "with an appearance of truth *and falsity* about all things" and claim that our knowledge of the world and "the world itself" are "one and the same" (*RS* 67; emphasis in original). Billy can only quaintly counter that "mathematics is the one thing where there's nothing to be afraid of or . . . think it's a big mystery" (*RS* 67). When LoQuadro leads Billy to Space Brain's void core, "where the dream originates" (i.e., "discrete retrieved entry-assembled memory"[*RS* 77]) — the link between Billy's Cartesian rationalism and Space Brain becomes evident: Billy too risks becoming a brain without a body. This "dream" also directs us to chapter 5 of *TLG*, when, after meeting Tweedledee and Tweedledum (corresponding to Shirl and Soma), Alice sees the somnolent Red King, and Tweedledee informs her that she is merely "a sort of thing in his dream" (Carroll 238). Billy's identity and the book we are reading are similarly composed of fragments of "discrete retrieved entry-assembled memory," which he and we must reassemble to "keep believing."

Billy resembles Descartes even beyond their shared rationalist faith: their common dreams suggest a close, even metempsychotic kinship. Billy recalls three dreams, the "last of them harbor[ing] a poem that pointed a way to the tasks of science" (*RS* 64). As LeClair has noted (*Loop* 128), these replicate the dream of Descartes who, while serving in the military in 1619, awoke one night with the "intense conviction that he had been presented with a magic key which would enable him to unlock the treasure-house of nature" (Hollingdale 126–27). The key symbolized both his application of algebra to geometry and his method of rigorous reasoning. Billy reenacts this dream in sections 21 and 22 of "Reflections," after he receives a piece of junk mail advertising "YOUR KEY TO ADVENTURES IN ELOCU-TION," along with a plastic key that unlocks Endor's room and thereby enables Billy to learn the significance of the star-message (*RS* 377).[13] Not only do Billy's meditations in Endor's room mirror Descartes's mathematical and philosophical advances; the key, as I suggest in more detail below, helps him to overcome a Cartesian mind-body dualism that plagues most of FENO's self-involved scientists.

Billy faces more dualities in chapter 5, "Dichotomy." The main event is his visit with Henrik Endor, who has become so discouraged by his failure to decode the star message that he has left FENO to live in a hole in the ground. Endor is both a Pythagoras figure and an avatar of Isaac Newton, co-inventor of calculus and codifier of the laws of gravitation; he has belatedly come to recognize the dread beneath scientific magic. For him, gravity means "everything wants" and seeks to "unite with all other matter" (*RS* 87, 84): he embraces the notion that science is a matter of faith as well as deduction.[14] Endor's diet has devolved along with his science: he now subsists on larvae, or "quasi-worms. Worms pro tem" (*RS* 85). This quirk leads us back to chapter 5 of *AW*, where Alice herself encounters a larva, the sagacious caterpillar who recites the poem about the Endor-like Father William (Carroll 70–71). In another sense, Billy is a larva — an immature creature who may metamorphose into adulthood — but he needs to heed Endor's words to achieve that metamorphosis. After warning him that "There is a dark side to Field Experiment Number One," Endor predicts that the message will "tell us something of importance about ourselves" (*RS* 91) and advises Billy, when he experiences his "inevitable terror," to visit Endor's locked room, which is both "in and of time" (*RS* 92).

Endor embodies a number of dichotomies, including logical (the difference between conjunction and disjunction, and versus or), epistemological (the close kinship between scientific knowledge and superstition), and narrative/historical (ending versus beginning). In the helicopter with Hoad and Poebbels Billy encounters others: first he learns that Ratner's Star has been discovered to be binary, thus creating a "three-body problem" (*RS* 93) of the kind considered by Newton (Motz and Weaver 155). A similar binarism is present in the relationship between Poebbels and Endor, who, as LeClair notes, represent Leibniz and Newton, respectively (*Loop* 128), and who, like them, have independently made the same discoveries. Poebbels has worked with both discrete and continuous things—with "Flow and grow" (*RS* 95). Likewise, Newton treated variables as flowing quantities changing with time, while Leibniz used sequences of infinitesimally close but discrete values (Hollingdale 273): their work displayed the dichotomy between continuousness and discreteness, both of which were necessary for the advent of calculus, which explains the "Rate of change every little instant" (*RS* 95). Poebbels hopes that the "star people" will teach them "how to join together discrete with continuous," but ultimately this is Billy's role: to be the "third body" who unifies dichotomies. He requires further enlightenment about his strengths and his weaknesses before he can assume that role.

A Grin Without a Cat

As the novel moves toward the late eighteenth century in chapter 6, "Convergence Inward," DeLillo depicts mathematicians as the isolated Romantic artists typical of the period. Thus Euler and Lagrange, the governing mathematicians of chapter 6, are praised for their "grim individual funneling of effort, [their] convergence toward an existential center" (*RS* 99), and Billy works on the code like a Byronic overreacher for whom "The only valid standard for his work, its critical point (zero or infinity), was the beauty it possessed. . . . The work's ultimate value was simply what it revealed about the nature of his intellect. . . . This was the infalling trap, the source of art's private involvement with obsession and despair, neither more nor less than the artist's self-containment" (*RS* 117–18).[15] Here Billy resembles DeLillo's other self-contained protagonists (Bucky

Wunderlick, Nick Shay), whose "convergence inward" is both symptom and cause of their alienation. His self-involvement also imitates that of mathematician Joseph-Louis Lagrange, a "detached gentleman content to die" whose "genius had been acclaimed by Napoleon" (*RS* 99), but who was plagued throughout his life by melancholia (Motz and Weaver 156, 161). The work of the prolific, one-eyed (eventually blind and thus necessarily inward-turning) Swiss mathematician Leonhard Euler (the "genial cyclops with a weakness for children" *RS* 99), however, more clearly defines DeLillo's use of "convergence." In mathematics, "convergence" refers to the way that infinite series "converge" in a finite value; they are the opposite of divergent series, in which the sum of the terms cannot be expressed except as a mathematical formalism (see Hayles, *Cosmic* 139). In other words, "convergence" refers to an infinitely diminishing sequence that never reaches zero. One of Euler's most significant advances was to refine the understanding of infinite series, which led to the discovery of "Euler's constant" (γ).[16] In this chapter DeLillo brilliantly weds the artistic and mathematical denotations of "convergence inward" to the "magic" of the unnamed aborigine who whirls inward until he vanishes or travels instantaneously to a star (or both). Even more ingeniously, DeLillo links these varieties of inward convergence with their perfect astronomical embodiment: the black hole. Collapsed stars that create gravitational forces so powerful that not even light can escape from them, black holes are invisible, and their existence can be determined only by measuring their disruptions of spacetime. DeLillo introduces black holes in chapter 6 to correspond with chapter 6 of *AW*, which contains its own famous illustration of convergence inward: the Cheshire cat, a massive "invisible object" (*RS* 101) that slowly disappears, leaving "a grin without a cat!" (Carroll 91). Black holes play a similar joke on the laws of spacetime. DeLillo's synthetic knitting of these intertextual threads generates a striking convergence between *Ratner's Star* and its intertexts.

Mutuka's speech introducing the aborigine crystallizes the novel's ambivalence about what exists "beyond the borders of rational inquiry" (*RS* 100). Mutuka claims that the aborigine will create "an alternative to space and time" (*RS* 102) by whirling and then traveling like a boomerang to Ratner's Star and back in the "timeless time of the dreamtime" (*RS* 105; his whirling foreshadows the slow spin of Skia Mantikos, the clairvoyant who appears at the end of the novel [*RS* 427]). The aborigine's journey (if that's what it is) also prefigures the novel's climactic discovery that the message is really an echo or boomerang. Blending "the primitive and the extraterrestrial" (*RS* 105), the aborigine embodies a potential alternative to the abstract and futile endeavors of FENO's residents.

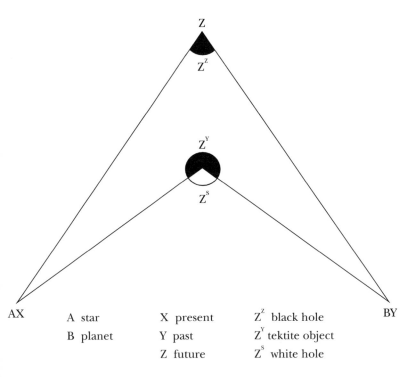

A	star	X	present	Z^z	black hole
B	planet	Y	past	Z^y	tektite object
		Z	future	Z^s	white hole

Figure 3. The aborigine's journey: a stellated twilligon.

One of them, the eyepatched (Euler-like) Celeste Dessau, is obsessed with "existing in the mind"—with the possibility of there being a "grin without a cat" (*RS* 113). She declares that "science avers that for every black hole there's a white hole" (*RS* 114), but also admits that "symmetry is [merely] a powerful analgesic" for primal terror (*RS* 115). That is, the existence of others as our mental projections and of white holes that balance black holes are as much matters of belief as the aborigine's boomeranging journey. To demonstrate this thesis, she sends Billy an envelope on which is inscribed the boomerang or "stellated twilligon" figure, which here represents the obsession with symmetry, as well as the aborigine's journey from star to planet and back through the opposed gravitational forces of a black hole and a white hole (*RS* 117; Figure 3). More significantly, it prefigures both Billy's inward convergence and the movement outward he must make in order to break his scientific solipsism. Compacting the personal and the cosmic, it illustrates the "complexity (simplicity)" of the cosmos (*RS* 116), and the self-reflexivity of scientific inquiry.

The next two chapters, "Rearrangement" and "Segmentation," introduce a number of "fabulous monsters" (Carroll 287) and initiate Billy's own "rearrangement," as his encounters with these "monsters" challenge him to acquire a sense of responsibility. Fabulous monsters also appear in Billy's recollections in chapter 7: a clogged sink containing a "vegetoid" mass that threatened to absorb the Terwilligers (*RS* 131–32); little Ralphie Buber as "Crabman" (*RS* 136); and Raymond (Nose Cone) Odle, a 7'2″ basketball player who suggests that Billy is himself "nothing but two eyes and a head" (*RS* 136). All of these "monsters" offer a looking glass in which Billy may see his own deficiencies and distortions.

The title of "Rearrangement" alludes to the absurd seating rearrangement at the teaparty of the Mad Hatter and March Hare in chapter 7 of *AW* (Carroll 102); similarly, math colossus Timur Nūt quizzes Billy with easy questions and nutty, Mad-Hatterish riddles. As LeClair notes, Nūt's questions allude to the work of Carl Friedrich Gauss, the presiding mathematician of this chapter (*Loop* 129). Gauss was a child prodigy who constructed the mathematical framework for the subject of Nūt's second question (*RS* 123), non-Euclidean geometry (Motz and Weaver 227), which Billy later invokes when he thinks of a piece of paper as a curved surface (*RS* 127). Nūt addresses the "irrational" elements of mathematics, such as the nonrepeating decimal created out of 1/7 (.142857—the same numbers as those in the "star-message" [*RS* 124]), particularly in his next-to-last question: "Do your dreams exceed your grasp?" (*RS* 125). Nūt is suggesting that the growth of mathematics depends not just on technique but on visionary imagination; it is a history of dreams coming true, and so far Billy's dreams remain juvenile. Nūt also cautions Billy that science is historically cumulative, a kind of metempsychosis reaching back to Ahmes the Scribe.[17] In short, he suggests, science is collaborative as well as competitive—a lesson that Billy must learn in order to decipher the message.

At the beginning of "Segmentation" Billy reads Softly's account of how mathematical and political revolutions in France deranged "the dreams of one slight child who later made his mark through exactitude" (*RS* 143–44). The child was Augustin-Louis Cauchy, who produced important mathematical papers despite being a victim of revolutionary politics (see also *RS* 348). Cauchy's work on the limits of convergence of infinite series immeasurably enhanced the rigor of calculus (Motz and Weaver 222); when, near the end of the chapter Harry Braniff tells Billy, "There is always a higher authority than you think. . . . No matter how far up or down the line you go, there's always someone else" (*RS* 166), he is ascribing a political meaning to Cauchy's infinite series. Indeed, this chapter generally dramatizes the economic, political, social, and religious responsibilities of science. Whereas at the end of the previous chapter Billy decided to "avoid responsibility for reflecting the world and all its grave weight" (*RS* 141), now he faces a series of challenges that provoke his involvement. Will he mature and, like Cauchy, balance his obligations to science and society, or will he squander his gifts like Cauchy's contemporaries Niels Abel (*RS* 164), dead at twenty-six, and Évariste Galois, killed in a stupid duel at twenty (see Motz and Weaver 182–86, 191–94)?

The first of these political challenges comes from "Elux Troxl" and his minion, Grbk, perhaps the novel's two strangest "monsters" (I place "Troxl" in quotation marks because it is not his name but only his "name's name" [*RS* 144–45]). "Troxl's" name games invoke the White Knight's segmentation of names in chapter 8 of *TLG* (Carroll 306), but he more strongly recalls Humpty Dumpty, who manipulates words as empty counters and baldly states the underlying point of "Troxl's" offer to "lease" Billy: "the question is . . . which is to be master—that's all" (Carroll 269). "Troxl" also performs the Dumptian role of translating the words of Grbk, FENO's Jabberwock (see Carroll 270–72). The nondescript Grbk is all body, while "Troxl" approaches pure, disembodied abstraction; robbed of features themselves, these two also want to rob Billy.

"Troxl" manages a cartel that aims to "manipulate abstract levels of all theoretical monies in the world" (*RS* 145). Like the terrorists in *Players* (discussed in chapter 5), he recognizes that "the concept-idée of money is more powerful than money itself" (*RS* 146), and incites revolutions that will "flux the curve our way." For him, science is a commodity and economics is merely mathematics made useful. "Troxl" thus represents not only the dangers of "an undrinkable greed for the abstract" (*RS* 146), but also the devouring maw of global capitalism, which at the end of the novel consumes even FENO itself. Billy must rouse himself to deflect "Troxl's" plans to "segment" Billy and connect him to Space Brain so as to manipulate the money curve more successfully (*RS* 146). When Billy declines, "Troxl" warns him that he'll face "the abysm itself. All limits twisted out of shapule" (*RS* 149): Billy will cease to exist. "Troxl's" "error" in calling Billy "Nilly" actually designates the way that unbridled capitalism reduces humans to ciphers and science to a struggle for power.

If "Troxl" threatens with physical segmentation, Armand Verbene, S.J., performs mental segmentations (for example, his analysis of the forms of ignorance: *RS* 157); his "monsters" are tiny red ants. Like the chess pieces in *TLG*, red ants have Red Queens and move according to preordained patterns that they don't understand; Verbene examines these patterns in hopes of finding "evidence of . . . selfward-tending teleological perfection" (*RS* 157). If Verbene's ants resemble the "Ratnerians" in that both generate patterns for no apparent purpose, from the cosmic point of view human activity looks just as insignificant and meaningless. That is, Verbene's ants are synecdoches of FENO, where scientific "pattern ants" self-reflexively create patterns for other ants to follow. In toto, Verbene's metaphysics points to a solipsistic God who has created a looking-glass cosmos in which every entity merely sees itself over and over, and all of them ultimately reflect Himself.

Verbene trusts that science will inevitably discover the meaning of the universe and the cosmic insignificance of human beings. Thus, when at the end of the chapter Billy asserts that Harry Braniff must have been sent by Celeste Dessau because "It fits right into the pattern," he is behaving like a red ant. The antidote to Verbene's theological positivism—and to his warnings about sex—comes from the bathing woman Thorkild, who questions the universality of mathematics and doubts whether the "star" pulses even constitute a message, and from Braniff, whose sardonic response to Billy's assertion suggests that his faith is as fabulous as Verbene's: "Keep believing it, shit-for-brains" (*RS* 167). Skepticism invites the humility bred by doubt.

An even better antidote to the destructive segmentations of "Troxl" are the symbolic, creative ones of Siba Isten-Esru (her name means Seven Eleven), who uses etymology to break down names and create new stories, new numbers, new identities. Like many of the other females at FENO, Siba, surrounded by "dust and shadow" (*RS* 151), is associated with the "reproductive dust" that rises from underground at the novel's end. Thus at first her nominal segmentations yield a trend toward "growing outward" (*RS* 153), but end with *n*, the mathematical sign for indefinites and infinities, thereby giving "birth to blank space and silence" (*RS* 153). Linguistic history is a boomerang. Moreover, her segmentation of "Twillig" into *Twi* plus *lig* (bind) points toward his destiny: "to bind together two distinct entities[.] To join the unjoinable" (*RS* 155). Billy must accept the story implicit in the history of his name; he must unify "Adventures" and "Reflections," synthesize diverse theories and bind together the halves of history. Both Verbene and Siba thus prefigure Billy's encounter with the mystic-mathematician Shazar Lazarus Ratner and adumbrate the charge he receives from Endor to bridge the gap between science and faith. Segmentation must yield to synthesis.

Chapters 9 and 10, "Composite Structure" and "Opposites," portray a new set of "monsters," including the ambiguous Orang Mohole and the ancient Ratner.[18] Now Billy's adventures begin to converge, as his interlocutors repeat the same ideas about mathematics and Billy's role at FENO. Chapters 9 and 10 are the key "Adventures"; here Billy, like Alice in chapter 9 of *AW*, must learn "mystery" along with history (Carroll 129; LeClair, *Loop* 130). The greatest mystery is Mohole's version of relativity, which implies that chaos governs the cosmos. His theory prompts a Conference on Invisible Mass and a panicky end-of-the-world party tape that ritually invokes the disruptions of conventional logic ("one that was different and the same"; "the set of all sets / Not members of themselves" *RS* 177, 176) and objectivity that Moholean relativity invites. Mohole's uncertain universe provokes dread; if seemingly invariant laws no longer obtain, we will all resemble the character Lepro, who cannot differentiate between cause and effect (*RS* 169). In such a universe, there is nothing left but to pray to the "Annihilator of Tautologies" (*RS* 176).[19]

Mohole disturbs Billy by informing him that Ratner's Star is a binary dwarf (the stars are red and white, like the royalty in *TLG*); it can therefore have no planets, and no Ratnerians. The "kingpin of alternate physics" (and avatar of the Red King of *TLG*), Mohole resembles a police composite sketch (*RS* 180); likewise his relativity theory is a composite of Einsteinian relativity and Heisenbergian quantum mechanics. He theorizes the existence of "moholes" that trap all the forces of the universe. Neither entities nor forces, moholes elude representation and compose what Mohole calls "the value-dark dimension," where space and time are "sylphed" or raised to a higher electrovalent power (*RS* 181). Eventually, as gravity overcomes the expansion left over from the Big Bang, all matter will collapse into a n-bottomed hole. But Mohole leaves things with "a chance to drip through," because "we're not so scientific that we can't have a little make-believe, right?" (*RS* 182). Mohole's picture of the universe yields another stellated twilligon or boomerang in which two triangles share the same invisible base (*RS* 241, Figure 4).

Just as his suite is full of mirrors, so Mohole postulates a looking-glass universe where one sees whatever one projects (*RS* 185). This is decidedly different from Einsteinian relativity, which, contrary to popular belief, does not mean that "everything is relative." Rather, general relativity saves the invariance of physical laws throughout the universe; indeed, at one point, Einstein considered calling it the "theory of invariance" (Hayles, *Cosmic*

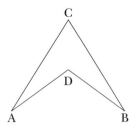

A big (or little) bang   AC matter expanding
B *n*-bottomed hole   AD gravity emergent
C present time   CB matter contracting
D exo-ionic sylphing compounds   DB gravity dominant
∠ ADB space-time sylphed

Figure 4. The Moholean cosmos.

45). Although relativity shows that measurements of time and space vary according to the observer, it does so to prove that the laws of motion and gravitation are absolute for any system in uniform motion (Hayles, *Cosmic* 46; cf. Rice 147–49). Thus the Einsteinian universe is an interconnected whole that lacks an objective frame of reference. Mohole inverts Einstein. Whereas in Einstein's universe "spacetime is the same for everyone" (quoted in Hayles, *Cosmic* 47), in Mohole's universe spacetime is different for everyone. Mohole's cosmos requires that one "keep believing": the observer creates whatever universe he or she wishes by interpreting indeterminate laws and phenomena. Heisenberg's famous uncertainty principle proved that observation alters what it observes (the principle obtains, incidentally, only at the microscopic level); Moholean uncertainty would mean that one can never be sure that anything exists to observe. Indeed, if moholes exist, we would all be living in a Wonderland where, as the Cheshire cat suggests, everybody is mad (Carroll 89). Moholean relativity is, in short, a realm of dreams that constantly change according to the dreamer's needs or desires.

    If Mohole's response to utter relativity is nihilistic hedonism, Endor, who phones Billy later in the chapter, offers salutary advice. Despite devolving so far that he now counts on his fingers, Endor still clings to a formalist vision of mathematics like that of Kronecker (*RS* 191), who claimed that "Mathematics builds its own universe . . . ; mathematical ideas are embedded in the human mind, outside which they have no separate existence" (quoted in Hollingdale 365). For Endor, mathematics is universal and beautiful; he finds solace in the fact that no matter how long you count, "beyond googolplex and glossolalia . . . there's always one more number" (*RS* 193). His peroration foreshadows the address to the reader—or to the "Ratnerians"—given by DeLillo's narrator near the end of the novel, which depicts mathematics as a supreme "expression of the will to live" (*RS* 194), or as Eric Lighter in "The Engineer of Moonlight" puts it, as "play toward the infinite" (45). Endor thus jesuitically urges Billy to compile elemental lists and celebrate the mystical, metaphysical quality of numbers. He declares that the history of mathematics is an underworld that nourishes us from below, a "history of nothing happening" that changes everything (*RS* 195). Mathematics is indispensable, because "[E]xistence would be sheer dread without [its] verifiable fictions." Finally, he urges Billy to assume his destiny, to "join the hemispheres. Bring logical sequence to the delirium, . . . language and meaning to the wild child's dream" (*RS* 195). In other words, although, like Mohole, Endor recognizes that mathematics is a product of the imagination, his ethos is the opposite of Mohole's: whereas for Mohole any belief is as good as any other, for Endor mathematics offers privileged fictions that are universally verifiable and that engender real-world improvements. Science is a kind of magic that, as in both Alice books, allows one both to believe impossible things and to make them happen—but only by the exercise of the imagination, which demands one's entire being. Endor exhorts Billy to give himself entirely to his labor, to balance creativity and order, logic and dreams.

As Billy moves from Mohole to the Great Hole where the Nobel laureates gather to honor Shazar Lazarus Ratner, his assumptions are undermined by that ancient mathematician and mystic whose middle name implies his potential for regeneration. A believer in kabbalistic number-mysticism, Ratner (an avatar of Pythagoras) appears in chapter 10 as if to verify the Pythagorean belief that 10 embodies perfection (Gorman 141). Ratner believes that "everything in the universe works on the theory of opposites" (*RS* 219), but that opposites converge, and "all things are present in all things" (*RS* 219; cf. Nadeau 175). Billy needs this lesson in mysticism, as his desultory version of Ratner's autobiography demonstrates. Indeed, Ratner and Billy, apparent opposites, embody this doctrine, and Ratner's story of overcoming an impoverished urban upbringing mirrors Billy's and offers a positive future path.

Like Verbene's red ant metaphysics, Ratner's science is teleological, seeking the ultimate secret that the universe is "the true name of G-dash-d" (*RS* 230). He believes that at the end of time humans will return to the stars from which we come, that all oppositions will be bridged in God, the Transcendental Signifier. But we can find this synthesis closer to home, in the "bottom parts" of the human body where "contradictions [are] joined and harmonized" (*RS* 222).[20] Ratner's understanding of the significance of "bottom parts" adumbrates the climax of "Reflections," when archaeologist Maurice Wu passes through "history's other end" to learn that regeneration begins with dust and excrement. Not only is "shit . . . universal" (*RS* 235), but it incarnates the dialectical or cyclical structure of the cosmos, manifesting a mystical order in which opposites mirror and contain each other in recursive symmetries. Waste reveals, as in *Underworld*, a subterranean history that reverses the visible one.

Ratner maintains, however, that we may discover this hidden harmony only through radiant trance states. But the consequence of this magical condition is the same as that of its absence, "terror" (*RS* 227), deriving from the awareness of human insignificance. Billy experiences a similar dread near the end of the chapter as he awaits the calling of his name in the Nobel laureates' procession: "Maybe he would not *occur.* . . . The name itself might assimilate his specific presence" (*RS* 229). This is the fear that Billy has been suppressing all along: that humans do not control our tools, but instead are made by them. Yet this confrontation with fear seems to be precisely what Ratner believes Billy needs: to humble himself before mystery, to learn that mathematics cannot explain every secret. Billy's eventual discovery of the irrationality of the universe, and his acceptance of his dialectical role in synthesizing opposites, will prove that he is one of Ratner's "stellar cinders"; once he learns to reconcile oppositions, Billy will *become* Ratner's Star.

Which Dreamed It?

Ironically, Billy responds to his fear of oblivion by seeking the "scantiest condition of existence" (*RS* 237–38), and soon faces another threat to his autonomy from Cheops Feeley, who wants to plant an electrode in his brain that will overstimulate the left hemisphere and produce an "overpowering sense of sequence" (*RS* 244). As LeClair has commented, the privileging of sequence over content refers to the work of Jules Henri Poincaré (*Loop* 131). More generally, chapter 11 foregrounds one of Poincaré's other obsessions: the nature of mathematical creativity (Motz and Weaver 291). Thus as Billy contemplates his own genius, he experiences an epiphany that the "star-message" uses base 60, like the arithmetical system of the ancient Mesopotamians (*RS* 239). The intuition comes in one of the "flashes" of insight that Poincaré described (and that Jean Venable later mentions: *RS* 297) as sources of mathematical inspiration. Such inspiration is also metempsychosis; it is as if Billy must momentarily reinhabit the ancient Mesopotamians' minds to solve the riddle of the Ratnerians.

Creativity is also associated with feminine reproduction throughout the chapter. Skip Wismer introduces the analogy when he discusses the death of his wife and his hope that after death there occurs a "turning inside out" or evagination (*RS* 242). Likewise, in creative acts convergence inward is followed by eversion, as the insulated mind is propelled outward from the womb of thought toward new consciousness. In "Reflections," time itself is evaginated as Wu and Billy are expelled from their caves; thus it is no accident that the matchbox inscribed with Mohole's diagram of spacetime "sylphed" appears during Wismer's speeches: it pictures cosmic evagination (*RS* 241). The last two chapters of "Adventures," then, not only foreshadow the grand fable of emergence that is "Reflections," but also reiterate DeLillo's ongoing fascination with narratives of containment and expulsion.

The counterpart to Wismer's deceased spouse is Cyril's wife Myriad Kyriakos, the chapter's fertility symbol. Myriad, like some of the other female scientists (Soma Tobias, Thorkild), is less interested in mathematics than in mathematicians, and particularly with the source of their intuitions. Thus she refers to Pascal's mystic hexagram and to the prodigies Galois and Ramanujan (*RS* 258). Pursuing "mathematics to its evanescent cave," she finds, like DeLillo, a close relationship between creativity and "the spirit of obsession" (*RS* 260, 258). A "[r]ose-white woman" who personifies the "radiant flux" of beauty and proportion (*RS* 256), Myriad is a dream-vision of feminine fertility (she also reincarnates Carroll's Red and White Queens in *TLG* [Carroll 256]). Her earthiness counteracts the sterility of the other scientists at FENO, and her fascination with the eccentricities of scientists exemplifies Endor's belief that mathematics expresses the will to live, offering a way of making dreams come true.

A different relationship between creativity and number emerges in Billy's final childhood memory, when he recalls confronting the neighbor called the scream lady and reading her cryptic "message." While recovering from a hysterectomy, she opened the door on Billy and (foreshadowing Wu's entombing/enwombing in the batcave [*RS* 391]) emitted a scream that expressed his dread and his father's paranoia. The scream lady's wail was her response to the terror that Kyriakos, Endor, and Ratner describe as the fount of scientific inspiration. She is particularly obsessed with the thirteenth chapter of the Gospel of Mark, where Jesus warns of "those days, after that tribulation, [when] the sun shall be darkened, and the moon shall not give light" (Mark 13:24). Ironically, her predictions of a solar eclipse turn out to be more accurate than the scientists'. Like Myriad's troubled geniuses, the scream lady embodies the kinship between madness and inspiration.

Madness also underlies the final chapter of "Adventures," which both boomerangs us back to the beginning and guides us through the looking glass to "Reflections." Here the suave Softly appears in person as Billy's mirror image, a "child-sized man" (*RS* 261). Billy's other counterpart in this chapter, which is entitled "Pairs," is the chimpanzee called Treeman; through their mirrored relationship DeLillo presents paradoxes of containment that adumbrate the cosmic evaginations of "Reflections." First Billy learns that his "canister" is actually an enormous sensor that has been used to observe him throughout his twelve days at FENO. Although the observers mistook Billy's readings for the chimp's, it may not matter if, as D'Arco states, in dreams you "glimpse a portion of your earliest being" (*RS* 264). The similarity between Twillig and Treeman becomes even more plausible when the chimp utters two seemingly nonsensical axioms (the "new kind of phonetic performance" that Rahda Hamadryad promised in chapter 3 [*RS* 53]) — "All in fi nite sets are in fi nite but some are more in fi nite than oth ers," and "The whole is e qual to one of its parts" (*RS* 268) — that turn out to be mathematically sound. The second phrase quotes Dedekind's definition of an infinite set (Hollingdale 360). The first phrase, which sounds even crazier, is not only a clever allusion to Orwell's *Animal Farm*, but marks an important moment in mathematical history by paraphrasing Georg Cantor's theory of infinite sets. Contrary to intuition, Cantor, who spent years in a mental institution, proved that the set of all whole numbers is smaller than the set of all real numbers; both are infinite sets (Kline, *Loss* 201). Hence, "all infinite sets are infinite but some are more infinite than others." Cantor also used set theory to discover paradoxes (or, as they are now called, antinomies) in the definition of infinity. For example, it has been shown that every set with more than one member must have a larger number of subsets than members. Thus the set {1, 2, 3} has six subsets: {1}, {2}, {3}, {1,2}, {1,3}, {2,3}. The paradox appears when one considers "the set of all sets." Since this set includes all possible sets, its number must be infinite. But if the set of all subsets of a given set is always larger than the original set, then the infinite set of subsets of "the set of all sets" must be larger than the infinite "set of all sets" (Kline, *Loss* 202). Once again, "all infinite sets are infinite but some are more infinite than others." The paradox occurs because the "set of all sets" *contains itself* and is thus irretrievably self-referential (Hayles, *Cosmic* 141; emphasis added). Cantor's work lays bare the limits of mathematical thinking; its ineluctable self-referentiality is that of a dream within a dream.

 Through the Looking Glass ends with a similar paradox, first presented by the twins Tweedledum and Tweedledee, who tell Alice, "you're only a sort of a thing in his dream" (Carroll 238). Indeed, the book's conclusion implies that the whole story may be either Alice's dream or the Red King's or both. We are left wondering "which dreamed it?" If it is both—if Alice's dream is contained within the King's, or vice versa—then all are implicated in an infinite regress of "two mirrors facing each other" (Gardner, in Carroll 239) that resembles Cantor's paradoxes of infinity. The mind balks at the notion that anything can contain itself; and yet a mirror facing a mirror shows how that may seem to occur. By presenting such paradoxes of containment, *Ratner's Star* deconstructs itself and mathematical logic, implying first that *Ratner's Star* may be Billy's dream, and second that, in the words of Joyce's Stephen Dedalus, history is itself a nightmare (*Ulysses* 28). "Reflections" now proceeds to ask: what happens if the dreamers awake?

It is just such "contaminations" of mathematical reasoning that Softly hopes to combat with the "scrub brush" (*RS* 272) of logic.[21] He recruits Billy to help devise a "logistic cosmic language based on mathematical principles" (*RS* 273) that will permit the scientists to communicate with the "Ratnerians," or, as they are now to be called, "artificial radio source extants"—ARSE. The Logicon project, as this enterprise comes to be called, aims to create yet another of the perfect structures that DeLillo's novels repeatedly criticize. Based on an already discredited positivism, Softly's project is doomed; ironically, for one who is well-versed in the history of mathematics, Softly fails because he ignores the history of science. Rather than trying to cleanse mathematics from contact with human culture, Softly would do better to embrace what Hayles calls the "field concept" of science, which assumes that discrete disciplines are "interconnected by means of a mediating field," such as language or mathematical symbols. To embrace the field concept is to admit that the observer participates in what is being described; it is to accept the inescapable self-referentiality of symbol systems (Hayles, *Cosmic* 41). Softly's vision of a pure logical language thus begs the question it is designed to answer: the inextricable relationship among "Algebraic number fields. Star fields. Electrical fields. Metrical fields. Field equations. Unified field theory" and the fields of grass through which he walks (*RS* 271). Billy goes with him, wearing a false mustache that implies his unfitness for the role. Ultimately, the Logicon projectors' discoveries will bear out the dire predictions of the mystics and mathematicians of "Adventures" and, paradoxically, speed Billy's maturity through a process of regression. Self-reflexivity will trap all of the other characters in "Reflections," which dramatizes life in the value-dark dimension.

Same Shape Upside Down

"Reflections" is a mirror-image of "Adventures" that takes place primarily in the deep sub-basement of the FENO building. Like its setting, the inverse of the visible building's cycloid shape, the section presents the "same shape upside down" (*RS* 282): as Tweedledee might say, it moves "Contrariwise" (Carroll 231), not only reversing the history of mathematics underlying "Adventures," but also inverting its structural principle, shifting from many discrete episodes to a single, continuous narrative broken only by "headlines" that attempt to present Billy's "reflections" as "adventures." The two parts are opposites in other ways as well, moving from outward movement to introspection, from several projects to one. With it DeLillo abandons the cartoonish cameos of "Adventures" to explore the inner lives of a smaller set of well-developed, more conventionally realistic figures. The continuous style effectively makes the characters' individual explorations and regressions reflect each other.

The frequent reappearance of the boomerang figure in "Reflections" represents a journey through the looking glass. The figure, as I have suggested, exemplifies "recursive symmetry," a key concept in chaos theory. Recurrence of the same shape "across many different length scales, as though the form were being progressively enlarged or diminished," eventually yields structures too complex to be calculated precisely and creates coupling mechanisms that rapidly transmit changes from one level to another (Hayles, Introduction to *Chaos and Order* 10). The results, called "fractals," epitomize how the repetition of simple designs may engender near-infinite complexity.[22] I want to claim that in *Ratner's Star* DeLillo deploys the boomerang or stellated twilligon figure similarly, as a literary fractal that not only embodies the novel's motif of reversals—in history, in narrative, in science—but that also illustrates the limits of positivism. Since the stellated twilligon is Billy's own invention, it also functions as a mirror inspiring him to make his own boomeranging journey, to converge inward and then move outward to merge with the "star-people."

"Reflections" exposes the inescapable self-reflexivity of human observation and inquiry through the failure of Softly's Logicon project, through archaeologist Maurice X. Wu's and chemist Walter X. Mainwaring's counterintuitive discovery of the self-reflexivity of the message, and through the characters' regressive inward journeys. Most importantly, it offers a self-reflexive investigation of fiction writing and reading: it reveals the futility of DeLillo's aim to create a novel that is a pure "piece of mathematics." Just as Softly's attempt to purify mathematical logic fails, so too does DeLillo's aim to create a schematic fictional equivalent of mathematics. Instead, in classical Menippean fashion, the novel suggests that "language is inadequate to express or define reality" (Relihan 23). And yet this failure produces a greater success, as the novel's subversion of its original principles reveals the potential for a new understanding of culture that celebrates the creative interrelationship among all its "fields"; like *Underworld* it shows that "everything is connected" (*U* 825). Both mathematics and fiction may offer stories in which "nothing happens" but through which everything changes. DeLillo's self-referential novel ends by turning its mirror upon the readers stationed "outside" the text, inviting us to observe our own observation. Through this self-reflection, it implies that accepting the fictional, provisional quality of symbol systems is more liberating than imprisoning.

A Binary Dwarf

As in the beginning of "Adventures," Billy again takes a "scary ride," but this time he descends to a cave below FENO where Softly and his collaborators reside. This descent not only recapitulates the subway rides of his youth, but invokes the fascination with underworlds manifest throughout DeLillo's oeuvre, from the subway rides in "Take the 'A' Train" and *Libra*, and the "small rooms" of Bucky Wunderlick and Glen Selvy, to the landfills and psychic hells of *Underworld*. As LeClair has noted (*Loop* 132), "Reflections" is organized around pairs: Softly and journalist Jean Venable; logicians Lester Bolin and Edna Lown; Wu and Mainwaring. Again Billy is the odd man out, the dialectical force who unites the "hemispheres." "Reflections" opens with the sexual coupling of Softly and Jean, which moves, like the entire section, from extreme abstraction ("the space between them seemed a series of incremental frames . . . man ostensibly engrossed in dressing, woman nude and on her side") to earthy concreteness ("the bottoms of her feet identically smudged with dust. . . . Softly rubbing his pale stubble" [*RS* 279–80]). Yet each remains alone during these "tunnelings," and Softly treats Jean as an object for narcissistic exploration. Thus the opening paragraph focuses less on their mutual interaction than on the space between them. Softly's bullying of Jean, however, typifies his role as a modern-day Pythagoras with a cabal of devotees.[23]

Softly has assembled this group of "supersavants" to realize his dream of a universal logical language. His phallic authoritarianism is congruent with his positivistic belief in the perfectability of science and its right to use any means needed to unearth the Truth. Yet he scoffs at Cantor's statement that mathematics can't be explained without metaphysics (*RS* 286) and ridicules any references to the mystical or imaginative capacities of number. Aggressive and confident, Softly also has crippling handicaps: dwarfism (harking back to Alice's shape changes) — perhaps the source of his belligerence — and manic depression exacerbated by promiscuous drug use. As Softly notes, he too is a "cycloid" (a bipolar personality; *RS* 301); like Ratner's star, he is a "binary dwarf" (*RS* 179) who embodies the novel's oppositions. Despite his intelligence and energy, he is radically unstable, veering toward and eventually succumbing to psychosis. He hates mirrors, partly because they expose his physical differences, but also because they remind him of the self-referentiality he dismisses. One of his strangest quirks is his habit of "talking in quotes," of saying words as though they were bracketed by scare quotation marks. This habit, as Billy recognizes, has a "source deeper than mere sarcasm" (*RS* 333); Softly isn't simply invoking the arbitrariness of all linguistic signs but "trying to empty an entire system of meaning" (*RS* 334). At the end of the novel, as he flees to Endor's hole, all of Softly's words become self-referentially framed. His blindness to the limits of objectivity eventually traps him in a strange loop of self-referential psychosis.

His partner, the equally neurotic journalist Jean Venable, also believes in objective truth, which she hopes to reveal in a book about the Logicon project. Her interviews (more of the "interview technique" central to *Americana*) with the scientists provide dialogic counterparts to the episodes of "Adventures." Jean claims to believe "in very little," but has not confronted the deep fissures that "the onset of . . . belief" might open (*RS* 298). She doesn't believe in love and in theory understands the importance of defenses; nevertheless, she allows Softly to exploit her. Behind her brittle irony lies a deep well of panic, a self-reflexive fear of "fear itself" (*RS* 338): her objectivity is nourished by dread. During her (now-ended) marriage, Jean would sometimes wound her spouse by pretending to be dead; ironically, her submission to Softly eventually sends her into a near-catatonic state that replicates this marital game. Her sex with Softly is simply another aspect of the solipsism that beckons her into a "coiled room" of mirror images (*RS* 331).

In another of the novel's self-reflexive turns, Jean remembers having been turned into a character in a friend's novel, and meditates on the disruptions of identity her fictionality produced. She searched the pages for signs of her character, feeling usurped by fiction's "capacity to gain possession of a person" (*RS* 311). Like Billy, she fears the capacity of language to imprison or resist its users. To wrest control of words, Jean decides to turn her nonfiction book into a game-like fiction, in which she is "free to make whatever rules I want as long as there's an inner firmness and cohesion. . . . Just like mathematics" (352).[24] Indeed, when Maurice Wu later backs out of the batcave (*RS* 394), his thoughts give way seamlessly to Jean's, as if "Reflections" is all Jean's fiction and her writing a form of cave art, the end of a process of "crawl, scratch and gasp" (*RS* 394).

But instead of grasping control through imagination, Jean retreats into a mirror: the fear of "fear itself" (*RS* 396). Now she perceives in the torture of stuttering (the subject of her first book) not only a representation of the " 'curse' of verbal communication," but an emblem of self-entrapment and loss of identity, as invoked in an apparently simple question: "What is your name, little girl?" (*RS* 397). Her "novel" too is a written stutter, a chaotic whirlwind of blank pages that is therefore "perfect" in its emptiness (*RS* 398). Paralyzed by panic, she envisions herself as a *"pupilla,"* a "female figure locked inside concentric rings, a lone doll in a coiled room, a little orphan girl . . . confined in the pupil of someone else's eye" (*RS* 399): she becomes Alice in the Red King's dream. Looking at others, she sees herself; looking at herself, she sees nothing. Unable to escape her imaginary confines, the diminished Jean becomes, like Alice, a "binary dwarf" whose imagined self mirrors Softly's physical one. Jean's demented "creeping logic" entraps her in a linguistic echo chamber, unable to do anything but enumerate synonyms for "insanity" (*RS* 414).

Breathe! Gleam! Verbalize! Die!

The second pair, mathematical logicians Lester Bolin and Edna Lown, are represented by a photo in which they pose, each with one leg extended as if dancing, partly toward each other and partly toward the camera: a human boomerang. Above the photograph is a banner reading "Breathe! Gleam! Verbalize! Die!" (*RS* 303). This dryly humorous caption reflects the pair's limited, linear thought patterns. Both are serious scientists who constantly speak of discipline and truth: Bolin doesn't laugh, instead tendering self-reflexive comments on laughter, like James Case in "The Engineer of Moonlight," who doesn't cry for help but shouts, "cries for help" (44). Yet Bolin, like some combination of Frankenstein and his creature, gives the impression of being "unmade" (*RS* 289). As he and Lown reach an impasse in their construction of Logicon, Lester becomes obsessed—like Victor Frankenstein—with building an artificial person who can speak his language (*RS* 340). He too seems to regress, eventually making childlike "advances" to Jean during their interview. Ironically, this linguist's most genuine communication is the "dreamy speech" (*RS* 401) in which he exhibits his genitals. Once he realizes that Logicon is a dead end, he enacts Endor's advice, making "simple lists" and uttering "numerical paternosters" to the nameless god of mathematics (*RS* 421). Far from demonstrating control over the world, Bolin's regression is a desperate response to the unwelcome realization that logic may be unable to cope with even so elemental an event as an eclipse.

Edna too loves "rules, regulations, formats," and understands mathematics as "an annex of logic" (*RS* 285). She has abandoned a husband and children for this project, which she initially believes to be her "true work, . . . a summation" of her career (*RS* 303). Logicon perfectly expresses her delight in "repetition, order, interval" (*RS* 319). Her work seems to her a fruitful example of convergence inward, and as she continues Edna imagines "entering herself just as surely as if she'd been able to bend her arms into her mouth and swallow them to the shoulders" (*RS* 329): she wants to contain herself like one of Cantor's infinite sets. This self-involution, however, leads her not toward Logicon, but back to the notes on childhood language she has been keeping for years. Near the end of the novel, Edna looks again at the photo of herself and Lester, and realizes that it is backward, apparently because of a reversal of the negative (*RS* 408). Pondering the photo, she feels that they have spent their years futilely dancing in a circle. The pointlessness of their enterprises is thus encapsulated by the photo's caption: having "gleamed" and "verbalized," all that remains is to die.

Logicon (examples of which are given in *RS* 308, 359, 378) is designed to eliminate noise entirely, and thus perfectly exemplifies Michel Serres's description of mathematics as "the kingdom of quasi-perfect communication, the *manthánein*, the kingdom of the excluded third man" (Serres 69). In this kingdom, empirical data are just noise. This purified condition is both its strength and its weakness: in stripping away all content, Logicon achieves a pristine clarity unapproachable through human language, but it is therefore incapable of referring to anything but itself.[25] DeLillo's projectors soon realize that they cannot verify the accuracy of Logicon without a meta-metalanguage to test it (*RS* 308, 340). What they need, in other words, is a "beneficially corrective infinite regress" (*RS* 316), a set of mirrors within mirrors. But such a project could have no end: the meta-metalanguage would then demand a meta-meta-metalanguage, and so on to infinity.

As James Robert Mendelsohn has noted, the Logicon project dramatizes the logical positivism of Hilbert, Whitehead, and Russell, who sought to devise a formal language with which to evaluate all mathematical theories, independent of content—to create a vantage point outside of mathematics with which to talk about mathematics (Mendelsohn 157). But in 1931 Kurt Gödel proved the impossibility of devising such a language by

△

Figure 5. Greylag's submarine.

demonstrating that any formal theory "complicated enough for arithmetic must be either incompletely described or contradictory" (Hayles, *Chaos Bound* 267). That is, any sophisticated and self-enclosed system will contain some statements that cannot be proven true.[26] Hence Logicon can do nothing more than create a strange loop of self-reference that reinscribes its creators' self-involvement. Its creators aim to devise a univocal language free from the social contracts and exchanges through which language evolves. But as Bakhtin notes, language is "not a neutral medium that passes freely and easily into the private property of the speaker's intention; it is populated—overpopulated—with the intentions of others" ("Discourse" 294). It is not merely a tool for our use, but a living organism that uses and shapes us; it can never be "purified" as long as people speak. In addition to misconceiving science, then, Logicon is also founded upon a misunderstanding of language.

Acknowledging the impasse, Softly seeks help from the "Supreme Abstract Commander," Nobel laureate Chester Greylag Dent, a ninety-two-year-old writer now living in a submarine far below the ocean surface—Dent too resides in a substratum, a value-dark dimension beneath the ocean's "flow." He is able to live so far underwater because of his submarine's unique "delta" shape: a "pair of sweptback wings or fins without a body proper" (*RS* 342). If we imagine its base removed, we see another variation on the boomerang (Figure 5). When Softly explains their problem, Dent paraphrases Gödel ("the more consistent the system, the less provable its consistency" [*RS* 349]), and advises him to "arithmetize" and thereby integrate the discrete and continuous as Cauchy did (*RS* 348). Dent also uses Cauchy to exemplify a key principle of "Reflections" that Logicon lacks: balance. But the hermitical Dent (a precursor, as his middle name suggests, to *Mao II*'s Bill Gray) is hardly a likely candidate to enlighten Softly about the social responsibilities of science, for he has himself withdrawn to seek a vantage point outside the system that, as always in DeLillo's work, proves futile.

Edna Lown stumbles upon a potentially more viable counterpart to Logicon in her notes on language. Perhaps, she thinks, the secret task of logic is "the rediscovery of play" (*RS* 332), because only "play-talk" can express the unspeakable. As in Jean's planned book, for Edna language is a game; but she conceives of it not as a means of mastery, but as a mode of freedom: "To break down language into its basic elements is to invent babbling rather than elementary propositions" (*RS* 365). Lown echoes DeLillo's assertion that non-signifying speech may be (as at the end of *The Names*) a "purer form" of language that invites regeneration (Interview with LeClair 24). Interspersed with Wu's archaeological excavation, her notes inscribe linguistically his archaeological discovery of "regressive development, or history inside out" (*RS* 366). As Wu explores the batcave, Edna begins to comprehend the "innate limitations of formal systems" such as Logicon, and the impossibility of freeing reality from human observation and limitations (*RS* 392). By the end, Edna grasps that it is these notes, not Logicon, that constitute her real life's work; belatedly, she realizes that she has until now been "a witness to [her] own adventure" (*RS* 425). Her recognition at least hints at rebirth: just as Wu and Mainwaring find in the reversal of history a potential for re-beginning, so Edna's notes end not with an abstraction but with a child's request—"give me a cookie" (*RS* 422). Or, as Bucky Wunderlick might say, "pee-pee-maw-maw."

Beyond Googolplex and Glossolalia

Alone of Softly's cadre, Billy remains aloof, until he adds his discovery about the message to Wu's and Mainwaring's findings. In "Reflections" Billy consummates the maturation process begun in "Adventures," and he does so, paradoxically, by regressing. Like Venable, Lown, and Wu, he turns inward. Increasingly obsessed with and confused by his body, he watches Softly and Jean having sex and hears with awe Jean's ecstatic noises, which he perceives as glossolalia. Their intercourse is for him both sacred and scary: sacred because it seems to offer genuine knowledge and communication beyond words, scary because it does "not have organized content... It did not represent anything or lead necessarily to a conclusion, a sum, a recognition" (*RS* 320). Disturbed by the threat to his containment, Billy builds a "hole within the hole" in his cubicle and retreats there, not just to wallow in despondency but to seek something beyond speech and number "beyond googolplex and glossolalia," with which to confront the nameless dread and dread of namelessness that have plagued him since the beginning of the novel.[27] Like *Libra*'s Lee Oswald, Billy perceives that there is "a life inside this life," something "in the space between what I know and what I am and what fills this space is what I know there are no words for" (*RS* 370). This is the value-dark dimension. Billy too is confronting the limitations of knowledge and language through infinite regress and self reference. These threats lead him to the source of his own creativity, sym bolized by the underground river from which Billy (like Alice) takes a drink (*RS* 373). The flow of water, rather than scaring him as did the shadow-flow at the beginning of the novel, soothes him; the awareness of disorder and inexhaustibility—and of our inability to understand these phenomena— now seems comforting.

Billy is recalled to the outside world by three pieces of "junk mail" he receives from "Elux Troxl." The first two—one a mock quiz that seems to predict the coming eclipse, the second a chain letter warning that one must not disrupt "a mass speculation . . . on the will to exist" (*RS* 294, 296)—are less important than the third, which has a singular significance in the novel: it is the "KEY TO ADVENTURES IN ELOCUTION" discussed earlier. Exhibiting "Troxl's" apparent omniscience and power, this piece contains the key to Endor's room that leads to Billy's solution of the "star-message" (*RS* 377). As I noted above, here Billy relives Descartes's dream, which in turn enables him to overcome his Cartesian mind-body problem; his opening of Endor's door occurs simultaneously with Wu's "nullifying plunge" into the darkened batcave (*RS* 382), implying an identity between their enwombments and subsequent emergences. Now Billy learns what Endor meant when he said that the room was "in time and of time": it features a clock stopped at 2:28:57 (14:28:57), revealing to him that the pulses from Ratner's star refer to a time of day, which turns out to be the moment when the eclipse will occur.[28] Billy's work provides the synthetic glue for the paired revelations of Wu and Mainwaring; he is the dialogical force, the "third man" who bridges oppositions. Nonetheless, the mailings point to another menace: they all derive from "Troxl," who is seizing control of both the money curve and one of its earthiest manifestations, bat guano. His cartel eventually engulfs FENO itself.

History's Other End

Chinese-American archaeologist Maurice X. Wu experiences a more corporeal enwombment and immerdment, as his physical motion into and out of caves recapitulates the other characters' psychic evaginations. As LeClair notes (*Loop* 132), Wu's initials form a palindromic pair with those of Walter X. Mainwaring, the chemist whose work on sylphing compounds complements Wu's. Like Softly and Billy, Wu embodies oppositions: East and West, science and magic, rational inquiry and prerational dread. Indeed, Softly values Wu precisely because his thinking manifests that reconciliation of opposites celebrated by Ratner and Pythagoras. For example, this scientist wears a *wu-fu*, or medallion, depicting a cluster of bats with wings extended, circling a tree of life, and polishes it superstitiously for exactly

Figure 6. Bats in flight.

17 minutes before spelunking (*RS* 338–39). Rather than embracing his hybridity, however, Wu has engaged in a "lifelong effort to become Chinese" (*RS* 392). Like Billy, he is seeking a "primary source" or "embedded part," as signified by the Chinese character 本 (pronounced /bəɕ/ [*RS* 393]).[29] Enwombed belowground, Wu feels the potential to "remake himself," to build "a receptive mentality that seemed to make him part of something more than the living cave around him" (*RS* 381). But when his lamp goes out while he is wedged deep in a cave full of dormant bats, Wu experiences Jean Venable's "fear itself." In an echo of the scream lady's tortured cries, Wu wails, losing himself in the sound. The result of this nullifying plunge is not annihilation but rebirth: he is psychically turned inside out and feels himself becoming "part bat" (*RS* 394); he reemerges with his fears gone and his creative insights formed. Undergoing an ordeal of purification and metempsychosis, Wu finds himself and the community he has sought (*RS* 356).

Along with personal identity and "countless decades of accumulated bat shit" (*RS* 313), Wu uncovers something of universal importance: "history's other end" (*RS* 382). The deeper he digs below a certain point, the more advanced the artifacts become: the data point to reverse evolution or historical evagination (*RS* 313). At the deepest level Wu has found a flat stone marked with a quartz engraving tip bearing the boomerang design in Figure 6 (see *RS* 322). "Bats in flight," concludes Wu, and in a sense he is right, since the bats' mass exodus from the cave signals the boomeranging of history that climaxes the novel. A little later Wu finds a circular bronze mirror engraved with abstract geometric designs, and traces in the dusty bat dung the pattern shown in Figure 7 (see *RS* 388). The boomerang is turned upside down to represent human evolution, which has passed through the looking glass to collide with itself. Wu's digging exposes recursive symmetries that illustrate an underlying order in which "each part . . . contains the whole" (quoted in Hayles, *Cosmic* 57).

The final implications of Wu's work, however, appear only in collaboration with Billy and Mainwaring. The latter has developed an "echo-

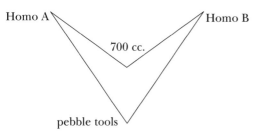

Homo A   Homo B

700 cc.

pebble tools

Figure 7. Evolution.

location quantifier" that pinpoints the origin of the "star-message" (*RS* 364). It is another "lesson in the effect of echoes"—the earthshaking news that the source is our own planet. The "star-message" is an echo, an aural boomerang sent thousands of years ago by the same humans whose artifacts Wu has uncovered; they "sent mail" to their descendants. Of course, echolocation—bouncing high-pitched sounds off objects—is the method that bats use to judge distances, and the message implies that modern humans are like bats, listening to echoes to determine our location, attempting to overcome blindness by screaming into the dark. Since this earlier civilization was destroyed, apparently by radiation (*RS* 404), the ARS extants may have been warning us that scientific arrogance will end in mass destruction. Mainwaring summarizes his and Wu's findings: "We get back only what we ourselves give. . . . We've reconstructed the ARS extant and it turns out to be us" (*RS* 405). The first phrase implies an ecological ethos—repeated in *Underworld*—that DeLillo's narrator echoes in the final pages, and that frames a Pythagorean philosophy of cosmic justice. The second phrase means that in looking for "history's other end," we have indeed found an ARSE, one whose waste products are human beings, the cosmic equivalent of bat guano. Star dwellers, star cinders, we are also cavedwellers and dungwaders.

Mainwaring then informs the others that he has used zorgs—Billy's allegedly useless mathematical concept—to determine that earth is in a mohole, and therefore that we "are part of the value-dark dimension" (*RS* 410). Zorgs provide a perfect mathematical model of "hole theory" because they blend "experience and pure thought," constructing dialectical pairs that combine particles and anti-particles (*RS* 418). Billy's work joins oppositions. But zorgs also reveal the absurdity of life in the value-dark dimension, where physical laws vary from observer to observer. Knowledge of this condition becomes even less consoling when the scientists learn that

"Troxl," now a "nonabstract proponent of actual living shit" with a monopoly on "guano stockpiling, price-fixing and eventual distribution," has acquired FENO (*RS* 413). All of FENO's projects have devolved into a by-product less valuable than batshit, which becomes a universal equivalent. Controlling both the money curve and this material substitute, "Troxl" has assumed the role of post-capitalist God, with batshit as his universal equivalent (see Goux 18–20). His earlier appearance in the same chapter as the Jesuit Verbene now makes sense: both signify the existence of an ultimate Authority. As J.-F. Lyotard notes, however, such technological control of symbol systems does not make reality more understandable; rather, it succeeds only in making the world "increasingly ungraspable, subject to doubt, unsteady" (255). In a mohole, even "God" grants no stability. And if earth really is "mohole-intense," then "Troxl's" mastery of economics is irrelevant.

Evagination

The radio announcement of an unforeseen eclipse throws the scientists into a panic. They turn to mysticism, bringing in a woman named Skia Mantikos, meaning "shadow-prophet" (*RS* 423), whose trances supposedly enable her to "perceive things beyond the range of the immediate present" (*RS* 422). This impoverished woman with her mouth stitched together first begins to revolve slowly, like Mutuka's aborigine; then she turns "completely inward" and begins to count on her fingers, à la Endor in his hole (*RS* 428). Finally freeing her mouth from the threads, she utters a single prophetic word: "Pythagoras" (*RS* 429). The invocation of the novel's guiding spirit at last unveils his covert presence and unites numerous thematic threads. The uttering of his name completes the reverse history of mathematics that underlies "Reflections," and implies the coincidence of science and spirituality, of mathematics and mysticism, that DeLillo has been dramatizing throughout the novel. She reminds these scientists of the limitations of rational thought, as if to suggest that Pythagoreans possessed a more "advanced" understanding of the cosmos than contemporary scientists.

In fact, the eclipse points back to the Pythagorean notion of the "counter-earth," the belief that a shadow-version of our earth moves around the "Central Fire," thereby balancing the cosmos and completing its numerology with 10 bodies. The counter-earth theory is a spatial version of Billy's zorgs: both permit the creation of dialectically opposed pairs that unite "[e]xternal reality and independent abstract deduction" (*RS* 418). Although the theory is, of course, factually false, as an explanation of observable phenomena (the early Greeks had no telescopes) it was "unsurpassable" (Burch 272). Indeed, the counter-earth theory constituted the "second great insight in the history of astronomy": that "the apparent motion of the heavenly bodies is due in part to the real motion of the observer" (Burch 277). Like Heisenberg's uncertainty principle, the counter-earth theory enabled scientists to acknowledge that observation affects what is observed, an insight taken to its furthest expression in Moholean relativity. The Pythagorean counter-earth theory beautifully illustrates *Ratner's Star*'s thesis of the existence of unseen worlds that not only affect the daylight world but even make it possible. Likewise, according to their philosophy of metempsychosis, existence is a "Wheel of Life divided into two hemicycles of light and darkness, through which the one life or soul continually revolves" (Cornford 161). Death gives way to life, darkness to light, and vice versa; humankind must continually relive our mistakes until we correct them. Thus combining science and religion, the Pythagoreans could account for the possibility—or even the certainty—that things could "go the other way." Skia Mantikos's invocation of Pythagoras sews together ancient and modern mathematicians, inasmuch as all must confront "the screech and claw of the inexpressible" (*RS* 22), which forcibly remind us of both our connection to the cosmos and our insignificance within it.

As time and space are evaginated, the scientists leave their holes to face the "endless uncertainty" of the Moholean universe (*RS* 432). For Softly, this means that "something here made no sense": why does the eclipse track seem to move in reverse? Softly resists this release from self-awareness and tries to hide in Endor's hole. Taking his most powerful drug, he gives in to the delirium of self-reference described earlier. Crawling into a hole within Endor's hole, he encounters the magus's maggot-ridden body: the man who ate larvae is now being eaten by them. Finally, even Softly feels the "sense of interlocking opposites, the paradox, the comedy, the fool's rule of total radiance" recommended by Ratner (*RS* 438). In a "zorgasm," the world passes through the looking glass and produces an explosion similar to the one that concludes Carroll's *Through the Looking Glass*.[30] The planet become a zorg, Billy Twillig madly pedals a white tricycle toward the white space between shadows, emitting a series of "involuntary shrieks" that echo Wu's and the scream lady's cries, as well as those of the bats as they exited their chamber. At the end—or beginning—the air is full of the "reproductive dust of existence" (*RS* 438).

What is most frightening here is not the eclipse (which is, after all, benign) but the overturning of expectations and predictability. Perhaps, as Mendelsohn (147) claims, it foreshadows the coming of a "dark age." But it seems more likely that the scientists' encounter with incertitude promises rebirth: the dust is "seminal," affirming material reality despite its unpleasant residue (Molesworth 149, 156). The experience certainly will dislodge Billy Twillig's formalism, and may push him toward a more humane awareness of his fellow creatures. Although Softly seems doomed, at least he is finally in touch with a genuine substratum, that nourishing layer that generates the fear of death and impels the pursuit of knowledge. Nor does the conclusion show the imaginative quest for beauty and certainty to be simply futile.[31] If mathematics expresses the will to live, then it is the enterprise itself, not its conclusions, that matter, because the history of science demonstrates time and again that answering one set of questions merely raises new ones. Most importantly, the conclusion of *Ratner's Star* celebrates the creative powers of belief.

Keep Believing It

As DeLillo's narrator traces the eclipse, he addresses "you" and shows you the real-world suffering and faith to which FENO's scientists have been blind. This long paragraph discovers in the Asian people it scans a sense of community in which "one experience pass[es] untouched through the soul of another" (*RS* 430), a metempsychotic belief that "the one life of the group . . . extends continuously" (Cornford 161). They possess wholeness, harmony, and radiance because they realize that each individual's activity forms an irreplaceable part of the whole—that everything is connected. These scenes thus illustrate not just deprivation but also richness and spiritual depth that the scientists lack (Molesworth 156). Theirs is not an abstract perception of coordinates or pure number, but a vision of the unity of theory and practice that "makes the way for the whittler's sleight, gives directional reference to the man at the bridge rail adjusting a small-boned instrument of navigation." It is here "at the contact line of nature and mathematical thought . . . where things make sense" (*RS* 431). Now the novel reattaches scientific abstraction to the dust and guano of material life, salvaging mathematics from its abuse by scientists.

In contrast, the addressee "you"—both the "hypothetical ARS extant" and the reader of the novel—is stationed Outside. Unlike those in the eclipse track, "you went beyond [mathematics's] natural association with the will to live and found that it contained a painless 'nonexistence'" (*RS* 432). Realizing their error, the ARS extants conveyed the limitations of "(y)our science" by relaying the time of an eclipse that would signal a new dispensation in which "you" now confront the minds of others and their cries of fear and pain. In such confrontations, those stationed Outside can re-experience the "richness of inborn limits" and may be thrust into a "tektite whirl" that provides "awareness of not being self-aware." This is the "metaphysical release at the center of the value-dark dimension" (*RS* 433), the key to unlock the prison of self-reference that traps *Ratner's Star*'s characters. Most importantly, those in the eclipse track recognize their involvement in something beyond reason, something that emerges from social exchanges, from a rooted sense of history, and from a belief in the unseen that recognizes that it *is* a belief.

Thus the interlude becomes a challenge to DeLillo's own readers, already tested by the demands of a difficult and elusive text. Moreover, in its conclusion *Ratner's Star* itself passes through a looking glass: by mirroring how reason inevitably collides with itself, it embodies its own limitations. That is, in attempting to write a novel that is "a piece of mathematics," DeLillo has subjected his text to the same self-referential paradoxes that stymie his scientists. A novel that is "naked structure" can finally be about only itself; it must defeat reader involvement. How then can we, stationed "Outside," learn a lesson from the effect of echoes? How does the novel avoid falling victim to the same sterility and abstraction that it so devastatingly criticizes? The text's recursive symmetries may provide an answer. As its mirrored structure and everting plot suggest, *Ratner's Star* is a boomerang, a zorg that combines the discrete and continous, that blends "experience and pure thought" (*RS* 418). It is a "stellated twilligon" whereby its hero (and inventor) recognizes his identity with Ratner's Star through repeated encounters with the shape. If we read *Ratner's Star* as a boomerang or zorg—as both a history of mathematics and a deconstruction of it— that wheels back to its beginning, we may also find a way out of the novel's looking-glass world of self-reference.

The novel implies that mathematics is a fiction that depends upon suprarational faith. Similarly, a fiction requires its readers to "keep believing," to accept provisionally its verbal constructs as a representation of reality. But *Ratner's Star* goes further, suggesting that reality is a function of our representations, and that both are constantly reshaped by observation. DeLillo's scientists err in mistaking their fictions for objective truth, in believing that human tools can exceed human limitations: they look into a mirror and think it is a window. They forget, in short, that their representations are fictions. But because *Ratner's Star* resists our attempts to make it "realistic," it never forgets—or lets us forget—its fictionality. It requires our active participation in making it cohere; it admits, in other words, that it is a "fiction whose limits [are] determined by one's perspective" (*RS* 3). In this regard, its failure to be a "piece of mathematics" is, ironically, its success, because now the looking glass or boomerang becomes an image of the echoing dialogue between readers and the text. We read ourselves reading it, just as DeLillo represents himself writing it; but we also see someone else standing behind us: the plural "you" he addresses. Because *Ratner's Star* explicitly locates itself within a "reinforcing grid of [other] works and minds" (*RS* 432), it embraces a community of readers that extends into the past and the future. These readers are dared to make difficult commitments, to read in several directions at once, to follow the boomerang, to reconcile the oppositions the author has constructed, or at least to hold in our minds mutually contradictory ideas. As this novel unfolds into cosmic mysteries, we find ourselves both believing it and realizing that we cannot; hence we must both make the effort to unify its disparate parts and recognize, like the Pythagoreans, their incommensurability. We grant that it is a dreamed history in which "nothing happens," but which may change our relationship to the waking world. As long as we "keep believing it," we dream ourselves anew, all the while recognizing that it is a fiction and thereby avoiding the scientists' failure. If we can make this commitment to examine ourselves in the process of reading, we may emerge from the value-dark dimension with some enlightenment.

Chapter 4
Observing Obsession, Questioning the Quest

I t has been suggested that most of DeLillo's novels are versions of the quest romance (see McClure "Postmodern Romance" 100). The description best fits *Running Dog* and *The Names,* his two most penetrating assessments of quest and obsession. As I noted in Chapter 2, DeLillo acknowledges his own obsessive nature; *Running Dog* and *The Names* likewise force us as readers to confront our attraction to quest plots. These two novels are thus self-reflexive studies of obsession: they question our desire for narratives of terror, and suggest how certain economies of representation may themselves promote it.

In the guise of a movie thriller, *Running Dog* relates a postmodern grail quest tale in which the icon is not a sacred cup but an allegedly porno-graphic film of Hitler and company—an unholy grail that symbolizes its pursuers' greed. Blending domestic drama, quest story, and expatriate novel into a profound meditation on language, *The Names* traces James Axton's emerging awareness of his complicity with systems of terror. Adapting Axton's son Tap's "counter-language"—Ob—as his own structural prin-ciple, DeLillo charts Axton's growth through a series of "ob" words that also outline a critique of the tyranny of writing. Whereas *Running Dog's* sar-donic conclusion suggests that quests are empty narcissistic exercises, the end of *The Names* offers resolution, perhaps even redemption. Here dread gives way to the magic of glossolalia, depicted as a gift that may restore community and mutual obligation.

DeLillo has stated that the pared-down prose, flat characters, and rapid pace of *Running Dog* reflect his intention to write "a thriller" (Interview with LeClair 23), and the novel indeed displays the violent actions and suspenseful structure of the genre.[1] Like many thrillers, it is a quest tale involving a competition for a valuable object. But *Running Dog* subverts the form: whereas classical quest tales—exemplified by medieval grail stories—depict a protagonist's search for identity through a series of ordeals that educates both hero and reader about proper conduct, the quest of Glen Selvy, this novel's ascetic soldier/monk and nominal protagonist, brings no purification or transcendence, but merely exposes him as the machine and trained animal of his masters. Moreover, while the Holy Grail inspires righteous behavior in those who seek it, *Running Dog*'s desired object— that home movie of Hitler and his minions filmed in the Führerbunker in April 1945—seems to contaminate all the characters and remold them in its image.

That the desired object is a film is appropriate to the world of *Running Dog*, where the ubiquity of the camera eye has created a superpanopticon that blurs the distinction between behavior and performance. DeLillo suggests that such omnipresent cinematic surveillance both replays the Nazis' staging of history as cinema and induces a similarly fascistic ideology. Propelled by what DeLillo elsewhere calls a "terrible acquisitiveness" ("Outsider" 64), the novel's questers serve an amoral, fascistic capitalism that turns humans into objects or "running dogs." In this postmodern pastiche of the grail quest in which the sacred icon is "the century's ultimate piece of decadence" (*RD* 20), DeLillo mounts a complex consideration of fascism's enduring appeal, of film's power to shape human history and subjectivity, and of the convergence of fascism and film in pornographic representation. The novel simultaneously investigates the fascinations of fascism and examines how such fascistic fascinations become marketable commodities. In sum, *Running Dog* explores both the obsession with marketing and "the marketing of obsession" ("Art of Fiction" 302).

The Unholy Grail

Running Dog's prologue offers the novel's sole instance of a character's direct narration: "You won't find ordinary people here. . . . Of course you know this" (*RD* 3). The use of second-person narration adumbrates the novel's depiction of postmodern subjectivity as a condition at once singular and plural, self- and other-directed, one in which the subject simultaneously acts and comments upon his or her performance.[2] The narrator, Christoph Ludecke, possessor of the Hitler film, is costumed in his wife's clothing while making his way toward an exchange of flesh. Similar exchanges, both commercial and narratorial, dominate the novel. An intertextual exchange also appears here: as his name indicates, Christoph is a parodic Christ figure dying for his God—"the God of Body. The God of Lipstick and Silk. The God of Nylon, Scent and Shadow" (*RD* 4); like Christ, he is the source of the Grail, and the abandoned building where he is killed serves as the Waste Land of the Fisher King (although Ludecke is dressed as a "queen" [*RD* 8]).[3] As in the Grail legends, his death comes by stabbing. At this point, however, the reader doesn't know Ludecke's identity, and both he and the cops who discover his body immediately vanish from the novel. Although Ludecke quickly loses his voice (just as he has lost his prized possessions in Germany), his nostalgia, self-consciousness, and dedication to a pseudo-spiritual ideal are repeated in several other characters.

The cop who finds his body laments that today "Everybody's in disguise" (*RD* 8). His description certainly fits Senator Lloyd Percival, whose surname suggests his role as seeker of the Grail. But unlike the youthful Percival of medieval Grail legends, this Percival is an expert liar. Although allegedly investigating PAC/ORD, a funding mechanism for U. S. covert operations that later plays a major role in the novel, he is actually obsessed with adding pornographic artifacts to his vast collection. No "righteous type" (*RD* 25), Percival is merely a skilled actor, as indicated by the orange TV makeup he is wearing when he first encounters journalist Moll Robbins, *Running Dog*'s second protagonist (*RD* 30). Like a TV actor, Percival is "all image" (*RD* 31), and he virtually disappears from the second half of the novel, just as Sir Percival vanishes from the second half of Chrétien's Grail story (see Weston 18). But Percival is the only character who recalls the source of the name *Running Dog*, the magazine for which Moll writes; this is appropriate, since he is one of the many "[c]apitalist lackeys and running dogs" who populate the novel (*RD* 30).

Moll also uses costumes to safeguard her true self, and as a journalist for a magazine that survives (barely) by trafficking in conspiracy stories, Moll too is involved in marketing obsession. As her first name indicates, she is fascinated by violent men such as her ex-lover, terrorist Gary Penner, perhaps because they appeal to her bloodhound curiosity about "whatever I don't see clearly" (*RD* 110). Like Pammy Wynant of *Players*, she values "transience and flash" over commitments (*RD* 109). Ironically, Moll's attraction to "men without a history" (*RD* 63) like Glen Selvy makes her complicit with the clandestine powers that her magazine claims to expose.

Tacitly aiding Selvy's obsessive behavior and secretly attracted to Percival, she has become the running dog of a capitalism that consumes its own opposition. But at least, Moll's curiosity and self-awareness permit her to observe the others' quests from a slight distance.

Glen Selvy is a late twentieth-century version of the knight in quest romances (cf. McClure, "Postmodern Romance" 107). Although his first name recalls that of Sir Gawain, he is playing a postmodernist Sir Percival. Like Percival, whose love for singing birds is emphasized in several Grail stories (Weston 40), Selvy is constantly associated with avians, including Robbins: he appears early in the novel surrounded by birds (*RD* 26), and near the end identifies with the birds of prey that presage his death. Initially involved in the quest for the Hitler film, Selvy eventually departs to pursue his own private quest. Displaying that "element of resolve and fixed purpose" (*RD* 35) typical of DeLillo's would-be ascetics, Selvy's elaborate rituals preserve a "fine edge to be maintained in preparation for—he didn't know what" (*RD* 54). A soldier without a war, Selvy is as transient as Moll, eschewing emotional attachments (he has sex only with married women) to protect "the severity of the double life" (*RD* 81); yet his refusal to consider consequences ultimately paralyzes him. These mental blinders recall Sir Percival, whose failure to ask the right questions in the Fisher King's castle prevents the King's full recovery (see Chrétien 99, lines 3582–90). Like *Libra*'s Lee Oswald, Selvy is a monkish devotee of a "theology of secrets" (*L* 442) who aims to "build . . . a second self" through a fetishistic identification with guns, his "inventory of personal worth" (*RD* 83, 92). Like Ludecke he refers to himself in second person, thereby betraying a deep self-alienation: a mechanism nearly as mindless as his weapons, Selvy has no self beyond his scripted rituals.

Thus as an actor he is not very believable, and Moll notices that his reactions are "just the tiniest bit mechanical" (*RD* 17). In fact Selvy is under double cover, pretending to be Percival's porn buyer while actually working for Radial Matrix, a secret arm of PAC/ORD, and reporting to Arthur Lomax, a man identified by his running dogs (see *RD* 29, 54, 108). Ironically, Selvy's expertise in dismantling surveillance devices (he "squashes the bug" that Earl Mudger, former head of Radial Matrix, uses to eavesdrop on Ludecke's widow) prompts his employers to hire hitman Augie the Mouse, who, like most killers in *Running Dog*, dons a costume (ear protection and shooting glasses) as he fires at Selvy (*RD* 65). But the motives behind Selvy's rituals are not political. As he and Percival contemplate an erotic statue of Saint Teresa, Percival comments, "her ecstasy always was sexual" (*RD* 46). Selvy's routine likewise springs from "sexual sources and coordinates" (*RD*

111), allowing him to become the star of his own private erotic film, and an object for observation and manipulation by people like Mudger.

Nazis in Motion

The unholy grail itself embodies the complex relationships among fascism, film, and subjectivity. All of its pursuers must approach it through a man named Lightborne, who runs a "worldwide network, buying and selling and bartering" (*RD* 16) fake erotica. The vain, dapper Lightborne tries to project an image of refinement and erudition, but his chronically flapping sole exposes him as the novel's pseudo-Charlie Chaplin. As his name implies, Lightborne is a faux-divine messenger who sets things in motion and caters to the others' acquisitive obsessions. If he symbolizes the spirit of capitalist exchange, his counterpart, Richie Armbrister, twenty-two-year-old "smut king" and "master of distribution and marketing" (*RD* 49), exemplifies its material flux. Entirely a creature of his appetites, Armbrister himself admits that he doesn't "exist as a person" (*RD* 50). Capitalists of lust, Lightborne and Armbrister are little more than matrixes of the profit motive.

It is Lightborne who delineates the fundamental aesthetic of twentieth-century erotica: it must have "Movement, action, frames per second. . . . [A] thing isn't fully erotic unless it has the capacity to move" (*RD* 15). Likewise, everything in *Running Dog* seems to be in motion, as the novel exploits film as both plot device and narrative paradigm. Like *Libra* and *Players*, *Running Dog* is structured as a series of cinematic crosscuts between characters and scenes that generates meaning through montage-like juxtapositions. Just as the plot revolves around a competition to possess the Hitler film, so the narrative stages a battle for the possession of voice, as though the text were also a commodity that the characters are vying to control. These narrative movements—the type that Ian Reid calls "dispossessions," which also figure prominently in *Players* and *Libra*[4]—reflect not only the novel's plot, in which each actor maneuvers for advantage over other prospective purchasers, but also the deeper spiritual dispossessions wrought by capitalism and cinema: everything is a commodity, everything is a surface.

A "student of the [Nazi] period" (*RD* 19), Lightborne speculates about the Hitler film: "Unedited footage. One copy. The camera original. Shot in Berlin, April, the year 1945" (*RD* 18). The film would be an historical document without precedent, and would possess the "aura" that Walter Benjamin famously describes as the source of classical aesthetic value (221).

Benjamin cites film as the most destructive agent of that aura: infinitely reproducible, cinematic images act like money, transposing use-value and exchange-value, and wrenching beauty from tradition (221). Indeed, when the film is finally found, it turns out to destroy the "aura" of originality in a multitude of ways, not least because Hitler, the lead "actor," is imitating a movie star who parodied him. Of course, Hitler was in some respects himself an actor who manipulated mass images of himself. By commissioning such propaganda films as Leni Riefenstahl's *Triumph of the Will* and *Olympia*, and by carefully staging his appearances, Hitler incited the adulation and "collective frenzy" characteristic of a "pop hero" (*RD* 147). Using cinema and simple icons, the Nazis trained the masses in a magical mentality in which "thoughts [were] replaced by moving images" (Benjamin 238).

As Lightborne puts it, "Those Nazis had a thing for movies. They put everything on film. . . . Film was essential to the Nazi era. Myth, dreams, memory" (*RD* 52). At the original headquarters in East Prussia, in fact, the Nazi elite showed a movie every night at 8 o'clock (Galante and Silianoff 41; ironically, the only person who never attended was Hitler). Eva Braun, who made 8mm home movies of Nazi leaders and arranged screenings of popular films, claimed that "cinema is an art" and imagined herself as an actress; her ultimate desire was to die and leave a beautiful corpse (Galante and Silianoff 64, 71, 63, 4). Moreover, the Nazis were inordinately concerned about the cinematic images they would pass down to posterity. During a conference at the Propaganda Ministry on April 17, 1945, for example, Joseph Goebbels reportedly predicted that "in a hundred years' time they will be showing a fine color film describing the terrible days we are living through. . . . Hold out now, so that a hundred years hence the audience does not hoot and whistle when you appear on the screen" (Bullock 728). As Susan Sontag asserts, the Nazis tried to turn history into theater ("Fascinating" 311). Of course this desire to turn themselves into filmed fetishes backfired, since it gave inarguable proof of their atrocities. Ironically, then, by obsessively filming themselves the Nazis condemned themselves through the same process that brought them to power. As Hannah Arendt argues, "the perpetual-motion mania of totalitarian movements which can remain in power only so long as they keep moving and set everything around them in motion" generates the fragmentation and restlessness that leads to their demise (4). The Nazis turned themselves into flickering images on the screen of history.

The fascist phenomenon fulfills Lloyd Percival's assessment of the "history of reform," in which "there's always a counteraction built in. . . . Always people ready to invent new secrets, new bureaucracies of terror"

(*RD* 74). *Running Dog* resurrects this history through individual characters' attempts to revise it. Ludecke's wife Klara, for example, believes that owning the film will bring her husband back to life and lend her some of the Third Reich's lost power (*RD* 97). Lightborne exploits a similar urge, telling clients that "History is so comforting. . . . Isn't this why people collect? To own a fragment of the tangible past. Life is fleeting, and we seek consolation in durable things" (*RD* 104). But collectors do not really recapture history; rather, they detach artifacts from the past and create a separate order that is both an elision and an emblem of history. In this regard, film plays a special role, because, as John Frow notes, it "seems to guarantee the solidity of history, to ensure a special access to historical truth" (Frow, *Marxism* 145); but as Riefenstahl's films brilliantly proved, filmed history is always staged history: cinematic images are constructed out of fragments, and thus can be made to "say" anything the filmmakers wish. A film therefore occupies a paradoxical temporal position: it is a solid object in time, but comes into being only when moving through a projector; while presenting itself as verifiable reality, a film is always an aesthetic construct.

History is crucial to *Running Dog*'s characters, because they are motivated largely by a yearning to recapture lost origins. Thus Selvy journeys back to Marathon Mines, the site of his training and the closest thing he has had to a home; Moll repeatedly tries to relive the thrill she got from consorting with a terrorist; Percival wants to own the past as a pornographic object. Even Mudger's fetish for surveillance is, as Patrick O'Donnell has observed, a "form of nostalgia" (O'Donnell 67) for the Vietnam War. Nostalgia transforms historical artifacts into souvenirs, into embodiments of personal emotions; and filmed nostalgia turns history into a "museum" or "supermarket . . . where people are free to shop around for their values and identities" (Cantor 41). As he does throughout his oeuvre, in *Running Dog* DeLillo anatomizes this symbiotic relationship between nostalgia and fascism.

For the characters in *Running Dog*, however, history is useful only if they can market it; thus Mudger, Lightborne, and the mob figures who later enter the chase want the film because they believe it will make money. And that exchange-value depends not only upon its historical veracity but also upon its alleged pornographic content, which in turn derives from a well-established association between SS regalia and SM pornography. As Lightborne notes, Nazis are "automatically erotic. The violence, the rituals, the leather, the jackboots. The whole thing for uniforms and paraphernalia" seems "endlessly fascinating" (*RD* 52). Why? In part because both fascism and sadomasochism stage power relationships in overtly theatrical form. Indeed, according to Sontag, both Nazi ideology and the aesthetics of sadomasochistic pornography "flow from (and justify) a preoccupation with situations of control, submissive behavior, extravagant effort, and the endurance of pain; they endorse two seemingly opposite states, egomania and servitude" (Sontag, "Fascinating" 316).[5] SM porn merely enacts more plainly the ontology of most pornography, which, as Keesey observes, generates an imaginary world where the viewer may be safely totalitarian (102). In short, just as fascism produces a pornography of power, so pornography, in *Running Dog*, is a form of fascist representation.

More generally, any transformation of bodies into instruments or sites for detached observation is fascistic. A prime example of this condition is Glen Selvy, who, as LeClair notes, "treats his body as a pornographic object" (*Loop* 174), a fungible medium of exchange. Seeking pseudo-religious self-transcendence, Selvy can find it only in bodily mortification and violence. He thereby fulfills the fascist ideal in which "everyday reality is transcended through ecstatic self-control and submission" (Sontag, "Fascinating" 313).[6] Selvy's zeal couples pornographic and fascist aesthetics: just as fascist art glamorizes death, so Selvy's pursuit of extreme states reduces subjectivity to a vehicle for a linear movement toward erotic self-annihilation. Like the Nazis, Selvy fetishistically transmutes dread into a form of magic.

Selvy's fanatic rituals weave together the novel's Grail plot with its anatomies of pornography and fascism; these links are more explicitly established in a conversation between Lightborne and Moll. As Lightborne outlines Armbrister's career, Moll comments, "Fascinating." Lightborne replies: "Fascinating, yes. An interesting word. From the Latin *fascinus*. An amulet shaped like a phallus. A word progressing from the same root as the word 'fascism'" (*RD* 151). Lightborne's fanciful etymology synthesizes the novel's themes.[7] That phallic amulet embodies the relationship between fascism and sadomasochistic eroticism, while figuring the way that Mudger, Lomax, and Selvy reenact the Nazis' reduction of human possibility to relations of dominance and submission. More significantly, the connection between fascination and fascism implies that the marketing of obsession—the shared business of Armbrister, Mudger, Percival, and Robbins—resembles the Nazis' mass-marketing of communal identity. That is, the fascination with fascism, with observing obsession, makes the observer complicit with the behavior and engenders a similarly objectifying relationship between audience and actors. Such fascination is itself fascistic. We readers of *Running Dog*, engaged as we are in observing the observers, are thus also implicated in its exploitative ideology. Fascinated by fascists, we play Nazi by proxy.

Running Dog further characterizes fascism, capitalism, and pornography as forms of power linked and amplified by technology. The figure who best embodies this connection is Earl Mudger, whose organization, Radial Matrix, a secret arm of PAC/ORD, operates as a "centralized funding mechanism for covert operations" against foreign governments (*RD* 74). Radial Matrix imitates its ostensible enemies, thereby fulfilling the "historical counterfunction" that requires new bureaucracies of terror (*RD* 76). But Radial Matrix really serves capitalism itself. Indeed, Mudger's greatest achievement is the way he combines "business drives and lusts and impulses with police techniques, with ultrasophisticated skills of detection, surveillance, extortion, terror" (*RD* 76). As Lomax later declares, in Mudger's domain business and spying don't just support each other — "one *is* the other" (*RD* 156). It is only fitting, then, that Mudger becomes interested in the pornography industry: where better to blend surveillance and surplus value?

Porn both depicts and embodies commodification by reducing human behavior to a series of "sexual *exchanges*" (Sontag, "Pornographic" 229; italics hers). We buy not only the bodies displayed and their sexual interaction, but also an ideology that makes eros consumable. *Running Dog* thus suggests that pornography is, as LeClair suggests, the purest expression of American consumerism (*Loop* 173). A man who views persons as objects, Mudger has always been a pornographer; and his military tactics are both mercantile and sexual, "a slam-bang corporate adventure" for which he needs "product" (*RD* 139). Mudger exercises power by controlling representations of identity. Thus the apparently meaningless name Radial Matrix — a geometric figure describing sets of numbers in rows that branch out from a common center — accurately captures the way Mudger's paramilitary program imposes "categorical definitions or functions upon that which is subsumed under [his] control" (Nadeau 179). In short, Mudger's organization mirrors the porn industry: both are bureaucracies devoted to the arrangement, manipulation, regulation and management of bodies by means of social categories (Stewart, *Crimes* 241).

Mudger's power is also pornographic in that it relies upon a surveillance network that transforms everyone into actors in his private movie. Although Mudger himself claims to worry that technological snooping makes us "feel like criminals" (*RD* 93), he is "close to religious" (*RD* 105) in his devotion to listening devices — which is why he targets Selvy for assassination when he dismantles his bug. Lightborne later adds the visual component to Mudger's analysis: "Go into a bank, you're filmed. . . . Go into a department store, you're filmed. . . . Everywhere. . . . Putting the whole world on film. . . . Everybody's on camera" (*RD* 149–50). Although *Running Dog* satirizes such paranoid philosophies even as it voices them, nonetheless it depicts the dire consequences of this condition—or the belief in it.

One consequence, as I have been arguing, is that all the characters in *Running Dog* exist in a cinematic world that conflates behavior and performance so that nobody lives in the first person. Yet these performances do not produce a consistent sense of self. Instead, like film actors, these subjects create their personae by bits and pieces. As Pirandello argues, because the film actor's persona becomes continuous only through editing, the actor always feels "exiled not only from the stage but from himself. With a vague sense of discomfort he feels inexplicable emptiness: the body loses its corporeality, it is deprived of reality, life, voice . . . in order to be changed into a mute image" (quoted in Benjamin 229). Their lives in the movies also prevent *Running Dog*'s characters from grasping their own motives. Not only is everyone an actor; everyone acts in a vacuum, alienated from other persons and from interior life. These characters exist, notes John Frow, as "stylizations" to whom the world appears *après-coup*, as after-effect or preview or déjà vu (Frow, *Marxism* 144). As in Baudrillard's domain of simulacra, subjectivity becomes an endless series of imitations without originals. The characters have no existence outside of their cinematic surfaces; all they can do is reshuffle the frames. This condition also makes them prone to manipulation by those for whom, in Foucault's description, "our society is not one of spectacle, but of surveillance. . . ; behind the great abstraction of exchange, there continues the meticulous, concrete training of useful forces." Thus in *Running Dog* "we are neither in the amphitheatre, nor on the stage, but in the panoptic machine" (Foucault, *Discipline* 217).

As in the penitentiary panopticon, in *Running Dog* the collective has been "abolished and replaced by a collection of separate individualities" in discrete cells (Foucault, *Discipline* 201). Subjects are unsettled by the awareness that they are being looked at, but even more by their inability to tell when they are being observed and when they aren't. If the initial result of panoptic observation is for creatures like Selvy the "penetration of regulation into even the smallest details of everyday life . . . [and] the assignment to each individual of his 'true' name, his 'true' place, his 'true' body, his 'true' disease" (Foucault, *Discipline* 198), the ultimate consequence is the dissemination of selfhood outward toward the camera eye, so that the observed identifies with the observer and becomes "the principle of his own subjection" (Foucault, *Discipline* 203). *Running Dog* depicts the world from inside the panopticon—an empty "inside" in a world "thoroughly exteri-orized" (O'Donnell 62). No longer can one say that everybody is in cos-tume; since subjectivity is indistinguishable from performance, disguise is no more possible than authenticity.[8] Hence, although I have been treating *Running Dog*'s named personages as characters, in a sense it really has no characters, only bundles of gestures, voices, and desires, radial matrixes of conflicting motives and forces.

The clearest embodiment of these effects is again Glen Selvy, who is simultaneously discipliner and disciplined subject.[9] The prize creature of Mudger's "royal menagerie" (Foucault 203), Selvy is the running dog of the title, as he himself tells Nadine, the young woman he rescues (in proper knightly fashion) from a nude storytelling parlor (*RD* 160). He bran-dishes this mock-Indian name as an emblem of autonomy, but the eco-nomic nature of his clandestine activities—paying secret commissions to foreign agents, financing terrorist bombings—demonstrates that he really runs to serve an anonymous, dehumanizing capitalism. Indeed, Mudger, his master, doesn't even know his name. The true nature of their relation-ship is dramatized in chapter 4 of the Radial Matrix section, where DeLillo intercuts Mudger's work on his knives with Selvy's encounter and escape with Nadine. The satisfactions of precision machine work and the recitation of knives constitute for Mudger a "near-secret knowledge" (*RD* 119), a reli-gion with its own litany. His meticulous labor reassures him of his power and reflects his ability to shape himself as a violent instrument, to become the "Mudger tip" (*RD* 92).[10] But his greatest weapon is Selvy, at once dog and machine, whom Lomax calls the "Best I've ever run" (*RD* 141). This juxtaposition of Selvy and Mudger identifies the former as the latter's magic blade and alter ego: they are knight and sword, Hitler and his prize Alsa-tian, Blondi.[11] Selvy's final journey back to Marathon Mines, the site of his training by Mudger, is thus at once a linear quest for termination and a loop backward toward his origins. Ironically, then, although Selvy views his life in the clandestine service as "a narrative of flight from women" (*RD* 135), his journey is a return to Mudger, his surrogate mother.[12]

True Believers

Eventually Mudger abandons the pursuit of the Hitler film, choosing in-stead to cultivate his private zoo. Lloyd Percival likewise backs off, find-ing his grail at the Medical Museum of the Armed Forces Institute of Pathology (a "[f]ascinating" place [*RD* 196]), where he feels "reborn, re-vitalized" by its collection of erotic artifacts, which enable him to replace "*Nazis in motion*" with "the art of mystics and nomads" (*RD* 222; italics in original). Nonetheless, Percival remains, in his devotion to the power of celebrity and the mystical force of erotic images, a true believer.

So are the organized crime "families" who eventually obtain the Hitler film. As Lomax says, they are "the only ones who believe in what they're doing. . . . They're totally committed" (*RD* 220). Their chief representative, Vinny (the Eye) Talerico, acquired his sobriquet because of partial facial paralysis that has rendered his sagging right side numb and expressionless. If Mudger's bugs make him all ears, Vinny's power is embodied by his right eye, which resembles that of a "hawk, a snake, a shark," and which evinces his simultaneously bestial and mechanical mentality (*RD* 175). Resembling an allegorical figure in a medieval romance, Vinny the Eye bluntly incarnates the most brutal aspects of postmodern capitalism. Not surprisingly, this incarnation of avarice models himself after a film actor (Richard Conte, who played numerous gangster roles in such films as *The Big Combo*: *RD* 177). Like the others, Talerico is a creature of images, a deadly caricature of movie mobsters.

But even he pales next to the truest believer, Selvy, whose terminal journey alternates with the screening of the Hitler film in the novel's final

scenes. As Lomax earlier pointed out, Selvy is the one who truly believes in that fascist faith that "transform[s] sexual energy into a 'spiritual' force" (Sontag, "Fascinating" 317; *RD* 141). Through Selvy's journey toward ritual suicide, the novel resumes its character as a metaromance, but now the aim of the quest, as McClure has observed, "is to find a viable romance form, a script that will enable Selvy, and perhaps the reader, to begin pursuing redemption" ("Postmodern Romance" 108). As Selvy travels toward an origin that is also an end, the barren terrain surrounding Marathon Mines is refigured as the Fisher King's wasted domain, with Nadine's angling father, Jack, in the regal role (*RD* 182). Just as Chrétien's Percival first discovers and speaks his true name only after his encounter with the Fisher King (Chrétien 98; lines 3570–76), here Selvy awakens to his true identity and purpose:

All those weeks at the Mines. . . . The routine. The double life. . . . The narrowing of choices. . . . It was clear, finally. The whole point. . . . All this time he'd been preparing to die. It was a course in dying. In how to die violently. In how to be killed by your own side, in secret, no hard feelings. It was a ritual preparation. (*RD* 183)

Selvy experiences that mystical transcendence sought by so many of De-Lillo's protagonists, that endland of purity and simplicity where he is freed from choice, that "subtle form of disease" (*RD* 192).

The conclusion of his quest is surrounded by symbolic trappings appropriate for an allegorical romance. As Mudger observes, the scene has the "foreordained character of some classical epic, modernized" to include that mechanical bird of prey, the helicopter (*RD* 209). Similarly, as Mudger's men, former ARVN soldiers Van and Cao (Portuguese for "dog"), pursue Selvy, he sees birds—a hawk (*RD* 184), a buzzard (*RD* 190), and a raven (*RD* 222)—that signify his condition as quarry. Selvy seems to accept his destiny, buying a Filipino guerrilla bolo knife because he finds the name "romantic" (*RD* 191), as if aware of its condition as twentieth-century version of the magic sword of the Grail romances. Selvy also seems to know that this dreadful blade will be used against him.

DeLillo even provides the stereotypical mystic sage in Levi Blackwater, who has survived torture to "the machine of self" and thus must have "knowledge to impart" (*RD* 231). But Levi's wisdom seems dubious, since his torture made him identify with his captors (*RD* 223), just as Selvy has devoted himself to a surrogate parent who aims to kill him. Levi exemplifies Foucault's "disciplined subject," who has internalized the punitive codes of his captors. But if DeLillo presents Levi's mysticism somewhat satirically, his pseudo-Indian creed of purification through pain still seems preferable to the brutal lust for power and possession—the marketing obsession—that runs the novel's other dogs. Levi himself knows that Selvy believes too "easily and indiscriminately, taking to things with a quick and secret fervor" (*RD* 245), and cautions him that if "you think you're about to arrive at some final truth. . . . You'll only be disappointed" (*RD* 233). Nonetheless, as Van and Cao approach, Selvy imagines himself in a movie Western (*RD* 186), and feels a "Strong sense of something being played out. Memory, a film. Rush of adolescent daydreams. He'd been through it in his mind a hundred times . . ." (*RD* 239). In the postmodern panopticon, even death, that consummately private moment, reels out as a movie.

The complex symbolic strands in Selvy's final encounter converge in his choice of apparel. As Selvy readies himself for his meeting with Van and Cao, Levi places a hood over his head. This combination of cowl and executioner's hood suits Selvy, a would-be monk whose execution is also a suicide. It also serves the avian symbology in the scene: Selvy resembles a falcon rehooded for return to his falconer. Most significantly, the hood again places him in a disguise that betrays his true identity: as Johnson comments, Selvy "becomes 'himself' by being executed" (78). But his death isn't merely personal; as Mudger might wish, Selvy's final struggle with Van and Cao allegorically replays the Vietnam War. Thus when Selvy thrusts his blade into Cao, he stabs him so deeply that he cannot pull out the blade and protect himself. "He was attached, in effect, to the man he'd stabbed" (*RD* 239), just as the American military became suicidally attached to the war and to the South Vietnamese government that sucked them into it. Two dogs of war, Selvy and Cao die in an ironic embrace.

After Van finishes off the paralyzed Selvy, he uses the man's chosen weapon to cut off his head as a trophy for Mudger. Selvy's maiming is ironically appropriate: a man who has closed off choice and made himself into a subject for observation and manipulation, his final destiny is to become a pornographic artifact, an emblem of *Running Dog*'s other fractured subjects.[13] Indeed, as Johnson points out (79), Selvy was effectively decapitated long ago. Levi hopes to leave the body for "the large soaring birds" (*RD* 245) after consecrating it in a Native American ritual that will free Selvy's spirit. Alas, one must begin the ceremony by "plucking a few strands of hair from the top of the dead man's head" (*RD* 246). Hence, even in death the luckless Selvy remains anonymous, denied both the body he has trained so rigorously and the solace of his spiritual ideology. With this sardonic conclusion, the novel eschews a thriller's resolution: Selvy's quest seems absurd, and the conclusion a grim jest on all concerned. DeLillo's violation of expectations thus not only subverts the genre's conventions and exposes its ideology, as John Frow argues (*Marxism* 146); it also reveals how the clandestine operations that inspire thrillers are themselves influenced by filmic representations. That is, thrillers are not so much modeled after real behavior as "real" behavior is modeled on thrillers.

An Accurate Reproduction

The conclusion of the other plot defeats our expectations as well. I am treating them separately, but DeLillo dramatizes their parallel qualities by crosscutting back and forth from Selvy's quest to the preparations for screening the Hitler film: Selvy's performance in Mudger's "film" enacts the fascistic mentality also displayed in the Hitler home movie; both events relive history as tragedy and macabre farce; both involve "radial matrixes," illustrated when the helicopter blades "dissolve" to the sound of the film in the projector (*RD* 234), as if Lightborne and the others are watching Selvy's movie. Both plots are also Grail quests in which the desired object is found but found wanting. And both quests disappoint Moll Robbins, who, by resisting Mudger's sexual blandishments, has been left out of the loop of observation and performance. Her "distinterested intelligence" (*RD* 188), however, allows her to furnish the novel's sole sliver of potential redemption, because she is forced to confront her own complicity in the exploitation she documents. Lightborne asks Moll to screen the film with him to help explain his fear that "It was all so real. It had such weight. . . . History was true" (*RD* 188). But although the film disappoints Lightborne, it offers a complex instance of the convergence of the artificial and the real, of history and theater, of "acting" and behaving.

These convergences also characterize the first film "shown" in the novel, Charles Chaplin's 1940 satire of Nazism, *The Great Dictator*, which Moll and Selvy watch just before the gun battle in Part 1. *The Great Dictator*, like *Running Dog*, juxtaposes two plots that comment upon each other. Chaplin portrays a Jewish barber and World War I veteran who is finally released from the hospital on the eve of the next war, just in time to be subjected to the Nazis' anti-Semitic atrocities. Chaplin also portrays Adenoid Hynkel, the Hitleresque dictator. The film implies that the infantile, self-absorbed Hynkel—who can't control his own underlings, engages in a hilariously idiotic struggle for authority with a competing dictator, and generally attempts to fulfill an image of magnificence beyond his powers—is merely a poor copy of a "great dictator." It thus suggests what Lightborne earlier stated: that Hitler, who modeled himself after cinematic versions of greatness, was only impersonating a great dictator. In the film's most *"celebrated scene,"* Hynkel performs an *"eerie ballet"* with a balloon globe, a performance suggesting that his *"vast romance of acquisition and conquest"* is really a form of child's play (*RD* 60; italics in original). Later in Chaplin's film, when the dictator falls out of his boat while duck hunting, the barber who looks just like Hynkel replaces him and addresses the multitude. In this famous and much-maligned speech,[14] Chaplin addresses the movie audience in his own persona, exhorting us to replace hatred with laughter and hope. That the barber can stand in for the dictator suggests again that Hynkel and Hitler are no more worthy of dictatorial powers than anyone else, and indeed that anyone, given the proper circumstances, can use images to exert power over the masses.

DeLillo's gloss on the film reveals a disturbing facet of Chaplin and his tramp. His narrator notes that even the humble barber *"studies his image"* in a bald man's head, as if deeply worried about his appearance. Moreover, the barber's replacement of Hynkel may imply that he, too, possesses the potential for megalomania, despite his championing of peaceful coexistence. More significantly, perhaps, Hitler and Chaplin shared features other than the *"world's most famous mustache"* (*RD* 60): they were born the same week, rose to fame through the global dissemination of images, and combined commonness with colossal ambition. Charles Maland notes that both Hitler and Chaplin "demanded strict control over subordinates when . . . they achieved positions of power (164). Just as the dictator was in some sense a comedian (*RD* 61), so the comedian could be a small-scale dictator. Chaplin's Little Tramp was probably the most recognizable figure in the world—aside from Hitler—and so when Chaplin addresses the multitudes, he is attempting to use the power of his image to sway audiences as Hitler did, albeit for diametrically opposed aims. Chaplin was an active antifascist. Nevertheless, in *The Great Dictator* even he exploited the growing fascination with Nazism; he too marketed obsession.

Chaplin's film foreshadows the highly ironic multilayered impersonation that appears in the underground Hitler film. Obviously, to imagine such a movie DeLillo is adjusting history.[15] But regardless of its historical plausibility, the film brilliantly consummates the novel's multiple themes. In its first segment, the stationary camera observes people behaving as themselves; in the second, the camera moves, and a subject performs; in the third segment, the subjects pretend to be an audience, thereby becoming, like the novel's characters, at once performers and observers of themselves and their own observers. In the initial sequence, amid flickering light caused by the bombing overhead, a room fills with children and a couple of adults setting up chairs for a performance. There is a cut to another room in which a woman, probably Eva Braun, sits reading a magazine and talking to someone offscreen. Moll Robbins finds this banal material fascinating: "it was primitive and blunt, yet hypnotic, not without an element of mystery" (*RD* 227). Mystery—a word frequently invoked in DeLillo's texts to suggest religious potential—is what makes the film "hypnotic." The viewers wonder who these people are, who else will appear, what will happen, why it was filmed. At the same time its primitiveness convinces Lightborne that "It's true. It's happening" (*RD* 229): the film is simultaneously an authentic document and an elusive artifact that resists comprehension. When the six children and five adults gaze at the camera,[16] they place themselves in the panopticon, submitting themselves to the verdict of history while at the same time staring down those future observers as if to say, "judge us if you can claim yourself free of sin."

Likewise, in the next sequence, the audience of eleven seem to watch their audience watching them, as they prepare for the entrance of the leading man. The camera slowly pans toward him and then up from his shoes: it is the Führer, playing Chaplin's Little Tramp. He shuffles toward the camera, flooded in light, and *"produces an expression, finally—a sweet, epicene, guilty little smile. Charlie's smile. An accurate reproduction"* (*RD* 236). This "ultimate postmodern moment" (Cantor 56) is not just Hitler playing Chaplin; it is Hitler impersonating Chaplin as the barber who impersonated Hynkel, himself an "accurate reproduction" of Hitler. The tragedy of history is again reenacted as farce (Frow, *Marxism* 145; Cantor 53), with Hitler as clown or pretender. This, along with the dictator's *"trembling arm, nodding head [and] stagger in his gait"* (*RD* 235), renders him ineffectual, even pathetic.[17] Hitler now becomes the aged Fisher King unable to restore his wasted kingdom. But the question arises: for whom is Hitler performing? For the children? For the adults? Or is he making a final appeal to posterity, as if to say, "I'm no monster, just a humble soul like Chaplin's clown"? The pitiful Hitler represents Nazism as a tired joke, a bad movie, a cheap imitation. But if Hitler has become merely an "accurate reproduction" of himself, this is a function not only of his impersonation, but of the nature of cinema: any filmed event, even if "true," can be no more than an "accurate reproduction" of reality. Thus while DeLillo is certainly depicting Nazism as a "derivative imitation" of greatness and power (Cantor 58), he is also demonstrating the difficulty of escaping from the radial matrix of representations that cannot distinguish the Little Tramp from the Great Dictator.

Blasé about Nazi pornography, Lightborne curiously finds "Hitler humanized" to be "disgusting" (*RD* 237). Perhaps this reduced Hitler repels him because he asks us to identify with him as "the subject of surveillance" (O'Donnell 60). Or perhaps, believing that the film will have no commercial value, Lightborne is disgusted by his own wasted effort. "I expected something hard-edged. Something dark and potent. . . . The perversions, the sex" (*RD* 237). If truth be told, so did we. The film both disappoints and intrigues for a number of reasons. First, it depicts Hitler not as he "really" was, but disguised, as if he could simply replace one persona—say, Dictator—with another. And if Hitler was himself an imitation, then was he really evil, or just a melodrama villain with a silly mustache? Indeed, because the masquerade works only if we know who is behind it, in portraying Chaplin/Hynkel/the barber, Hitler is playing himself, playing. Hence it becomes impossible to separate the real from the representation, and we seem no closer to understanding the fascinations of fascism—at least not if we insist upon looking outside of ourselves. But the film's final segment hints at a more complex relationship between audience and performer. In this final setup, the "*sole attempt at 'art'*" (*RD* 237), the filmed audience members silently "*applaud the masquerade*" (*RD* 238) taking place offscreen. We readers watch the audience of the Hitler film watch another audience (the viewers within the film) "watch": we view a mirror image of ourselves, riveted to the screen while history passes in front of them but remains beyond their and our possession. We cannot own it; we cannot even own our own observation of it, because the film has appropriated it from us in advance. The newsreel of history turns out to be just another mirror; events are staged to be observed by actors.

DeLillo's hall of mirrors contains another figure who stands for us: Lightborne, who has admitted to his fascistic fascinations throughout the novel. As the film travels through the projector, Lightborne acknowledges that, like the Nazis, he has "put powerful forces to work" (RD 237–38). Not only, then, is he another running dog, but in collaborating to rewrite history as Ludecke (and Hitler) would have liked, he has also colluded with contemporary authoritarian programs. And if we have read this far, we have probably shared Lightborne's fascinations. Thus DeLillo implies that we readers and viewers, fascinated by these lightborne images, are ourselves "Lightborne." This is not the same as saying, as Bruce Bawer claims, that "we are all Hitler" (40). It means, rather, that Hitler and the little Hitlers who populate the novel express not only our fascination with, and even nostalgia for, larger-than-life figures who epitomize grand abstractions such as Good and Evil, but also that fascism continues to manifest itself in late capitalism's obsession with marketing. It also means that we are inextricably imbricated into the matrix of images that exists between history as event and history as representation, because a novel or a film can have meaning only if we choose to "set it in motion." Hence the neutrality with which the camera presents its material seems to accede ineluctably to a nihilism that cannot differentiate between hilarity and horror.

If the conclusion of the film plot at first seems as anticlimactic as Selvy's quest, it does satisfactorily synthesize most of the novel's themes. But Moll remains disappointed: after the first reel, she departs, leaving Lightborne to meet Augie the Mouse on the fire escape. Augie too makes clownish gestures (wiping his nose on his lapel) and speaks of himself as if he were a film image in slow fade-in: "There's nobody here. . . . I'm beginning to hear. . . . I'm taking form. . . . You're beginning to see me" (RD 242). His words, echoing those of the cop in the prologue, bring the novel full circle. Although Augie's lines seem to have been learned from movie gangsters, they prove again that the "families," those true believers, do not need to "audition" (RD 244) for a part they have played for centuries. For them, Hitler and the unholy grail are only commodities like any other, and Augie is merely a middleman, a facilitator of exchange—another Lightborne, who readily switches gears to contemplate marketing outlets for the film. What else could he do? "Could he tell them people like to dress up? Could he tell them history is true?" (RD 244).

Both quests, then, end in ironic irresolution. Just before she watches the Hitler film, Moll contemplates quests in a passage that describes DeLillo's theme in both Running Dog and The Names:

At the bottom of most long and obsessive searches, . . . was some vital deficiency on the part of the individual in pursuit, a meagerness of spirit. . . . Whether people searched for an object of some kind, or inner occasion, or answer or state of being, it was almost always disappointing. People came up against themselves in the end.

Nothing but themselves. Of course there were those who believed the search itself was . . . the reward. (*RD* 224)

In *The Names* the "search itself" inspires Axton's renewed appreciation of conversation and community. But in *Running Dog* the outcome is frankly nihilistic. All of this novel's questers seek the film as way of extending power and ownership, and hence ego, into the world: Percival wants to complete his collection, and thus to extend his own body through objects; Lightborne wishes to make a name for himself; Mudger, conceiving capitalism as guerrilla warfare, craves the thrill of the hunt; Talerico and Armbrister want to expand their empires. In each, the desire for the film reveals an absence that can be filled only by a commodity that reaches across time; even Selvy searches for a fullness of being that he senses he lacks. Moll's words also mark a confrontation with her own "life in the movies" (*RD* 224). She is self-aware enough to recognize her complicity with the running dogs of capitalism and their nihilistic machinations. But it is not clear whether she gains anything from it: her fictional existence ends indeterminately when, accompanied by a flock of pigeons (*RD* 242), she leaves Lightborne's gallery dissatisfied that nobody is watching her, that nothing remains but bare ugliness, "the blatant flesh of things" (*RD* 244). On the one hand, this seems a victory: Moll has awakened from the nightmare of history-as-commodity and has checked out of the panopticon. She is free to become somebody other than a "moll." On the other hand, even the "blatant flesh of things" now looks like another bad porn movie.

Moll's thoughts about quests also turn the lens back at readers to challenge our expectations about plots, novels, and genre. As McClure notes, the novel "reminds us that we are, as a culture, addicted to fantasies of quest, conspiracy, and illumination" ("Postmodern Romance" 107). Why are we? Moll, awaiting the screening, muses that "the anticipation was apart from what followed. It was permanently renewable, a sense of freedom from all the duties and conditions of the nonmovie world" (*RD* 224). We pursue quests for the same reason: because through them we inhabit narratives that lead to clearly defined goals. In reading about or observing quests, we come to share the questers' fascinations, to possess them like a Grail—which now becomes anything that permits us to authorize our own destinies. As in *End Zone*, *Players*, and *The Names*, DeLillo interrogates the value of plot, and scrutinizes his and our participation in the games of novel reading and film watching. He does so by withholding satisfaction: like Selvy, we are denied the self-renewal of the completed quest. Instead, he indicates that the desire to read and write quest plots presupposes a yearning to dictate material and form and is thus itself fascistic; that it presumes a longing to compress history into ownable objects, and a need to turn others into artifacts. And yet, by showing how obsession and marketing converge in postmodern capitalism, he questions his own activity—for isn't he too marketing obsession, fascinated with fascism?

It may seem, then, that DeLillo exposes the marketing of obsession and the obsession with marketing but then shrugs his shoulders, as if admitting that one can do nothing but succumb to the radial matrices of the late capitalist panopticon. Likewise, his thriller may not transcend its reductive treatment of character and structure. But while it is true that the novel's restless motion and relentless cynicism render it a touch facile, Moll's incremental growth—she resists Mudger's seduction and thereby escapes her previous role as a "Mafia wife" (*RD* 131)—and her self-aware comments about quests and plots self-critically articulate how narratives can be liberating as well as ensnaring. Precisely because the characters in *Running Dog* are so two-dimensional, the reader strives to give them depth, instinctively sensing that the mysteries of subjectivity extend beneath and beyond the tentacles of capitalist representations. Indeed, because we live in the cinematic panopticon and perceive ourselves as filmed images, we require at least the illusion of freedom. If films and novels furnish that, they enable us to imagine ourselves as other, to be free from our daily obsessions, and even, perhaps, to recapture the mystery that transfigures dread into magic, that transforms "the blatant flesh of things" into an accurate reproduction.

THE GIFT OF TONGUES: OBLITERATING *THE NAMES*

In the opening paragraph of *The Names*, narrator James Axton, an American working in Greece as a risk analyst for a multinational insurance corporation, explains why he has avoided the Acropolis: "the weight and moment of those worked stones promised to make the business of seeing them a complicated one. So much converges there. . . . There are obligations attached to such a visit" (*N* 3). A risk analyst by temperament as well as by trade, Axton shuns obligations of all kinds, but undergoes a series of life-altering experiences that move him toward toward commitment and community. His passive character is destroyed and then restored by a newly liberating comprehension of language as the necessary ligature of filial and communal bonds.

As its title implies, *The Names* concerns the ways that linguistic exchanges construct identity and social relations. Axton, who learns little Greek, resists such exchanges. His containment resembles that of his nine-year-old son, Tap, who speaks Ob, a kind of pig Latin ("frobeeze tobo dobeath") he has learned from his mother, Axton's estranged wife Kathryn.

Ob functions for Tap as a "substitute Greek or counter-Greek" (*N* 11) that both proves his tie to his mother and protects him from outsiders — including his bemused father. Tap's Ob also is an obstruction or objection to the smug, insular "lexical trafficking" (Saltzman, *Designs* 45) of Axton and his friends. I want to argue that the prefix "ob," meaning "in the way of" or "against," comes to signify the dialogical and transformative power of linguistic exchange. Indeed, I hope to show that DeLillo writes his own novel, metaphorically, in Ob; that is, he employs a series of "ob" words to chart the geographical and psychic movement of Axton and his friend, archaeologist and epigrapher Owen Brademas (whose initials are O.B.), toward transformative encounters with linguistic mystery.[18] Denying both domestic and political obligations, Axton also objectifies the citizens of the countries where he works. But through a shared obsession with a murderous cult, Axton and Brademas find their identities obliterated; then, by reading Tap's novel about Owen's experiences in a Pentecostal church during the ritual of tongues, Axton achieves a new awareness of language as an oblation, which forces him to revise his perception not only of the Acropolis, but of all human history and culture. In this novel DeLillo considers the political and economic consequences of the tyrannies of textuality, and contemplates both the power of communal speech and the consequences of its disappearance. As in *Running Dog*, DeLillo employs a quest plot to investigate the need for quests, and through his characters' obsessions engineers a self-reflexive investigation of writerly obsessiveness. But *The Names* offers a counterforce to bureaucracies of terror, a pathway out of the earlier novel's crippling ironies: language is the magic that defuses dread.

Obligation

Axton avoids the Acropolis because it seems to demand involvement in Greek culture. The procession of tourists up the hill appears to him as an unpleasant "pilgrimage" or "commitment" (*N* 5). For Axton, "obligation," a word formed by adding "ob" to *ligare* ("to bind"), signifies bondage. His friends — banker David Keller and his young second wife Lindsay, corporate consultant Charles Maitland and his wife Ann — likewise eschew meaningful encounters with Greek culture, instead creating a little world with its own verbal rituals, which DeLillo captures in their sophisticated, sterile dialogue. While their words are designed not to promote intimacy but to prevent it, for the Greeks "conversation is life, . . . a shared narrative . . . too dense to allow space for the unspoken, the sterile" (*N* 52). Lindsay Keller admits that she and her friends are beginners in this Greek art of genuine dialogue (*N* 63). Hence the title of Part 1, "The Island," refers not only to the place where Kathryn and Tap live, but also to the isolation of the American expatriates, who live in foreign places but remain insulated from their real life (cf. LeClair, *Loop* 181). In short, Axton's friends are all "risk analysts."

This insularity suits their activities in Greece. As Axton puts it, "Americans used to come to places like this to write and paint and study, to find deeper textures. Now we do business" (*N* 6). As in *Running Dog*, capitalism subsumes all other human enterprises, so that the characters' various activities—making investments, destabilizing governments, visiting tourist sites—are all euphemistically described as "business." And one "does business in English" (*N* 42). Axton's "business" uses actuarial divination to "protect the investments" of insurance companies by collecting information about the stability of foreign countries. His job enables him to remain a "perennial tourist" who can "escape accountability" (*N* 43), a feat that, ironically, results from the financial accounting—compiling and weighing statistics, analyzing figures, assessing the balance of payments—that constitutes his occupation (*N* 33–34). Risk analysis is thus merely an economic version of Axton's earlier profession as a "Renaissance hack" (*N* 48). He has traded in this innocuous verbal production to traffick in fear and the value of human lives.

Axton's boss, George Rowser, is less certain about freedom from accountability: he travels under a false name and hides behind layers of bogus documents. These "investments," the clothing of the secret life, help him generate profitable financial investments for his clients. Rowser assesses the "cost-effectiveness of terror" (*N* 46) and then convinces insurance companies to sell ransom policies to corporations. If the risk of enrolling is lower than the risk of kidnappings, his company makes money, so he must convince his clients that the risk is high. Secrecy is crucial, because if a terrorist group believes that a corporation is insured, they are more likely to kidnap an executive. Rowser protects "the parent" by selling portions of the original policies, thereby spreading "risk and generat[ing] whatever cash flow the parent did not supply" (*N* 48). His use of "parent" for his corporation is telling: familial and domestic ties have for all the expatriates been replaced by affiliations to nebulous capitalist institutions. Yet Rowser's elaborate mechanisms of protection imply a deep-seated guilt that is also shared by his colleagues. Although they pretend that "nothing sticks to us but smoke in our hair and clothes" (*N* 7), when foreign governments confiscate their property they secretly feel that they had it coming (*N* 41), as in privately regretting their detachment and hoping that forces beyond their control will deprive them of their ill-gotten gains. Their "investments" in foreign goods thus allay their guilt and allow them to rationalize their business practices. As Axton comments, "America is the world's living myth. There's no sense of wrong when you kill an American or blame America for some local disaster. This is our function, to be character types. . . . People expect us to absorb the impact of their grievances" (*N* 114). This is less an explanation than an excuse: by presenting American imperialism as a myth, he deflects responsibility for his activities.

Kathryn Axton not only contests this sophistry; she believes that "There's something secret and guilty about investing. . . . It's the wrong use of the future" (*N* 12). She also perceives the double meaning of "investing," comprehending that James's telexes and calculations disguise violent interventions. Unlike James, moreover, Kathryn welcomes risk and commitment (*N* 128). She is currently committed to archaeology and is in Greece working (without pay) on a Minoan dig headed by Owen Brademas. She also knows that James's avoidance of obligation extends to his domestic life. Whereas the philandering Charles Maitland produces the word "wedlock" like "a gold coin between his teeth," Axton thinks of marriage as no "state at all," because "we'd broken out of states and nations" (*N* 39). As LeClair notes, marriage is for him another mode of tourism (LeClair, *Loop* 181).

One way that Axton avoids confrontation is by pre-empting Kathryn's criticisms. Thus he has compiled his "27 Depravities," a list containing his version of Kathryn's accusations. Although many of the allegations are accurate (he is indeed *"Uncommitted,"* and *"Politically neuter"* [*N* 16–17; italics in original]), the point is that he presumes to speak for her, just as he and his friends presume to speak for the Greeks, Arabs, and Turks. Kathryn is right to call the list a "masterpiece of evasion": by codifying her supposed criticisms, he can defuse them and subdue her. Still, sometimes their conversations, especially when they quarrel, reach deeper levels. Thus the argument that ends "The Island" contains their "history in words" (*N* 123), a narrative of obligations and losses, an account of shared sadness.

Kathryn and James also speak through Tap and Owen Brademas. However, Owen's patriarchal presence troubles Axton, whose avoidance of obligation makes him a diffident father. He envies his hotel doorman and his friend Anand Dass for their confident way with children; he also objects to Kathryn's and Tap's use of Ob, and warns Tap not to become "Obsessed" with it (*N* 88). Tap's language further reveals his allegiance to his mother: in contrast to James's careful, anonymous hackwork, Tap "collides with the language" in "flamboyant prose" (*N* 32). Although Owen's relationship with Tap makes James jealous, eventually Owen becomes a surrogate father to both Tap and James by providing a compelling character for their narratives and for DeLillo's.

Owen engages in a form of linguistic archaeology that unearths the original meanings of words. For example he tells Tap that "character" comes from a Greek word meaning " 'to brand or sharpen.' Or 'pointed stake' if it's a noun" (*N* 10). Thus a character is both an alphabetic letter and an imaginary personage—a double meaning that the Names cult's murders enact in their murderous identification of letters and persons. As befits a novel entitled *The Names*, Owen's definition not only signifies that identity is a function of naming, and that characters are "literal"—made of letters (Bryant 18)—but also alerts us to the names of DeLillo's characters. Thus, for example, "Axton" includes "ax," a sharp instrument used for chopping or engraving; "Brademas" incorporates "brad," a name for a small nail. Both names suggest penetration, violence, rigidity. On the other hand, "Tap" connotes a fluidity also exhibited in the language that flows from him. This contrast between stone and liquid persists throughout the novel as a symbolic representation of opposed attitudes about language. Perhaps more importantly, the etymology of "character" suggests that naming involves power—the ability to create characters (in both senses) by violent marking. Naming others means mastering them, making them into objects, and wielding over them the power of creation or destruction. The definition of "character" even implicates readers in such power or violence, which is executed when we master the characters on the page. In any case, "Brademas" fits this character, who scratches his name onto others through persuasive speech.

If in some respects Owen, who yields completely to things (*N* 20), is Axton's opposite, they share the fascination with mystery and purity seen in many other DeLillo characters. But although they are fascinated by religion—"All that reverence, awe and dread"—each remains an "observer," a theological tourist (*N* 24), hemmed in by reason and "rockbound doubt" (*N* 92). Owen's initial description of the pivotal scene of his childhood in the Pentecostal church displays this skepticism. Speaking of glossolalia, he first admits that not just the rural poor but also dentists and Dallas executives can practice it to become "carriers of ecstasy," but then dismisses it as "a life focus for depressed people" (*N* 173). Axton comments that Owen measures what he is saying "like a man determined to be objective" (*N*173) and in fact Brademas fears to confess his longing for a magical transcendence and community lost when he failed to speak in tongues (Morris 117). Despite his objectivity—his throwing of words "in the way" of his real emotions—he is drawn to the Names cult out of that inchoate spiritual yearning.

His attitude toward the epigraphs he reads also demonstrates this mixture of objectivity and obsession. In his earlier years as an epigrapher, the stones offered "a form of conversation with ancient people" that seemed to "uncover ancient secrets." But what the stones recorded—"grain payments, records of commodities. . . . a desire to keep accounts. . . . Bookkeeping" (N 35)—began to seem banal.[19] Owen is no longer interested in the meanings of epigraphs, instead finding "mysterious importance in the letters as such, the blocks of characters," especially their tactile beauty (N 35).[20] Owen's epigraphy, then, is motivated not by a desire for historical knowledge but by a flight from history, a need to see in letters something timeless, insular, and perfect. Thus although Owen recognizes the historical and cultural connections among Europeans, he avoids the bonds that archaeology and etymology expose. Similarly, the Names cultists, despite asking prospective members how many languages they speak, are really fascinated by "the alphabet itself. . . . letters, written symbols, fixed in sequence" (N 28). By reducing human beings to letters, they can erase any obligations to them and freely treat them as objects.

Objectification

In one sense, Owen's pursuit of the cult is an extension of his and Kathryn's archaeological goal of "find[ing] objects" (N 73). Like the Minoans,[21] who "saw the beauty in . . . [p]lain objects" (N 84), Kathryn appreciates objects, suggesting to Axton that their otherness "dispel[s] our sadness" (N 133). Perhaps, Axton meditates, "objects are consoling" because. . . . [they] are the limits we desperately need. They show us where we end" (N 133). As the etymology of the word indicates, objects are "thrown in the way" of human beings; though we use them, they resist our attempts to appropriate them. Objects embody or speak a counter-language—Ob—that eludes decryption. But unlike Kathryn, who respects the integrity and dignity of Otherness, the remaining Westerners in the novel respect objects only insofar as they can own them. Worse, they view people of other nations as objects.

The essence of this objectifying mentality emerges in a story that Owen tells about an Englishman who wanted to copy inscriptions from the Behistun rock. Unable to climb the rockface without falling, he coerced a Kurdish boy—at the risk of death—to read the stones by clinging to the rock, using the very letters as handholds. Owen claims that this is a story about "how far men will go to satisfy a pattern, or find a pattern, or fit together the elements of a pattern" (N 80): for him it is an allegory of reading, a fable of obsession that adumbrates his attempt to read the Names cult's work. "All the noise and battle and spit of three spoken languages," says Owen, "had been subdued and codified, broken down to these wedge-shaped marks" (N 80). The English imperialists, he claims, were enlightened conquerors because they "preserved the language of the subjugated people." Tom LeClair argues that this need to subdue and codify typifies written, as against spoken, words. Walter Ong further suggests that literacy inevitably separates the knower from the known by setting up "conditions for 'objectivity' " (46) and objectification, whereas orality tends to create connections between people.

But here the tyranny of print is part of a broader objectification that Edward Said has famously called Orientalism, in which the East is reconstructed as a "textual universe" (Said 52) for Westerners. Indeed, "subdue and codify" is the Orientalist creed, as Said demonstrates when discussing English explorer William Jones: "To rule and learn, then to compare Orient with Occident: these were Jones's goals . . . with an irresistible impulse always to codify, to subdue the infinite variety of the Orient to a 'complete digest' of laws, figures, customs, and works" (Said 78). Thus Kathryn is right to describe Owen's story as a "political allegory" (*N* 80), because it dramatizes what Arnold Weinstein calls the "brutal 'inscription' of the Kurdish boy into the Englishman's design, the kind of invisible, systematic exploitation that has conditioned the stage now occupied by James and his cohorts" (295). To read the Other is to master and rewrite it. Axton's and his friends' dealings similarly textualize and codify the countries in which they operate; to "do business" in the Middle East is to turn each Greek, Turk, Arab and Kurd into an " 'object' of study, stamped with an otherness . . . of an essentialist character" (quoted in Said 97).

Axton's circle enacts this objectification of Otherness in several scenes that amount to a lesson in Orientalism for beginners. Athens is an appropriate location for such a lesson because it is what Mary Louise Pratt calls a "contact zone" where "cultures meet, clash, and grapple with each other, often in contexts of highly asymmetrical relations of power" (34). From their base in Athens, Axton and his friends travel around the Mediterranean and return with "one-sentence stories" (*N* 94) that fix each place in a single phrase. For example, Nairobi becomes a story about people greeting Tanzanian forces with flowers and fruit and beating their own troops to death. As James Clifford argues, such "metonymic freezing" is dangerous because it employs a single aspect of a people's life to "epitomize them as a whole, constituting their niche in an anthropological taxonomy" (Clifford 100). The expatriates jokingly frame their activities as guerrilla war: Keller tells the others that he will lead a group of "credit officers with blackened faces" into post-revolutionary Iran (*N* 131). But their jokes mask their frightened awareness that "there was around us almost nothing we knew as familiar and safe. . . . [W]e could only register the edges of some elaborate secret" (*N* 94). Although Axton echoes the exaggerated inscrutabilities of

Conrad's Marlow, the danger is real: the Turk Vedat Nesin tells Axton that he is a "marked man" outside of his country, because as an American he can easily become a character (named with a pointed stake) in the "world's living myth" (*N* 195).

But DeLillo's expatriates would be alienated in any surroundings. Although Axton wants to believe that there is something "rich and living" in their entanglements (*N* 259), they know that their bonds to each other are tenuous. In fact, each tries to create a "private Cyprus" by acquiring some internal property or making some psychic investment that offers a protective shield (*N* 161). Their metonymic freezing expresses what Robert Young calls "internal dislocation": that is, the objectification of the Other manifests Westerners' fear of their own Otherness (Young 139–40). They try to counteract this dislocation in diverse ways: Ann Maitland finds a lover in each locale; Dick and Dot Borden invest in objects, as if to hide behind them and their monetary worth (*N* 219). For them, Orientalism is a "systematic discipline of accumulation" (Said 123) that masters Otherness by consuming it. These are the forms of magic with which they ease their dread.

Axton's internal dislocation is dramatized in a scene at a New Year's party in which he seduces Janet Ruffing, the wife of an American banker, who belly dances for the group while costumed in "Arabian" garb. Axton seduces her by asking her to say "the names"—"Say belly. I want to watch your lips. . . . Say thighs. I want to watch your tongue curl up in your painted mouth" (*N* 222–23)—and by asking for her underpants, that "vivid and intimate . . . object" (*N* 224). The dialogue of this seduction (or rape) dramatizes Orientalism by proxy. In seducing an American disguised as an "Oriental" Axton can safely play out his fear and attraction to the Other, "investing" in the Orient just as Janet is invested in Oriental clothing. But if the scene seems to conform to the Orientalist habit of representing the East in tropes of "feminine penetrability . . . [and] supine malleability" (Said 206), Axton's attraction is more complex: he wants her precisely because her transparent disguise reveals his own internal division. Thus he wants her to call him "James" in order to afford an image of himself as "still twenty-two years old" (*N* 223). He wants to thinks of himself as a linguistic beginner like Tap.

The seduction scene also stages David Keller's view of "business": he says he loves being "intimately involved" with "[m]y countries" (*N* 232). This ownership is not just a figure of speech; as the Greek Andreas Eliades remarks, "Our future does not belong to us. It is owned by the Americans" (*N* 236). So, the Westerners believe, is the past. Thus Maitland gets angry when postcolonial nations change their names: "Every time another people's republic emerges from the dust, I have the feeling that someone has tampered with my childhood" (*N* 240). How dare Persia, with its aura of Oriental romance, change its name to Iran (*N* 239)? For these Westerners, the East is an "unchanging, uniform, and radically peculiar object" (Said 98). Glib phrases, such as the way dark people come "sweeping out of Central Asia" (*N* 260), pin the Orient down like a butterfly in a book and safely distance it for the dispassionate discussion of Westerners. Like the "program" of the Names cult, these phrases exemplify Bakhtinian "authoritative discourse," which "permits . . . no gradual and flexible transitions" (Bakhtin, "Discourse" 343); naming reduces Others to letters in a text authorized by the namer. Of course, the result of this objectification is not clearer understanding but deeper mystery, so the final humiliation, declares Eliades, is that "the occupiers fail to see the people they control" (*N* 237).

Ironically, this blend of objectification and fascination arises from a "reconstructed religious impulse" (Said 121) like the one that Owen feels for the Pentecostal tongue-speakers of his childhood. The textual Orient embodies Westerners' yearning for coherence, ceremony, and community. A similar religious longing underpins the obsession with the cult that grows in Brademas, Axton, and Axton's friend, filmmaker Frank Volterra. When Axton travels to Amman and then Jerusalem to seek information about the Names cult, he initially feels oppressed by the "tumult and pulse, the single living voice" of the Islamic call to prayer (*N* 146), but eventually longs to hear what that voice is saying. Thus it is no accident that most of the cultists who speak about it are Europeans, driven by a spiritual desperation so deep that only murder can stir them from sleep. In this sense, the Names cult is the novel's most concentrated example of Orientalism, a textualizing of the Other that enacts the objectifying mentality of the Westerners obsessed with it.

Obsession

The middle section of *The Names* becomes a quest story, extending the shrewd analysis of the obsessive mentality begun in *End Zone*, *Great Jones Street*, and *Running Dog*. As we have seen, an obsessed person is for DeLillo "an automatic piece of fiction" who resembles "the natural condition of a novelist at work" (Interview with LeClair 29). Similarly, the Names cult, whose members obsessively match their victims' initials with the place of the murder, becomes a blank page upon which each of its commentators compulsively writes his own initials. Each one propounds an interpretation of the cult that reflects his individual fears and obsessions (O'Donoghue 3).

If the cultists' acts of naming give them the magical power of authorship—they create "characters" by matching initials to place—and the power to kill, their interpreters ultimately usurp that power, for by naming the cult and narrating its activities they eventually dissolve it.

A young man "obsessed by film" (*N* 106), Frank Volterra is another person who tests the relationship between James and Kathryn. James realizes that Volterra has arrived when he sees Kathryn wearing one of Frank's old shirts, a metonymy of Volterra's "investment" in the Axtons' marriage. Volterra requires emotional investments, too, by listening so closely that he "implies an obligation on the speaker's part" (*N* 118). Frank's desire to make a film about the cult furnishes Axton with a protective investment, whereby he can "conceal myself in Volterra's obsession as I had in Owen's unprotected pain" (*N* 205). Frank's pursuit allows Axton to remain passive, to trail the cult by proxy, just as he was able to have safe sex with an "Oriental" by seducing a banker's costumed wife. But despite his single-mindedness, Volterra has a history of failing to complete his projects, and acknowledges that he can "never surrender myself to places. . . . I'm always separate" (*N* 143). Like Axton and the others, he remains a tourist. Thus his worst nightmare is to own a drycleaning business in a small town where everybody knows him: here he would be "investing" (in) a community rather than in himself.

Volterra's vision of the cult reflects his vanity. He imagines them in an Antonioni-like film about "emptiness," in which the "space is the desert, the movie screen, the strip of film. . . . This space, this emptiness is what they have to confront" (*N* 198), and envisions the cultists as cinematically literate murderers like those in "The Uniforms," who would welcome a film about their actions. But although Volterra claims to realize that "film is not part of the real world" (*N* 203), he cannot imagine anything not part of the reel world. Thus, as Jacqueline O'Donoghue points out, he describes his picture not as an investigation of murder, but as an "essay on . . . what film is" (*N* 198; O'Donoghue 23). His planned film is just another form of narcissism.

Volterra apprehends the cultists as "secular monks" who want to "vault into eternity" (*N* 203). Perhaps, he thinks, their murders are a means of approaching divinity through sacrificial offerings. The oracular Vosdanik, a former guide and archaeologist whom Axton and Volterra interview, offers a similar interpretation, presenting the cult's actions as a response to the terminal geography of the desert: "wherever you will find empty land, there are men who try to get closer to God" (*N* 149). Vosdanik imagines the cult to be imitating the inscription of the Divine Word: "If you will know the correct order of letters, you make a world, you make creation. . . . [Y]ou make all life and death" (*N* 152). As authors rewriting the world, the cultists gain the power to create or erase a "character"; their victims are just objects whose fatal destiny is inscribed in their names. According to Vosdanik, the cult kills in an attempt to dry up God's "river of language" (*N* 152), to counter His Word with their letters.

Earlier in the novel, Kathryn, James and Owen debated the cult's possible religious motives. Owen had suggested that the cultists "fear disorder" and, like the secret societies in *Running Dog* and *Libra*, kill to "be part of some unified vision. . . . . Safe from chaos and life" (*N* 116). As Georg Simmel argues, insecure people are drawn to such rituals because they remedy a perceived "excess of freedom" (371). Owen claims, however, that the cultists are not trying to generate authorial meaning, but are interested in letters for their own sake. He recalls discussing with them the theory that letters began as "objects in the world" (*N* 116). If so, the cult seeks to reverse the history of language by turning letters back into objectified bodies. Indeed, this notion of linguistic history parallels that of religion and economics, and may be elucidated by the work of Jean-Joseph Goux.

Goux charts a complex set of homologies among the histories of several symbolic systems, including the psychic, linguistic, religious and economic. In Goux's terms, the cult's sacrificial victims—turned into bearers of letters—would resemble ideograms, the linguistic "characters" that predominated in the period between pictorial and alphabetic forms of writing, and which accompanied the "magico-cosmological" world of polytheism (72, 84). Goux argues that modes of writing are equivalent to modes of signifying exchange (72); ideographic writing is historically concurrent with the pre-monetary "extended form of value," in which certain privileged objects (e.g., livestock, wheat, oil) serve as general economic equivalents (67). A trace of each stage is today exhibited in specific neuroses (80), which are thus remnants of archaic forms of consciousness (83). Fittingly, ideographic writing—the linguistic expression of the "extended" value-form and the polytheistic worldview—is manifest in modern times by the kind of obsessional neurosis exhibited by Axton and his friends (81–82).[22] Since the movement toward a single deity corresponds to the emergence of a single universal economic equivalent (the money form), the cult's murders, in reverting to an earlier linguistic form, also deny the existence of a single God and return to an earlier stage of economics that antedates the centralization of economic exchanges in money. In both respects, then, they subvert the Authority of the Universal Equivalent—the economic mode in which Axton and his cohorts operate—for a "primitive," decentralized form of value based upon objects. Their fetishization of letters reverses history by creating Others—objectified, "Asiatic" ideograms—that seem to embody a more "authentic" language of sacrificial objects but that also reflect the obsessional neuroses of the cultists and their interpreters.

Perhaps, says Owen, their choice of victims—the senile, the mentally deficient, the disabled—means that "these acts are committed outside the accepted social structure, . . . and should be paid scant mind" (*N* 171). They kill only those abject beings whom Georges Bataille refers to as the "accursed share"—the excess in a human or social body that cannot be usefully employed—who may be sacrificed as a safety valve that ensures the body's health (Bataille 59, 72). Bataille argues that such sacrifices re-sacralize that which "servile use has degraded, rendered profane . . . has made a *thing* (an *object*) of that which, in a deep sense, is of the same nature as the subject" (55; emphasis in original). Perhaps, then, the cult's objectification of victims is a fleeting stage on the path toward a resacralization; the victims become things to be sacrificed in a ceremony that restores both parties' humanity through mortal deeds and thereby produces a deep intimacy between sacrificer and victim (Bataille 56). Such consecration can occur only through violence. Whereas, as Axton earlier argued, American homicides are merely "the logical extension of consumer fantasy" (*N* 115), the cult's crimes, which reinstate an earlier cultural stage when murdered bodies were sacralized signs of value, reject capitalism and Axton's cost analysis for a sacrificial gift made to gods whose power they usurp. According to this interpretation, the cult merely dramatizes the condition of the sacred in a godless world, one where "only ultimate acts of destruction can affirm the void that opens in God's absence" (Webb 70).

But Owen rejects this reading, arguing that "they weren't god-haunted people. . . . [There was] no sign of ritual. What god could they invent who might accept such a sacrifice, the death of a mental defective? A street mugging, in effect?" (*N* 116). No, they are "people intent on ritualizing a denial of our elemental nature. To eat, to expel water, to sense things, to survive" (*N* 175). Far from celebrating risk and expenditure, the cult performs an "austere calculation" (*N* 171) in which their human texts function not as gifts but as accounting ledgers. Rather than consecrating the accursed as way of restoring multivocality or humanity, they are trying to reinstate literality, to extract language from the mire of reference. By this reading, the cult is engaged in a counter-sacrifice that turns subjects into objects with no intention of resacralizing them. Perhaps Owen's interpretation merely reflects his self-image as a disinterested observer who analyzes epigraphs, glossolalia, and murder with the same scientific detachment. Perhaps he cannot imagine the cult to be religiously motivated because he has repressed his own encounters with religious mystery. In this case his objectivity expresses his own internal dislocation. Axton's growing obsession with the cult exhibits a similar ambiguity. Although his quest gives his narrative and his life a plot, he frequently halts his story to question his authority and interrogate the relationship between plot and obsession. And he protects himself by allowing others to act out that obsession, just as, when he goes to interview Andahl, another former cult member, he takes care to cloak himself in "denim and sheepskin" (*N* 206), protecting his psychic investment with sartorial ones.

Nevertheless, Andahl knows that Axton recognizes himself in the cultists: "Our program evokes something that you seem to understand and find familiar, something you can't analyze. We are working at a preverbal level, although we use words" (*N* 208). As Dennis Foster observes, the cult is trying to generate a language that functions "without symbolic representation" (159), a primal language that in some respects resembles glossolalia.[23] Andahl thus describes himself as an "Abecedarian" and the cult as "learners of the alphabet. Beginners" (*N* 210): by conflating character and object in their initialed victims, they aim to eliminate the deferral of meaning inherent in signification and destroy referentiality itself, which involves that unbridgeable gap between the signifier and signified. These radical readers seek to restore the innocence that precedes writing; says Andahl, "We are inventing a way out" of history (*N* 209). The cult means to erase language by obliterating "literal" victims. Hence, as they commit their murders, they feel a deep "frenzy of knowing, of terrible confirmation" (*N* 211), a rapture beyond language that resembles religious ecstasy, which is, "by definition, more than can be known or felt, described or contained" (Webb xiv). Their magic emerges from their dread of language: absorbing the mortal fear of their victims, they transcend their own and transform it into seemingly godlike power.

And yet Andahl's description of their actions as a "program" invokes not religious rapture but the rigid calculus of a machine (LeClair, *Loop* 193). Their "ritual"—like *Ratner's Star*'s Logicon—is all structure. Their violent inscriptions lack narrative threads; thus, Andahl suggests, what Axton might provide for them is an "interface with the world" that will outlast them and produce "Something to contain the pattern" (*N* 212). That is why Andahl calls him "Axstone": James is to be their tool, both the stone on which they engrave their story and the ax that will chisel their name into history (*N* 212). Once Andahl departs, however, Axton begins to realize that the last thing they need is "an account of their lives" (*N* 215). The cult's power is based on absence, and permits "No sense, no content, no historic bond, no ritual significance" (*N* 216). A book about the cult would violate the very secrecy that gives it cohesion. To write an account of the cult—to place the murders within a book or a ledger—would be simultaneously to "literate" and to obliterate them: once the pattern becomes a narrative, it ceases to lie outside of semiosis and the social body. Their ecstatic economy of objectified gifts would be transformed into mere accounting. Thus Axton decides that Andahl, "the apostate" who "manages his own escape by revealing a secret of the organization" (N 216), must be trying to abolish the cult.

Indeed, Andahl allows Axton to discover the name of the cult, painted on rocks. It is a self-referential name that resembles one of the nominalist conundrums in *Ratner's Star*, one that names its own infinite regress— *Ta Onómata*, or "The Names" (N 188)—a non-name that epitomizes what another cultist calls a "self-referring" world (N 297). By gaining knowledge of their name—a knowledge that Owen never acquires on his own—Axton obtains one of the secrets that defines the group. Likewise, when he discovers the alphabetical pattern behind the cult's murders, he keeps it a secret because the knowledge "confers a culthood of its own" (N 247); that is, by learning the cult's secrets and sharing their obsession, Axton becomes a member.

His obsessive reading of the cult's texts, of course, does eventually produce writing—the book we are reading. Thus his obsession creates an obligation that he cannot deny, as etymology reveals: the Sanskrit word for "knot," *grantha*, eventually took on the meaning "book." Hence a book binds author, subject and reader. Transmitted through the Greek *puxos* or "box-tree," the word "book" once referred to "alphabetic symbols incised in wood. The wooden ax shaft or knife handle on which was carved the owner's name in runic letters" (N 291). Similarly, Axton writes himself into the cult with his "ax," carving "The Names" into the book of his identity. In first reading and then writing about the cult, Axton becomes a character— a pointed stake, an ax that writes and a stone that is written upon—who authors himself. If to be named is to be marked and victimized, then Axton is at once author and object. But ultimately Axton yields his authorship to Tap, thereby obliterating himself as a character in his own book.

Obliteration

In the novel's third section, "The Desert," Axton follows Owen to India and listens to the tale of his final encounter with the Names cult. Although both make geographical journeys, it is their psychic journeys that enable them to confront the Other within, as Owen relates his confrontation with the source of his obsession. He wandered all over India feeling "the nightmarish force of people in groups, the power of religion—he connected the two. Masses of people suggested worship and delirium, obliteration of control" (*N* 276). This description of faceless masses implies that Owen too dehumanizes and objectifies "Orientals" (Morris 119), but also expresses his ambivalent desire to lose himself in something larger. Indeed, his experience in India eventually overwhelms his "Greek gift" of objectivity (*N* 280) and makes him "feel like a child" again (*N* 278). Near Rajsamand Lake he finds the epic poem he had sought; as he looks at the inscription, a woman near him beats clothes against a rock, and the motion reminds him of something he cannot quite recall. As Foster suggests, the recollection is both that of the cult's lethal hammer strokes and of the Pentecostal preacher who in his memory "strokes the air as he speaks, then cuts it with emphatic gestures" (*N* 305; Foster 164) The inscription strikes "through to him from some uncycled memory where the nightmares lay, the ones in which he could not speak as others did, could not understand what they were saying" (*N* 284).

Owen then finds the cult in the desert of northern India, where he becomes "their strength in an odd way and also their observer and tacit critic" (*N* 299). Through Owen's admission of his "likeness" to the cultists (*N* 293), Axton confronts his own fascination: "My life is going by and I can't get a grip on it. . . . My family is on the other side of the world. . . . The cult is the only thing I seem to connect with. It's the only thing I've been right about" (*N* 300). As Owen remarks, they "overlap" (*N* 293), having turned to the cult for the same motives that, according to Bataille, underlie sacrifice: both are "in search of a lost intimacy" (Bataille 57). As he continues, Owen similarly imagines surrendering his ego to "the chanting wave of men" worshipping at the Grand Mosque (*N* 296). His traumatic encounter with the cult's most fanatical members destroys the last shred of his carefully constructed objective identity, so that when the cultist Emmerich asks him who he is, Brademas answers not "Owen" but "No one" (*N* 292). In the cult's erasures Owen finds the obliteration he has sought.

But neither of the cultists who speaks to Owen—the brilliant megalomaniac Emmerich or Avtar Singh, aphorist of last things—justifies the cult's actions in Volterra's and Vosdanik's quasi-religious terms, nor presents it as a source of fellowship. Instead, they describe the killings as a "blunt recital of the facts" that "follows logically upon the premise" they have given themselves (*N* 302). The "logic" of their premise is apocalyptic: an unveiling and annihilation of meaning like the one sought by *End Zone*'s Gary Harkness. Yet in telling their story Owen begins to move beyond this apocalypse towards restoration, as if his account of the cult's murder revivifies their desert of objectified human letters. Owen also withholds the de-

132
Chapter 4

nouement, as if signifying his resistance to the cult's apocalyptic antinarrative. He did not follow them to observe the murder of Hamir Mazmudar in Hawa Mandir, but waited in a silo that sent him back to the silos of his Kansas childhood. As Singh and Emmerich kill the old man, Owen relives his primal moment of terror and alienation in the Pentecostal church. If he can just "recall the bewilderment and ache, the longing for a thing that's out of reach," he may begin to "repair [his] present condition" (N 304). At once detached from and enthralled by his memory, he reads the past both to observe and to obliterate it. In so doing he becomes a character who scratches out one identity and scratches in another.

Through a kind of metempsychosis—a word that contains the root of "to breathe" and is hence related to "spirit" (N 113)—he hears the voice of a young preacher exhorting the worshippers to "talk as from the womb"— to receive the gift of tongues, which Pentecostals call "praying in the Spirit" (N 306). (This is the same scene that Tap narrates in the novel's coda.) As rains fall from above, the preacher pleads with the worshippers to "get wet" metaphorically by becoming vessels for divine glossolalia (N 306).[24] Figured as water, the gift of tongues seems to wash away the Names cult's desiccated language and barren rituals, so that through his memories Owen finds an "escape from the condition of ideal balance," one in which "Normal understanding is surpassed, the self and its machinery obliterated" (N 307). The last word recalls his earlier, horrified image of religion as the "obliteration of control" (N 276), but now he welcomes this condition in which rockbound language becomes "spat stones" and finally pure liquid (N 307). Counteracting the Names cult's rigid calculus is the possibility of pure excess, of a fluid gift that can be received only by suspending the will. It is the antithesis of both the stone's accounts and the expatriates' euphemized exploitation: this language comes "like nobody's business" (N 307).

In blessing the people of his memory, Brademas accepts his failure to speak in tongues and acknowledges the value of communal experience. He also recognizes that he is forever barred from this Edenic speech. Now he comprehends why the Names cult has failed to satisfy his longing for spiritual sustenance, community, and self-erasure: their executions merely "mock our need to structure and classify, to build a system against the terror in our souls. They make the system equal to the terror. The means to contend with death has become death. . . . They intended nothing, they meant nothing. They only matched the letters" (N 308). In pursuing a purified language without syntax that tries to liberate humans from moral obligation, the Names cult confirms only a desert of self-reference. Worse, they replicate the abuses of tyrannical textual systems like insurance companies and the CIA. Rather than providing an alternative to the covert violence of Axton's associates, the cult just reinscribes their "subdue and codify" mentality, verifying Simmel's insight that subversive secret societies inevitably imitate the institutions that they claim to oppose (Simmel 360). Far from writing a new world, the Names cult copies that other cult of letters, the CIA (Saltzman, *Designs* 46).

But Owen's obliterating encounter with the cult frees him from obsession and rejuvenates Axton through a narrative exchange (*N* 309). It is as if Owen's authorial sacrifice magically transfers the power of creation to Axton: listening to Owen, Axton begins to grasp that denying one's obligations only enables others to construct them. Returning to Athens, he feels more sharply the pain of his estrangement from his family, and decides that "This is what love comes down to, things that happen and what we say about them. Certainly this is what I wanted from Kathryn and Tap, the seeping love of small talk and family chat" (*N* 312). But his reawakening is not yet complete; two more events converge to push him toward a new understanding. The first is his reading of the excerpt from Tap's fictional version of Owen's childhood, a scene that I will analyze in the final section of this chapter. The second is the discovery of his ties to the CIA—America's own "living myth" (*N* 317)—and the near-fatal consequence of those ties.

Earlier Axton had met Rowser, who indirectly warned him that he was in danger and should resign. Rowser presented it as a matter of accounting: "the parent is a collector. They acquire companies, they adjust, they seek a balance. We're one of the companies, that's all" (*N* 268). Hostility toward Rowser's company, he predicts, will make Axton a target. The message that Axton fails to comprehend is that his firm has all along maintained a "back-channel dialogue with the CIA" (*N* 315), which Axton finally discovers when he returns to Athens. Stunned, he desperately tries to justify his involvement as mere grammar, the innocent manipulation of "grids of virgin numbers" (*N* 317). But he knows the truth: just as his interest in the cult helped them further their murderous aims, so his unwitting complicity with the CIA has made him a silent partner in their actions. Ousted from his obligation-free island, Axton now understands that the world is, in Lindsay Keller's words, "one big tangled thing" (*N* 323) in which everybody overlaps. His passive neutrality destroyed, Axton must learn a new grammar.

But this language may also be a death sentence (Weinstein 296)—one that is nearly carried out in the assassination attempt he witnesses during his morning run. Whether Axton or Keller is the target remains unclear and perhaps doesn't matter: as Axton noted earlier, they're all "serving the same broad ends" (*N* 70). What does matter is that, like the cult's victims, he has been marked as belonging to a place — the United States of America — and so experiences the same essentialist objectification he and his associates directed at others; he has been appropriated into the myth of America as great Other. Like cult's victims, he becomes a character named and authored by others — the CIA, the Greek Nationalists who may be responsible for the attempt — a sacrificial ox like those on the Parthenon's friezes (see Bruno, plate 27).

With his CIA connection revealed and his commitments partially restored, Axton vows to "return to the freelance life" of "higher typing" (*N* 318). *The Names* constitutes the fruits of that typing; Axton has used his "pointed stakes" to recreate both himself and his friends as characters: "These are among the people I've tried to know twice, the second time in memory and language. Through them, myself. They are what I've become, in ways I don't understand but which I believe will accrue to a rounded truth, a second life for me as well as for them" (*N* 329). Through narrative metempsychosis, he reincarnates and rereads himself and his associates in a book — a *grantha* — that affirms the knot of obligations he has denied. Perhaps, as Saltzman observes, Axton now "matures into an artist like DeLillo himself, who extols the opportunity afforded the writer 'to shape himself as a human being through the language he uses' " (*Designs* 49; see Interview with LeClair 23). But the final reshaping comes only when Axton finally visits the Acropolis, where he achieves a rejuvenating apprehension of language and history.

Oblation

As Owen Brademas concludes his tale, he sits detached, "owl-eyed" (*N* 309). The metaphor links him to Athena, the Greek goddess of wisdom who was associated with owls and whose temple was the most important building on the Acropolis. Supplicants brought oblations to her temple that were kept in the Parthenon and tallied by epigraphic accounts engraved on stone (B. F. Cook 35). When James Axton makes his long-delayed pilgrimage to the Acropolis, he perceives its ancient role within its contemporary one:

the Parthenon was not a thing to study but to feel. It wasn't aloof, rational, timeless, pure. . . . It wasn't a relic species of dead Greece but a part of the living city below it. . . . I hadn't expected a human feeling to emerge from the stones but this is what I found, deeper than the art or mathematics embodied in its structure. . . . I found a cry for pity. This is what remains to the mauled stones in their blur surround, this open cry, this voice we know as our own. (*N* 330)

The shift from "I" to "we" here signals Axton's new appreciation of the communal, which he hears as a voice resounding from the stones that echoes all those who bring offerings. The Acropolis, he perceives, is less a place than a process that constantly recreates "the fallen wonder of the world" (*N* 339). As LeClair points out (*Loop* 196), here Axton moves from literality to orality, from reading to listening, from writing to speaking.

In Axton's reconceived Acropolis, "everyone is talking" and "no one seems to be alone" (*N* 331). As it was in ancient Greece, the Acropolis remains "a place where representatives from all parts of the . . . world might come together in a spirit of pride . . . to celebrate and to do honor to the gods" (Bruno 65). How do we do honor today? According to Axton, "Our offering is language" (*N* 331). Hearing this polyglot profusion, Axton perceives language as a mode of communion that creates and confirms obligations. Unlike the monolithic, objectifying intentionality of the cult's letters or Owen's unliving stones, this spoken language is fluid, revivifying; its currency is not literal but lingual. Just as the ancient visitors to the Acropolis left gifts for the gods, so today we leave the gift of tongues, oblations that "unite[ ] people in groups" (Ong 69).[25] And these oblations are indeed gifts, according to the paradigms outlined by Lewis Hyde, who argues that unlike market exchanges—which use money as objectified instrument and which separate humans into competitors not personally invested in their transactions—gift exchanges involve the full human being, and hence bring together people as a "copula: a bond, a band, a link by which the several are knit into one" (Hyde 10, 153). Such "anarchist property" embodies an economic alternative to the cost accounting and the exploitative investments of capitalism (Hyde 84). Equally importantly, according to Chris Gregory, gift exchanges inevitably involve persons in a condition of "reciprocal dependence that establishes a qualitative relationship between" them (104); as gifts, spoken words carry an obligation to reciprocate and thereby forge bonds of community.[26]

In recognizing language not as a tool for subjugation but as a sign of community, Axton achieves a self-obliteration more potent and positive than does the Names cult. The offerings he now observes are not murdered bodies who empty the desert of meaning, but exchanges in which each participant receives something in return for what is given. This language is not a weapon to be wielded but a present to be yielded, whose circulation may bring riches back. Although we cannot return to Adamic speech, we may take comfort in the proliferating richness of human talk. In Bakhtin's terms, Axton now understands language as a dialogic function in which every word is "overpopulated with the intentions of others" ("Discourse" 294), through which the islanded individual merges with the subjectified

Other.[27] Dramatizing the meaning of "Parthenon" (from the Greek *parthenos*—"virgin"), this recognition may engender a rediscovery of primal innocence; just as the Parthenon's entrance commemorated the birth of Athena (Harrison 225), so Axton's new conception of the Acropolis may open a passage to his rebirth.

But it is Tap's writing that generates the dialogical force that prods Axton to this new realization. Tap's novel revisits Owen's experiences in the Pentecostal church during the speaking of tongues. The setting is appropriate, since modern Pentecostalism is founded on the vision of an imagined community strikingly similar to Axton's conception of the Acropolis.[28] According to scripture, as the apostles gathered, "suddenly there came a sound from heaven as of a rushing mighty wind, and it filled all the house where they were sitting. And there appeared unto them cloven tongues like as of fire, and it sat upon each of them. And they were all filled with the Holy Ghost, and began to speak with other tongues, as the Spirit gave them utterance" (Acts 2:2–4). All the people—whether "Parthians, and Medes and Elamites" or Galileans—who heard the words understood them in their own tongue (Acts 2:9). Like Axton's Acropolis, Jerusalem on Pentecost was a site where, it is believed, the "lost unity of humanity" was restored (Cox 24, 40). Pentecostalism, in other words, seeks to confirm and consecrate community through lingual oblations. This condition is suggested in the opening of Tap's excerpt, when the protagonist, Orville Benton, finds himself "in the middle of a crowd, tongue tied!" (*N* 335). Orville means that he can't speak, but the others are "tongue tied" in the sense that tongue-speaking acts as a gift, a "bonding device, tying people together in a beloved community" (Cox 95). Glossolalia unbinds the tongue in order to bind it to a spiritual fraternity.

Pentecostal worship also fits the novel's dichotomy between orality and literacy. Although Pentecostalism is often viewed as a form of fundamentalism (and is based upon a literalist reading of certain scriptures), it differs from fundamentalist sects that believe in the primacy of texts. Pentecostals center worship around oral testimony, ecstatic speech and bodily movement, subscribing to a theology of pure presence. As I noted above, they view speaking in tongues as a sign that the speaker has been "baptized in the Holy Spirit," which they cite as one of the four "charismata" or gifts of the Spirit (Dayton 24–25). Thus Orville hears the glossolalists as inspirited, as "out of breath and breathing words instead of air" (*N* 335). Similarly, in praising Tap's "spirited misspellings" (*N* 313), Axton suggests that the boy's words have been infused with that same "spirit." Axton finds these misrenderings "exhilarating. He'd made them new again, made me see how they worked, what they really were" (*N* 313). For example, Orville sees a man in a "daise"—both dazed and blooming like a daisy (*N* 335)—"realing" in a corner, as if only in ecstasy does he truly become real. Such linguistic archaeology opposes Brademas's by textualizing the same gift of tongues he is describing. Indeed, I would argue that Tap's novel is therefore metaphorically written in Ob, in a counterlanguage in which the disregard for the tyranny of spelling stands "against" or "in the way of" the obsessive logocentrism of the Names cult and Western literacy.

Tap's liberating language exemplifies what Paul Maltby has described as DeLillo's "Romantic metaphysics," whereby, as DeLillo states elsewhere, "children have a direct route to . . . the kind of natural truth that eludes us as adults" ("Outsider" 302). Similarly, the preacher in Orville's church exhorts the worshippers to engage in "Childs play" (*N* 336).[29] The gift of tongues—a "transcendent commerce" of "recreation" and renaissance (Hyde 93)—comes as a "graceful provision" for those too inarticulate to pray in their own words (Cox 87). In this sense, the answer to Orville's question, "whose words were they?" is—nobody's. Freeing speakers from the bounds of ego, the gift of tongues is an endlessly circulating stream that issues from the Divine and returns as an oblation. It is not a possession or investment, but an "abundant divestiture of the self" (Webb 60). That is why the preacher exhorts them to "yeeld": they must relinquish control to let the spirit enter.[30] The misspelling is again meaningful and implies the communal nature of the act: it is something only "ye" (plural) may do together. And when they do, glossolalists seem to experience a Bataillean liberation, an "expenditure that knows no boundaries" (Webb 60), a sense of "fantastic release" akin to orgasm (Kildahl 46, 51). Gaiety transfigures all that dread: spontaneous expression counteracts the programmatic rituals of the Names cult precisely by removing the iterative qualities—the repetition and obsession—from sacrificial practices. Spontaneity turns obl[iter]ation into oblation.

Tongue-speakers seek a fluid language, and so the images in the final section revolve around flow and liquidity, as the preacher urges Orville to "get wet" in the spirit that resides in the "river and the wind" (*N* 336–37). This imagery is appropriate not only to the novel's antinomies of rock and water, but also to Pentecostalism's millenarian theology. Drawing from the apostle Peter's allusion on the day of Pentecost to the prophet Joel (Acts 2: 16–18), Pentecostals view glossolalia as a sign of the imminent approach of the "latter rain" (Joel 2:23), when God will "shower fresh gifts of the spirit on the faithful" (Cox 49) as prelude to the final "harvest" of souls at Christ's Second Coming (Dayton 27). In *The Names* these liquid metaphors display DeLillo's insistence on the linguality of this speech, a quality that again emerges through Tap's misspellings. For example, Orville imagines wild creatures ready to "lick and saver" a wanderer (*N* 337): the tongue may be either digestive or redemptive, just as to lick is both to whip and to comfort. Similarly, Orville's verbal incapacity is brilliantly termed a "strange laps of ability" (*N* 338): unable to use his tongue, the boy cannot "lap" the river of divine language and instead lapses into the "the nightmare of real things, the fallen wonder of the world" (*N* 339). Orville's resistance to the gift of tongues is thus metonymized by a "gift" he received of "black leather boots with canvas lining" (*N* 337). Like Axton in his denim and sheepskin, Orville's "investments" in textiles and textuality prohibit the divestitures needed for glossolalia. As a result, "the gift . . . the whole language of the spirit," is not his, and his tongue and ears are "rocks" (*N* 338)—lithic, not lingual.

Orville experiences not the "raptured" self of mystical excess but the ruptured self of post-Edenic humanity, for whom the perfect gift can be glimpsed but never reached. As usual in DeLillo's work, the attempt to discover a purified language—whether it be the Names cultists' matching, Bucky Wunderlick's silence, or *Ratner's Star*'s Logicon—fails. For Orville, as for Axton, Brademas, and DeLillo's readers, there will be no new Pentecost; we must content ourselves with the "fallen wonder of the world." But the ambiguity of the final passage's pronouns—"This was worse than a retched nightmare. It was the nightmare of real things" (*N* 339)—suggests an even deeper ambiguity, because we do not know whether "fallen wonder" includes only objects or language as well. The ambiguity perhaps implies that the "fallen wonder" lies precisely in the unbridgeable gap between word and thing, that language always reflects the post-lapsarian incommensurability between experience and narration. But what is to be our attitude toward this post-Babelian condition? Is DeLillo suggesting that, since primal language is out of our reach, we must settle for infinite semiotic deferral and the violence of a naming that inevitably alters—or kills—what it designates? Or can we celebrate our fallibility and the transformative power of language that results from it? The answer seems to be that we cannot retrieve language from its "laps," but may find a secondary transcendence through verbal oblations—lingual "laps"—that test and confirm our obligations to Others. Indeed, perhaps it is only our alienation from primal purity that permits us to be free from enslavement to a univocal Word. The world has wonder only because it is fallen; it is magical only because we can never fully name it.

But this possibility exposes another problem: if, as DeLillo seems to imply, only living speech can fill the void with meaning, then how does a novel—not a voice, after all, but a text—avoid the textual tyrannies it analyzes? LeClair suggests that DeLillo turns characters into "voices," so that we do not see but only hear them (*Loop* 203). Tap provides a better answer. In the boy's florid prose both his and DeLillo's readers find liquid refreshment because the words seem to *be* the real things: in their condensation of multiple meanings and encapsulation of linguistic history they nearly become metamorphosing objects. They may "dispel our sadness, temporarily" (*N* 133) because through them we gain access to an ob-reality in which words yield tiny explosions that also mark readers as "characters" containing conflicting forces. By immersing readers in heteroglossia, Tap's tale throws off the objections and obstructions to dialogic interplay. The language of the final section thus epitomizes Bakhtin's description of internal dialogism, in which each word encounters "an alien word and cannot help encountering it in a living, tension-filled interaction" ("Discourse" 279). We cannot read such words as obsessive trackers of univocal meaning. Indeed, through their internal tensions, Tap's words become epigraphs announcing the marriage of oppositions, including that of orality and literacy.

Orville's inability to "yeeld," to accept the gift of tongues and its obligations, mirrors Axton's. But Tap's narrative now stands "in the way" of Axton's story, making the father's entire narrative appear to be little more than an elaborate intratextual frame around the real story—Tap's. Tap's narrative thus stands as an obversion (both an inversion and an Ob-version) of his father's tale, an obstetrical counternarrative in which he gives birth to (or fathers) a new father by pushing him toward a new appreciation of language. Tap's novel—a story of O[wen]B[rademas] written in Ob— also fathers Owen, who as Orville Benton is given an emotional life much deeper (if more melodramatic) than Owen's own memories tap. Owen becomes Tap's character in a liberating renaming. Thus by depicting Owen's originary dislocation, Tap ob-literates (both erases and rewrites) Owen and Axton as authors and characters; Owen Brademas becomes Orville Benton in an "ob" text—one written "in front of" or "against" the literalist view of language promulgated by the Names cult—that revises not only Owen's and Axton's story, but our entire experience of the novel. Similarly, as I have been insisting, by tracking the "ob" words in Axton's story, we too may read "against" it, or object to it, and thereby object also to the subdue-and-codify mentality of bureaucracies of terror like the Names cult and the CIA. Finally, then, Tap's writing both restores the filial obligations in the novel and embodies DeLillo's vision of the author's vocation: to object to patriarchal authorities; to place verbal magic in the way of paralyzing dread.

Axton's epiphanic reading of Tap's liberating language, then, provides a model for our own reading. By offering an inconclusive ending, DeLillo defeats our desire to make reading a way of closing off meaning. We are not allowed to assume ultimate authority, to objectify the text and turn it into a closed system. We too must read in "Ob"—object to pre-emptive authorities, reject the desire to read obsessively, obliterate the patriarchal reader—to receive the gift of tongues. And to do that, we must participate in dialogic verbal exchanges that risk full obligation, that make reading a conversation. When we do, we participate in a "child's play" that makes language new. To read or write a book with full engagement in the novel possibilities of language may produce a *grantha*—a knot—that will render us all "tongue tied," shorn of our old language, but newly obligated. If in "yeelding" his authority to Tap, Axton finally acknowledges the obligations he has denied, so DeLillo's "yeelding" to Tap declares his authorial creed: to resist consumption and force readers to rename the world. Only by reciprocating that challenge do readers pass from obliteration to oblation, from accounting to the gift of tongues.

Chapter 5
The Theology of Secrets

David Bell's suspension between retreat and reemergence in *Americana* initiates a recurring pattern in DeLillo's novels: Bucky Wunderlick disappears midtour to hibernate in a small room in the Bowery, reappearing only after a harrowing experiment with silence and immobility; the Wynants (*Players*) withdraw from their previous lives only to involve themselves in parallel betrayals; in *The Names* James Axton attempts to revoke all commitments, but is ultimately implicated in the violence of the terroristic cult that gives the novel its name; *Libra*'s Lee Oswald generates secret identities that simultaneously confirm his alienation from the world and permit him to merge with history; *Mao II*'s Bill Gray surfaces after years of isolation only to become an anonymous sacrifice to terrorist violence. Threatened by waves and radiation, by the aggressive manipulations of media, institutions, and their discourses, DeLillo's characters seek safe islets of privacy and introspection. His work repeatedly explores the conflicts and boundaries between the public and the private, between collectivity and individuality, between concealment and revelation.

Defined as the condition of "being protected from unwanted access by others" (Bok 10), privacy is generally considered a consensual condition in which society permits individuals to erect barriers to the flow of information (Warren and Laslett 27–28). But DeLillo's characters, even on their islands, usually find true privacy to be fleeting or impossible. Their withdrawal is deemed subversive or hostile; or, as in both *Great Jones Street* and *Mao II*, privacy itself becomes a media event or fad. To discover true privacy, then, DeLillo's characters resort to a more active, even aggressive, form of protection and concealment: secrecy. As DeLillo has stated, his work is informed by "the secrets within systems" that are also "the secrets of consciousness" ("Outsider" 61). But unlike privacy, secrecy is considered illegitimate, and the information or condition concealed is usually threatening, shameful, or criminal (Warren and Laslett 27–28). Social theorists also inform us that secrecy is more typical of "lower status persons," children, and the institutionalized (Warren and Laslett 31); if so, DeLillo's habitual concern with secrecy implies a vision of postmodern social life in which virtually all citizens have become disenfranchised, alienated and childlike. Yet the concealment in secrecy is not total; rather, information is merely withheld for "limited and privileged sharing" (Calinescu 235); that is, secrecy is a form of communication (Calinescu 245) that simultaneously prevents and promotes socializing by restricting it to a limited domain.[1] A secret, in short, generates an alternate society, a magic shield, "a world inside the world" *(L* 13). As I intend to argue, however, because the institutions against which DeLillo's characters react are themselves cloaked in secrecy, their secret lives eventually mimic and are engulfed by the same systems from which they seek protection.

Secrecy is related historically and etymologically to the sacred (Bok 6). "Secret" is derived from *secernere*—to separate, to divide off—and related to *sacramentum* (the Latin translation of the Greek *mysteria*), which comes from *sacrare* (to consecrate, to set apart religiously). Both secrecy and the sacred elicit that combination of magic and dread called "numinous consciousness" (Bok 6). We have already remarked on DeLillo's recurrent fascination with varieties of religious experience, so it makes sense to argue that, in exploring the value and need for secrecy, DeLillo's novels also examine the place of the sacred—or more accurately, its absence, its replacement by simulacra—in postmodern culture. How, DeLillo repeatedly asks, can mystery be maintained in a world without privacy? The two novels I want to discuss in his chapter—*Players* and *Libra*—perhaps best exemplify DeLillo's analysis of what *Libra*'s Nicholas Branch calls the "theology of secrets" (*L* 442).

The two novels' similarities are both thematic and formal: both use narrative exchanges—quasi-cinematic crosscutting—to depict the characters' personal and interpersonal exchanges and crossings; both involve conspiracies in which characters create secret plots to lend their lives shape and meaning; both plots leave their protagonists suspended between revelation and concealment, privacy and publicity. Rather than building to a climax that resolves events, reveals secrets and explains mysteries, their plots "open out onto some larger mystery" (Interview with LeClair 26). That is, these texts withhold their own secrets, at once critiquing the secrecy system and embodying it in their own economy of reading.

TRANSIENTS: THE ECONOMY OF SECRETS IN *PLAYERS*

Like its companion novel *Running Dog*, *Players* questions "the value of secrets by investigating the 'double life' [its] characters lead" (LeClair, *Loop* 146).[2] It begins with a section called "The Movie," a miniature version of the novel: cool, detached, and impersonal, it depicts its characters "in transit," watching an airline movie during which (in a scene recycled from "The Uniforms") terrorists gun down golfers. A "lesson in the intimacy of distance" (*P* 6), the prologue introduces the novel's spatial patterns, acknowledges its debt to film techniques, and, perhaps most importantly, exposes one of its larger themes: "the glamour of revolutionary violence . . . the secret longing it evokes in the most docile soul" (*P* 8). As mysterious double agent J. Kinnear plays music of "simple innocence" on the piano, the other characters watch the "folly of second childhood" (*P* 5) unfold on the links; even their feigned detachment is an attempt to recapture the innocence and wonder of childhood. Thus, even as bodies are blown to pieces, the action seems a "little bit like cowboys and Indians" (*P* 9)—at once playful and serious, farcical and deadly.

As we are introduced to these characters in their "real" lives, the novel adopts film techniques for its narrative form. The first half crosscuts within chapters from Lyle Wynant to his wife Pammy, as each pursues occasionally joint but usually separate parallel activities. These narrative crossings capture not only the individual characters' constant motion, but also their transience in each other's lives. When the two do talk, their dialogue is the brittle, superficially witty conversation of a movie script. Indeed, the textual crossings (and forms of "cross" or "crossing" appear with marked frequency in the text) again exemplify those narrative exchanges that Ian Reid terms "dispossession": strategies for "pre-empting or usurping interest as to whose side of the story will be heard" (27). These dispossessive narrative exchanges dramatize the absence of genuine human exchanges between the Wynants, and between them and the other characters, as well as their shared feeling of dispossession. Thus, although stringently economical in its narration, *Players* resembles those postmodern novels of excess analyzed by Tom LeClair that are concerned primarily with "communication exchanges" ("Mastery" 101). Indeed, *Players* uses economic exchange both as a metaphor for social exchanges and as an explanation for its characters' secret lives: their failure to engage in authentic exchange compels them to create second selves, and to contrive plots designed to regain their lost spiritual and emotional property.

As LeClair has noted (*Loop* 157–58), Lyle and Pammy seem distanced from their own bodies, and are increasingly unconsoled even by the compilation of consumer opportunities and experiences that has previously provided them comfort. Lyle is fixated on watching television, finding in it a ritual, a "secret of celestial energy" (*P* 17) that simulates religious practices. But like *White Noise*'s Jack Gladney, Lyle remains anxious and paranoid, believing that everyone knows his inner thoughts, "not an uncommon feeling among older children and adolescents" (*P* 22). While Lyle labors on the Stock Exchange, Pammy works for the Grief Management Council, a group that quantifies and channels mourning by giving it a "clerical structure" (*P* 19) and by assigning "per diem rates for terminal-illness counseling" (*P* 42). Like Lyle, Pammy is self-estranged, believing that others communicate to her "from some unbounded secret place" (*P* 51) that she does not have. Pammy defines her world architecturally, in terms of "spaces" and "places" (elevators, for example, are places), but all her places seem to be constantly in transit (*P* 23).

The irony is that, although they feel bereft of privacy (or even of separate consciousness) the Wynants are both boxed in. Lyle, for example, is happiest when tapped into the "idiot box," and seems to be living in a self-scripted movie, often referring to himself in the third person and supplying the attributives ("he replied," etc.) for his own conversations. He epitomizes that "universal third person" described in *Americana* and, as I suggest in the next chapter, further explored in *White Noise*. An architect of privacy, Lyle builds "a space between himself and . . . the people he was likely to deal with in the course of daily events" (*P* 72). Pammy likewise tries to rise above all the "souls of the living" in her office high in the World Trade Center (*P* 24). Yet her compulsive yawning silently dramatizes her desperate alienation, as if she were attempting to talk but unable to produce words even to describe her own ennui. The couple take refuge in their apartment—itself a box among other boxes, its windows only occasionally open to the world—and find in objects some "partial sense of sharing" (*P* 53). But even at home Lyle merely replicates the forms and postures of popular media, and places scare quotation marks around his actions: having sex means he must "perform" in order to "service" and "satisfy" her; they must make an effort to "interact" (*P* 35). Merely playing at intimate exchange, each has retired to a private box.

At least Lyle's job at the Exchange makes him feel part of "a breathtakingly intricate quest for order and elucidation" in which "Everyone reconnoitered toward a balance" (*P* 28). In this compact economy "there was always a final price"—a narrative resolution. Manipulating these figures, Lyle feels mastery: numbers and symbols become "an artful reduction of the external world to printed output" that magically refines away "aggression . . . [and] the instinct to possess." Inked paper (this economy's excreta) becomes "property in its own right, tucked away," boxed in (*P* 70). For him, even to pay a bill is to "seal off the world," simultaneously to become part of a network and to retain private space (*P* 75); it is at once to give money and to accumulate immaterial property. In contrast, Pammy feels guilty, oppressed, and paranoid whenever she visits the bank, as if her entire personality were being exposed to hostile scrutiny (*P* 52). Thus while Lyle responds to the necessity of exchange by abstracting it, Pammy simply avoids economic exchanges whenever possible.

Both, however, are responding to a close affiliation between money forms and secrecy that has been compellingly analyzed by social theorist Georg Simmel. According to Simmel, ever since "traffic in economic values has been carried on by means of money alone, an otherwise unattainable secrecy has become possible" (335). Conversely, since secrecy is a process that "constantly receives and releases contents" (Simmel 335), it is itself an economy—the informational equivalent of economic exchange. Three aspects of money are particularly pertinent for Simmel: its compressibility (a check or bill can be slipped secretly into someone's hand), its abstractness and qualitylessness (exchanges of property can be effected without any goods being shown and without any human contact taking place), and its "effect-at-a-distance" (an electronic transaction in Baltimore is credited in Hawaii; Simmel 335). The totally dematerialized financial exchanges that Lyle "handles" generate an even more impersonal and abstract economy. The dematerialized money circulated by the Exchange likewise seems to dematerialize human beings, to make them just currency in its ghostly economy. As he types in the Stock Exchange codes for Grief Management, he imagines the Great Board turning humans into numbers for consumption—"Eat, eat. Shit, eat, shit" (*P* 64)—just as Grief Management turns mourning into a commodity. Stripped of personality, Lyle, like Lee Oswald, needs secrets as what Simmel calls "inner property," as "adorning possessions" (332, 337) that are valuable not for the information or value they conceal, but merely because they constitute something that the secret-keeper alone possesses. Secrets are magic designed to arrest invasion by immaterial agents that turn humans into bills or bytes.

Despite his feeling of control, Lyle seems ambivalent about his participation in The Exchange: precisely because his "inner property" has become so systematized, so much a part of the Exchange's "[c]urrents of invisible life" (*P* 107), his identity is in danger of dissolving altogether. And so, perhaps to reassure himself, perhaps to test himself, he begins first a secret sexual affair (not coincidentally, with a *secret*ary named Rosemary), and then a clandestine liaison with the terrorist group that he has witnessed shooting an acquaintance on the Exchange floor.[3] An escape from commitment that requires a set of new commitments, Lyle's involvement is intercut throughout Part 2 with Pammy's retreat to Maine with their friends, a gay couple named Ethan and Jack. Pammy perceives her withdrawal as "a separation from the world of legalities and claims, an edifying loss of definition" (*P* 88): she too commences a second, secret life outside of the social and economic bonds that seem to box her in. Part 2 also extends the cross-cutting structure, but now alternates chapters for Pammy (2, 5, 8, 10) and Lyle (1, 3, 4, 6, 7, 9), their physical separation slowing the narrative pace but preparing them and the reader for more significant movements and exchanges. Both Lyle and Pammy are about to cross over, to form new bonds; each is writing and performing in a private movie. And yet both are becoming increasingly transient, establishing obligations only to betray them and learning secrets only to divulge them.

As Lyle meets the terrorist Marina and the mysterious J. Kinnear, he feels that his involvement is less a movie than "a play" (*P* 100) in real space.[4] Delivering secret information to federal agents, Lyle realizes, is the "secret dream of the white collar" (*P* 100). That dream draws from the appeal of the secret society that, according to Sissela Bok, "like play, . . . offers the freedom to trust and to be creative, and the excitement of transcending ordinary limitations" (49). In joining this group, Lyle aims to give himself a plot, a fictional existence that will open "secret possibilities of self" (*P* 88). His involvement with these terrorists places him within a meaningful and dramatic narrative, just as it initiates the real plot of *Players* itself. As DeLillo has remarked, "there is a deep narrative structure to terrorist acts" (quoted in Passaro 77), along with a sense of "rules and boundaries" that powerless people need ("Art of Fiction" 289). "You need this, don't you," says Kinnear to Lyle. "A sense of structure" (*P* 106). Lyle's secret life makes him feel simultaneously liberated and contained, at once more real and more fictional.

This group wants to attack the capitalist system by planting a bomb on the Stock Exchange. Their aim, says Marina, is to disrupt

"the idea of worldwide money. It's this *system* that we believe is their secret power. . . . Currents of invisible life. . . . The electronic system. The waves and charges. . . . This is . . . their way of continuing on through rotting flesh, their closest taste of immortality. Not the bulk of all that money. The system itself, the current. 'Financiers are more spiritually advanced than monks on an island.' . . . It was this secret of theirs that we wanted to destroy, this invisible power." (*P* 107)

In its dematerialized condition, money is closer to sorcery than to currency. As "Elux Troxl" puts it in *Ratner's Star*, "the concept-idée of money is more powerful than money itself" (*RS* 146). Now when Lyle revisits the Exchange, he visualizes money passing "from a paper existence to electronic sequences, its meaning increasingly complex, harder to name. It was condensation . . . a paring away of money's accidental properties, of money's touch" (*P* 110). It is no longer matter, but merely data to be stored. He realizes that, as "spiritual indemnity against some unspecifiable future loss," money exists "in purest form in his mind, *my money*, a reinforcing source of meditation" (*P* 110): like a secret, money is "inner property." But those who participate in this immaterial economy can never be sure to whom the property belongs. No longer anchored to any material signifier, money, as Jean-Joseph Goux has shown, floats free and becomes pure transience (114). Thus, in removing the connection between money as a circulating medium and money as a standard of value (what Goux calls its Symbolic and Imaginary functions, respectively) and its condition as physical wealth (its Real function; see Goux 47–48), finance capitalism produces only "disaffected, depersonalized, asignificant relations between abstract individuals who are not mutually delineated by any 'symbolist' rite" (Goux 123). These terrorists want to attack the same economic system that has appropriated and reshaped Lyle's consciousness; he is, in effect, to obliterate himself. But it matters little, since the economy has already effectively depersonalized him. It seems better, then, to replace this slippery "property," this dematerialized money, with the more tangible (though still immaterial) inner property of secret information, the content of which matters less than the simple fact that he possesses it. And yet by becoming currency in the economy of secrecy, Lyle is again reduced to a medium of exchange.

As he walks through the financial district at night, Lyle realizes that it too is boxed in, "sealed off from the rest of the city. . . . The district grew repeatedly inward, more secret, an occult theology of money, extending ever deeper into its own veined marble . . . . At the inmost crypt might be heard the amplitude pulse of history, a system and rite to outshadow the evidence of men's senses" (*P* 132). The placard-bearing man whom Lyle repeatedly encounters outside the Exchange dimly understands this condition, his sloganeering bearing witness to a recognition that DeLillo presents in several novels, from *Ratner's Star* to *Underworld*: that the pulse of history is really underground, a secret economic function of capitalism that belies its democratic institutions (see *P* 151–52). And like any religion, capitalism has its central secret, its Mysterium Magnum (Bolle 5). Indeed, the Financial District is a church designed to protect its crypt, wherein lies its sacred heart, the engine driving the circulating immaterial exchanges that produce postmodern culture. The secrecy that surrounds that heart is thus both a necessary barrier and an essential component of its sacredness.[5]

Although seeming to collaborate in the underground's subversion of secret money, the elusive, Jesuitical (*P* 115) Kinnear is actually planting "disinformation" within the terrorist group; he is a double agent, working both for the terrorists and for the "police apparatus." Ironically, as he withdraws ("I'll be sort of transient"—*P* 132) from actual contact with the group and becomes a mere "voice" or "vibratory hum, coming from nowhere in particular" (*P* 133), he imitates the immateriality of the capitalist medium of exchange the group aims to attack. Like a cunning priest, Kinnear expertly manages the "complex geography" of disclosure, so that his selective revelations confirm only "the material existence of the space he'd chosen to occupy" (*P* 145). Likewise, Lyle's secret life generates a second crossing, a betrayal, a secret within a secret: he passes information to a man called Burks, a government agent tracking the terrorists. Thus, even more ironically, Lyle's "secret" life is not secret at all, not only because he betrays the underground organization, but because that organization is merely part of a totalizing system that contains its own opposition. What Patrick O'Donnell observes in regard to *Running Dog* is also true here: "in this system, nothing is really 'secret' or 'unknown'"; instead, what is called "secrecy" becomes the name for "what is anticipated as the 'always-already' known" (62). The secrecy of terrorist crime is merely the necessary countersign to the system of secrecy that the Exchange propels. It is as if economic or governmental institutions must invent terrorists in order to give themselves a reason for secrecy, and hence for their own existence; this process in turn makes their own activities more sacred.

In contrast to Kinnear, Marina believes in the group's aims and expects total devotion. Her faith in this "exchange of intense commitments" is sealed with a directness that produces "cross-channeling, a lane of immediate reciprocity" (*P* 145). She also offers to Lyle "other exchanges"—sexual ones—that confirm his obligation: she exchanges "her body for his risk" in planting the bomb (*P* 187). Thus, as they have sex he begins to realize that she holds "secrets he would never know" (*P* 188), and is mystified and impressed by her genuine (if childish and brutal) dedication. Because their sexual exchange makes "him feel more deeply implicated in some plot" (*P* 188), for a few moments Lyle actually feels himself "occupy his body" (*P* 189). But this liaison is merely a stratagem in Lyle's self-scripted movie: all the while, he imagines himself narrating the events to a third party. Thus, although he experiences his orgasm as a "great shoaling transit" (*P* 190) that signals a true metamorphosis or genuine exchange, in fact this sexual transaction is merely part of his more general transit: immediately after their encounter Lyle reports Marina's address to his government contact and flies to Canada. This literal "border-crossing" (*P* 192) indicates Lyle's doublecross, in which he reveals first the secrets of the Exchange and then those of Marina's group. And yet, by the end of the novel, it becomes clear that Lyle's secret game is merely part of a larger drama in which he is not a player but a pawn.

While Lyle is assessing his "clandestine potential" (*P* 114), Pammy acts in her own domestic drama with Ethan and Jack. In Maine she begins to explore the messages of her body and the physical world. She is also confronted with others' secrets, when Jack claims that he is not really gay — that his life with Ethan is just a play. His importunities prompt Pammy to rehearse the common excuses people make for disloyalty (*P* 143): emotions are just transient conditions, one should always act out one's fantasies. Thus, at the same time that Lyle is carrying out his betrayal of Marina, Pammy is betraying Ethan and Jack: she and Jack retire to a beach marked "PRIVATE" (*P* 163) and have sex. "The child in Jack was what she would seek, the starry innocent" (*P* 165), she thinks; their sexual exchange is to her no more than "game-playing" with a "make-believe" lover (*P* 166). Jack is merely a toy, a simulacrum. The clinical description of their intercourse thus reflects Pammy's denial of responsibility, reducing their emotionally fraught sexual exchange to body parts in shifting arrangements, a "crossing over. The recomposition of random parts into something self made" (*P* 168). Like Lyle's border-crossing, Pammy's is an attempt to deny commitment. But as the several forms of "cross" that appear on this page suggest, her decision to have sex with Jack is really a double cross, a sacrifice of friendship on the altar of ego.

Jack's repeated declarations that Ethan "is responsible for me" (*P* 170) imply both his child-like helplessness and Pammy's moral failure. But the ramifications of her act dawn when Ethan and Jack begin to "team up" against her (*P* 176). It occurs to her that "this was the secret life of their involvement. It had always been there, needing only this period of their extended proximity to reveal itself. Disloyalty, spitefulness, petulance." But no matter: "Everybody's involvement with everybody had a secret life," she tells herself. "Don't be so dramatic, so final. It would fix itself, easily, in weeks" (*P* 177). Her training in grief management has served her well; within her, "a place was being hollowed out, an isolated site, and into it would go the shifting allegiances of the past week" (*P* 177): Pammy retreats back into her box. Her violation of their secret life prompts a return to her own. The truth of this withdrawal and unwilling involvement in the "intimacy of distance" is dramatized when she observes three boys playing miniature golf (*P* 178): although she claims that her betrayal of Ethan and Jack is just a game, in fact it is a domestic version of the prologue's massacre of golfers. Like both Lyle and the dispassionate watchers of "The Movie," she has committed an act of terrorism, an assassination of emotion and trust all the more damning for her disavowal of responsibility.

When Jack is found dead by self-immolation, arms and hands crossed (*P* 197–98), Pammy is forced to face her complicity, and she realizes that she may have been no more than a tool in Ethan and Jack's lethal game. If Jack is the sacrificial victim, she is both Judas and Pontius Pilate. Simultaneously a protest and an act of emotional terrorism, Jack's suicide both mirrors the terrorist act on the Exchange and exposes his own secret life of emotional torture, an "extreme analogue of Pammy's own, in its denials and their effects" (LeClair, *Loop* 159). Pammy's emotional suicide is less dramatic, but just as deadening. Once again she boxes out, placing her hands over her ears and returning to "her chalky encasement for the world of children" (*P* 199): this is a secret that she refuses to hear. She thinks of comforting objects and is seized by a paroxysm of yawning. Then, after mouthing the platitudes of her profession to Ethan, she eagerly returns to her apartment where, "closed away again" (*P* 204), she watches an old movie and weeps uncontrollably over its canned tragedies. Like Lyle (see *P* 123), she can experience grief only electronically, by channeling social interactions directly into the box, which speaks her secret feelings. Her grief purged, Pammy ends her fictional existence beneath a flophouse marquee announcing its clientele: "TRANSIENTS" (*P* 207). As I have been arguing, the denatured, depersonalized exchanges of money and secrets she and Lyle have executed designate precisely such a radically transient condition, one in which even secrets are no more than a medium of circulation in an economy of shifting betrayals. Indeed, Pammy proves the word's aptness by barely registering its meaning, as if the signifiers are themselves transient units that evade "the responsibilities of content" (*P* 207).

At least her final condition shows signs of re-emergence. In contrast, Lyle is left suspended, awaiting further word from Kinnear. The motel room where he waits is the architectural expression of his transience and characterlessness. Lyle claims to like motels for the "the blank autonomy they offered" (*P* 196–97), but this autonomy is illusory. In the epilogue, entitled "The Motel," Lyle is stripped even of his name, his game of secrecy and betrayal having stolen even that essential social signifier. He is a blank bill, a gray screen. As former secretary Rosemary emerges from the bathroom wearing a dildo, exchanges seem about to become sexchanges. But Rosemary's "playlet of brute revelation" discloses the secret that Lyle has missed all along: like Rosemary, he is merely an instrument, a toy of Kinnear as well as his substitute. "Dil-do. A child's sleepy murmur. It was as

151
The Theology
of Secrets

collaborators that they touched, as dreamers in a sea of pallid satisfaction" (*P* 211): Lyle's fantasy of secret commitment—like the economy of secrets itself—is exposed as child's play. The artifical phallus fits the economic relationship I have been attempting to describe. If, as Goux argues, the phallus plays in the psychic register the same role as gold-money in the financial one (54; 116–21)—both are "general equivalents" that establish the value of other commodities in their respective economies—then Lyle, depersonalized by his contact with immaterial money and shorn of his selfhood by trafficking in disclosure, has himself become a dildo, a phallic credit card in the economy of secrets. Detachable, exchangeable, transient, he is a simulacrum, an artificial medium of exchange.

More broadly, the end of *Players* implies that the postmodern economy of secrecy makes all human subjects crave such substitutes for real involvement. At the novel's conclusion, the sun comes through the window, and Lyle seems to vanish into the light, thereby "absolving us of our secret knowledge," so that "Spaces and what they contain no longer account for, mean, serve as examples of, or represent" (*P* 212). Like the observers in "The Movie," we watch as the Wynants take residence in a derelict theater for the terminally transient. Our involvement in their secret fantasies is now called into question: we too are players, voyeurs secretly indulging in their drama of exchange and betrayal. DeLillo's final withholding of meaning and resolution suspends us as well. The novel's plot is not concluded, and thus defeats our desire to read it as one of Ethan and Jack's cheap spy novels or Lyle's juvenile fantasies. We are not allowed merely to consume the text, to make it a plastic toy for our secret satisfaction. At the moment that Lyle's secret life is exposed as an empty fantasy, ours is likewise revealed as a game, or mere gossip-mongering. The text's final movement is therefore riskily self-reflexive, as DeLillo removes the veil from his own secret: that novel reading may be no more than a retreat into the same sterile box as Lyle's television watching, yet another futile variety of magic that doesn't defeat dread but only exposes it. But not quite. In the novel's final self-reflexive turn, DeLillo suggests that the revelation of his own game and our complicity with it is the real subject of *Players*. Therefore the novel is not boxed in: we too are writing the plot of *Players* in a private world that shares information with Lyle's and DeLillo's but that belongs to neither of them. What Glen Scott Allen suggests about *Ratner's Star* is also true of the end of *Players*: we are asked to "build upon an interpretive principle which is secretive, elusive, coded, with a potentially totalizing or 'universal' agenda" (paragraph 26)—to find, like Pammy, a meaning that is at once social and secret. If we can apprehend DeLillo's secret and recognize our own role as plotters and secret-keepers, perhaps we can be more than transients in the commerce of secrecy.

"A WORLD INSIDE THE WORLD": *LIBRA*'S SECRET HISTORY

As he gathers data to write the "secret history" of the Kennedy assassination, retired CIA analyst Nicholas Branch comes to realize that "there is much here that is holy" (*L* 15). The Kennedy assassination is America's Mysterium Magnum; like any religious mystery, it is both radiantly overdetermined and heavily shrouded. Thus, on the one hand Branch begins to understand, as DeLillo himself did in researching the novel, that "every revelation about the event seems to produce new levels of secrecy, unexpected links" ("Art of Fiction" 299). The more facts (or factoids) that Branch uncovers, the more branches he must trace, until it begins to seem that "Everything belongs, everything adheres" (*L* 182) to the conspiracy. But on the other hand, he comes to suspect that material is being withheld even from him and wonders "if there is some limit inherent in the yielding of information gathered in secret" (*L* 442). While doing research on *Libra*, DeLillo faced Branch's dilemma, discovering that "the landscape was crawling with secrets," while keeping "this novel-in-progress [as] my own precious secret" ("Art of Fiction" 292). Both a reader-surrogate—a researcher delving into the secret intrigues surrounding the Kennedy assassination—and DeLillo's alter ego, Branch must perform two conflicting tasks: he must strive simultaneously to unearth secrets and to keep that history a secret. His investigations therefore imply two seemingly contradictory positions: first, that in postmodern America nothing is secret; second, that the most essential information is always that which nobody shares.

The nature of *Libra*'s secrecy is, therefore, paradoxical. Its paradoxes may be understood in terms of Ian Reid's description of textual frames. Reid defines four types of framing: circumtextual (the physical format of the text, its binding, photos, cover, etc.); extratextual (the genre of the text or reader's expectations about that genre); intratextual (paragraph breaks, typography, and tale-within-tale formats); and intertextual (historical and linguistic signs of allusion, citation, reference; 44–52). Although framed intratextually (by Branch) as a "secret history," *Libra* is framed intertextually as yet another of the seemingly endless semifictional documents about the assassination; it is framed "extratextually" and "circumtextually" (for example, by the cover photo of Oswald) as a revelation of hidden truths. One of the novel's revelations, indeed, seems to be that all history is secret history. But such a revelation is selfcontradictory: once revealed, it is no longer secret, and hence no longer history, since we can be sure that the "real truth" remains protected. Thus *Libra* both presents and parodies such mythmaking, simultaneously offering a plausible "secret history" and a critique of secret histories. That is, the novel is both a conspiracy theory and a theory of conspiracies, at once promulgating the existence of a secret "world inside the world" (*L* 13) and critically analyzing the desperation that motivates the belief in such worlds. Like *Players*, then, *Libra* both presents a plot and forces us to question our need for plots; also like *Players*, *Libra* links secrecy with the sacred, analyzing two conflicting human needs: the powerful human craving for belief in mystery and magic, and the need to penetrate such mysteries.

Libra refines the cinematic crosscutting employed in *Players*, generating two converging plots: the aimless story of Oswald's plotless life—identified by places—and the linear, intention- driven plot of the conspiracy to assassinate Kennedy—identified by dates (Lentricchia, "*Libra*" 201). Oswald's stated intention to merge with history is signaled by the overlap of the two plots, and by his appearance in "time"—in the segment dated 6 September (*L* 291). The two plots, in fact, offer different forms of secrecy, which, borrowing from sociologists Warren and Laslett, we might call private-life secrecy and public-life secrecy. Private-life secrecy—the kind pursued by Oswald—involves "the concealment of attributes, actions, or relationships that, if discovered, might bring harm"; in contrast, public-life secrecy—practiced by Win Everett and his coconspirators—is "secrecy on the part of those in power and their agents" (Warren and Laslett 29) Private-life secrecy is allegedly "passive and protective," while public-life secrecy is "active and directed at others" (Warren and Laslett 30).[6] In these terms, Oswald's quest to merge with history signifies a desire to move from private-life secrecy to public-life secrecy; likewise, Win Everett, banished to early retirement in Texas, is attempting to emerge from the secrecy of his private life back into the public-life secrecy that was his vocation.

Lee Oswald discovers the power of secrecy early in his life, while riding the New York subways: "the view down the tracks was . . . a secret and a power. The beams picked out secret things . . . . Never again in his short life . . . would he feel this inner power, rising to a shriek, this secret force of the soul" (*L* 13). The underground passage of the subway—an image that encompasses DeLillo's career from "Take the 'A' Train" through *Under-world*—provides a perfect image of his secret "world inside the world" (Bernstein, paragraph 11). A misfit and mama's boy, Lee, like Lyle Wynant, uses secrecy to draw a "veil between him and other people" (*L* 12). Russia thus attracts him as a vast mirror, a "secret that covers one sixth of the land surface of the earth" (*L* 33), and he is similarly fascinated by Lenin, Trotsky, and Stalin, who invented aliases that first placed them outside of history but ultimately enabled them to re-enter it more lastingly. Lee knows that he will need a "secret name" (*L* 41) if he is to imitate his heroes. Indeed, there is a kind of heroism in secret-making: as Simmel notes, because the secret offers "the possibility of a second world alongside the manifest world," it can be described as "one of man's greatest achievements" (Simmel 330). The Marxist books that teach Oswald this lesson are similarly precious precisely because they are forbidden, and like a "lucky piece that contains the secret of who you are" (*L* 41), they help him create a secret society of himself and his heroes. They are magical, and hence accrue value only because they seem to stand outside the consumer system from which he feels alienated. While Bill Millard may be right that Oswald conceives of Communism as a consumer item (paragraph 13), it also speaks to his realization that he himself is valueless as a commodity, a "zero in the system" (*L* 40). As for Lyle Wynant, so for Lee Oswald secrets are adorning possessions that bolster his identity and give him worth, but do so only because they cannot be shared.

As a Marine in Atsugi he gives a name to his secret self. "Hidell means don't tell" (*L* 89) is his childlike mantra of concealment. Hidell (Oswald's Mr. Hyde) is born when Lee reveals information about the U-2, the very name of which suggests his own division: "the more he spoke, the more he felt he was softly split in two" (*L* 90). Hidell means "hide the L"— hide the Lee—just as Ls and other letters seem to hide from the dyslexic Oswald. If Lyle Wynant's secret life mimics the depersonalized symbolic order of money, Oswald's secret name reflects his word-blindness, his alienation from the linguistic order. Both his secret-keeping and his dyslexia thus contain within them what Matei Calinescu describes as a "nostalgia for transparency" (245). That is, Oswald creates secrets chiefly to give himself an opportunity to reveal them, and thereby to enter the linguistic realm (and thus the world of social exchange) from which he is otherwise barred. But his experiences in the brig teach him that even confession does no good because "there are no right answers" (*L* 104). Both sympathizing with and despising the guards, Lee feels "secret satisfactions" (*L* 100) in watching his own punishment and humiliation; here he learns again how to be a patsy. Indeed, he realizes that "the brig was invented just for him. It was just another name for the stunted rooms where he'd spent his life" (*L* 100). The brig becomes a private religion, a "counterforce to politics and lies" (*L* 100), at once a second world inside the public world and its mirror image. Like those in *Players*, Oswald's boxes, his sites of concealment, create not only his identity, but also a dogma and a central mystery that simultaneously express his alienation and protect him from it. They are magical charms to ward off dread of himself and others.

His defection to the Soviet Union seems to be an attempt to enter the world outside of his box. What he wants is to be made new—as Alek, perhaps—to be scripted into another self, a secret identity who both is and is not the nobody Lee H. Oswald (see *L* 162, 166). Before long, however, he is confronted again with his ineluctable anonymity and powerlessness. As he attempts to conjugate the Russian verb for "have," he realizes that he is "in the midst of a vast secret" (*L* 156). The juxtaposition is telling, again linking his linguistic failures to his social estrangement: Lee is comprehending that, as always, he does not "have" much at all. Again he is a zero in the system. Moreover, he suspects that once he reveals the military information that has given him power—once he reveals that he even has such secrets—both he and the secrets will become worthless (*L* 159). Thus his analysis of captured U-2 pilot Francis Gary Powers obviously refers to himself: "crushed by the pressure exerted from opposite directions," both are becoming "chapter[s] in the imagination of the state" (*L* 198). In Lee's case, the pressures are not only globally political, but personal and social: should he reveal or conceal? He attempts to resolve the conflict by writing his Historic Diary. But its very title illustrates his contradictory aims: he calls it a diary, which is private writing, but also imagines its being read by posterity. Of course, the act of writing constantly reminds him of (and reveals to us) the one "secret he'd never tell" (*L* 83): the dyslexia that places "limits everywhere" (*L* 211). Oswald's secret-making and -keeping efface his initial identity as a means of generating new ones; but those secret selves initiate processes that ultimately lead to more radical erasures. Secrets are Lee's medium of exchange not only between his private world and the "world in general," but also between one identity and another; and yet, like Lyle's money, they fail either to be secret or to make him truly new.

Upon returning to the United States, Lee denies that he gave secret information to the Soviets (*L* 231), ironically disowning the inner property that had given him power. While he berates Marina for making their life public (*L* 239), nevertheless he realizes that "the only end to isolation was to reach the point where he was no longer separated from the true struggles that went on around him" (*L* 248). Thus Hidell reemerges, ordering Communist tracts that dredge "a channel to sympathetic souls, a secret and a power. [They] gave him a breadth and reach beyond the life of the bungalow and the welding company" (*L* 236). Joining a secret society provides him (as it does the other conspirators) with all the satisfactions of a religion; they may be simultaneously secret and, within the organizational confines, sociable. Hidell also orders the guns that ultimately transform Oswald's private-life secrecy into the aggressively public secret that we all know, or believe we know. As Win Everett asks, "If the world is where we hide from ourselves, what do we do when the world is no longer accessible? We invent a false name, invent a destiny, purchase a firearm through the mail" (*L* 148). As they are for Jack Gladney in *White Noise*, Oswald's guns are a "secret," a "second life, a second self, a dream, a spell, a plot, a delirium" *(WN* 254). Hidell/Oswald's firearm purchases permit him to flirt with history by attempting to assassinate right-wing general Edwin Walker. Afterward he visits one of Walker's rallies, his .38 under his jacket. Standing anonymously at the rally, "the secret he carried with him made him feel untouchable" (*L* 372); but the secret is not so much the gun as the knowledge that he has it and nobody else knows about it, and that he is the one who shot at Walker. "Bet you don't know who I am," he thinks, the knowledge of "how strangely easy it is to make your existence felt" granting Hidell a charmed feeling of invincibility (*L* 373). At the Walker rally, Hidell/Oswald is at once anonymous and powerful, secretive and public. His secret at once expands and effaces Oswald's identity, glorifying his new self as one who knows something that nobody else knows. And yet, because he cannot share it, the secret merely confirms his lack of power and worth.

Hidell lives in a small room, a place to develop a "design, a network of connections. It was a second existence, the private world floating out to three dimensions" (*L* 277). This is the mirror-image of Branch's small room; both chambers contain the "world inside the world" where secret history is written. Indeed, the Hidell documents—tiny narratives of economic transactions through which he inscribes himself as a secret revolutionary hero—are Oswald's only effectual form of writing; these accounts furnish his aimless life with direction and value. Eventually, however, his private plot is usurped by the secret society into which he blunders; yet at the same time their careful script is appropriated by Oswald.

Win Everett, the architect of the assassination plot, is likewise a self-conscious philosopher of secrecy. He believes that "it was a natural law that men with secrets tend to be drawn to each other, not because they want to share what they know but because they need the company of the like-minded, the fellow afflicted—a respite from the other life, from the eerie realness of living with people who do not keep secrets as a profession or duty" (*L* 16). He seems well aware of the cultic aspects of his secret society, which exists less to protect a secret than to create a secret to protect, so that the ultimate secret is the existence of the organization itself (*L* 23). But even within the small society, secrets spawn "like reptile eggs" (*L* 21), engendering multiple layers to shield the Mysterium Magnum; it is as if the existence of secrets automatically generates more. Everett is another of *Libra*'s novelist figures, and his authorial function provides him with a fictional existence that "speaks to something deep inside me. . . . It's the life-insight, the life-secret" (*L* 28). As do Lee's and Lyle's, Everett's secret life demands the exercise of imagination that permits him to be at once author and character. Thus his plot produces not only an identity, but also a private history and a community of fellows—a world inside the world.

All the conspirators are obsessed with the commerce and theology of secrecy, imagining themselves as martyrs and saviors. Former FBI agent Guy Banister, for example, describes the thrill of clandestine life as the ability to have "secrets to trade and keep, certain dangers, an opportunity to function in tight spots" (*L* 63–64). He believes JFK is powerful because "he holds the secrets. . . . Take his secrets and he's nothing" (*L* 68). Larry Parmenter is interested in the way the language of conspiracy "constantly found a deeper level, a secret level where those outside the cadre could not gain access to it" (*L* 117). But he more capitalist than cryptographer, trading secret information for "pieces of promising action" in places where the CIA has operated (*L* 126). Most of all, Parmenter understands the religious satisfactions of secret societies: "The deeper the ambiguity, the more we believe, the more we trust, the more we band together" (*L* 259). In other words, whereas individually held secrets isolate the individual, secret societies counterbalance the effect of secrecy by offering each member support against disclosure as well as a sense of shared superiority over those who do not know the secret (Simmel 355). The conspiratorial group creates a sense of community, and provides an orderly hierarchy that acts as a stabilizing force against the chaotic world. At the same time, however, it offers a measure of freedom within its ritualized and rigid hierarchy (see Simmel 356–57, 360–61). The plotters' secret society thus constitutes a separate world, a form of social magic, in which its alienated members can discover the sense of belonging, meaning, and order that postmodern American life so rarely provides.

Watching his daughter Suzanne deal with secrets, Everett tells Parmenter that "secrets are an exalted state, almost a dream state. They're a way of arresting motion, stopping the world so we can see ourselves in it. . . . [T]here's something vitalizing in a secret. My little girl is generous with secrets. I wish she weren't, frankly. Don't secrets sustain her, keep her separate, make her self-aware? How can she know who she is if she gives away her secrets?" (*L* 26). Everett's words (which strikingly echo Simmel's) imply several key insights about secrecy: first, that secrets offer a means of controlling the unmanageable world outside the self; second, that they bring to life new aspects of the self, constructing a bridge between private life and social life; third, that secretkeeping is really a form of communication in which information is withheld for privileged sharing: it combines privacy and sociability. Of course, Win understands his daughter's childish behavior because he is practicing it. As Bok notes, secret societies discourage self-criticism, and hence promote rigidity and freeze members into immature stages of development (Bok 54). As Parmenter observes, their conspiracy is "a natural extension of schoolboy societies, secret oaths and initiations" (*L* 30). Thus, although fetishizing secrecy seems to create new identities, it is actually regressive, childish, schizoid. Later, when Suzanne is depicted with her Little Figures, it appears that she has learned her father's lessons well: like Lee's aliases and books, her Figures seem to protect her; they are not toys but tools to be used in case her alleged parents are really somebody else (*L* 366). At once pathetic and chilling, her need for the figures mirrors her father's fetishization of secrecy: she controls them as her father does his Oswald-figure. In sum, like *Players* and *Running Dog*, *Libra* suggests that the obsession with secrecy is a particularly dangerous form of child's play that often leads to fascistic violence.

Perhaps the most important point in Everett's analysis, however, is his implication that secrets provide the "radiance in dailiness" ("Outsider" 63) that DeLillo's novels often reveal, an "exalted" or mystical state that opens onto the sacred. Secrets, like religious mysteries, gather congregations around them. Indeed, as Simmel shows, secret societies are usually characterized by "usages, formulas and rites" that act like a magical "body round [the] soul" of the central mystery (Simmel 358, 359). Everett's conspiracy is merely a smaller cabal of the larger religion—the CIA itself, whose power to "fertilize minds and hearts with a central mystery" (Bolle 10) marks it as a religion whose theology blooms from its fetishization of secrecy. Indeed, according to Parmenter's wife, Beryl, the CIA is "the best organized church in the Christian world, [with] a mission to collect and store everything that everyone has ever said and then reduce it to a microdot and call it God" (*L* 260).[7] Parmenter is the high priest and chief theologian who constantly professes his faith that "the Agency understands" (*L* 259). And yet he believes that "nothing can be finally known that involves human motive and need. There is always another level, another secret, a way in which the heart breeds a deception so mysterious and complex it can only be taken for a deeper kind of truth" (*L* 260). This passage exposes both the organization's central truth and its most dangerous mystification: if motives are incomprehensible and utterly private, then nobody is comprehensible, and nobody is culpable for anything. Their theology of secrets disseminates blame, offering guilt-free confession and total absolution.

As we have seen, the secrecy process involves an economy of withholding and release; secrets thus contain a tension that is dissolved in the moment of revelation (Simmel 333). Secrets are capsules of condensed energy that cry out for expression. The plotters' liaison between conception and action, T. J. Mackey, recognizes this secret in the secrecy process: "the thing that hovers over every secret is betrayal" (*L* 218).[8] Thus almost as soon as the plot is fully formed, Everett longs to reveal it, to "lose control" of it (*L* 221). As Mackey removes himself from the original plotters, changing the plan from a near miss to an actual hit, Everett increasingly yearns to "be found out. . . . He feared and welcomed the chance to be polygraphed" (*L* 361). The Agency would be pleased, he thinks, by the complexity of his plan and by his repentance (*L* 363). Like Oswald's Historic Diary, then, his plot is at once a private fetish and a message to posterity, both secret history and public autobiography. He is the communicant in Parmenter's ritual of mystery and revelation, and his ordeal of retention, confession, and betrayal demonstrates the cultic, religious nature of secrecy. But when Everett is taken "out of the loop," the novel exposes a major irony, one that Simmel terms a "ubiquitous sociological norm" (*L* 360): underground organizations invariably come to imitate the very structures of the institutions they aim to subvert. Hence, once the plot is put in motion, Everett is "retired" back into his insignificant private life.

The ultimate goal of their secret society, of course, is to create an Oswald out of "scissors and paste," to write a narrative in which he will play the patsy; in this script he will be simultaneously inside and outside the secret organization. Thus Everett is displeased when he discovers that "Lee Oswald existed independent of the plot" (*L* 178), with his own secret names and forged documents. Oswald is in fact writing a competing narrative line that ultimately merges with Everett's. Given Oswald's leftist politics, his affiliation with Mackey and the others seems contradictory. But such strange concatenations are typical of conspiratorial coteries. As Kenneth Fidel observes (193), what unites such secret groups is less a common politics than a shared feeling of alienation. Moreover, Oswald's presence here—under the new cryptonym, Leon—is seemingly ordained by some more powerful plotter, some mystical destiny or fate. As co-conspirator David Ferrie explains, "there is a third line. It comes out of dreams, visions, intuitions, prayers, out of the deepest levels of the self. . . . It has no history that we can recognize or understand. But it forces a connection" (*L* 339). This magical "no history" is that underground or secret history that Lyle Wynant perceives at the center of the Exchange, one that resembles the counterhistory that DeLillo himself writes in *Underworld*. Just as a kind of shadow society exists beside the prosperous, happy one, so a secret history exists alongside institutional history as the "sum total of all the things they aren't telling us" (*L* 321). As if ordained by this magical history, on the night before the assassination Lee watches *Suddenly*, Lewis Allen's 1954 movie about a failed presidential assassination, which speaks to him "like secret instructions entering the network of signals and broadcast bands . . . . They were running a message through the night into his skin" (*L* 370).[9] While these beliefs sound like megalomaniac fantasies, DeLillo uses them to suggest one of the novel's most resonant themes. For *Libra* is ultimately less about the conspiracy, or about Oswald, than it is about the darker secrets and deeper divisions of American culture.

These secrets are voiced by KLIF disk jockey Weird Beard, a guerrilla truthteller like *Americana*'s Warren Beasley or *Underworld*'s Lenny Bruce, who intimates that "You're out there in the depths of the night, listening in secret, and the reason you're listening in secret is because you don't know who to trust except me. We're the only ones who aren't them. . . . We're the sneaky little secret they're trying to uncover" (*L* 266), a "little itchy thing" seeping out beneath the complacent surface of American society (*L* 382). There are other Oswalds; indeed, Oswald's condition as a Libra, one who is "ready to be tilted either way" (*L* 319), exemplifies the divided consciousness of America itself. Entering Dallas on the way to his death, JFK senses this "deep division, the country pulled two ways" (*L* 393), as well as the sacrificial offering that may suture it. The deep division is represented not only by the novel's structure, but also by the juxtaposition of JFK and LHO. As Stanton Tefft notes, "social divisiveness which is generated by conflicting interests creates the social conditions under which secrecy thrives" (67). Thus in depicting Lee Oswald, nobody and American Everyman, along with a conspiracy of nearly anonymous secrecy fetishists whose combined trajectories violently intersect with the most public figure of all, the president, DeLillo composes a secret history of American society—a society infected and impelled by secrets. But he also dramatizes how the addiction to secrecy creates the very conflicts that spawn these dangerous divisions.[10] The secrecy system, in other words, is both a cause and an effect of the fissioning of American consciousness. DeLillo returns to this theme in *Underworld*, where he depicts FBI director J. Edgar Hoover as the embodiment of this pathological system. *Libra* suggests that the nation can unite only through what Hoover most dreads: "a contagion," or "some mystery of common impulse" that can bring together "so many histories and systems of being." The nation must participate in a purgation of blood, and "receive some token of the bounty of [JFK's and Oswald's] soul" (*L* 393–94). And yet this violent sacrifice creates only a fleeting unity that, like Oswald's secret-making, ultimately explodes any lasting coherence.

Oswald's secret action in his "kid's snug hideout" in the Book Depository Building (*L* 395) effects his final emergence into history. Even as he pulls the trigger he is "already talking to someone about this. He had a picture, he himself telling the whole story to someone" (*L* 400): he longs to share his secret, to turn private fantasy into public fodder. During the brilliant narration of the assassination, DeLillo constantly juxtaposes cameras and rifles, suggesting that everyone is being "shot" here, indeed, that the whole event is a spectacle staged for public consumption. Thus, after Oswald is arrested, the public waits for news because "only news could make them whole again, restore sensation" (*L* 414). The assassination creates a brief electronic community, "an instant surface that people can see and touch together" (*L* 414). But for Lee this phenomenon both creates him and tears him apart: "Lee Harvey Oswald, Lee Harvey Oswald. . . . They were talking about somebody else" (*L* 416). He experiences the dissemination of self into images so prevalent in *Running Dog* and (as I will show in the next chapter) in *White Noise*. Oswald realizes (as he has perhaps known all along) that he is again a zero in the system: he is the plot's scapegoat, the cipher who makes the entire system possible—"Hide the L."

And yet, since nobody outside the conspiracy knows the facts, Lee retains the final secret: who did it and why. Realizing that he "could play it either way" (*L* 418), he now recognizes that this is his life's work: manipulating the theater of concealment (*L* 434). Ironically, since he dies without ever revealing his ultimate secret, it is precisely his unwilling maintenance of secrecy, his withholding of crucial information, that allows him to merge with history. He remains mysterious, his position as "zero" paradoxically giving him the public, historic (if not heroic) role he has always craved.

Lee dies on TV, at once public spectacle and private sacrifice, momentarily uniting the viewers (including himself) in both ignorance and shared knowledge. As Beryl Parmenter watches his death replayed over and over, she feels that Oswald's own alienation, his mystery, his nobodiness, has put "him here in the audience, among the rest of us, sleepless in our homes— a glance, a way of telling us that he knows who we are and how we feel, that he has brought our perceptions and interpretations into his sense of the crime. . . .[It] tells us that he is outside the moment, watching with the rest of us. . . . But he has made us part of his dying" (*L* 447). If Lee, like Jack Gladney, is a "stranger in [his] own dying" (*WN* 142), ironically this estrangement effaces that "borderline between one's own personal world, and the world in general" (*L* epigraph) that he has so long sought to demolish. The secret he carries with him to the grave adorns his presence, intensifying and enlarging "the impression of the personality by operating as a sort of radiation emanating from it" (Simmel 339). At once victim and confessor, clown and holy icon, Oswald has become the overdetermined emblem of America's divided consciousness, now indelibly inscribed into its secret history and its public religion of celebrity. Even the boys who steal dirt from his grave sense the power of his name, and repeat it "like a secret they'd keep forever" (*L* 456). Oswald, finally possessed of his desire for fame at the very moment of ultimate dispossession, is buried as William Bobo, a fitting name for a clown.

Branch's conclusions about secrecy are partly DeLillo's. Branch concludes that the CIA has "built a vast theology, a formal coded body of knowledge that was basically play material, secret-keeping, one of the keener pleasures and conflicts of childhood. Now he wonders if the Agency is protecting something very like its identity—protecting its own truth, its theology of secrets" (*L* 442). Secrets, thinks Branch, are "childish things," a diagnosis that *Libra* and *Players* bear out. In both novels, characters create secret lives that function as what D. A. Miller calls a "spiritual exercise by which the subject is allowed to conceive of himself as a resistance: a friction in the smooth functioning of the social order, a margin to which its far-reaching discourse does not reach" (Miller 207). They pursue ritualized behaviors in the service of a theology of secrecy that is also a fantasy of subversion. But both novels show, like *The Names*, how such resistance is ultimately appropriated and subsumed by the very institutions it is meant to subvert: Lyle Wynant is used as a tool by Kinnear, who may be working for FBI; Lee Oswald becomes a patsy of the intelligence organizations; Win Everett turns his alienation into a public spectacle of atonement that reinforces the CIA's ceremonial position as keeper of institutional secrets. What Oswald's final role and final secret imply, in fact, is that the CIA's world inside the world both imitates and produces the larger world: it protects its secrets to protect its definition of American culture—a self-perpetuating ethos of clandestine power. In these novels as in *Underworld* DeLillo depicts the secrecy system as a totalizing phenomenon that infects not only public life, but also the very foundations of subjectivity.

And yet, if DeLillo implies that the child's play of secrecy detaches power from responsibility and is thus dangerously fascistic, he also suggests that such play is necessary to achieve individual selfhood. Indeed, the novels themselves use secrecy as an essential part of their effects. A writer who fiercely guards his private life, DeLillo also withholds important information within his texts. He resists resolution in *Players*—we'll never know if Lyle ever receives his final directive—and manipulates our responses in *Libra*: we know the factual outcome, but the circumstances behind them must remain fictional, mysterious. Indeed, like Branch, we both want to know the truth and want it to remain a secret so that we can invent our own.

Suspended between secrecy and revelation, between ignorance and understanding like Beryl Parmenter and Lyle Wynant, we become the players in these novels' games of secrecy. Oswald's creation of secret selves is in fact a function of our desire to find out who he is, to penetrate his masks and expose him. Thus, to the degree that DeLillo's novels withhold final explanations, and instead open out onto some larger mystery, they too participate in this theological game of secrets, becoming thwarted reciprocal exchanges that prompt us to examine our own expectations of disclosure. Our role is the likeness of Oswald's, Wynant's, and Everett's: we too make up plots, imagine ourselves as "heroes," authoring our own fictions in secret as we privately read the texts. This secrecy is priceless: it enables us to participate in social life without feeling anonymous, transparent, exposed. In this sense, the reader's world inside the world is an indispensable haven, a magical protective shield against the dreadful waves and radiation that bombard us. Perhaps, then, these texts of secrecy create their own secret society of readers, and thereby constitute a medium of exchange between secret play and social participation.

Chapter 6
The American Book of the Dead

Channeling *White Noise*

W*hite Noise* is DeLillo's most tightly focused treatment of "American magic and dread" (*WN* 19). As in DeLillo's other novels, but more desperately, the characters of *White Noise* try to counteract dread by mouthing chants and litanies, practicing pseudo-religious rituals, crafting narratives that deflect or purge their fear, performing violent or death-defying actions. The source of dread was named in the novel's early working title: "The American Book of the Dead" (LeClair, *Loop* 228); DeLillo seems to agree with Ernest Becker—an acknowledged influence (LeClair, *Loop* 213)— that "of all things that move man, one of the principal ones is his terror of death" (Becker 11). But when death is everywhere, it becomes more frightening. Thus *White Noise* depicts postmodern mortality not as a glorious struggle, but as "daily seeping falsehearted death" (*WN* 22) heard as white noise, as a "dull and unlocatable roar" (*WN* 198, 36) of spirits who may be appeased only through magical spells like those found in *The Tibetan Book of the Dead* and the *Ancient Egyptian Book of the Dead* (*WN* 72, 221). These sacred texts provide detailed prayers and rituals to protect the dying on their journey beyond the body; DeLillo's American Book of the Dead listens to the sounds and lists the products and places that reveal the presence of the sacred in postmodern life.

The Tibetan Book of the Dead describes the space between lives (the "dharmata bardo," or "island in-between") as an experience of "luminosity" (11). Likewise, in *White Noise* DeLillo seeks to unveil "the radiance in dailiness" ("Outsider" 63) by examining those "American forces and energies" ("Art of Fiction" 304) beneath the surface of the banal. The novel dramatizes how this "extraordinary wonder of things is somehow related to the extraordinary dread, to the death fear we try to keep beneath the surface of our perceptions" ("Outsider" 301). The sources of "radiance" are not in Asia or Africa, but across the street and in the living room: the supermarket, the shopping mall, the TV set. In *White Noise*, characters seek luminous moments through consumption, and television functions not only as the main medium of information—one responsible for those "waves and radiation" that infiltrate their minds and derealize the real—but also as the chief disseminator of capitalist ideology. Television and other sites of consumption muffle, as well as amplify, the spiritual yearnings of consumers and audiences. It seems appropriate, then, to address the themes of death and of consumption through the metaphor of the channel.

The term refers first, of course, to TV stations or cable networks that regale viewers with commercials bearing the gospel of consumerism: that consumption provides therapy for body and soul. Advertisements create what Stuart and Elizabeth Ewen call "channels of desire"—mental grooves that deflect political and social desires into the wish for commodities (27). The term also describes a popular form of New Age spirituality, the practice of "channeling," in which dead souls (sometimes the past lives of the speaker, sometimes alien beings) allegedly speak through living humans, or "channels." Both television and spirit "channels" are mediums through which disembodied voices purvey advice, remedies, and consolation. TV and spirit channels both claim to bring fragments of the inner self together and infuse "life with magic" (Michael Brown 84). All three channels—television channels, consumer desires, and spiritual channels—converge in the tabloids, those garish magazines loaded with lurid tales of celebrity indiscretions, UFOs, and miracles that shout at us from supermarket checkout stands. In fact, DeLillo has stated that tabloids, which syncretically blend a myriad of pseudo-religious beliefs into a curious species of postmodern faith, lie "closest to the spirit of the book" (quoted in James 31). Thus *White Noise* gains much of its remarkable resonance by compelling us to listen again to the "noise" of our own popular culture, and to revisit those postmodern temples—the supermarket, the mall, the TV, the motel—where we seek "peace of mind in a profit-oriented context" (*WN* 87).

DeLillo ventriloquizes the voices of the culture through three types of inserted phrases. The first are triads—usually brand names, but sometimes descriptions of commodities or acronyms—that have no clear origin. They are not simply quoted by the narrator, Jack Gladney; rather, he seems to be a medium manipulated by some distant source (Lentricchia, "Tales" 102). These interpolations may be Jack's later observations on the action for, as I hope to suggest, they usually comment on the scenes in which they appear. The second insertions are television or radio voices that punctuate the action with pointedly satirical phrases. For example, as Jack and his fourth wife Babette try to decide what kind of pornography to read before having sex (Babette protests, "I don't want you to choose anything that has . . . men entering women. 'I entered her.' 'He entered me.' We're not lobbies or elevators" [*WN* 28]), Jack ludicrously gets an erection. At that moment the TV "enters": "Until Florida surgeons attached an artificial flipper." A parallel between pornography and prostheses is inserted here that compliments neither Jack's endowment nor the couple's connubial life. The third sort of inserted phrases are spoken by living people, either in the supermarket (*WN* 38), on the street (*WN* 262), or in the motel room when Willie Mink channels the voices of TV. All three varieties function not only as commentary and imitation of electronic media, but also as holy chants that invoke commodities for protection or supplication. Through them, *White Noise* becomes a book of spells, a box of products, a literary TV set that channels the discourse of commodities. By channeling the "spells" in *White Noise*, I hope to suggest that a fruitful critical analysis of DeLillo's dialogue with culture must acknowledge, as DeLillo does, its own implication in the culture that it critiques.

THE TOTAL PACKAGE

White Noise is a book of spells, but it is perhaps equally a book of packages—a thesis on the kinds and uses of intellectual, linguistic, commercial, personal, and televisual packaging. Packaged commodities in *White Noise* radiate an aura. In the novel's opening set piece, for example, a description of station wagons bringing students to college depicts not the students but only their possessions, implying not only that higher education is a commodity, but also that the students have disappeared into the glow of their tennis rackets, drugs, computers, Dum-Dum pops and Mystic mints (*WN* 3); in that sense only they and their parents are "a collection of the like-minded and spiritually akin, a people, a nation" (*WN* 4). Jack Gladney, a professor at the College-on-the-Hill and founder of Hitler studies in America, watches this spectacle with bemused admiration; he knows he is another commodity they are buying. Indeed, Hitler has helped Jack to package himself as an attractive item on the curricular shelf (see Cantor 44), and Jack's chancellor (the same title that Hitler held) urges him to grow into the Führer's figure by wearing heavy dark glasses, assuming the more authoritative name J. A. K. Gladney, and wearing his academic gown when he teaches. Hitler and these trappings become Jack's "artificial flipper" propelling him to the forefront of his field. As in *Running Dog*, in *White Noise* history is also packaged for ready consumption in Jack's courses about the "continuing mass appeal of fascist tyranny" (25). "Mass," a word that appears in almost every key scene of *White Noise*, signifies how Hitler's stature depended upon large crowds and the religious nature of his allure; as the word recurs in the novel, its meaning expands to encompass the complex relationship between consumption and death. One thing is clear, however: Hitler has enhanced Jack's value in the academic market.

"And other trends that could dramatically impact your portfolio" (*WN* 61).

Hitler is perhaps the preeminent author of spectacles in our century, and the Nazis' manipulation of twentieth-century technologies points, as we saw in *Running Dog*, toward the postmodern condition; not only is Hitler's image still on TV, but "we couldn't have television without him" (*WN* 63). Thus Jack conceives of Hitler as a "medium of revelation," a channel for collective desire (*WN* 72). Once again Hitler is figured more as a pop star than as a mass murderer, because the proliferation of images makes all forms of fame equivalent. Thus Jack and his colleague Murray Jay Siskind (the ex-sportswriter first introduced in *Amazons*) can carry on a "dialogue" juxtaposing Hitler and Elvis, the Führer and the King. But there was something peculiar about those "masses [Hitler] once called his only bride": they gathered so the assembled could construct "a shield against their own dying" (*WN* 73). Jack uses Hitler similarly, at once hunkering in his penumbra and inflating his own "aura" by appropriating his image, his language, and eventually his murderous impulses as a "protective device" (*WN* 31).

Jack named his first son Heinrich because the name has "a kind of authority" that might protect the boy (*WN* 63). But Jack is not alone in yearning for authority.[1] Heinrich himself trusts the electronic media more than his father or his own senses, as he demonstrates in his hilarious conversation with Jack about rain (*WN* 22–24). He also cultivates friendships with people who seem to possess the concentration that he lacks, such as Orest Mercator, who plans to set the world record for the longest time sitting in a cage with poisonous snakes. While Jack skeptically challenges him, he also admires his "aura of inspired risk," and wonders if such people, "in building toward a danger . . . escape it in some deeper sense" (*WN* 268, 267). Orest knows that he's "nothing without the snakes": like spirits or demons, the snakes provide an "aura" that enlarges and protects him.[2] Heinrich explains that "People are getting interested. . . . Like they believe him now. The total package" (*WN* 268): like Jack with his Hitler and academic garb, Babette with her running clothes, Murray with his little beard and speeches, Orest is packaging himself. As Reeve and Kerridge note, the characters in *White Noise* use such prepackaged lifestyles to express their need for "authentic" being (315). Thus Orest desires at once to expand the self and to protect it by wrapping it in the clothing of TV shows and fashionable "sports."

"Dacron, Orlon, Lycra Spandex" (*WN* 52)

Murray Jay Siskind is the most persuasive live authority in the novel, and when he and Jack visit "the most photographed barn in America," Murray astutely explicates its condition as Baudrillardian simulacrum. "Once you've seen the signs about the barn," he declares, "it becomes impossible to see the barn. . . . We're not here to capture an image, we're here to maintain one. Every photograph reinforces the aura." This ritual replication is a "religious experience, in a way, like all tourism. . . . They are taking pictures of taking pictures. . . . We can't get outside the aura. We're part of the aura" (*WN* 12–13).[3] "Aura" refers to a quasi-divine radiance or halo that lends a patina of authenticity or mystery to material phenomena; but this glow of authenticity depends upon mediation (Duvall, "(Super)Marketplace" 140). The most photographed barn is, in short, not a barn at all, but a package with a "barn" in it.

Other "American environments" in *White Noise*—the airport, the supermarket, the motel—function similarly. As we have seen in earlier chapters, DeLillo has long been fascinated with motels, which, like malls, are architectural equivalents of the denatured, "modular" postmodern self. Indistinguishable from other modules, the motel room is often DeLillo's preferred site of violence or sexual exchange. Motels fit perfectly into postmodern capitalism because they are simply packages for people (Hine 170). When motels are first mentioned in *White Noise*, they exemplify the transient, postnuclear family. For example, Steffie and Bee, Jack's daughters from different marriages, barely know each other, but Jack reassures Steffie it's okay if Bee visits because they "met at Disney world" (*WN* 15). Shuttling between parents, the children need to be resilient, to be able to "land lightly" (*WN* 15). The Gladney house thus resembles an airport, a switching yard, or motel where the children can learn to shift allegiances, to redesign their filial and familial packages, as if they live in

"The Airport Marriott, the Downtown Travelodge, the Sheraton Inn and Conference Center" (*WN* 15).

Murray Siskind, like the other faculty in the "American Environments" department who "read nothing but cereal boxes" (*WN* 10), believes that packages are "the last avant-garde. Bold new forms" with "[t]he power to shock" (*WN* 19).[4] But he resists the lure of packages by buying only generic products, whose stark black-and-white surfaces seem to place them beyond the radiance of commodities (Duvall, "(Super)Marketplace" 144). But in fact generic packaging is merely an especially shrewd form of packaging—anti-packaging, if you will—that furnishes spurious reassurance to those who believe they are too smart for advertising. Yet the appeal of generic packaging depends upon the consumer's hard-earned disgust with the usual garish packages.[5] Jack is more honestly enthralled, finding in the "mass and variety" of his purchases, in "the familiar package designs and vivid lettering, the giant sizes, the family bargain packs with Day-Glo stickers" a "sense of replenishment . . . of well-being" (*WN* 20) unshared by those who have not been freshened by

"Clorets, Velamints, Freedent" (*WN* 229).

It's no accident that this list appears just as Jack and his colleague Winnie Richards discuss the fear of death: these three products are imbued with natural properties—clouds, light, fresh air—that are antidotes to the olfactory sign of physical decay that is bad breath. The supermarket is full of such magical products and packages. Even the "burnished, bright" fruits and vegetables, displayed under lights as "indivisible units

of consumption" (Hine 17), take on "the *form* of packaging" (Frow, "Last Things" 189). "[A]wash in noise," the supermarket contains "some form of swarming life just outside the range of human apprehension" (*WN* 36) that prompts Murray to recall the Tibetans, who believe that "death is a waiting period" (*WN* 37). The *Tibetan Book of the Dead* describes death as a "bardo" or gap between lives, during which one hears a roar "like a thousand thunders" (11, 15). The rituals and spells collected in the *Tibetan Book of the Dead*—"a guide to dying and being reborn" (*WN* 72)—are meant to be spoken into a dying person's ear and thereby promote "The Great Liberation Through Hearing" (15). The "dull and unlocatable roar" in the supermarket similarly lends a spiritual quality to the mundane task of buying groceries.

Murray plays the Tibetan priest who whispers in Jack's ear: "this place recharges us spiritually, it prepares us, it's a gateway or pathway. Look how bright. It's full of psychic data" (*WN* 37). Very full. According to Thomas Hine, a shopper on an average trip to the supermarket encounters 30,000 different products vying for attention (1). Packages must appeal instantly to the consumer's emotions, rather than to her or his intellect. Thus, intimates Murray, "all the letters and numbers are here, all the colors of the spectrum, all the voices and sounds, all the code words and ceremonial phrases" (*WN* 38). The product codes and small print seem to enhance the products' power by giving them an aura that is the last vestige of the patina by which Renaissance Europeans proved their lineage, except now patina derives not from age but from novelty, not from originality but from perfect replication.[6] This aura is not cultural but religious. Thus Murray claims, "The place is sealed off, self-contained. . . . Chants, numerology, horoscopes, recitations. Here we don't die, we shop. But the difference is less marked than you think" (*WN* 38). In linking shopping with religion, Murray seems to be performing his own magic act, asserting kinship between utterly unlike entities. But, as Hine shows, the history of packaging is inextricably related to the history of religion. For example, the monstrance is itself a package designed to call attention to, as well as to contain, its divine contents (see Hine 37–41). Modern packaging similarly attempts to exploit associations between boxes and arks, or cups and chalices (Hine 39). People desire containers that fulfill their spiritual yearnings, and consumer packaging fills the void created by the disappearance of traditional religious icons. Thus if for the Tibetans "death is the end of attachment to things" (*WN* 38), for Jack and many contemporary Americans, consuming attaches persons to the things whose reproducibility betokens immortality.

The supermarket is "sealed off" in another respect, too: it "purges sociability, which slows down sales," and "replaces people with packages" (Hine 2). Grocery shopping becomes less a means of engaging in interpersonal exchanges than a way to enlarge the self through narcissistic satisfactions. Later in the novel when Jack visits the Mid-Village Mall with his family, shopping lets him "grow in value and self-regard. I filled myself out, found new aspects of myself" (*WN* 84). But if such consumption expresses "the desire *for*, as well as the desire *of*, the self," it also fragments consumers into a collection of discrete "needs" (Ferguson 27, 35). Thus, as they shop, the members of Jack's family catch glimpses of their misshapen, multiplied images in "mirrored columns, in glassware and chrome, on TV monitors in security rooms" (*WN* 84). Here shopping produces a simulated self who is not an individual agent but an element of the system of capitalism. By generating that "universal third person" to which advertising appeals (*A* 270), consumption turns persons into packages radiating and receiving psychic data. We become spectacular commodities who consume everything we see, but most of all, ourselves.

"This creature has developed a complicated stomach in keeping with its leafy diet" (*WN* 95).

Shopping is thus both a private activity and a brand of self-dramatization. This is especially true in malls, where shopping trips become spectacles that mirror the "theatrical display of goods and commodities within the stores" (Shields, "Spaces" 7). The mall offers a safe and sanitized version of Bakhtinian carnival that actually reinforces the capitalist ethos (Shields, "Spaces" 9). Subjectivity is a performance in which consuming supplants other forms of social signaling, and creates "dramaturgical simulacra of social life, hyper-real expressions of selfhood" (Langman 63): the universal third person is constantly rehearsed and re-enacted to engender a community of reproducible selves. Malls bring together leisure and consumption activities previously held apart, thereby generating a spatial facsimile of the swift, jarring juxtapositions of television, where dramas about abortion collide with commercials for Kool-Aid (Shields, "Spaces" 6). They can therefore be frightening places to people like the Treadwells, an elderly couple who disappear, only to be found several days later, abandoned and frightened, in the mall, where "the vastness and strangeness of the place . . . made them feel helpless and adrift in a landscape of remote and menacing figures" (*WN* 59).

Jack doesn't feel helpless there, however. Indeed, as the shopping trip continues, he spends "with reckless abandon," building his prestige like a chieftain in a potlatch ritual: "I was bigger than these sums. . . . These sums in fact came back to me as a form of existential credit" (*WN* 84). He earns capital by dispensing "gifts, bonuses, bribes, *baksheesh*," so that consumption is magically transmuted into production (Williamson 141). "My family gloried in the event," Jack exults. "I was one of them, shopping, at last" (*WN* 84). Thus, as Ferraro argues, the radiance in this scene derives not just from shopping but from the "energy of familial interaction" that exudes an "aura of connectedness . . . an illusion of kinship." Eventually, however, this radiation "renders one unable to feel either the sacredness or the tyranny of the family bond" (Ferraro 31, 20–21): thus, when Jack tells the kids to pick out their Christmas gifts, they become "private, shadowy, even secretive" (*WN* 84). And when they return home, each retires alone to his or her room, thereby exemplifying how "Consumer capitalism brilliantly exploits the need for strengthening family bonds that it has itself, in part, destroyed" (Ferraro 36).

What postmodern consumption most of all mystifies are the social and economic exchanges involved in purchase; hence, no exchanges of money are depicted in any of the shopping scenes in *White Noise*. Instead, credit seems to dispel material facts such as aging, while at the same time it regulates consumer choices and inflates desire with colorless, odorless currency. But Jack is less troubled by the dematerialization of money than are the Wynants in *Players*; instead he feels anointed by the electronic system, perhaps because ATMs are so much like television. Thus, when he checks his balance there, he feels "waves of relief and gratitude" flowing over him. "The system had blessed my life. It felt its support and approval. . . . I sensed that something of deep personal value, but not money . . . had been authenticated and confirmed. . . . [W]e were in accord, at least for now. The networks, the circuits, the streams, the harmonies" (*WN* 46). Along with voices, then, Jack "channels" the postmodern economy in which money bestows "peace of mind in a profit-oriented context" (*WN* 87) and permits spiritual travel like the kind in the Books of the Dead. Do you fear cosmic darkness? You need only use your ATM or credit card to be transported elsewhere, not to another womb, or to the Egyptians' Field of Reeds, but to anywhere you can travel by

"MasterCard, Visa, American Express" (*WN* 100).

By mystifying the actual workings of the economy, brand names likewise become prayers or spells. Their supernatural function perhaps explains why the commodity lists that punctuate Jack's narrative always appear in groups of three, a magical number in many religious texts, including the *Tibetan Book of the Dead* (34). The mantras in DeLillo's Book of the Dead likewise evoke "the essence of a particular deity or power" (*Tibetan* 108) — a "Red Devil" or an "Ultra" (*WN* 159, 167). These trinities usually comment on the scenes where they appear; but it is not clear if we are meant to read them as extradiegetic insertions or as issuing from Jack himself.[7] If the latter, Jack is being depicted as a channeled consciousness, a human TV set who epitomizes what Leonard Wilcox calls a "new form of subjectivity colonized by the media and decentered by its polyglot discourses" (348). These "spells" thus dramatize Ewen and Ewen's claim that consumerism creates channels of desire that reflect and produce a "palpable system of belief" (46).

This mediated subjectivity corresponds to the "protean" self promoted by New Age religions, which celebrate the novel shapes and channels that each soul occupies as it evolves (Brown 24). Both kinds of "channels" reveal the religious yearnings beneath postmodern culture. In *White Noise*, product names yield a form of magic; but to perform these rites one needs a prayer book or archive of spells, and TV fulfills this function in both *White Noise* and in our world. Jack futilely tries to use television as a pedagogic tool and aid to familial unity, hoping to counter the medium's "narcotic undertow and eerie diseased brain-sucking power" by mandating that the family — a mutated sitcom family consisting of two of his kids and two of Babette's, none of whom are full siblings — watch together on Friday evenings (*WN* 16).

On one such evening, Jack is perplexed by the children's unusual attentiveness to "documentary clips of disaster and death"; "every disaster made us wish for more, for something bigger, grander, more sweeping" (*WN* 64). Jack's colleague Alfonse Stompanato claims that this phenomenon results from "brain fade. We need an occasional catastrophe to break up the incessant bombardment of information" (*WN* 66). TV is, after all, a box containing other little packets of information that have no necessary relationship to any other packet; it is an electronic form of packaging not only because it stimulates consumption, but also because of its disconnected, paratactic narrative method.[8] Thus the kids' fascination with televised disasters may be attributed to a deep need for a certain type of narrative. In a culture full of information bits in which "nobody actually knows anything" (*WN* 149), people yearn for cohesive stories with a beginning, middle, and end. As I argued in Chapter 2, apocalyptic events fulfill this need for simplified narratives particularly well. But televised apocalypses wrap social problems into tidy narrative parcels, reducing frightening events to formulaic fables. In packaging mass death, TV at once derealizes it and makes it more real, so that genuine catastrophes such as the near plane crash that Jack hears about at the airport seem to come prepackaged for the camera as "four miles of prime-time terror" (*WN* 92). If there are no cameras, there is no event. Ironically, televised disasters eventually become part of the ambient noise, just another package; hence, "a forest fire on TV is on a lower plane than a ten-second spot for Automatic Dishwasher All" (*WN* 67). Medicine, natural disasters, even nature herself, cannot be distinguished from "CABLE HEALTH, CABLE WEATHER, CABLE NEWS, CABLE NATURE" (*WN* 231).

For Murray, television is another source of mystery; it is "Sealed off, timeless [the same words with which he describes the supermarket], self-contained, self-referring. It's like a myth being born right there in our living rooms" (*WN* 51). As Delfina Treadwell, the talk-show host in *Valparaiso* puts it, "there is something in these grids of information that strikes the common heart as magic" (*Valparaiso* 109). Television evokes "memories of world birth, [and] welcomes us into . . . the network of little buzzing dots." Murray urges Jack to "look at the wealth of data concealed in the grid, in the bright packaging . . . the coded messages and endless repetitions, like chants, like mantras. '*Coke is it, Coke is it.*' The medium practically overflows with sacred formulas if we can remember how to respond innocently" (*WN* 51). He exhorts Jack (and his students) to become as children, to open themselves to this marvelous synthesis of priest and parent. Since the novel is narrated from a later time, the interjected voices and spells suggest that Jack has indeed tuned in.

The children don't need the advice; their habits (such as Steffie's attempts to mouth the words on TV) and fears prove that they are already devotees. TV is their counselor and priest. But Babette's toddler son, Wilder, plays a more momentous, perhaps even oppositional, role in *White Noise*. In contrast to Murray's bogus naivete, Wilder is a true innocent whose inability to speak somehow permits him to expresses the family's emotional condition with stark honesty, as when he ululates for no apparent reason for seven hours. After a while, Jack no longer wants him to stop, and instead lets it "enfold and cover" him, like a concerned mother (*WN* 78). The child stops as suddenly as he began, evoking the reverence one might feel for a holy man who has "just returned from a period of wandering in some remote and holy place" (*WN* 79). Wilder clearly acts as a medium or channel for the others' nameless dread, and although DeLillo's attitude toward such mystical states is complex, *White Noise* does depict childhood as "a form of magic" (quoted in James 31). Jack certainly thinks of the whole family as a "magic act . . . sharing unaccountable things" (*WN* 34), and of the children as the sources of redemptive mystery.[9]

Yet they are also highly susceptible to the blandishments of consumer culture. Wilder, for example, first appears in the novel surrounded by discarded packages, as if he is another disposable consumer good (*WN* 7). To him the world is a series of "fleeting gratifications. He took what he could, then immediately forgot it" (*WN* 170): his transient attention makes him the perfect target for advertisements. Such childlike behavior prolonged into adulthood yields the frivolities of the "American Environments" faculty, who turn memories into prepackaged responses. *White Noise* depicts the results of the cultural regression that produces this "amusement society" (Langman 62)—an "essentially childish" culture in which most activities have become elaborate forms of play and in which adults are encouraged to indulge in nostalgic self-gratification (Reeve and Kerridge 317). Such regression produces an even deeper alienation and frustration when adults become estranged from the products they consume (*WN* 50). Wilder thus epitomizes the tensions in *White Noise*: on the one hand it asks us to become as children—to respect, as Weinstein notes, "the dignity of surfaces" (310) and appreciate the "waves and radiation" of commodity culture and hear its deeper, mystical emanations; on the other hand, it alerts us to the terrifying, numbing and infantilizing qualities of those voices, to the capacity of consumerism to transform subjects and behavior into packages and to replace familial interactions with acts of consumption.

In this regard, the most highly charged moment in Part 1 occurs near the end when Jack, Murray, and the kids watch Babette teach her class on sitting and standing on the local cable channel. Disembodied but visible, Babette seems to have floated in from the spirit world; behind the postmodern altar of TV, she glows like a goddess, guru, or ghost, "shining a light on us . . . coming into being, endlessly being formed and reformed," a soul preparing for rebirth beyond the grave. Broadcast through each family member, she is magnified and immortalized: "We were shot through with Babette. Her image was projected on our bodies" (*WN* 105). This scene

—an instance of "radiance in dailiness"—emphasizes the family's conflation of television and parents. Television teaches, consoles, lectures: thus Babette's appearance on TV dramatizes how television has assumed the maternal role in the family. But her framed image also disturbs the family deeply, particularly when she is muted by a technological glitch that imitates her own ineffectual denials of death. Only Wilder remains calm, perhaps because he does not distinguish between the televised mother and the real woman. But he too is profoundly upset when the program is over, and his weeping again expresses the others' deepest fear: Mother could go off the air at any moment. Babette's "disappearance," then, exposes the repressed dread of death that lurks beneath the surface of Part 1, as well as the desperate remedies undertaken to quell it—the bodily obsessions, the simplifications, the dabbling in Eastern religions.

"Let's sit half-lotus and think about our spines" (*WN* 18).

MANUFACTURED AWE

Part 1 of *White Noise* has no discernible plot. In fact, Jack resists giving his narrative a plot because he believes that "all plots tend to move deathward" (*WN* 26). Near the end of Part 1, when Jack visits the Blacksmith burial ground and muses on the dead, he ends with a benediction: "Let the seasons drift. Do not advance the action according to a plan" (*WN* 98). Sensing the need for closed narratives that Gary Harkness exemplifies in *End Zone*, Jack understands the implied menace in the apocalyptic tales that the children crave. He resists "events" in general, which in *White Noise* consist of any occurrence that can be packaged or mediated. This resistance to plot is also a response to the ominous undertone in Part 1, which surfaces in such incidents as the elderly Mrs. Treadwell's death from "lingering dread" (*WN* 99), the evacuation of the school, and especially in the question that increasingly obsesses Jack and Babette: "who will die first?" (*WN* 15). Plotlessness ends in Part 2, when a toxic cloud marking the "end of uneventful things" (*WN* 151) threatens Blacksmith. In its wake, mortal panic emerges as the novel's most potent theme; with that dread come ever more desperate forms of magic.

Heinrich, attired in his camouflage jacket and cap, seems to anticipate the disaster even before he sees it. The cloud also wears camouflage, but it is a verbal form supplied by the authorities who give it euphemistic names. At first Jack sees the cloud as a "heavy black mass," invoking something shapeless but also demonic, like a satanic rite (*WN* 110). A name so threatening surely won't do, so the authorities redub it a "feathery plume," which makes it seem natural, birdlike, even friendly (*WN* 111). The "plume" gives way to a "black billowing cloud," a slightly more honest but still euphemistic term that focuses on its aesthetic properties rather than its toxicity (*WN* 113). At last the plume acquires its final *nom*: the "airborne toxic event" (ATE: *WN* 117). Of course, this phrase doesn't describe the cloud, but only the "event," as if the poison has already been obscured by the media cloud surrounding it. Jack and Babette also deny the danger for as long as possible, Jack deferring to the authority of television news (where one never sees college professors evacuating their flooded homes) and Babette taking comfort in packages with "familiar life-enhancing labels" (*WN* 119).

"Kleenex Softique, Kleenex Softique" (*WN* 39).

When the Gladneys finally evacuate, they join a caravan of cars ironically reenacting the opening procession of station wagons filled with students and their property, only these people are leaving their possessions behind. When Jack gets out to fill the car with gas, the cloud comes into view, lit by army helicopters like a movie premiere or "sound-and-light show" (*WN* 128). "The enormous dark mass moved like some ship in a Norse legend. . . . It was a terrible thing to see, so close, so low, packed with chlorides, benzines, phenols, hydrocarbons, or whatever the precise toxic content. But it was also spectacular, part of the grandness of a sweeping event. . . . Our fear was accompanied by a sense of awe that bordered on the religious" (*WN* 127): they experience the mixture of dread and wonder that marks the numinous.[10] Since the thing itself is hidden in a cloud of unknowing, Jack must package it in the language of TV commercials (LeClair, *Loop* 219). Thus when next appears this "bloated slug-shaped mass," it assumes its true role as a "national promotion for death, a multimillion-dollar campaign backed by radio spots, heavy print and billboard, TV saturation" (*WN* 157).

Not only is the cloud described in the language of advertising; advertising and television seem to exist for just such events, and create them as "events." As all the euphemisms imply, the toxic cloud seems to elude description; people are fascinated with it because only such catastrophic occurrences escape the mediation that turns everything else into tired formulas. The cloud seeps out of the frame within which advertising language tries to contain it. Jack's family desperately tries to recontain it by thinking of it "like a flood or tornado" (*WN* 127), but the cloud is not a natural disaster. Rather it is an an unintended consquence of the manipulation of nature, a byproduct of the insecticides that speed the growth of all that burnished fruit at the supermarket. In the toxic cloud the death that hides in commodities erupts like the return of the repressed.

Jack is buying death's "national promotion": when filling the tank with gas, he inhales some toxic gas. He learns the consequences of his exposure when the SIMUVAC ("simulated evacuation") man who analyzes his level of exposure tells Jack that he is "generating big numbers" on the computer (*WN* 140) Like the products in the supermarket whose price and composition are infallibly revealed by the holographic scanner, Jack is hereby reduced to "the sum total of [his] data" (*WN* 141). He becomes a TV star—or rather "pulsing stars" (141). But he doesn't feel like a celebrity; instead, he feels alone and alienated: "It is when death is rendered graphically, is televised so to speak, that you sense an eerie separation between your condition and yourself. A network of symbols has been introduced . . . . It makes you feel like a stranger in your own dying" (*WN* 142). Even in death, Jack remains the "universal third person"—or rather the universal second person: again the use of second person suggests the inner estrangement that this mediation produces. Technology is doubly alienating: not only does it give us the lethal chemicals that lead to early death but it then takes death away by turning it into data. The toxin soon comes to embody Jack's nebulous dread, giving it local habitation and a name: Nyodene D.

In cultures such as Tibet and ancient Egypt, interment rituals enable the dying person to "own" death and see it as the fitting end of a life-narrative. Bereft of such rites, postmodern Americans are dispersed into the ambient radiation (Hayles, "Parataxis" 412). Death, like some televised conspiracy, is just "out there." Murray explains that "the nature of modern death" is to adapt and seek "new outlets," like a product discovering its marketing niche. He tries to reassure Jack by recalling Lao-tse, who taught that "there is no difference between the quick and the dead. They are one channel of vitality" (*WN* 150). But there is a difference between Lao-tse and SIMUVAC, between the old and new ways of death: one perceived life and death as a spiritual continuum; the other turns it into a TV channel. The shows on the death channel are neither mine nor yours, but belong to a spectral alter ego that speaks in white noise; this death at once omnipresent and unreachable. So menaced by the cloud and the computer, is it any wonder that Jack yearns for a protectant?

"Krylon, Rust-Oleum, Red Devil" (*WN* 159).[11]

Some evacuees have a different attitude toward the cloud, welcoming it as a sign of imminent Armageddon, when the elect will know each other by their shared "neatness and reserve" (*WN* 135). Grace will be a matter of the good grooming that prevents "the rotting" of human packages (*WN* 136). Their apocalyptic stories reinforce capitalist values. The same mixture of marketing and missionary impulses is displayed in the tabloid newspapers that Babette reads at the camp. America's Books of Revelations, the tabloids offer commodified renditions of sacred writ. One story, headlined "Life After Death Guaranteed with Bonus Coupons," concerns two researchers who hypnotize subjects to enable them to recall their past lives. The subjects become "channels" who speak the languages of ancient cultures. The most successful subject, five-year-old Patti Weaver, even solves fabulous "crimes," such as the "murders" of Marilyn Monroe and Elvis (*WN* 142–43). Babette goes on to read predictions in which aliens and Bigfoot replace the angels and apostles of traditional tales, and dead celebrities offer salutary lessons for the masses. "Out of some persistent sense of large-scale ruin, we kept inventing hope" (*WN* 146–47).

These postmodern prophecies repackage death and turn it into magic. It's no accident that the lead story concerns channeling, for tabloids are the textual equivalent of such postmodern religions: both provide an "improvisational alternative to formal religious institutions" and "reject habits of mind based on analytical reasoning" (Brown 10, 42). As their name suggests, tabloids are pills, scriptural medications that release a "spirit of imagination. . . . We began to marvel at our own ability to manufacture awe" (*WN* 153). The tabloids "detoxify" the Cloud by conjuring up stories in which technology saves us from itself. It is easy to laugh at these magazines and their readers, but neither Jack nor DeLillo simply mocks them, nor do the 25 percent of Americans who, according to Michael Brown, believe in past lives (6). Indeed, DeLillo is fascinated with the way that the tabloids "ask profoundly important questions about death, the afterlife, God . . . in an almost Pop Art atmosphere" (quoted in James 31). They can be purchased like any other commodity in the supermarket, and, with an estimated 20 million readers per week, are evidently quite successful in getting themselves purchased (*Tabloid Frenzy*).[12] Like the varieties of postmodern religion they describe, the tabloids do not distinguish between karma and Kapital, but blend them to proffer peace of mind in a profit-oriented context.

Still, something about them fails to satisfy. Perhaps it is that, unlike the ancient Books of the Dead, tabloids give readers nothing to do, no rituals to ensure permanent security. That is where shopping comes in: we have to buy a new one each week. Thus, even though a feeling of "desperate piety" sweeps over Jack, he remains unpacified, and continues to seek signs of spiritual comfort (*WN* 154). Since watching children sleep always makes him feel "devout, part of a spiritual system," he goes to observe his daughter Steffie. He hears her speaking, uttering something in her sleep that seems to be "part of a verbal spell or ecstatic chant."

"*Toyota Celica*" (*WN* 155).

Jack knows that it is just a computer-generated brand name, a part of "every child's brain noise," and yet the moment still seems "beautiful and mysterious, gold-shot with looming wonder. It was like the name of an ancient power in the sky, tablet-carved in cuneiform." Duvall observes that this scene again expresses how "art's magic function has merely migrated to the marketing of consumer goods" ("(Super)Marketplace" 135); I would replace "art" with "religion." As Raymond Williams shrewdly noted many years ago, "if the meanings and values generally operative in the society give no answer to, no means of negotiating, problems of death, loneliness, frustration, the need for identity and respect, then the magical system [of advertising] must come, mixing its charms and expedients with reality in easily available forms" (190). The phrase is "tablet-carved"—a pill, a package, a form of verbal Dylar. The children are able to plumb "substatic regions too deep to probe," mining moments of "splendid transcendence" from the aural junk of consumer culture. The brand-name mantras that punctuate the text, however, imply that Jack, narrating the events from a later date, has learned from Steffie's channeling. Although Jack seems credulous, DeLillo wishes us to recognize the absurdity of a frightened parent finding comfort in the name of an automobile. DeLillo doesn't explicitly ridicule either Jack's method or his madness, as if to grant that one discovers consolation wherever one may.[13] But Steffie's mantra is not meant to be shared, for consumerism, like other postmodern religions, does not incorporate its believers into a community (Michael Brown 68–69). Despite its demographic research and messages about joining "generations," consumerism offers decidedly private satisfactions (Schudson 221).

Since the ATE is a consumer byproduct, it seems only fitting that scientists aim to destroy it with organisms that "literally consume the billowing cloud"—no more literally, however, than Jack (*WN* 160). This news so much resembles a story in the *National Enquirer* or the *Star* that Jack and the family feel "glutted in an insubstantial way, as after a junk food spree." Like fast-food fries, consuming engorges us but leaves a more profound hunger in its place. Babette doesn't doubt the plausibility of "little organisms packaged in cardboard" like tiny McDonald's burgers (*WN* 160). In any case, she has already demonstrated her belief in the miraculous powers of technology by taking the experimental drug Dylar, a supplement designed to satisfy that hunger.

"The radio said, 'excesses of salt, phosphorus, magnesium'" (*WN* 236).

Although tabloids and TV news render events in tidy packages, the "real" ATE—like the cloud itself—resists narrative consolations. After the evacuees flee to Iron City, they learn that the disaster wasn't even disastrous enough to be televised. A man walks around with a TV on his shoulder, shouting, "Do they think this is just television? . . . Don't they know it's real?. . . Even if there hasn't been great loss of life, don't we deserve some attention for our suffering, our human worry, our terror? Isn't fear news?" (*WN* 162). The comedy is clear enough; but the tragedy is that the others share his feeling of emptiness. They can't understand their own experience without electronic mediation, without the knowledge that they are being observed. Stripped of the universal third person, they are trapped in a first person they no longer recognize. The cloud's enormous mass will remain nebulous because television news has not wrapped it for general consumption. But the experience of the ATE cannot be packaged or safely filed away with the videotapes. Jack's later obsession with the internal "nebulous mass" that the cloud has produced is thus related to his need to see his terror televised, where it can be made harmless. Instead, he experiences something almost worse than death: the dizzying alienation of insignificance.

"There are forms of vertigo that do not include spinning" (*WN* 56).

PANASONIC

In the wake of the ATE, life gains an added edge. The ominous undertone of Part 1 grows louder and more ubiquitous in part 3, as if those dead souls "babbling at the edge of a dream" (*WN* 4) now intrude into daylight life, building a massive cloud of panic. The noises become "panasonic" (*WN* 241)—ubiquitous and full of panic—a brand name that was also one of DeLillo's working titles for the novel. And as their dread expands, the characters seek more potent magic. Babette, for example, teaches a new course in "Eating and Drinking: Basic Parameters," because people need "to have their beliefs reinforced" (*WN* 171). Devout in her victimhood, Steffie acts in SIMUVAC's disaster scenarios, believing that "the more we rehearse disaster, the safer we'll be from the real thing" (*WN* 205). Jack continues to take German lessons from Howard Dunlop, who piles furniture around his doors, reads the *Ancient Egyptian Book of the Dead* (a "best-seller in Germany" [*WN* 221]), and investigates others who seem less fearful.

Babette's dread, however, antedates the toxic cloud, and several months ago she sought help in the form of Dylar, an experimental drug created to quell the fear of death. Before confronting her about it, Jack takes one of the pills to chemist Winnie Richards, who tells him that Dylar is not just a pill, but a "drug delivery system" in which the medicine is encased so that the chemical is released gradually over time (*WN* 187); Dylar, in other words, is a medicinal package that Babette learned about in the expected way: through an ad in a tabloid (*WN* 196). Dylar promises the same sense of well-being as others find in the tabloids, and when Babette explains its function, she echoes TV ads for pain-relievers, saying Dylar "speeds relief" to the "fear-of-death" part of the brain (*WN* 200). Quintessentially American in her belief that "everything is correctible" (*WN* 191), she also possesses the American faith that pills can defeat even death—or the fear of death, since in this fully mediated world death matters less than its shadowy forerunner, dread. But the cure seems as bad as the disease: if Jack's televised death means that we are the sum of our data, Dylar signifies that we are merely "the sum total of our chemical impulses" (*WN* 200).

As Jack quizzes her about the drug, he seems upset less that she is taking it than that her scheme has disrupted his package of beliefs about her character: "The whole point of Babette is that . . . she reveals and confides" and "says yes to things" (*WN* 192, 220). Jack appropriates her story (Reid 61), fixating not on her desperation, but on the "capitalist transaction" to exchange sex for Dylar that she completed with a "composite" man she calls Mr. Gray (*WN* 194). They entered the "grubby little motel room," and then "he entered you" (*WN* 194), says Jack. Trumping her dread even more forcefully, he announces that he is "tentatively scheduled to die" (*WN* 202), as if death were a department meeting (and as if we were not all so scheduled). Their panic is deepened by the nebulousness of postmodern death, which is "Electrical noise. . . . Uniform, white": everywhere and nowhere, death is the white noise of the title (*WN* 198). Clinging together in terror, Jack and Babette engage in the age-old answer to death, the movements of their love-making counteracting the "chaos in [their] souls" (*WN* 199). If "all plots move in one direction," perhaps they can deflect that deathward trajectory by igniting a countermotion.

"Leaded, unleaded, super unleaded" (*WN* 199).[14]

Jack also visits his internist because, as Stompanato tells him, "internal medicine is the magic brew" (*WN* 217) of postmodern life, and he makes a pilgrimage to a gleaming medical facility called Autumn Harvest Farms (where the Grim Reaper works?). But its high-tech medicine makes Jack feel more like a commodity than ever, and the technicians remind him of the bag boys at the supermarket, that other postmodern temple. He learns that his exposure to Nyodene D is likely to nourish within him a lethal "nebulous mass" (*WN* 280), as if its "enormous dark mass" (*WN* 127) has taken up residence inside his body to give physical form to his nebulous dread.

Unconsoled by the medical profession, Jack must conjure up his own magic. Despite Babette's insistence that Dylar doesn't work, he becomes obsessed with getting some of it. A perfect symmetry takes shape in his mind: since his impending doom was caused by consumer technology, the fear it triggered should be erased by Dylar, "the benign counterpart of the Nyodene D menace." If the cloud looks like the fearsome visage of some vengeful god, Dylar is "technology with a human face" (*WN* 211). In an anticipation of the landfill scenes in *Underworld,* Jack searches through the trash compactor to find the last of the pills, but instead encounters an "oozing cube of semi-mangled cans . . . and other refuse. The bottles were broken, the cartons flat. Product colors were undiminished in brightness and intensity" (*WN* 258). Though the products are dead, the packaging remains radiant. This is the eerie, Dorian Grayish afterlife of commodities: the soul dies but the shell lives forever. Jack can't believe that this reeking mound belongs to his family, and picks through it, "mass by shapeless mass, wondering why I felt guilty, a violator of privacy. . . ." Here is

Some kind of occult geometry or symbolic festoon of obsessions. . . . Was this the dark underside of consumer consciousness? I came across a horrible clotted mass of hair, soap, ear swabs, crushed roaches, flip-top rings, sterile pads smeared with pus and bacon fat, strands of flayed dental floss, fragments of ballpoint refills, toothpicks still displaying bits of impaled food. (*WN* 259)

But no Dylar. The "mass" of smashed and discarded commodities not only reincarnates the toxic cloud, but also evokes the "nebulous mass" he may be carrying within. The house's entrails seem to provide a frightening X-ray of Jack's body, also bearing the traces of a lifetime of consumption. This is what happens to the bright packaging and burnished fruit; this is what it does to one's mortal frame.[15]

"Meanwhile here is a quick and attractive lemon garnish suitable for any sea food" (*WN* 178).

Disgusted, Jack decides that the Tibetans are right — possessions have a "mortality" attached to them (*WN* 262) — and so begins throwing things away in order to sever that mortal connection to matter. These "divestment rituals" (McCracken 87) — replaying again the purgative rites of Gary Harkness, Bucky Wunderlick, and Glen Selvy — are his attempt to generate by material means the spiritual transcendence that the Tibetans obtain from religious practices. If earlier in the novel Jack accumulated commodities to shield him from death, now he throws objects away as if demonically possessed. But the same motive lies behind each valence of this psychic economy: both accumulation and attrition are meant to clear his system, muffle his dread, anesthetize his pain.

"A decongestant, an antihistamine, a cough suppressant, a pain reliever" (*WN* 262).

Whereas the Tibetans and ancient Egyptians invoked spirits to guard the dead on their journey to the next life, the only invisible presences that Jack encounters issue from the spectral economy that blesses his ATM card. Twice in Part 3 he channels such postmodern spirit guides. In the first, an anonymous authority provides twelve-step directions to insure proper

183
The American
Book of
the Dead

payment to Waveform Dynamics. Like ATM cards, checks are a form of credit that require faith in some suprarational or superhuman (or corporate) entity that monitors and safeguards debts and payments. The second intrusion, occurring just after his last divestment, warns him to await his new ATM card and above all to "Reveal your code to no one. Only your code allows you to enter the system" (*WN* 295). His check properly on its way and protected by his secret code, Jack feels capable of conquering his fear. Yet even these pieces of inner property are inadequate; what he really needs is to write himself into a story, to create a narrative in which he is the protagonist.

Death could provide such a narrative. When Winnie Richards discusses Dylar with Jack, she sensibly suggests that it would be a mistake to lose one's fear of death. "Isn't death the boundary we need? Doesn't it give a precious texture to life, a sense of definition?" (*WN* 228): isn't death the sharp terminus that gives our life-narrative its necessary shape? But postmodern death—just a panasonic quality in the air—yields no clean denouement, so Jack must manufacture a better one. But he still needs two things: a narrative engine and a villain. The engine of his plot arrives when Babette's father, Vernon Dickey (a man hilariously wracked with his own litany of deficits and diseases), gives Jack "a 25-caliber Zumwalt automatic. German-made," an instrument that endows Jack with a "fresh design, a scheme, . . . a secret . . . a second self, a dream, a spell, a plot, a delirium" (*WN* 253-54): at last a magic wand to wave away death. Next he conjures up his villain, "Mr. Gray," the composite scientist with whom Babette betrayed him. Jack watches him on the TV channel of his mind as a "staticky, unfinished" figure "flared with random distortion" (*WN* 241). Neither black nor white but only a bland gray, this is an unsuitably nebulous villain. Better to confront his rival physically, and with his magic wand win the spoils—Dylar. With one more ingredient, Jack will be primed to complete his masterpiece.

"Using my palette knife and my odorless turp, I will thicken the paint on my palette" (*WN* 309).

That ingredient comes from Murray Jay Siskind, who suggests that Jack needs something as cathartic as one of his car-crash movies to offset his "shallow, unfulfilling" death (*WN* 283). Dismissing Winnie's notion that death gives life shape, Murray argues that "every death is premature" (*WN* 283).[16] He outlines several options: "You could put your faith in technology," because it has the divine capacity both to create an appetite for immortality and to threaten universal extinction. Or he could sample a variety of religions and "pick one you like" (*WN* 286). It is appropriate that Murray offers these choices as they windowshop at a shoe store, since he is suggest ing that Jack shop for a religion, and is himself windowshopping into Jack's dread, passing lightly from alternative to alternative without incurring any obligations. In a similarly nonchalant but penetrating way, he explicates Jack's relationship with Hitler: " 'What have you been trying to do all these years?' " he asks. " 'Put myself under a spell, I guess,' " Jack answers. " 'Some people are larger than life. Hitler is larger than death. You thought he would protect you. . . . On one level you wanted to conceal yourself in Hitler and his works. On another level you wanted to use him to grow in significance and strength' " (*WN* 287). Becker dubs this phenomenon the "spell cast by persons," and suggests that such grandiose figures emit a "magic aura" that seems to protect their followers and make them feel as children (Becker 127, 130). A similar regressive longing, Murray argues, explains Jack's desire to be with Wilder: the toddler doesn't know he's going to die, and lives in a cloud of unknowing that obscures nebulous masses and mutes white noise (*WN* 289–90; cf. Becker 22). At this moment, Jack and Murray are walking through the supermarket; Murray is also "marketing" something to Jack, repackaging his fears to prepare for his most dangerous suggestion.

According to Murray, there are two kinds of people in the world: killers and diers; Jack confesses that he has been a dier all his life. Violence might spur rebirth; indeed, Murray proposes, "to kill a person is to gain life-credit. The more people you kill, the more life-credit you store up" (*WN* 290). Already feeling blessed and oppressed by the immaterial economy, Jack is struck by this metaphor; murder might be the secret PIN number that allows entry into the banking system administering the economy of death. If so, plotting is related to death in a different way than Jack has previously believed. There is something compelling about this theory, despite its speciousness (we are all diers, after all); but, as several critics have noted, there is also something fascistic about a philosophy that turns someone's death into fodder for individual self-enhancement (Heffernan 179; Dewey 215). As Becker might explain it, Murray is playing mini-Führer, urging his follower to perform the "magic of the initiatory act" and deflecting the follower's guilt by standing as a colossal example (135–36). But for Murray, viewing Jack's panic through his theoretical screen, murder is just an exercise or educational TV show.

"Now watch this. Joanie is trying to snap Ralph's patella with a *bushido* stun kick. She makes contact, he crumples, she runs" (*WN* 257).

So Jack invents a story, a "reality [he can] control, secretly dominate" (*WN* 297) one that will allow him to package death in a plot. DeLillo is suggesting that plot is Dylar, a container for dread that gives it a tangible—and therefore manageable—shape. As Jack tries to localize his fear by proceeding with his plot, *White Noise* gathers momentum for its own plot, and begins to circumscribe its readers' dread within its covers. In so doing it becomes an American Book of the Dead, replete with instructions for how (and especially how not) to approach one's inevitable demise. Similarly, Jack's plot becomes for him an anchor for floating anxiety, a thread to guide him through the labyrinth that his life has become.

"If you keep misplacing your ball of string, cage it in a Barney basket, attach some organizer clips to your kitchen corkboard, fasten the basket to the clips. Simple" (*WN* 296).

But one cannot kill a TV image. Fortunately, Winnie tells him that "Gray" is actually a renegade scientist named Willie Mink, who conducted "interviews in a motel" (like David Bell of *Americana*) to find suitable subjects for Dylar. Armed with his gun and his secret code, Jack drives to confront Mink, on the way channeling the words "Random Access Memory, Acquired Immune Deficiency Syndrome, Mutual Assured Destruction" (*WN* 303)—RAM, AIDS, MAD.[17] The acronyms suggest that violence, a "sardonic response to the promise of consumer fulfillment" ("Outsider" 295), has infected Jack like a virus. He has become an instrument of the technology he once feared: rather than using the gun, the gun is using him. Feeling "lighter than air, colorless, odorless, invisible" (*WN* 303), he has become his own "airborne toxic event" (Keesey 148), a menacing cloud of unknowing.

Throughout the confrontation with Mink, Jack repeats his plan again and again: find Mink, shoot him three times, put the gun in his hand, steal the Dylar, drive the neighbors' car back to their garage. Although it's a ridiculous plan (how many suicides shoot themselves repeatedly in the stomach?), in executing it Jack feels himself "part of a network of structures and channels" (*WN* 305)—TV channels, for the plan smacks of nothing so much as a bad TV movie (see Keesey 147–48; LeClair, *Loop* 222). Despite its silliness, the plot furnishes Jack with a narrative design that works like the prayers in the Books of the Dead to provide a method of mastering death. As he enters the motel room (that embodiment of the modular self), he feels a "density that was also a transparency" (*WN* 307). Willie Mink feels the same way, but only because his ingestion of Dylar has impaired his ability to distinguish between the denseness of the real and the transparency of a TV screen. Like the straitjacketed character in Act 2 of *The Day Room*, Mink "channels" the voices of TV (Moses 76). Interrupting himself with quoted instructions or descriptions from TV, Gray/Mink is a living "schizogram" who also expresses the fragmentation of his alter ego, the gray-coated Gladney. As Duvall comments, Mink's condition reveals that "television itself . . . is Dylar" ("(Super)Marketplace" 146). Moreover, with his Budweiser shorts and "Planter's peanut" skin, Mink is a shell, a empty can: a "composite" (*WN* 307), an amalgam of the advertised products and technologies that glut and sedate us.

Many of Mink's hilariously incongruous phrases expose the hidden currents of the scene. For example, when he declares that "Some of these sure-footed bighorns have been equipped with radio transmitters" (*WN* 306), he is describing his and Jack's plugged-in condition. His formulae and instructions ("To begin your project sweater . . . ; "To convert Fahrenheit to Celsius. . . "[*WN* 307, 308]) imply that Jack needs guidance; his elliptical comment about wisdom teeth (*WN* 312) suggests Jack's lack of such wisdom, and so on. More directly, Mink announces that, because Dylar failed to win its market share, death will become "more effective, productwise. This is what the scientists don't understand, scrubbing their smocks with Woolite" (*WN* 308). New Improved Death: this is the kind that won't soil scientists' hands with moral responsibility, instead leaving everything clean and white (*WN* 308). Jack shares the scientists' elevated sense of ethical freedom, albeit for a different reason. Moreover, as we readers vicariously participate in this violent encounter, we too resemble both TV audiences glued to luridly violent programs, and those scientists detachedly observing suffering subjects. Perhaps we too root for Jack's conquest, which may purge our own dread of death.

"Not that I have anything personal against death from our vantage point high atop Metropolitan County Stadium" (*WN* 308).

Mink's spells, however, don't work. What's worse, he can no longer distinguish signifier from signified: hence, when Jack says "hail of bullets," Mink ducks in terror. Endowed with such godlike verbal authority—"let there be fire"—Jack feels spiritually purified, sensorily powerful. "White noise everywhere. . . . I understood the neurochemistry of my brain. . . . I believed everything" (*WN* 310). For once he "knows who [he is] in the [TV] network of meanings" (*WN* 312), and fires "the gun, the weapon, the pistol, the firearm, the automatic," as if the gun is a crazed word processor riddling Mink with words as well as with bullets (Dewey 217). But once Jack places the gun in Mink's hand, his victim starts writing his own script, and shoots Jack in the wrist. Suddenly the "world collapsed inward. . . . The old human muddles and quirks were set flowing again. Compassion, remorse, mercy" (*WN* 313). With grandiose nobility, Jack decides to save Mink, even giving him mouth-to-mouth resuscitation; eventually it is "no longer possible to tell whether the blood on my hands was his or mine." With this mystical transference, Jack feels "epic pity and compassion" flooding into him (*WN* 315).

"And this could represent the leading edge of some warmer air" (*WN* 313).

But his magnanimity is just another aspect of his narcissism, his aid disguised infection, his "life-credit" merely a form of "inflated . . . income" (*WN* 316), and his compassion a species of nostalgia. During his treatment at the hospital, however, a nun shatters his complacency by telling him that even the sisters no longer believe in the old verities; they only make believe. "If we did not pretend to believe these things, the world would collapse" (*WN* 318). Nevertheless, their pretense is a "dedication. Someone must appear to believe. Our lives are no less serious than if we professed real faith. . . . Those who have abandoned belief must still believe in us." They surrender their lives "to make [his] nonbelief possible" (*WN* 319). Rejecting the miraculous cures and bourgeois Armageddons of tabloid Christianity, the nun espouses a pragmatic devotion for a postmodern age. But it's also a disturbing one. Is faith no more than a performance, and religion as much a simulacrum as the most photographed barn in America? To what is she dedicated? To healing the sick and dying? To disabusing smug professors of fascistic nostalgia? Or perhaps DeLillo is suggesting that the impulse to believe, a faith in the bare potential for sacredness or transcendence, will always endure. Tabloids, TV, supermarkets, toxic clouds—like it or not, these are the sites where spirits live and the shapes that spirits take.

Disgusted by Jack, the nun starts to speak in German, growing ever more animated, finally assaulting him with "Litanies, hymns, catechisms. . . . The odd thing is I found it beautiful" (*WN* 320). At last a living being utters the words that Jack has been straining to hear, intimating the presence of something truly "larger than death." This is the "purer speech" that consummates so many of DeLillo's novels, except that here it cannot be accepted as a simple celebration of innocent language, but must be read through Jack's self-delusion and DeLillo's irony. Perhaps the words are compelling only because they are unintelligible. Or perhaps DeLillo is suggesting that the most powerful mysteries can never be fully understood. In any case, the nun's verbal assault humbles Jack by reminding him of his limitations and his last end. Are these the words that elude commodification, the echoes of dead souls, a true spirit channel, uttered in the language of the untellable?

"They're not booing—they're saying 'Bruce, Bruce'" (*WN* 269).

The denouement of the novel deepens the mystery by depicting three discrete scenes that are narrated without comment, just as Jack's violent adventure seems (somewhat implausibly) to produce no legal or moral repercussions. Each one depicts both potential redemption and an accompanying danger. In the first, the "mystically charged" Wilder rides his tricycle across the interstate, miraculously escaping harm, only to fall into a baptismal ditch (*WN* 322–23). Does his ignorance of death protect him, as

Murray believes? Or is he shielded because he is one of those "holy fools," an ancient soul whose actions provide guidance for others? Wilder's epic journey through the traffic—those "dead souls babbling at the edge of a dream" (WN 4)—may even symbolize the possibility of reincarnation, described in the *Tibetan Book of the Dead* as a passage through the "great wilderness" of death (we duly note Wilder's name), beyond "the bardo's dangerous pathway" (96–97, 100). But even if Wilder's trek represents a spiritual journey, or points to the possibility of redemption beyond the body, how many are brave or foolish enough to undertake it with him?

The second scene returns to those colorful "postmodern sunsets" mentioned earlier in the novel (WN 227) and imbues them with the aspect of eternity. The highway overpass has become an outdoor cathedral where "the middle-aged, the elderly"—those confronting their mortality—gather to watch the sky, which seems "under a spell, powerful and storied" (WN 325). Nobody speaks, white noise ceases. This veneration of sunsets recalls the many prayers in the *Ancient Egyptian Book of the Dead* in which the sun god Ra or Re is asked to "dispel cloudiness" and to allow the deceased to merge with "this one who traverses the sky towards the West" (Faulkner trans; 120).[18] Each pilgrim seems to gain some mystical protection for the journey through death by contemplating the force above. Just as important, the community meets together here and suspends individuality until darkness falls and restores all to their "separate and defensible selves" (WN 325). And yet, if there is "awe, it is all awe, it transcends previous categories of awe, . . . we don't know whether we are watching in wonder or dread" (WN 324). Why dread? Because the colors that produce this sublime aesthetic effect are another byproduct of the toxic cloud. This residue contaminates the view (WN 325): the god of nature has been soiled by the devil of technology. The sunsets retain the blend of terror and wonder, of dread and magic, first borne by the toxic cloud; as Frow remarks, we could as "well say 'another *poisonous* sunset,' or speak of an 'airborne *aesthetic* event'" ("Last Things" 176). But has the human relationship to the supernatural ever been unmixed with fear?

At last we revisit the supermarket, where the "shelves have been rearranged," causing panic in many shoppers (WN 325) An "aimless and haunted mood" pervades the temple, and people feel betrayed. But in the end it doesn't matter, because

the terminals are equipped with holographic scanners, which decode the binary secret of every item, infallibly. This is the language of waves and radiation, or how the dead speak to the living. And this is where we wait together, regardless of age, our carts stocked with brightly colored goods. A slowly moving line, satisfying, giving us time to glance at the tabloids in the racks. Everything we need that is not food or love is here in the tabloid racks. The tales of the supernatural and the extra-terrestrial. The miracle vitamins, the cures for cancer, the remedies for obesity. The cults of the famous and the dead. (*WN* 326)

Now death—or life—has truly become a "waiting period," a *bardo* or island between two states. Fittingly, the novel ends at this terminal, the commercial/technological gate of heaven where not people but products are judged by omniscient gods. If Wilder's journey and the glorious sunsets seem miraculous and mollifying, the supermarket remains menacing. Do the scanners and lights induce the peace that, in the *Tibetan Book of the Dead*, lets us hear "All sounds as my own sound" and see "All the lights as my own light / All the rays as my own ray" (102)? Or do they interpose an alienating authority between the seeker and mystical knowledge? Do those waiting truly share anything? DeLillo describes no persons, but only waves, radiation, and the tabloids' sacred writ. Thus the comfort provided in this temple seems decidedly impersonal and mass-produced. What is most disturbing about this scene, however, is not the disappointing nature of the epiphany, but the neutral tone of the narration. Again Jack seems to channel another voice, his dazed (or ironic) acceptance echoing Murray's earlier comments, or perhaps issuing, like a spell sung in deadpan timbre, from the ectoplasmic mouth of some long-dead spirit.

"Panasonic" (*WN* 241).

This conclusion has generated much critical debate.[19] Is Jack—and, by proxy, DeLillo—resigned to the reduction of religion to tabloid tales, to late capitalism's distortion of familial and community bonds? Is he dourly exposing the pathetic delusions of contemporary Americans? Or is he probing the recesses of the religious impulse, accepting the viability and authenticity of postmodern faiths, despite (or because of) the "Pop Art" aspects of their expression? Certainly the absence of authorial comment here signifies DeLillo's recognition of his own imbrication in white noise: he admits that there is no privileged position—or at best a fleeting and fluctuating one—from which to comment. Maybe tabloids and commercials do fulfill a religious need. Whether "genuine" or not, such things sometimes provide comfort, authority, a sense of something larger. What's more, they explain death and rob it of its sting. The final passage perhaps best exemplifies how DeLillo operates from the inside of American cultural institutions to instigate a dialogue with them that takes place in the very language they speak, albeit one more beautifully rendered and ironically gauged.

Masking its critique in celebration, *White Noise* inhabits the heart of postmodern culture to weigh its menaces against its marvels, to alert us to its wonder as well as its waste. Yet what it most of all affirms is the power of fiction itself. That is, DeLillo's fiction, like the nun's dedication, is an act of faith; but unlike the nun, he credits his readers with the ability to discriminate. By refusing to provide his readers with the anesthetic of violent resolution or melodramatic resurrection, DeLillo prevents his fiction from being thoughtlessly consumed like Dylar or Wonder Bread. Instead, he forces us to make our own negotiations with all species of nebulous masses. *White Noise* neither simply satirizes nor sedates, but does something more difficult than either: it makes us work, shining a reflected light back from the TV set that compels us to question our own beliefs, satisfactions, and desires, to perceive the radiance in dailiness but not be dazzled by it. If fiction is not merely Dylar, DeLillo suggests that it nonetheless possesses a privileged power to transfigure the real, to make us listen again. *White Noise* thus dramatizes how the yearning for mystery and meaning hasn't gone away; like the dead, it has merely changed form. Finally, then, the elusiveness of *White Noise* embodies the magic that DeLillo seeks to understand, those same ghostly voices and sacred sounds that we barely discern beneath the babble. Perhaps they are mere simulacra, and perhaps their channels are never free from static. But if we have heard them at all, then his fiction has given us a bonus coupon that promises something beyond the trash compactor.

"Void where prohibited" (*WN* 303).

Chapter 7
Becoming Incorporated

Spectacular Authorship in *Mao II*

When DeLillo was asked in 1979 why he withholds information about himself, he answered, "Silence, exile, cunning, and so on" (Interview with LeClair 20). His response, of course, echoes Joyce's Stephen Dedalus, who in *A Portrait of the Artist as a Young Man* proclaims that he will use silence, exile, and cunning as the "only arms" with which to defend his art from the "nets" of politics, family and religion (247). As we have seen, DeLillo's fiction repeatedly treats the press of publicity on privacy, the fetishization of celebrity and the commodification of art. But his 1991 novel *Mao II* for the first time directly addresses the position of the writer in postmodern culture through the character of reclusive novelist Bill Gray, who exemplifies the Romantic or Dedalian model of authorship in its death throes.

Since publishing two slim novels thirty years previously, Gray has exiled himself from the public, cunningly hiding his whereabouts and refusing to speak about his work. Until recently, DeLillo has cultivated a similar anonymity, shunning interviews and television appearances and rarely giving readings. Indeed, the parallels between the two seem almost too obvious: DeLillo used to tell friends that he was going to "change my name to Bill Gray and disappear" (quoted in Passaro 38). Critics of *Mao II* have thus argued that Gray is DeLillo's mouthpiece (Edmundson 123) for an "argument about the future" that pits "the arch individualist" against the "mass mind" in a battle for the "imagination of the world" (Passaro

76; "Art of Fiction" 296), and have claimed that DeLillo too clearly favors Gray over the characters—photographer Brita Nilsson, bewildered would-be mystic Karen Janney, terrorist leader Abu Rashid—who represent the future.[1] I want to argue in this chapter the contrary proposition that *Mao II* demonstrates the inadequacies of Gray's Joycean model of authorship by dramatizing how it does not elude the "nets" of politics and celebrity, but actually makes Gray more exploitable by what Guy Debord famously calls the "society of the spectacle." More broadly, *Mao II* announces—with mixed emotions—the end of the grand narrative of modernist authority and its replacement by what I am calling, after Jennifer Wicke, "spectacular authorship": the power to use photographic or televised images to manufacture, as if by magic, spectacular events that profoundly mold public consciousness.[2]

The second part of Bill's (and allegedly, DeLillo's) argument consists of the charge that terrorists have supplanted novelists as the shapers of culture. In the second part of this chapter, I want to challenge this claim as well by showing how terrorism—itself a form of spectacular authorship—is irretrievably mediated by the journalistic and photographic gatekeepers who record and comment upon terrorist actions. Yet if *Mao II* shows, as Joseph Tabbi claims, the "impossibility of achieving a wholly literary opposition" to mass culture (173), it also suggests the potential for a more viable form, represented not by Gray but by Brita Nilsson. Indeed, in this novel DeLillo employs photography, Brita's creative medium, both to criticize more sharply the culture that gives rise to spectacular discourse and to acknowledge his own inevitable incorporation within such discourse. Here as in all his work DeLillo imitates the discourses he aims to deconstruct and thereby generates a dialogue with those cultural forms that both criticizes their consequences and appropriates their advantages. Again DeLillo's critique emerges not from Dedalian exile but more cunningly from within the culture itself.

TERRIFYING AUTHORS

A reader first opening *Mao II* must immediately be struck by the book's physical format: Andy Warhol's famous Mao silkscreens decorate the cover, and a series of interpolated photographs (a rally in Tiananmen Square; a Unification Church mass wedding; the Sheffield soccer disaster; a crowd of Iranians in front of an enormous poster of Khomeini; three boys in a bunker, one aiming a camera or a gun) demarcate its sections. These "circumtextual" framing devices (Reid 44) immediately suggest the novel's concern with the nature of mimesis. Because it is not only about photographs but also composed of them, it invites us to consider writing and photography as contrasting or complementary modes of representation and authorship. For example, whereas writing is linear and requires the use of a reader's imagination, photos seem to project us immediately into the scenes pictured. And yet, while photos seem to give us instant access to the real, they also remind us, as Susan Sontag has noted, of its remoteness ("Image-World" 356), and of the layers of representation that always intervene between subjects and the phenomenal world. The physical form of *Mao II*, then, embodies the paradox of photography: its mimetic quality is always accompanied by a realization of its artificiality, of the photographer's authority, of the subject's performativity, and of the mediated nature of "reality."

If the dust jacket and interpolated photos—all but one of them crowd scenes—illustrate the novel's argument that "the future belongs to crowds" (*M* 16), they further suggest, as DeLillo states elsewhere, that "the photographic image is a kind of crowd in itself" (Interview with Nadotti 88). That is, photos both represent crowds and, by inviting the viewer into the picture, generate and incarnate them. Moreover, photographs seem not to issue from an individual author but from a dynamic collaboration between photographer and subject that captures a moment of embodied theater. Thus, just as *Ratner's Star* was designed to be a "piece of mathematics" that interrogated mathematical authority (Interview with LeClair 27), so *Mao II* presents itself as a multimedia event, as a text that is also a crowd of photos, one that enacts Debord's thesis that to analyze spectacle one must speak its language (Debord, *Society* 15). But DeLillo's aim is not mere documentation, but rather to use the discourse of images to redefine them, denaturalize them, and subject them to a dialectical reading.[3] DeLillo's use of photos thus discloses his participation in the culture of images that Gray abhors, and his construction of a novel form of authorship—one we might call "corporate," since it is collective, and at once corporeal and simulacral—shared with photographers and their massed subjects. The text incarnates DeLillo's participation in spectacular discourse and in the economy of subjectivity that such discourse demands.

The first photograph after the frontispiece shows a crowd of brides and grooms lining up in Yankee Stadium to be married by the Reverend Sun Myung Moon. "Here they come" (*M* 3): like *White Noise*, this novel opens with a procession tracked by the narrator's roving camera. "[T]he effect is one of transformation. From a series of linked couples they become one continuous wave," an "undifferentiated mass" (*M* 3). A key word in this novel as it is in *White Noise*, "mass" refers both to crowds and to the mass-produced images that consume and are consumed by them. As Roger

Janney, Karen's father, recognizes, "They take a time-honored event and repeat it, repeat it, repeat it until something new enters the world" (*M* 4); extravagant replication turns ritual into spectacle or "sculptured object" (*M* 7). The sculptor is Moon himself, the novel's first spectacular author, who has organized the wedding and conducts it to create a specific aesthetic effect. Indeed, the couples have been arranged to render them indistinguishable, or to imitate an imaginary photograph: as Karen later admits, Moon "matched us by photograph. So I thought how great, I have an Instamatic husband" (*M* 183). The couples aren't people but photos come to life, mere actors in Moon's colossal comedy. As the spectators snap their photos, Karen imagines that the couples are "already in the albums and slide projectors, filling picture frames with their microcosmic bodies" (*M* 10). The parents photographing them try to "neutralize the event" (*M* 6), to reassert origins and family history, but it is too late: Moon's spectacular authority, his fatherhood of the image, has enabled the couples to be "lifted by the picture-taking, the forming of aura" (*M* 15), to become a luminous outline limned by the Great Photographer.

Distributing auras like gold coins to beggars, Moon provides one answer to Roger's question (one DeLillo asks repeatedly in his work): "When the Old God leaves the world, what happens to all the unexpended faith?" (*M* 7).[4] For Moon isn't just their leader; he "lives in them like chains of matter that determine who they are" (*M* 6). Like the authoritarian leaders in DeLillo's earlier novels (for example, *End Zone*'s Emmett Creed), Moon gives his followers a supportive community that lends meaningful order to their lives. And like the terrorist leaders profiled later in the novel, Moon furnishes his acolytes with what Khachig Tololyan calls a "projective narrative"—an apocalyptic tale that maps out "future actions that can imbue the time of individual lives with transcendent collective values" (Tololyan 218)—one that will lead them out "past religion and history" and bring the "End Time closer" (*M* 15–16). Requiring that they abandon their possessions, parents, and personal histories, Moon becomes a protector who writes for each acolyte what Tololyan terms a "regulative biography"—a new personal narrative that is policed to ensure the effacement of natural genealogy and its replacement by Moon's surrogate paternity (Tololyan 218, 224). With Moon as their doctor, they are quarantined from the American ethos of individualism, "immunized against the language of self" (*M* 8).[5]

But if in one sense Moon's followers are united in their resistance to American values, in another sense his spectacular authorship exploits the American entrepreneurial spirit. Hence, he has his children memorize chants such as "We're the greatest, there's no doubt; heavenly father, we'll sell out" (*M* 13). Even Karen, who thinks of marriage as a TV-like "channel to salvation" (*M* 10), unconsciously registers how Moon diverts his children's addiction to consumerism into his own capitalist religion. Because spectacle is already a "specious form of the sacred" (Debord, *Society* 20), Moon can readily transmute it by encouraging his followers to spend their unexpended faith on his behalf, and uses their labor to forge a new economy of subjectivity and a new measure of value that nevertheless owes much to American consumerism and its fetishization of images. Rechanneling and expanding the ethos of entrepreneurship, Moon promotes himself as a Divine Salesman or Capitalist of Faith.[6] His aura is the reflected glow of money. Thus while in some ways Moon's church emits a "long, low cry from the past: a demand for a return to a simplified world over and against . . . a complicated and fragmented present-day society" (Horowitz xvii), in other ways it trumpets a frightening future that "belongs to crowds" (*M* 16).

But not all crowds, as proven by the horrifying photo of the 1989 Sheffield soccer stadium disaster that introduces Part 1. In this centerless mob (created when the authorities abdicated their responsibility for crowd control) the spectators become the spectacle. Yet these celebrants neither possess nor bestow auras, because their subjectivity seems to emerge only from their rush to mass suicide. As subjects, they both draw us in and defeat our involvement, as the spectator's role is transferred from the crowd to the photographer to the viewers of the photograph; we detachedly look on while the denouement for this "mass of bodies" (*M* 33) unfolds. The replication of the event on TV (and later in photos) aestheticizes it, re-rendering it, according to Karen (always our eyes for such spectacular images), as "a religious painting . . . composed and balanced and filled with people suffering," a "crowded twisted vision of a rush to death as only a master of the age could paint it" (*M* 33, 34). What was once a documentary record becomes a Bruegelesque work of art like *The Triumph of Death* in *Underworld*, as the photo evokes Aristotelian pity and terror but freezes and deflects them by positioning us beyond the chain-link fence along with the photographers. Consequently, the photo seems magically to have authored itself, or to have been authored by the event, which in turn seems to exist solely to engender the photo. The people die for the camera, as the new tragic narrative is played out not on the field or the stage, but in the audience. And yet we feel no Aristotelian catharsis but only a horrified revulsion, a two-dimensional emotion that imitates the form that invokes it. Magic only reproduces dread. This is the chaotic crowd that Moon's indistinguishable devotees replace; lacking a center to give it meaning, the mob devolves from the spectacular to the sickening.

Bill Gray himself first appears as an anonymous spectator watching from his window as a car approaches (*M* 28). Another of DeLillo's men in small rooms, he has acquired an iconic "second self" (*M* 37) through silence, exile, and cunning that makes him a god for people like Scott Martineau, his factotum and now his captor. Because "the image world is corrupt," Bill believes, the "writer who won't show his face is . . . playing God's own trick" (*M* 36–37): Gray is enacting Stephen Dedalus's godlike author who exists "within or behind or beyond or above his handiwork, invisible, refined out of existence" (Joyce, *Portrait* 215). But this god's disappearance has, paradoxically, only made him more visible: precisely *because* he hasn't published or appeared in years, "Bill is at the height of his fame" (*M* 52). Like the real-life Thomas Pynchon or the fictional Bucky Wunderlick, his very resistance to celebrity has made him one. Gray now realizes that his isolation has allowed others to manufacture an aura for him grander than he will ever be.

Later Bill distinguishes between "the life and . . . the consumer event," declaring that "Nothing happens until it's consumed. . . . All the material in every life is channeled into the glow" (*M* 43–44). If, as these words imply, his life has become a TV show, then it is only fitting that Bill doesn't step onstage until after we have met Scott, who seems to have "popped out of a package" (*M* 197). Thus in the opening scene of the novel proper we find Scott in a bookstore, scanning the shelves "for Bill" (*M* 20). As Peter Baker points out, the phrase is ingeniously multivalent, suggesting simultaneously that he is "Checking for Bill's works, checking the shelves on Bill's behalf, or checking for some kind of commodified version of Bill's corpse" (paragraph 12). Bill has been usurped by his brand name which, with its neutrally colored surname and common first name, inscribes his position as a commodity or medium of exchange: he is just a "bill," a universal equivalent, a blank counter upon which others can write and from whom others profit. "Bill Gray" (not even his real name, we later learn) is a non-name, a neutral counter like paper money, a mass of documents that Scott manages.

Bill's invisibility has also become an excuse for his failure to do any meaningful creative work. Although he claims that "the language of my books has shaped me as a man," he no longer recognizes himself in the book he has been writing for the last twenty-three years (*M* 48).[7] The critical "surgeon with a bright knife" (*M* 38), Scott plays Mephistopheles to Bill's Faust: by disparaging the book, he claims to be saying what Bill "deep down wants me to say" (*M* 74). Unfailingly "shrewd in his fervors" (*M* 19), Scott refuses to let Gray publish it, arguing that "the withheld work of art is the only eloquence left" (*M* 67). This Beckett-like epigram may sound impressive (and Beckett is later held up as the last literary author to shape culture), but we can't be sure whether Scott belittles the book because it really is weak or because in writing it Gray has dared to challenge the fetishized image that Scott worships. Nonetheless, Scott keeps the flame, maintaining a sacred crypt in the basement for manuscripts of the work in progress (*M* 32). Formerly trapped in Bill's "material mesh," Scott now holds him hostage, taking over the way a "disease takes over a life" (*M* 60, 45). It is perhaps appropriate that during Brita Nilsson's visit they eat lamb, since Bill's role in the novel (and perhaps in culture) is to play the sacrificial victim to Scott's brand of voracious consumerism.

From images of Bill, Scott turns to those of Bill's artistic antithesis: Andy Warhol (Keesey 180), the second of the novel's spectacular artists. Unlike Gray, Warhol deliberately courted fame, but also effaced himself by retaining control over his public identity, cunningly crafting the image of a vacuous idiot-savant that both drew and deflected media attention. Warhol also borrowed the aura of his celebrated subjects to pre-empt their fame. His oeuvre may thus be read as a meditation on celebrity and spectacle, a composite "portrait of the artist" that reveals the altered conditions of postmodern authorship. Although DeLillo's public profile seems close to Gray's, his work more closely resembles Warhol's: both DeLillo and Warhol comment on fame and authority by imitating the discourses of publicity. Both also share a fascination with crowds, as illustrated by the first Warhol work that Scott sees, the 1963 silkscreen called *Crowd* (*M* 21; a photograph of the print can be found in MacShine 306). This work both exemplifies DeLillo's earlier-cited remark that photos are themselves crowds and, like the Sheffield photo, illustrates how spectators may become spectacular. It seems to Scott that the crowd is "being riven by some fleeting media catastrophe" (*M* 21), but actually the tears in the fabric are part of the design, since this silkscreen, like the Moonie wedding, consists of a single event (or photo) repeated over and over until it becomes something else, something at once phantasmal and corporeal, singular and corporate.

The same is true of the famous silkscreen series of Chairman Mao that is used for the novel's dustjacket art. Scott thinks that the series reveals the "deeper meaning" of Mao (*M* 21): that he was both a singular authority (one who occupied the masses "at a molecular level") and also a crowd, a different Mao for each viewer.[8] As the series continues, Mao's face is painted over amateurishly in garish colors that turn him into a clown or madeup celebrity like Elvis or Marilyn Monroe. Simultaneously beautifying and defacing the image, the paint smears are the sole traces of "originality" or "creativity" in the series. But the point is that Mao has already been "painted over" by everyone who observes him, that his "identity" has been subsumed by his stature as demigod. Thus while Mao's discourse was "spectacular" in seeking to foreclose all but a single response (Debord, *Comments* 28–29), his image invites decoration or desecration. But for Warhol, who knew that Mao's image as a hated and threatening adversary would enhance the work's value to capitalist collectors in the West (Bourdon 317), the series was above all a shrewd business move. The Mao series, then, is a self-portrait: at once homage and parody, it both exemplifies the leveling, commodifying tendencies of a culture that equates a Communist leader and a movie star, and critiques the image-fueled celebrity that produces that leveling. Borrowing Mao's authority to generate "aura," Warhol depicted his own spectacular authorship.

Warhol's work provides a test case for Walter Benjamin's famous analysis of the demise of originality in photographic and cinematic reproduction. For Benjamin, reproduction eliminates the "aura" of a work, which derives from its placement within an historical tradition of individual creativity derived from myth and ritual (223).[9] Scott similarly finds the Mao series "liberating" because it is "unwitting of history" (*M* 21). But in fact the series *wittingly* challenges the Romantic tradition of individual originality. As Arthur Danto suggests, Warhol and pop art demonstrated that "Art was no longer possible in terms of a progressive historical narrative. The *narrative* had come to an end. But this . . . liberated artists from . . . having to follow the 'correct historical line.' It really did mean that anything could be art" (Danto 9). DeLillo similarly states elsewhere that Warhol succeeded in taking an image and "liberating it from history. . . . In the same way that soup is packaged, Warhol packages his Maos, his Marilyn Monroes, and his Elvis Presleys." He goes on to declare that this repackaging of history as commodity is "a little frightening" (Interview with Nadotti 96–97). It was meant to be: as Bourdon notes, Warhol's art was "an intentional provocation" that used surprise and the willful violation of accepted standards to generate publicity; in short, it performed a kind of artistic terrorism. Yet in another sense it is not terroristic, but deeply democratic. By splashing paint on Mao or celebrating Campbell's Soup cans, Warhol reveals the wonder of everyday life, or what DeLillo calls "the radiance in dailiness" ("Outsider" 63). Indiscriminately appropriating everything from the Old Masters to Brillo boxes, Warhol erases the distinction between high and popular culture, showing how art is anything packaged as such.

But DeLillo then suggests that when "the images are identical to each other consumerism and the mass production of art in their most explicit form take over" (Interview with Nadotti 97): in other words, Warhol's work offers too little resistance to commodification. Warholian seriality, DeLillo suggests, too easily slides into a mode of mass production that turns "Warhol" into a fetish. *Mao II* dramatizes such a transformation when Brita contemplates a Warholian piece called *Gorby I*, which seems to embody the "maximum statement about the dissolvability of the artist and the exaltation of the public figure" (*M* 134): even Andy's "aura"—itself a consequence of his demolition of originality—becomes a commodity. What was once revolutionary is now trite; what was once a comment on consumerism is now consumed by it.

And yet, by anticipating the inevitable backlash—by parodying himself—Warhol remains immune from pastiche: originating in kitsch, his work preempts its own kitschification. Moreover, Warhol's "true" identity remains elusive, as his innumerable "self-portraits"—usually multiple images of the artist, sometimes with one face in shadow—demonstrate.[10] He once said, "If you want to know all about Andy Warhol, just look at the surface: of my paintings and films and me, and there I am. There's nothing behind it" (quoted in MacShine 457). On the other hand, he is quoted in *Mao II* as disclosing that "the secret of being me is that I'm only half here" (*M* 135). Perhaps Warhol cultivated his vapid public image in order to protect the other half: the Roman Catholic son of Czech immigrants who visited the church of St. Vincent Ferrer in New York almost every day and gave generously and anonymously to the homeless at the Church of the Heavenly Rest (Rosenblum 36). Warhol's "nutty" (his term) blandness multiplied his faces and extinguished any simple correspondence between artist and work: Andy Warhol became a crowd. "You should always have a product that has nothing to do with who you are, or what people think about you," he once said. "[Y]ou should never start thinking that your product is you, or your fame, or your aura" (quoted in MacShine 459), because "everything is sort of artificial"—including Andy Warhol (quoted in MacShine 461). Warhol cunningly exploited the culture of simulacra by constructing silkscreens to hide behind; unlike Bill Gray, he never entirely believed his own self-dramatizations. By manipulating the packages he purveyed, Warhol carved out a private space within or behind or beyond celebrity and thereby controlled the self-image that was his greatest artistic creation. Warhol's method—courting publicity but recognizing that publicity is inevitably performance—thus resists appropriation more successfully than Gray's.

Even Bill has now realized that his seclusion has backfired and, in either a gesture of resignation or a last-ditch effort to wrest control, has decided to allow Brita Nilsson to take his picture. The fourth author to appear in the novel, Brita occupies a crucial position in its argument about the future. Formerly devoted to photographing atrocities, she eventually recognized that "No matter what I shot, how much horror, reality, misery, ruined bodies, bloody faces, it was all so fucking pretty in the end" (*M* 24–25).

Like the Sheffield photo, her photographs derealized the real by aestheticizing it and distancing the observer from the horror. Now afflicted with a "disease called writers," she travels around the world taking photos of authors, recording a moribund cultural form that her own work is also helping to destroy (*M* 24–25). She aims to present her photographs as unmediated objects by eliminating "technique and personal style," but secretly knows that she is "doing certain things to get certain effects" (*M* 26). In fact her apparent artlessness is the source of her art, which is held up for comparison to that of Gray and DeLillo.

If, as Walter Benn Michaels notes, early photographers justified their work by calling it a form of writing, nowadays it is more common to think of writing as a form of photography (Michaels 220, 239). Thus when Scott thinks of Bill's writing, he conjures up "photographs of tract houses at the edge of the desert"—referring to a specific photo by Garry Winogrand called *New Mexico, 1957* (Keesey 181) that blends innocence and foreboding into an evocative meditation on American magic and dread. (The dustjacket of this book reproduces the photo.) Like Brita and Gray, Winogrand adhered to a "snapshot aesthetic" (Szarkowski 31) that sought the spontaneous and serendipitous. Thus his photographs of writers capture them unposed, in activities that both glorify and reduce them.[11] Likewise, Brita aims both to magnify and diminish Bill. No wonder he feels threatened by her work, which he believes turns him into a "bad actor" creating a "sentimental past for people in the decades to come" (*M* 42). He worries that she is stealing something from him, that their exchange will transfer authority from writing to photography. He may be wise to worry: as Sontag has observed, a photograph offers a "potent means of acquiring [its subject]" that yields "possibilities of control that could not even be dreamed of" in writing ("Image-World" 351). Just as Bill created a "second self" in his work room by writing himself into (and out of) existence, Brita now prints a different Bill, a new currency in which "Nature has given way to aura" (*M* 44). But she is merely confirming what Bill already knows: that he is already incorporated, commodified in his books and in his reclusive image.

If photography is a form of writing and writing is a form of photography—as DeLillo's use of photographs in his book also implies—then the photographer's authorship must be as important as the writer's. Indeed, by the end of the novel it becomes clear that, as Joseph Tabbi puts it, Brita is a more "culturally central artist" than Gray (198), largely because, like Warhol, she appropriates spectacular images for her critical purposes. Although she participates in the image world's raiding of consciousness, she also respects her subjects and shares authorial control by turning the session into a dialogue. Unlike Bill, whose silence and exile only make him more available for appropriation, Brita's work both rests in and resists the cultural evolution that makes writers anachronistic by cunningly acknowledging its complicity in that evolution. While she is certainly shaped by the historical changes that victimize Bill, she also plays a significant role in shaping them: she is *in* the society of the spectacle, but not entirely *of* it. Later in this chapter I elaborate on these claims and suggest that Brita represents a privileged authorial position that resembles DeLillo's own, one we are encouraged to read as the most viable source of creative resistance remaining in the society of the spectacle.

With his image captured, Bill is free to visit his editor, Charlie Everson, who thinks that Bill has a "twisted sense of the writer's place in society. [He] thinks the writer belongs at the far margin, doing dangerous things" (*M* 97). In contrast, Charlie declares that the way to "create a shift in rooted attitudes" is not by writing essays or novels, but by staging "public events" (*M* 98). Thus he plans to exploit Bill's image as a "hunted man" (*M* 97) by mounting a publicity stunt in which Bill will contribute to a public reading of the works of Jean-Claude Julien, a Swiss poet and UN employee who has been taken hostage by a terrorist group: "one missing writer [will] read the work of another" (*M* 99).[12] Bill agrees to participate less because he cares about the hostage or freedom of speech than because he wants to escape from his own captors—which he does at the end of Part 1 by joining the "surge of the noontime crowd" (*M* 103).

AUTHORING TERROR

Part 2 advances another argument about authority, one illustrated by its introductory photograph: a mass of Iranians in front of a huge photo of the Ayatollah Khomeini. That is, it considers the appeal of totalitarian authority, manifest in Khomeini, Mao, and the terrorist leader Abu Rashid. As the novel moves out of Bill's hermitage into the larger world that consumes him, it depicts (as do *Players* and *White Noise*) characters' attempts to reauthorize themselves, to wrest control of the story by contesting or consenting to dominant authorities. Also as in *Players*, DeLillo uses a series of narrative "dispossessions"—cinematic shifts from character to character (Reid 27)—to stage a battle for control of the narrative that mimics the larger struggle for "the future." The framing photo, however, implies that the outcome is a fait accompli: Khomeini's visage glares at us in an arrogant proclamation of his victory.

Yet this part opens instead with another man in a small room—the captured poet Jean-Claude—thus moving from a voluntary hostage (Gray) to an involuntary one. At first full of plans, Jean-Claude soon forgets them and begins to identify with his captors (the so-called Stockholm syndrome). This breakdown of his mental story ("there was no sequence or narrative" to his days [*M* 109]) leads him to lose control over his identity. Thus his hooded anonymity proves the authority of his captor, whose invisibility imitates Joyce's godlike author. As Jean-Claude's initials indicate, his role is to be a sacrificial victim, a martyr to the same economy of authorship that destroys Bill. By the end of the novel Jean-Claude, like *Libra*'s Oswald, becomes a character in somebody else's book, but remains unsure who the "author of his lonely terror" really is (*M* 111). Worse, he ultimately becomes only a "digital mosaic in the processing grid" (*M* 112).

These scenes suggest that terrorist leaders generate a revolution in authorship and character: Jean-Claude is remade not of written words but of electronic bits. In this new mode of circulation, characters are disassembled, disseminated, and then reassembled by reporters, photographers, and cinematographers; authorship is no longer a matter of lonely individuals pecking out words on typewriters, but of invisible leaders giving orders and producing messages, which are then altered and relayed by the media and passed on to consumers. The final products are media events in which the messengers play a crucial "gatekeeping" role (Weimann and Winn 68): by selecting which stories get told, they collaborate in authoring the events. Both characters and audiences are thereby drawn into the electronic mesh.

Karen represents those audiences, whose members imagine themselves in or as crowds. Thin-boundaried and permeable, she lacks a singular identity, insteading acting as what Mark Edmundson calls a "conductor, a relay point . . . for currents of [penetrating] force" (108). She "believe[s] it all, pain, ecstasy," whatever floats through the airwaves; she both carries and transmits "the virus of the future" (*M* 119). When Scott first found her after her brutal deprogramming, he recognized her as "something out of Bill Gray" (*M* 77). But with Bill gone, she is a character in search of an author, and so travels to New York City, stays in Brita's apartment, and roams the streets around Tompkins Square Park, mingling with the homeless and disenfranchised. This city-within-a-city resembles the centerless, desperate crowd in the Sheffield photo—or, in a refrain that runs anonymously through the text, "it's just like Beirut" (*M* 146). To Karen, these people are just a "set of milling images with breath and flesh" (*M* 149) indistinguishable from the poor she has seen on TV. But she accurately grasps that this "life-and-death terrain where everything is measured for its worth" (*M* 151) constitutes a junkyard crammed with the leftovers of America's consumer paradise; as DeLillo elsewhere notes, these people exemplify the "consequence of not having the power to consume" (Interview with Nadotti 93).

Nevertheless, capitalist images retain a vestigial presence here in, for example, the youthful drug-dealer Omar's Warholian T-shirt, with its rows of Coke bottles; in his attempts to sell marijuana; in the shopping carts full of meager possessions; in the "homes" made of discarded TV boxes. If, as DeLillo shows in *Americana*, to consume in America is to dream, these are people whose dreams have been stolen or lost. And dreams are what Moon and other spectacular authors promise to give them back.

While immersing herself in the lives of these lost souls, Karen also studies photographs of disasters, crowds, and holy men. Watching the Tiananmen Square demonstrations on TV, she understands that they illustrate the "preachment of history" which pits "[t]he motley crowd against the crowd where everyone dresses alike" (*M* 177): the novel's argument about the future is staged as a TV show. A little later, Karen watches Khomeini's funeral on television, and imagines herself going "backwards" into the lives of the mourners, feeling their grief (*M* 188). "Here they come, black-clad, pushing toward the grave" (*M* 192): the echo of the novel's opening words solidifies the link between Moon's and Khomeini's authority. In both crowds ancient rituals of community (marriage, funerals) have become media events. Karen understands the mourners perfectly—"the living do not accept the fact that their father is dead. They want him back among them" (*M* 189)—wondering if "we share something with the mourners, know an anguish, feel something pass between us, hear the sigh of some historic grief" (*M* 191). As she did when watching the Sheffield disaster, here again Karen experiences Aristotelian pity and terror from televised images. No longer Bill's creation, she has become, like Jean-Claude, a character in a global electronic narrative, captured by a spectacular authority that extends beyond the nation, beyond the moment, even beyond the grave.

Drawn by these images of disaster, death, and apocalypse, Karen interprets the words of the homeless as "formal prayers" couched in the "ragspeak of shopping carts and plastic bags" (*M* 151, 180). She responds with the zeal of a missionary who knows that "Only those sealed by the Messiah will survive" (*M* 153), and whose "task is to prepare for the second coming . . . [when] all doubt will vanish in the arms of total control" (*M* 179). The transmitter of the "virus of the future," Karen ingests and relays the projective narratives and regulative biographies that patriarchal authorities produce. At first she carried "many voices through New York" (*M* 172), but now the chorus of cries is drowned out by a single sound: like the dog in the famous RCA logo, she has "Master's total voice ready in her head" (*M* 194). Although DeLillo's entire career has been a critique of authoritarian thinking, nonetheless in his portrayal of Karen, as in those of the would-be ascetics in *Running Dog, End Zone,* and *Great Jones Street,* he exhibits genuine sympathy for her spiritual impulses. Indeed, along with Jean-Claude, she is the only character in the novel who is motivated by altruism rather than money or ego. Thus while Karen exemplifies the losses incurred in becoming a spectacular subject, her selflessness and compassion also epitomize its attractions.

If Karen's response to the loss of her "Master" is to revert to older ones, Scott's is to keep the faith, to prepare for Bill's canonization by making lists and waiting for the god's inevitable return. Believing that Bill is "hiding from his photograph" (*M* 143), Scott understands his absence as a "simulated death" like that of Mao (*M* 140). Just as Mao used photographs to announce his return, so, Scott believes, Bill's photo will be his means of "transformation" (*M* 141). But as Scott blows the traces of Bill from the typewriter keys (*M* 143), it is clear that he no longer needs the "real" Bill, because the only one who matters resides in the books and manuscripts under Scott's control. Once Brita delivers the contact sheets of her photo session, Scott owns Bill's image as well. Moreover, the apostle Scott possesses his god's Mysterium Magnum—the knowledge of Bill's real name, Willard Skansey, Jr. "Gray" has been sublimated from a person to a name to an unspoken secret, an adorning possession, a piece of internal property that magnifies not Bill's but Scott's radiance. Thus if Scott is to write a secular gospel that will "sustain and expand" the apostle (*M* 185), Bill's novel must "stay right here, collecting aura and force, deepening old Bill's legend, undyingly" (*M* 224). Bill's "escape" has freed Scott to author *his* Bill Gray.

Charlie's plans for Bill, however, are constantly disrupted by the terrorists, and so Bill is forced to move eastward to London and then to Athens, along the way engaging in a series of discussions with George Haddad, an academic whose affiliation with terrorist groups is certified by his having been "photographed in [their] company" (*M* 131). Bill's dialogues with Haddad dramatize the other debate in the novel, introduced when Bill declared to Brita that "there's a curious knot that binds novelists and terrorists. In the West we become famous effigies as our books lose the power to shape and influence. . . . Now bomb-makers and gunmen have taken that territory. They make raids on human consciousness. What writers used to do before we were all incorporated" (*M* 41). Now, he claims, we need narratives that are "larger and darker" than what novelists can provide (*M* 72), so fictional texts have been replaced by news stories, and books by "tape recorders and cameras" (*M* 42). With Haddad he expands upon his earlier remarks: "What terrorists gain, novelists lose. The degree to which they influence mass consciousness is the extent of our decline as shapers of sensibility and thought. The danger they represent equals our own failure to be dangerous" (*M* 157).

What do Gray and DeLillo mean by "terrorists"? According to Gabriel Weimann and Conrad Winn, terrorism involves three major elements: the use of violence or its threat toward some political end; the transgression of accepted rules of humanitarian conduct; and the use of publicity, along with surprise or unpredictability, to generate fear (Weimann and Winn 22).[13] In contrast, terrorism specialist Walter Laqueur declares that "there is no terrorism *per se*," only "different terrorisms" (9). But Haddad doesn't question the term, and even enlarges on Bill's argument by asserting that writers above all people feel affinity for "the violent man who lives in the dark" (*M* 130): both are men in small rooms who "think[ ] a thought" that "bleeds out into the world" (*M* 132).[14]

Although in interviews DeLillo has similarly remarked on the way that terrorist acts permit needy people to give their lives order ("Art of Fiction" 289), as we have seen, he also challenged the affiliation between terrorists and artists in his early work, satirizing artists like Jean-Luc Godard who believe that art should be "terroristic" (see Chapter 1). Thus I want to argue, along with Peter Baker (paragraph 19), that Gray's remarks about novelists and terrorists are at best halftruths and that DeLillo knows it. For one thing, this part of Gray's "argument about the future" contradicts his earlier charge that the individual has been supplanted by the mass mind. For if the latter is true, then terrorists are no more capable of individually authoring events than novelists are, because their authority depends upon the collaboration of conveyers and consumers. Indeed, because journalists need good stories and terrorists need publicity, terrorists have a symbiotic relationship with the media: reporters court terrorists, explain them, and sometimes even become them (Weimann and Winn 52, 62); conversely, terrorists—like those in "The Uniforms"—play to the cameras.[15] I submit, then, that terrorists don't finally control their own spectacles, because the coherence of act and image that they rely upon for their dissemination of dread requires the collusion of the photographers, producers, and executives who transmit and own the images. In fact, control of the public mind (always fleeting and partial) really belongs to the media corporations who authorize the images that terrorists produce.

Gray claims that Samuel Beckett was "the last writer to shape the way we think and see. After him, the major work involves midair explosions and crumbled buildings. This is the new tragic narrative" (*M* 157). But even if we grant the somewhat dubious premise that Beckett profoundly shaped popular consciousness, it seems obvious that he did so not through his difficult and little-read novels, but through his plays. Likewise, terrorist spectacles—with their scripts, living characters, props, and interviews—resemble not novels but theatrical events (Weimann and Winn 52). To revert to Stephen Dedalus's terms, the art of terrorism is not epic but "dramatic," because its authors' images are present in "immediate relation" to others, while the authors themselves remain distanced and usually invisible (Joyce, *Portrait* 214–15). Haddad, however, claims that we admire terrorists for "their discipline and cunning" (the latter word, we note, is one of Dedalus's principles): "In societies reduced to blur and glut, terror is the only meaningful act. . . . Only the terrorist stands outside" (*M* 157).

But they do not stay there. Not only do terrorists depend upon the cooperation of the media to distribute their spectacles, but their narratives, which are typified by rapid movement from tension and anger to grief and release, also follow the formulas of television shows (Weimann and Winn 97). Adapting Elihu Katz's typology of media events as coronations (which borrow the format of soap operas), conquests (imitations of Westerns), or contests (events that resemble quiz shows), Weimann and Winn describe terrorist actions as "coercive" media events (the true "must-see TV"!) and point out that they employ the same graphic violence, mystery plots, and flashy villains as television crime dramas (Weimann and Winn 91; 107–8). This striking comparison not only exposes how terrorists are spectacular authors; it also suggests that, far from being "outside" of capitalism, terrorists perfectly exemplify how it engulfs even those discourses that seem to oppose it. Like Bill Gray, terrorist authors are already "incorporated"; their dread is but another brand of consumer magic. Haddad himself betrays this fact in describing hostage-taking as a "business" (*M* 155): for him and the terrorist leaders he represents, hostages and their pictures are just commodities like any others. Terrorists and their media collaborators thus prove Debord's assertion that images have become the chief commodity of our culture (*Society* 16).

Bill seems vaguely to recognize the contradictions in Haddad's vision of the terrorist as a "solitary outlaw" (another image taken from Westerns), replying that they aren't individualists, but "perfect little totalitarian states" (*M* 158). Haddad then shifts his ground, citing Mao as a model author who wrote "the history of China . . . on the masses" and provided the regulative biographies and projective narratives "every culture needs in order to survive" (*M* 162). But words were for Mao only weapons to be wielded on "front of the pen" (Mao 251). Thus he demanded that the author hide his or her face in a different way from Dedalus or Gray; according to Mao, an ideal leader accepts the views of the masses, refines them, and then reflects them back with an enhanced aura reflecting *his* image (Mao 272). Thus for Mao words are instruments of domination shaping not the author but the audience. If so, then terrorist leaders are the Mao II of the title: each seeks to be a miniature Mao, creating little replicas of himself who echo his words and mirror his identity.

Bill rejects Maoist "total being" because, he says, "the experience of my own consciousness tells me how autocracy fails . . . how my characters deny my efforts to own them completely, how I need internal dissent, self-argument" (*M* 158–59). The novel, he counters, must be a "democratic shout" in which one voice is "unlike the next" (*M* 159). Against Maoist or terrorist monologism, Bill champions a Bakhtinian heteroglossia in which a word "enters a dialogically agitated and tension-filled environment of alien words, value judgments and accents," where language always lies "on the borderline between oneself and the other" (Bakhtin, "Discourse" 276, 293). For Bill, a novel is a crowd of voices.

Yet this conception of the novel as a locus of "internal dissent" and democratic cacophony also reveals the limits of authorship. In this portrait of the artist, no writer maintains complete control over his or her slipping signifiers or characters, let alone over the fate of his or her books once they are published. Thus, in contrast to Foucault, who defines the author as "the principle of thrift in the proliferation of meaning" ("Author" 159)—a textual function that limits the incessant generation of significance by allowing readers to ascribe them to a named source of ownership and intention—Gray depicts an author as the moderator of an ongoing debate who incites rather than quells the proliferation of meanings. And yet it is this very proliferation that Bill has attempted to stifle by withdrawing from public life. Gray now suggests that such attempts to inhibit linguistic polyvalence—a danger DeLillo has anatomized repeatedly in his work—are embodied in the figure of the hostage, a man in a small room who has lost the ability to shape words and author his identity. In eliminating dissenting voices, terrorist kidnapping constitutes a "rehearsal for mass terror" (*M* 163). But if so, Gray too has rehearsed terror, violating his own principles by seeking to retain sole ownership over his texts; in so doing he has become his own hostage.

Finally, Bill defends the labor of writing, the difficult task of finding authentic expression. Terrorist authority, he argues, is built on an inauthenticity symbolized again by Haddad, for whom words are not material objects to be wrenched forcibly from the soul, but weightless electronic signs one can "fling . . . back and forth" (*M* 164) with a word processor. For Haddad, words are just commodities, and writing is a way to promote power. But if words are commodities that also mold their authors, then terrorists must be subject to commodification precisely *because* of their authorship. Once their acts or images are circulated, they too become others' material—the possessions or characters of those who own the means of dissemination. Spectacular authorship, then, is subject to an economy of identity and authority in which the origin of any event or text is overdetermined and its authorship exploded by the circulation of images; in this economy every message is corporately owned. The error in Bill's novelist/terrorist equation is therefore multiple: not only do terrorists not possess the singular authority that he claims; no brand of authorship does. Imbricated in global capitalism and its culture of spectacle, terrorist authorship submits to the same proliferating mediation as do other forms, and terrorists, like their victims, become commodities.[16]

Bill himself seems ready to become a commodity, to trade himself for Jean-Claude Julien and become a martyr to Romantic authorship. After he is struck by a car in Athens, and even after he is informed—in a wonderfully staged scene in which he "pretends" to be a character in his own novel—that he has a lacerated liver and will soon die unless he gets treatment, he refuses to help himself. Like Hamm in Beckett's *Endgame*, he accepts that there is "no more medication" (*M* 159; cf. Beckett 71). Then, in one of the novel's strangest turns, Bill tries to write about Jean-Claude in a style indistinguishable from the one DeLillo uses at the beginning of Part 1. Bill interprets Jean-Claude's captivity as a self-annihilating fiction that begins to "empty the world of meaning and erect a separate mental state, the mind consuming what's outside itself, replacing real things with plots and fictions. One fiction taking the world narrowly into itself, the other fiction pushing out toward the social order, trying to unfold into it" (*M* 200). But now Jean-Claude is reconstituted as one of Bill's works, as if Gray has "read" the text of his terrorist captor, Abu Rashid, and now embellishes it, using Jean-Claude to "increase the flow of meaning" (*M* 200), and thereby contest Rashid's authority. In this sense Bill's "authoring" of Jean-Claude is actually a desperate attempt to reinvent himself. And yet, according to Bill's earlier remarks, a novelist's duty is to free her or his characters, because to exert authoritarian control over one's creations is not only impossible, but also leads to bad art. Torn by these conflicting models of authority, Bill fails in his attempt to wrest control over the hostage; constantly distracted by the boy captor, he is unable to imagine the captive.[17]

In seeking to inhabit Jean-Claude, Bill is also trying to take his place, confirming his willingness to sacrifice himself. But for what? The significance of Bill's gesture is obviated when his identifying documents are stolen from his corpse. Of course, Bill lost his identity long ago, and so this erasure is merely the terminal point of a fated trajectory, one perhaps ordained by his own god-like Author. But Bill's anonymous death may be his only way out of captivity: he is finally free from the tyranny of "Bill Gray" and the rapacities of his interpreters. Or is he? As Karen and Scott shuffle through Brita's photos of Bill, they discover not his authorship but hers, seeing in them "glimpses of Brita thinking" (*M* 221). In one sense, her authorship follows Bill's liberatory model, because in taking his picture she tried to "deliver her subject from every mystery that hovered over his chosen life" (*M* 221). But because all the photos "might easily be one picture repeated" like Warhol's Maos (*M* 222), in another sense Brita has turned Bill into Bill II, an icon subject to the exegeses of the apostles who own his texts, his photos, and even his name.

Does Gray's fate mean that all authors are inevitably and irredeemably coopted by commerce? Does authority ineluctably pass into the hands of image-mongers and capitalists? In interviews DeLillo has insisted that writers must refuse to be "incorporated into the ambient noise. This is why we need the writer in opposition, the novelist who writes against power, who writes against the corporation or the state or the whole apparatus of assimilation" ("Art of Fiction" 290). But given the conditions outlined in *Mao II*, how is such opposition to be maintained? Certainly not through silence and exile. As DeLillo stated in a 1993 interview, "I don't think that a writer can allow himself the luxury of separating himself from the crowd. . . . It is indispensable to be fully involved in contemporary life, to be part of the crowd, of the clash of voices" (Interview with Nadotti 88). The novelist's response, in other words, must be dialogical: to contribute from within the culture a voice that challenges conformity. The question is not whether, as Scanlan puts it, a novel is "complicit in the process it criticizes" (245)—every novel is a commodity once it is published, and every novelist is subject to commodification, just as every work of art must confront its exchange-value—but rather what one does with this condition. In this regard, all of *Mao II*'s examples of postmodern authorship—Moon, Gray, Warhol, Mao, and Abu Rashid—are deficient in some significant respect.

But the novel does not end with Bill's death. Instead it follows Brita to Beirut, where she plans to photograph Rashid. Brita's abandonment of her nostalgic writers' project seems to confirm the death of the old authorship and her acceptance of a future given over to crowds of people and images. And yet she may also represent a glimmer of hope—albeit an ambiguous one—that authentic authorship and opposition are not dead. For Brita does not just follow trends; she also acts as a weathervane: "everything that came into her mind . . . seemed at once to enter the culture, to become a painting or photograph or hairstyle or slogan" (*M* 165). She molds the culture even as it molds her. Thus, even if she exudes the "contagious glow" left by the virus of the future (*M* 165), she is not merely a Typhoid Mary, but also a potential healer who can diagnose if not treat the contagion.

Brita's role is revealed in the final section of the novel, "In Beirut," which is narrated in present tense to suggest not only its temporal distance from the rest of the novel, but also the eternal present in which this world seems to exist. The section is framed by a photo of three boys in a bunker, flashing either the peace or the victory sign. One boy aims something at us: is it a gunsight or a camera viewfinder? The epilogue identifies the two, as well as the "camera-toters and . . . gun-wavers" who wield them (*M* 197). They are both weapons: but whose? That is the question Brita must now confront.

At first they seems to be Abu Rashid's, as her decision to photograph him seems to magnify his importance. As Barthes notes, "photography . . . photographs the notable; but soon, by a familiar reversal, it decrees notable whatever it photographs" (*Camera* 34). However, his image is only one of many in Beirut's "millennial image mill" (*M* 229), where military groups shoot at the photographs of the leaders of rival groups, where pictures of martyrs and clerics lie next to movie posters and ads for Tahiti vacations, where the red lettering of ads for Coke II (perhaps a reference to Warhol's first important work) reminds Brita of Maoist placards (*M* 230). This latter association beautifully illustrates how capitalist spectacles level differences by "incorporating" everything, so that political leaders are as interchangeable as advertisements. In that sense, photographic images don't magnify but rather diminish what they portray, as crowds of images become as indistinguishable as crowds of people.

Abu Rashid himself is shielded (or trapped) by little boys wearing his photo on their shirts and by his interpreter, who translates and explains his words as Scott does Bill's. When Brita asks Abu Rashid why the boys wear his picture, the interpreter answers that it means "They are all children of Abu Rashid" (*M* 233): Rashid provides the regulative biographies and projective narratives also bestowed by Mao and Moon (*M* 235), and the boys surrender their features to the master's. He argues that his new nation must begin with such children who have no sense of history, and who can be more easily convinced to die for the future. In this ephemeral, image-driven world, history is a commodity ("we do history in the morning and change it after lunch" [*M* 235]), just as hostages are as fungible as "a Rolex or a BMW" (Jean-Claude, for example, has been sold to fundamentalists [*M* 235]). This is, according to Abu Rashid, evidence of a new economy in which terror replaces labor as the source of value. But he doesn't seem to grasp how this new economy also incorporates himself. Indeed, the vagueness of his portrayal suggests his interpellation in the economy of terrorism: he too could be replaced by somebody else with a stronger image or more memorable slogans.[18] And if there is something terrifying about these cold-eyed children, the immaturity of Abu Rashid's minions also suggests the limits of his authority: if he were really so powerful, wouldn't he command adult men and women? He is not Mao but Mao II—a simulacrum, a circulating image soon to be supplanted by another.

Abu Rashid seems to suspect as much, as his repeated queries about what Brita thinks of him imply. Neither he nor Brita seems to believe his declarations. And it is here, in her skepticism about Rashid and her role as mere recorder, that Brita asserts a subversive authority. As she is leaving, "on an impulse" she removes the hood of one of Rashid's boys and snaps his picture (M 236), at once restoring the boy's original identity and re-authoring the boy by acquiring his image, which she is now free to alter or exploit as she wishes. Before she leaves she also makes a point of shaking Rashid's hand and "pronouncing her name slowly" (M 237) as if to say, "I am not a child of Abu Rashid, and I contest your authority, even as my camera records it." Her act reminds Rashid that he is nothing without her, just as the boy is nothing without Rashid: the real author in this scene is not Rashid, but Brita.

The impulsiveness of Brita's decision to photograph the child suggests both an exertion and a suspension of will. And indeed, her authority may lie precisely in the spontaneity of her act, which dramatizes John Berger's analysis of the creative essence of photography. Photographs, he argues, are the products of a "single constitutive choice"—the moment selected to push the button—and thus their meaning is necessarily ambiguous. That is, because the choice of the moment is instantaneous, and because the photographer cannot know for certain how the photo will turn out, photography is "weak in intentionality," and thus permits interference and accident to dilute the photographer's creative authority (quoted in Michaels 237). In turn, this dilution of authority invites (even requires) each viewer to interpret a photograph differently, and thus defeats any attempt—whether by authoritarian leaders or multinational corporations, and whether the photograph is a portrait or an ad—to reduce the image to a univocal meaning. Thus the photograph both expresses the subjectivity of the photographer and demands the superimposition of the viewer's: it is both social and personal, at once a document and an interpretation.[19] Brita's photos therefore reduce Rashid as much as they magnify him; her authorship, with its multivalence and spontaneity, resembles Gray's dialogue of voices more than the authoritarian mastery of Moon or Mao. More significantly, her skeptical gesture of defiance sketches some hope for oppositional authorship. In fact, her authority is more viable than Gray's precisely because she recognizes her involvement in the society of spectacle and, rather than hiding from it, uses it to her own—and perhaps to society's—advantage.

DeLillo's appreciation of her potential is evidenced not only by his giving her the final word in the novel, but also by his incorporation of photographs into the text, a gesture that acknowledges his (reluctant but definite) participation in the society of spectacle. Both Brita and DeLillo, then, practice a modified form of spectacular authorship, at once retaining creative control and relinquishing some of it to the audience, raiding the "raiders" of consciousness. Both work from the inside of the discourse of images to engage in a critical dialogue with it.

At the end of the novel Brita returns to a friend's abandoned apartment and listens to the city, a place where gunshots and mortars compete with radios and TV in a cacophonic aural equivalent of its visual clutter. The repeated phrase "Our only language is Beirut" signifies not only the clash of cultures and ideologies and the apocalyptic yearnings that have wasted the city, but also its allegorical role as the landscape of the future. But the last scene in the novel returns us to the beginning: a tank rolls down the street, not to shoot at the apartment buildings, but to celebrate a wedding party (*M* 239–40). This time, however, it is not an illustration of spectacular authority but an assertion of the vitality of community. Unlike the brides in Yankee Stadium, this woman looks "surpassingly alive . . . [and] free of limits" (*M* 240). Although this moment of joy and freedom is fleeting, nevertheless its presence suggests that ancient rituals endure despite the glut of images and the din of explosions. If the Moonie wedding manifests how capitalism and spectacle have altered subjectivity and sociability, this Beirut wedding suggests how sociability in turn resists and modifies spectacle. The "new tragic narrative" of bombs and hostages has briefly been ousted by comedy.

Turning away from this scene, Brita sees a flash. It is not the day's first exchange of gunfire but a camera and flash unit that reminds us that she owns a weapon with as much power as Rashid's rifles. Likewise, by using her weapon in his text, DeLillo demonstrates how authors may incorporate spectacle without being entirely incorporated by it. If, as Gray maintains, an author's identity may be reshaped by his or her work, then we may see DeLillo, through Brita, remodeling his vision of authorship and imitating her position at once within and against spectacular culture. If his gesture signals an acceptance of the ubiquity of spectacle and commodification, it also suggests how novels may push out toward the social order, not to become part of the crowd, but to engage the crowd in remaking that order.

Chapter 8
"Everything is connected"

Containment and Counterhistory in *Underworld*

Near the climax of his drug-aided epiphany on a desert gunnery range, *Underworld*'s Matt Shay concludes that "everything connects in the end, or only seems to, or seems to only because it does" (*U* 465). Although this insight—repeated in slightly different words several times in the novel (*U* 289, 408, 825)—may resemble nothing more than the paranoid fantasies of loony conspiracy theorists, in fact it describes the major theme and organizational principle of *Underworld*. Two examples will illustrate this convergence of technique and theme. Matt is fascinated with a videotape depicting a murder committed by the so-called Texas Highway Killer. The victim, a man in his forties driving a medium Dodge, is (we later learn) Judson Rauch, who once owned the ball that Bobby Thomson hit into the seats at the Polo Grounds to beat the Dodgers and win the 1951 National League pennant for the Giants (see *U* 179–80). The ball passes through several hands, including those of advertising executive Charles Wainwright, his son Chuckie, and memorabilist Marvin Lundy, who sells it to Matt's older brother, Nick. These characters are connected in other ways as well: during the Vietnam War Chuckie serves as navigator on a B-52 bomber nicknamed "Long Tall Sally"; this same bomber is later transformed into a work of art by Klara Sax, who in 1952 had a brief affair with Nick Shay. In 1974 Klara watches another home movie—the notorious Zapruder film of John F. Kennedy's assassination—in which another "man in his forties" (*U* 496) is shot while riding in a car. "The two rivers meet" (*U* 179):

the ball and the murders form a circuit linking Matt, Rauch, Marvin, the Wainwrights, Nick, and Klara, while also connecting them to the most important public events of the era. Yet none of them could trace the entire chain, because the connections lie underground, visible only through the lens of art.

A second example: Chuckie Wainwright's plane "Long Tall Sally" drops Agent Orange on the jungles of Vietnam; during his stint in Vietnam, Matt remarks that the drums of Agent Orange resemble "cans of frozen Minute Maid" (*U* 463); a few years earlier, one of the elder Wainwright's clients was Minute Maid orange juice (*U* 532). In 1974, as Klara watches Sergei Eisenstein's long-lost film *Unterwelt*, she recognizes the soundtrack as Prokofiev's overture for the opera *Love for Three Oranges* (*U* 442), and during her work to transform "Long Tall Sally" into an artwork she wears an orange T-shirt (*U* 67). Near the end of the novel, in the 1990s, the aged nun Sister Edgar—Matt Shay's former grade-school teacher who lived in the Bronx the same time as Klara—sees what she believes to be an angelic apparition on a billboard. The billboard is selling Minute Maid orange juice (*U* 820–22). This complex skein indicates a unity linking advertising, war, religion, and underground art, yet no character grasps the unity. Everything is connected in the novel and in the society it portrays—but only in the underworld.

One could list dozens of such motifs, which in one sense are the kind of devices that give shape and coherence to any novel as long and complex as *Underworld*. But in this novel they point to a deeper level of connection that Matt senses when he asks: "how can you tell the difference between orange juice and agent orange if the same massive system connects them at levels outside your comprehension?" (*U* 465). Two such massive systems—capitalism (and the consumer society it has engendered) and what President Eisenhower called the "military industrial complex"—combined in the Cold War era, whose history is underwritten by the mountains of waste it left behind. The architects of the waste and weapons systems also colluded to devise a totalizing ideology of containment: just as the U. S. government tried to contain the Soviet Union by building more and more nuclear weapons that it could never use, so we also built landfills to house the remains of our rampant consumption. The ideology of containment thus encompasses weapons and waste, whose devastating physical and psychological repercussions constitute DeLillo's primary theme in *Underworld*. The novel dramatizes how the proliferation of weapons and waste has fueled a rigid binary thinking, an "Us versus Them" mentality, that has alienated us from nature and from our own better nature.

Near the end of *Underworld* Nick Shay, now a fiftyish "waste analyst," visits the former Soviet Union, where Viktor Maltsev, his Virgilian cicerone to the Russian underworld, declares that "waste is the secret history, the underhistory" of civilization (U 791). Here engineers dispose of radioactive waste by blowing it up with nuclear weapons. Nick senses that in destroying waste with atomic bombs they are bringing about "the fusion of two streams of history" (U 791). But the convergence of weapons and waste was there to be discovered all the time, so that the emergence of this underhistory only exposes what we should have known all along: "what we excrete comes back to consume us" (U 791). What makes "everything connect," then, is not only quasi-magical objects such as the Thomson baseball, but the broad streams of weapons and waste, and the shared sense of *un*connectedness—of loss, alienation, dread, and confusion—that those streams feed. These implacable powers mold individuals invisibly, making us feel that forces beyond our ken control our actions, beliefs, and desires.

Yet *Underworld* also dramatizes how waste cannot finally be contained. Uncontainable energies drive people to construct interlocking underworlds that resist oppressive institutions, to write a counterhistory that undoes official narratives. Nourished from below, the spirit of resistance wells up to mount guerrilla attacks on the dominant culture. Outcasts and artists, ignored or discarded by the mainstream, respond to unseen waves and radiation, and fashion from dread varieties of redemptive magic. This spirit of resistance is embodied, DeLillo suggests, in works such as Eisenstein's *Unterwelt*, Klara Sax's repainted B-52s, and Sabato Rodia's Watts Towers. These works—salvage operations, recycling projects—redeem and transmogrify the refuse of consumerism and the Cold War. DeLillo offers *Underworld* as a similar act of resistance and redemption, submerging us in the culture of weapons and waste so that we may reemerge transformed. To carry out this difficult act, he borrows from the artists he depicts, organizing the text by juxtaposing fragments in a quasi-Eisensteinian montage, and adopting Rodia's method of bricolage to build his text from the debris of the past. *Underworld* thus presents a series of fragments—displayed mostly in reverse chronology—that dialectically guide the reader toward a synthetic fusion, so that we too must labor to make everything connect. The slogan that "everything is connected" thus describes both DeLillo's working method and the social philosophy to which the novel points, an ecological ideal in which recycled waste represents a form of grace.

DeLillo's artistic design thus reveals the undercurrents from which a truly oppositional art may arise, and suggests that only an art that critically examines those "massive systems" from the inside can escape recontainment. Thus although *Underworld* amply documents the devastation wrought by weapons and waste, it also demonstrates how the fusion of these two streams engenders what DeLillo calls, in an essay on the novel, "counterhistory" ("Power of History" 63). That is, *Underworld* embodies how fiction can generate a "version of the past that escapes the coils of established history" ("Power of History" 63). Modifying the despairing conclusions of *Mao II*, it dramatizes how an art that pits the "idiosyncratic self" against oppressive institutions can become an "agent of redemption" ("Power of History" 62, 63) by recycling the waste of consumer society and detoxifying the psychic fallout from atomic weapons. And yet, precisely because of its mosaic-like structure and the insurmountable isolation of its major characters, *Underworld* stops short of conclusively affirming a communal salvation. Its final, pacific word is offered hopefully but tentatively as an ideal that may nonetheless remain out of reach.

PROLOGUE: LONGING ON A LARGE SCALE

DeLillo found the seed for *Underworld* in a pair of headlines from the October 4, 1951 *New York Times* ("Power" 60). One the left side of the front page was a story headlined "Giants Capture Pennant, Beating Dodgers 5–4 in 9th on Thomson's 3-Run Homer"; on the right side a headline read "Soviet's Second Atom Blast in 2 Years Revealed by U.S.; Details Are Kept a Secret." Bobby Thomson's homer, which provided the climax to a thrilling tale of underdogs prevailing, long ago passed into public consciousness as a shared American moment like the Kennedy assassination. In contrast, the Bomb was "born secret" (Bok 166) and was often depicted in popular journalism as the era's biggest secret (see Hilgartner et al. 33).[1] Baseball versus The Bomb, public events versus secret information, joy versus the "Triumph of Death": DeLillo plays these oppositions in counterpoint throughout *Underworld*, but also implies that they partake of each other.

Despite government suppression, stories about atomic power filled the *Times* that week in October 1951. The stories bear witness to an uneasy mixture of fascination and fear. For example, a series of stories beginning on October 3 reports on the dislocations South Carolinians are undergoing to make way for the Savannah River nuclear weapons plant (Freeman, "15,000 in Carolina" 22).[2] In the second story of the series citizens refer to themselves as "the first displaced persons of World War III" (Freeman, "Atom Plant" 7). They wouldn't be the last. The revelation of the Soviet test occurred just as the U.S. military was announcing a new series of atomic tests in Nevada that would "include experiments designed to show the effect of a tactical weapon against frontline combat units" (Lawrence 6, column 2). The paper fails to mention that these effects were to be measured by using American soldiers as guinea pigs.[3] The October 4 issue also depicts the debate over weapons containment or proliferation: on the one hand, Senator Brien McMahon urges the mass production of atomic bombs so that we can "make our country invincible in full-scale war and exempt from the cold-war threat of bankruptcy" ("A.E.C." 7); on the other hand, Bernard Baruch is quoted as retaining hope for "atom control" (6, column 1). This anxiety and ambivalence is even displayed on the entertainment pages, which feature an ad for Robert Wise's film *The Day the Earth Stood Still*, in which an alien comes to earth and delivers an ultimatum: live in peace or be destroyed. Clearly the fall of 1951, with Senator McCarthy on the rampage and weapons testing accelerating, was a watershed period for Cold War culture. Indeed, John Duvall may be correct in suggesting that October 4, 1951, when the United States had to acknowledge that the Soviets were regularly testing atomic weapons, was the first day of the Cold War (Duvall, "Baseball" 294).

The early 1950s were also the Golden Age of baseball, especially in New York, which boasted three perennial contenders—at least one New York team was in the World Series every year between 1947 and 1956—within a few miles of each other. But while atomic weapons stir a deep unease about the future, baseball channels the communal awareness of an ideal past that acts as anodyne to atomic anxiety. "Longing on a large scale is what makes history" (*U* 11), DeLillo's narrator states at the beginning of *Underworld*. What better emblem of such longing than baseball? The game bears more history than any other American sport, and Bobby Thomson's home run off Ralph Branca to win the National League pennant for the Giants is perhaps the most storied moment in the history of the game. Its fame derives from the dramatic fashion in which the game ended, from its location in the media center of New York City, and from the way the Giants charged from 13 1/2 games back on August 11 to catch the Dodgers on the last day of the season. Yet DeLillo adduces this particular game as much to dramatize myth as to document history. Baseball has long been associated—sometimes unconvincingly—with fundamental American myths and ideologies: rags-to-riches individualism, the relationship between fathers and sons, the demise of the pastoral, and most of all with a nostalgic desire to return home that is incorporated into the very structure of the game.

In baseball mythology the park or field becomes, according to Deeanne Westbrook, a "consecrated piece of ground" set off from the profane world, a "space and a structure where the unconscious can make itself heard," a place "hospitable . . . to the sacred" (45, 53). In such a place "local yearnings" like those of Cotter Martin, the fourteen-year-old African-

American boy who crashes the gate to attend the Dodgers-Giants game, are blended with those of the assembled spectators, each of whom carries "some solemn scrap of history" (*U* 11, 16). DeLillo indicates this shared history by narrating in present tense—as if implying that the game continues to take place in the minds of Americans—and sporadically in second person, as his camera eye zooms and cuts from the field to the stands. The cheering spectators, like the crowds in *Mao II*, become "the force of some abject faith, a desperate kind of will toward magic and accident" (*U* 36) that muffles and vents anxiety.

These magical aspects of the game are presented by Giants announcer and baseball theologian Russ Hodges, who thinks of a souvenir ball as "a priceless thing . . . that seems to recapitulate the whole history of the game every time it is thrown or hit or touched" (*U* 26). Hodges chronicles the game for the radio audience and also furnishes DeLillo's readers with the historical "narrative that lives in the spaces of the official play-by-play" (*U* 27). He recalls broadcasting simulated games in which he invented most of the action by filling in the gaps left by statistics (*U* 25). Yet his narrative of the real "thing that happens in the sun" (*U* 25) is no less a salutary collective fiction, based upon the belief that the game brings communities together.[4] But baseball has also been employed to promote less sunny ideologies. John Duvall shows how the game was used to sell cultural imperialism and instill the "mythos of capital," as well as to whitewash racism and present a mythically unified nation, even though African Americans were barred from playing in the major leagues until 1947 (Duvall, "Baseball" 288–89, 295). Nonetheless, Cotter is able to strike up a brief friendship with the white businessman Bill Waterson, who invokes the same terms— history and faith—that Hodges uses to appeal to his listeners (*U* 31).[5]

More importantly for my purposes, baseball and atomic energy were affiliated in the popular press and in people's minds. For example, one journalist observer of the American nuclear tests at Bikini atoll described the bombs as "atomic baseballs" (quoted in *Radio Bikini*). The October 4 *Times* also featured a story that describes the upcoming Nevada atomic tests as "atom games" ("Secrecy" 6). And in an "as-told-to" newspaper story in the same issue, Bobby Thomson states that he didn't run the bases after his homer, but "rode around 'em on a cloud" (43). He probably was not thinking of a mushroom cloud, but it is difficult not to draw the connection, especially since elsewhere in the *Times* the home run is referred to as a "blast" and soon became popularly known as "the Shot Heard 'Round the World" (see *U* 669, where Albert Bronzini confuses the two blasts).

The kinship between the ball game and The Bomb, as well as the broader relationships between publicity and secrecy, between community and the "Triumph of Death," are shown most clearly when FBI director J. Edgar Hoover learns of the Soviet test. The Director, attending the game with Frank Sinatra, Jackie Gleason, and Toots Shor, realizes that "fame and secrecy are the high and low ends of the same fascination" (U 17). A connoisseur of all forms of power, he imagines the explosion as a "red bomb that spouts a great white cloud like some thunder god of ancient Eurasia" (U 23). At almost the same moment that Thomson wins the pennant for the Giants and Jackie Gleason vomits his late repast, some torn pages of Life displaying a color reproduction of Peter Bruegel's painting The Triumph of Death float down on the Director (U 41). Bruegel's picture of souls writhing in damnation and bodies descending to the underworld flutters from the sky like the lethal radioactive fallout that rained on Americans throughout the 1950s. In its foreground a skeletal throng is being herded into the gates of hell, which the Director likens to a "subway tunnel or office corridor" (U 41), but which also looks much like a stadium gate (See Marijnissen and Seidel 124–25). The picture thus reminds Hoover that all the people at the game share one thing at least: they are all "sitting in the [Bomb's] furrow of destruction" (U 28).

Hoover is attracted to this display of "Terror universal," which brings to mind the barren Kazakh site where the Soviets tested their device (U 50). But he is even more fascinated by its invocation of the theology of secrets: "what secret history are they writing? There is the secret of the bomb and there are the secrets that the bomb inspires, things even the Director cannot guess. . . . [T]he genius of the bomb is printed not only in its physics of particles and rays but in the occasions it creates for new secrets. For every atmospheric blast . . . a hundred plots go underground, to spawn and skein" (U 50–51). As I noted in Chapter 2, the atomic bomb, because of the secrecy with which it has always been surrounded, has become the Deus Otiosus—Hidden God—of the twentieth century (Chernus 18). The secrets of atomic weapons are not only those of design and production, but also those about fallout and radiation that the American government hid from its citizens, who remained in a cloud of unknowing about what their leaders were doing to them and their environment.[6] The Bomb engendered underworlds—not only the secrets of powers and dominions, but also the private fears of Americans and the remedies sought to quell them. Indeed, Spencer Weart argues, as nuclear energy became the "modern Arcanum," it came to represent all "the cruelest secrets of the heart: forbidden aggressive prying; treachery; the drive to master others; and the urge to destroy . . . even one's own city" (Weart 391, 126). Hoover embodies these cruel secrets as well as the desperate quest they fostered for a perfect security, one that instead created a "world of total insecurity" (quoted in Boyer 351).

This desire for absolute security readily mutates into a rigid form of dualistic thinking in which absolute good battles absolute evil (Chernus 32). Hoover thrives on such binaries, on the feeling of "deep completion" (*U* 51) that having an enemy brings to one. A man with an air-filtration system and an elevated toilet (to ward off infection) in his house, the real Hoover pictured his foes as dirt, as "rats, vermin, regurgitating their filth to despoil the clean picture of American manhood and womanhood"; their viciousness would lead to "filth in mind, filth in living, filth in morals and bodily health" (quoted in Dumm 83). J. Edgar Hoover conceived of his job as waste containment. "Containment" was also the name of the official policy that the United States adopted toward the Soviet Union in the postwar period. In the words of its primary architect, George Kennan, containment was designed to dam the "fluid stream," to check the Soviets' dangerous impulses (quoted in Nadel 16). But Kennan's words suggest that the real source of those impulses lay not in Russia but in our own secret urges to overcome the dam. Thus was nourished a terror of the unseen that, as DeLillo locates it in Hoover's neurotic psyche, is projected outward from one's hidden yearnings and onto dark Others. Hoover and other Cold Warriors parleyed a pathological fear of invasion into a public policy whereby all outsiders were seen as threats to the bodily purity of the United States. It scarcely matters whether the invaders are bugs or Communists; as Hoover comments before attending the Black-and-White Ball later in the novel, "the sense of infiltration was itself a form of death" (*U* 557). By the end of the 1950s, however, the fear of contamination had migrated in the public mind from Communism to nuclear energy itself (Weart 189), as citizens gradually became aware that the bounties of consumer society—the Packards, Playtex bras, and Motorola TVs advertised in *Life* next to *The Triumph of Death* (*U* 39)—could also produce their own creeping death. The spectators at the game are thus unified not only by baseball, commodities, and language, but by a shared dread that the ideology of containment encouraged.

Hoover thus symbolizes how Cold War history is founded upon acts perpetrated in secret. Thomson's homer seems to nurture an opposing history. According to Hodges, it "makes people want to be in the streets, joined with others, telling others what has happened" (*U* 47). He muses that the spectators will carry something "out of here that joins them all in a rare way, that binds them to a memory with protective power" (*U* 59), and believes that "this midcentury moment enters the skin more lastingly than the vast shaping strategies of eminent leaders" (*U* 60). Against the public-life secrecy enacted by Hoover and his ilk, Hodges invokes "the people's history" written in communal rituals like baseball. Although, as I have noted, DeLillo acknowledges the mystifications in this history, nonetheless he portrays the game as a significant form of what Westbrook calls "crisis art": works that permit humans to "shape, control, and hence to live with or beyond absolute, zero-degree terror" (148). Still, baseball alone cannot resist institutional oppression and remold community. That task requires idiosyncratic individuals—especially artists—who respond to and reflect shared desires; *Underworld* depicts a number of such crisis artists in its pages. Only such art, DeLillo asserts, can counteract "the enormous technology of war" ("Power" 63). And such resistance can be executed only by an art of crisis that embodies the fusion of waste and weapons, and that dramatizes the inextricable relationships between small-scale sins and large-scale longings.

WASTE

Fallen Angel

Sixteen-year-old Dodgers fan Nick Shay did not attend the game at the Polo Gounds, but only listened to the radio broadcast from his rooftop. Nevertheless the Dodgers' loss and the Thomson baseball, which he eventually comes to own, symbolize the trajectory of his life. The Polo Grounds for him restages the *Aeneid*'s "Groves of Blessedness," where heroes of old engage in contests surrounded by the accouterments of their professions (Westbrook 109; Virgil 6.845–54; pp. 159–60). Even in the novel's present, some forty years after the game, Nick maintains that he "died inside when [the Dodgers] lost" (*U* 93). Yet the Thomson baseball is the "only thing in my life that I absolutely had to own," because for Nick it is not about the triumph of the underdog but about "Branca making the pitch. It's all about losing . . . about the mystery of bad luck, the mystery of loss" (*U* 97). At a later Dodgers-Giants game in Los Angeles, Nick and his friends sit behind a glass window, as insulated from the crowd physically as Hoover was emotionally. One loss that the ball signifies, then, is that of the vital interlinked community and connections across races and classes that the 1951 game briefly enabled. Further, Nick synecdochically represents a larger American pattern of loss and incomplete redemption that characterizes the Cold War era. But these collective aspects are for Nick less significant than its personal meaning: the ball elicits an overwhelming nostalgia that both verifies his identity and ratifies a personal narrative of the fall. A vestige of his first life, the ball also signifies the living death that he now leads.

For Nick has "fallen from grace" (*U* 95), and the novel's title indicates his metaphoric place of residence: like Satan (also called Old Nick), he is a fallen angel, a once-bright star who begins in glory but ends in the darkness of self-imposed damnation. His original sin is a careless or unconsciously deliberate murder committed in his youth against George Manza, an older friend who introduced him to a peculiar form of manhood. In Dante's underworld, Nick would thus be relegated to Circle 7 of upper hell, reserved for those who commit violence against their neighbors (*Inferno* XII; 111–14). But Nick tours a series of underworlds in the novel, guided by a diverse set of cicerones: Simeon Biggs, who welcomes him to the waste management industry and takes him through African-American night life in Los Angeles; Brian Glassic, who introduces him to Marvin Lundy and mediates his purchase of the baseball; Viktor Maltsev, a Russian engineer who shows him the Kazakh test site and the Museum of Misshapens. Nick also reincarnates other visitors to the underworld, particularly Aeneas, who descends to the lower world in search of his dead father; unlike Virgil's pious hero, however, Nick never finds his progenitor. Nor does he ever fully ascend from the domain of Dis, despite living in the symbolically named city of Phoenix (one of many bird symbols in the novel). Rather, he remains in a self-made penitentiary, torn between his desire to contain waste and his need to wallow in it. Thus, even though he has risen from the ashes of his delinquent youth, he still looks back with longing to those "days of disarray" (*U* 810) before his Paradise was lost.

We first meet Nick in 1992, as he drives his Lexus (a striking contrast to the dilapidated stolen Chevy he drove in his youth) across the desert. Nick is seeking Klara Sax, with whom he had a brief affair in 1952, aiming to "discharge the debt to memory" (*U* 64). His most troubling memories, however, are those of his father, bookie Jimmy Costanza, a dodger of responsibility who went out for a pack of Luckies when Nick was eleven years old and never came back. Like Aeneas, Nick repeatedly undergoes a "ritual replication of his experience" in order to be free of his past (Macdonald 29). But he never exorcises his New York ghosts, and although he jokes that he lives a "quiet life in an unassuming house in a suburb of Phoenix. Pause. Like someone in the Witness Protection Program" (*U* 66), the humor does not conceal the underlying truth: though he tries to convince himself that he lives "responsibly in the real" (*U* 82), Nick is hiding from himself.

It is difficult to recognize in this haunted, solitary man the gregarious, delinquent adolescent of 1951. The youthful Nick is eager to leave the past behind: as early as the day after the playoff game, Nick recognizes that the Dodgers' loss marks the end of his childhood, "the last thin thread connecting him to another life" (*U* 679). After quitting school to hang out in pool halls and on the street, he takes a job unloading trucks, which eventually leads to his sexual initiation with Klara, then the thirty-two-year-old wife of his former science teacher, Albert Bronzini. These two encounters take place under the watchful eye of a print of Whistler's *Arrangement in Gray and Black*—the famous portrait of his mother—which foreshadows for Nick and recalls for us the older Nick's own condition at the opening of the novel: as Klara asserts, the woman in the painting is "lost . . . in memory" (*U* 748).[7] During their second rendezvous Nick places a pair of nylon stockings over his face, his thief's disguise signaling his attempt to assume an adult role for which he is unprepared. In contrast to Nick, who perceives the affair as proof of manhood, Klara views it as one attempt to forge a private space free from a husband who thinks of her painting as a hobby. She envisions her life as an artwork in progress, with Nick playing "The Young Man, like a character in a coming-of-age novel" (*U* 747). Nevertheless, she thus plays the same Oedipal role for Nick that the sculptor Sully does for *Americana*'s David Bell. In having sex with her, Nick can both replace his father and take revenge on the mother who wasn't attractive enough to keep him.

Nick's conversations with his pal, the garbageman's son Juju, exhibit the bravado of a teenager who is "angry about . . . the thing that ran through his mind even in his sleep" (*U* 705): the missing father who always "kept a distance . . . Like he's somewhere else even when he's standing next to you" (*U* 691). Adhering—despite strong evidence to the contrary (see *U* 765)—to the belief that Jimmy was executed by mobsters to whom he owed money, Nick unconsciously seeks a replacement father on whom he can release his anger and shame. He finds one in George Manza, a waiter who serves as his Virgilian guide to crime, "that particular life. Under the surface of ordinary things" (*U* 761). But George is no mere visitor, as Bronzini discovers when he happens one day upon him, nodding out on heroin, in his squalid lair: George lives in the underworld (*U* 770). This condition is further represented by his use of heroin, associated throughout the novel (via the Yiddish *shmek*, or "shit") with waste and death (*U* 594, 329). When George discloses his habit to Nick, the latter feels that "George had cut him down to size . . . had taught him a lesson in serious things" (*U* 727). George thus embodies the delightful danger of the underworld that Nick's father courted and that the middle-aged Nick strives mightily to deny.

When George shows Nick his sawed-off shotgun, the most important event of Nick's life takes place. Aiming the weapon at the older man, Nick seems to see a rare "brightness in [George's] eye," as if he were urging him silently to shoot (*U* 780). Weapons and waste converge as Nick pulls the trigger, fatally shooting George through the head. Nick rewinds the moment over and over again in the videotape of his mind, but no matter how often he relives it, he never fully grasps the reasons for his act, or even determines whether he had a reason (see his explanation to Donna—*U* 299). The psychiatrist at the reform school to which he is sent tells him that his father was "the third person in the room" that day (*U* 512), and indeed the Oedipal motivations behind the crime seem almost too obvious: Nick must kill the surrogate father out of rage at the real one; or perhaps he must kill George for not being up to the task. The murder of George completes the Oedipal pattern, and both marks the end of Nick Shay's boyhood and closes the curtain on the Bronx as it was—a lively community where everyone was connected. By the time we revisit it in late 1980s, the Bronx has become a wasteland of missing men and lost lives; yet its squalor represents only a different form of the same disease that plagues Nick Shay.

In reform school, Nick craves the reassurance of a functioning penal system, because "we weren't worth much if the system designed to contain us kept breaking down" (*U* 502–3). But he eventually learns to "contain" himself when he is sent to a special school in Minnesota run by Jesuits, where Bronzini's friend Father Paulus takes Nick under his wing and, in a pedagogical scene that recalls Stephen Dedalus's conversation with the Dean of Studies in Joyce's *Portrait*, requires Nick to recite the parts of a shoe. Through such exercises one discovers how to "escape the things that made you" (*U* 543). According to Paulus, "rage and violence can be elements of productive tension" (*U* 538); thus to gain "an ethical strength that makes him decisive, that shows him precisely who he is," he must not dismiss his appetites, but harness them. He must experience all passions, "if only to contain them" (*U* 539). The lesson is that in containment lies virtue and power, just as, according to his partner Clyde Tolson, Hoover's authority derives from "the rejection of unacceptable impulses" (*U* 573).

Although Nick doesn't entirely control his impulses (his later fling with Amy Brookhiser, for example, results in a Mexican abortion and an enormous load of guilt), he is generally quite successful at self-containment. For example, when in New York during the 1965 blackout, he resists a friend's blandishments to visit the old neighborhood (*U* 620). Nick prefers to "black out" his past, so that thirteen years later he can proudly proclaim himself a "country of one" (*U* 275). By 1978, when he accepts a corporate position with Waste Containment (Whiz Co), Nick pictures himself as an Aeneas, a "sturdy Roman wall," a "made man" (*U* 275). This section, "The Cloud of Unknowing," titled after a late medieval theological work, aptly describes Nick's condition: a man as blind as Oedipus about his own motives.[8] No matter what he does, he still feels like an "imposter" (*U* 339).

During his sojourn in Los Angeles (a suitable home for a fallen angel) Nick seduces a "swinger" named Donna by quoting to her from *The Cloud of Unknowing*. According to its anonymous author, God gains power by withholding Himself from us, so that one can never understand Him by the use of reason. He may be approached only when the seeker places a "cloud of forgetting" between him- or herself and all earthly things (*Cloud* 128). To perform this exercise, the supplicant should focus on a single word, preferably of a single syllable, such as "God" or "love" or perhaps "peace" (*Cloud* 134; cf. *U* 295), which will be "your shield and your spear, whether you are riding in peace or in war. With this word you are to beat upon this cloud and this darkness above you" (*Cloud* 134; later I argue that DeLillo uses the final word in *Underworld* similarly, as a spear and shield against weapons and waste). Through this text Nick learned to think of God as a "long unlighted tunnel"—as the pathway to a psychic underworld. He discovered that we "cherish [God's] negation," the very fact that He seems beyond us or absent. In other words, Nick has determined that God's power comes from His secrecy—from the way that He contains Himself (*U* 295). Nick's ascetic self-containment thus again parallels Hoover's fascination with the atomic Deus Otiosus: he not only imagines God as his missing father, but also imitates Him by hiding in a dark tunnel and living in a "cloud of unknowing."

However, Nick uses *The Cloud of Unknowing* and a phrase from St. John of the Cross—*todo y nada*—not to arrive at a contemplative state, but to make a sexual conquest, to prove something to himself, and perhaps to give himself a chance to confess his sins. Thus he ends up telling Donna the story of his murder and penitence, a tale he has never shared with his wife, Marian. Afterward, back in Phoenix, he admits to Marian his adultery, but still never tells her the larger truth about his past. Although he claims that "silence is the condition you accept as the judgment on your crimes" (*U* 345), it is obviously also a means of self-protection. How fitting that Nick works for Waste Containment: he is engaged in a similar enterprise with his personal waste. Just as his company works to package and restrict hazardous waste, so Nick tries to contain his memories within carefully guarded boundaries that nonetheless permit traces of his internal poisons to leach from his psychic subterranean and taint his life. When it is so effortfully contained, waste spawns a near-phobic fear of contamination—a "condomology"—that is forcefully dramatized when Nick's colleague Brian Glassic brings him to an emporium for prophylactics that wears that name (*U* 109).[9] When Nick visits a colossal landfill that seems to him to function as a "giant prophylactic device" for the ejaculations of consumer society (*U* 285), it becomes clear that condoms and landfills are equally forms of "containment." In Nick's case, the condom is psychic more than physical, and although it keeps him safe, it also renders him sterile.

Nick's need for a "faith to embrace" attracts him to Waste Containment, whose operations give to garbage a "whisper of mystical contemplation" (*U* 282).[10] But the true magnitude of his new mission is conveyed when Simeon Biggs takes him to the large sanitary landfill just mentioned. Covered by an "immense shimmering sheet," the landfill carries a "drastic grandeur, even a kind of greatness"—a power and magic that derive both from its size and from its secrecy (*U* 285). Landfills hide garbage under a cloud of unknowing that increases its dimensions and mystery. This religious attitude toward waste is further enhanced by the provocations of Jesse Detwiler, a "waste theorist" and formerly one of the garbage guerrillas who plagued Hoover. *Underworld*'s Murray Siskind, Detwiler understands the relationship between secrecy and awe; he knows that waste, the "best-kept secret in the world" (*U* 281), evokes the radiance and dread we associate with divinity. He urges that we bring waste out into the open, demystify it, acknowledge our relationship with it; but he also believes that we should isolate the most toxic waste, because containment will make it "more ominous, more magical." Eventually, he predicts, toxic and radioactive waste sites will be viewed as sacred places, a "remote landscape of nostalgia" for the "brute force of old industries and old conflicts" (*U* 286). More important, Detwiler claims that "we have everything backwards": waste isn't a by-product of civilization but its wellspring; human beings constructed civilization as a means of coping with garbage (*U* 287). Waste disposal has made us what we are, midwives of a culture whose mandate is "consume or die" (*U* 287).[11]

Brian Glassic reaches a similar conclusion when he visits the mammoth Fresh Kills landfill on Staten Island, and senses a "poetic balance" between the mountain of garbage and the World Trade Center. He recognizes that the "container ships, all the great works of transport, trade and linkage were directed in the end to this culminating structure" (*U* 184).[12] Waste managers, therefore, make up an "esoteric order" of adepts who deal in "people's habits and impulses, their uncontrollable needs and innocent wishes" (cf. *WN* 259). By the time Nick reaches his mid-fifties, he is a priest of this order, one of the "Church Fathers of waste in all its transmutations" (*U* 102), entombing "contaminated waste with a sense of reverence and dread" (*U* 88). And just as he has a "religious conviction . . . that these deposits of rock salt would not leak radiation" (*U* 88), so he believes that he can securely contain his past. But Nick ultimately faces the same problem confronted by consumer society: "how to keep this mass metabolism from overwhelming us" (*U* 184). Both physical and emotional waste are underground streams that always eventually surface. According to Detwiler, we can understand ourselves and attain a more authentic relationship to the environment only by accepting that consumption and waste are inextricable counterparts—that "everything's connected" (*U* 289). Here, then, this thesis not only describes how large-scale actions have broad consequences that we cannot fully predict; it also hints at a personal truth that Nick Shay has not grasped: what we discard always comes back to haunt us.

The middle-aged Nick obsessively restages his losses. While he and his family fastidiously sort their recycled waste, he constantly recycles his past, with the same icons—the number 13, the imaginary swamp, the baseball— repeatedly surfacing in his mind like tires in a landfill. Even a cab ride is haunted. When an L.A. cabbie says "Light Up a Lucky. It's light-up time," Nick recollects his father's favorites brand of smokes (*U* 333). He cannot dodge his past; it seeps ineluctably into his meditations: "The more hazardous the waste, the deeper we tried to sink it. . . . The word plutonium comes from Pluto, god of the dead and ruler of the underworld. They took him out to the marshes and wasted him" (*U* 119). Like plutonium, with its half-life of thousands of years, Nick's radioactive memories resist decay, mutating into haunted obsessions. He is ruled by his waste, a word that contains such derivatives as "empty, void, vanish and devastate" (*U* 120). One can almost hear him repeating the words of Aeneas: "My father, it was your sad image / so often come, that urged me to these thresholds" (Virgil 6.919–20; p. 161).

When he first arrives in Los Angeles, he visits Watts Towers, a visionary blend of sculpture and architecture built over thirty-three years by an illiterate Italian immigrant named Sabato Rodia, who constructed the towers (the tallest of which is almost a hundred feet high) singlehandedly out of mortar and discarded cups, tiles, bottles, shells, and other recycled objects (Goldstone and Goldstone 59). Strangely, however, Nick does not recognize the similarity between Rodia's achievement and his own work as a waste analyst and designer of containers. Instead it strikes him as an emblem of his father: both Jimmy and Rodia were Italian; both were "missing men" (Rodia also abandoned his first wife and children, went by various names, and disseminated false information about himself [Goldstone and Goldstone 31, 37]). But unlike Jimmy, Rodia left a tangible landmark, a "memory-trigger" that verified his existence and attached him to a new home (Goldstone and Goldstone 19). It is a trigger for Nick, too, who sees his "ghost father . . . living in the walls" of Rodia's work, but misses an opportunity to see in Rodia's productive recycling of waste an example he should follow.

Hence, at the end of the novel's first section he sits at four o'clock in the morning clutching the Thomson baseball, purchased from Marvin Lundy for $34,500. If in *The Names* objects tell us where we end, this object—a fragment he has shored against his ruin—also declares where Nick began. Given the game's mythology of father/son atonement, the ball perfectly embodies his filial yearning. But while it seems to offer consolation, it also promotes Nick's futile obsession with the past. As a magical object that both palliates and reproduces Nick's emptiness, the baseball fits Susan Stewart's description of souvenirs, which are objects that speak "a language of longing" and that arise "out of the necessarily insatiable demands of nostalgia" (*On Longing* 135). The demands are insatiable because the object is incomplete and must be supplemented by a narrative of its possessor (*On Longing* 136). Nick's narrative imbues the ball with all his losses: it marks for him the beginning of the "Branca luck" that he believes characterizes his life (*U* 132). The Thomson ball allows Nick to "be a tourist of [his] own life, . . . to appropriate, consume, and thereby 'tame' the cultural other"— in this case his own wild adolescence. And yet, in creating an "exoticism of the self," the object at once "mourns and celebrates the gap between [itself] and context of origin" (*On Longing* 146, 148, 164): that is, it brings back the past, but only insubstantially, and thus instantiates the irretrievability of loss. The ball seems to retransmit the voice of the vanished community of Nick's childhood (*U* 132). Using the second person to imply this collective loss, Nick realizes that the ball is "connecting many things" (*U* 131): not only how a single act can transform a life, but also how totemic objects epitomize larger historical longings. Like a reverse crystal ball, it contains Nick's rooftop view, from which he imagines the players and field of "crisp blues and elysian greens," all "gone to black and white in the film fade of memory" (*U* 134). He grips the ball, but those Groves of Blessedness forever elude his grasp.

Even at the novel's conclusion, Nick remains consumed by that "desire for something fled or otherwise out of reach" (*U* 803). As his son Jeff visits a website devoted to miracles, Nick revisits his past, seeking not so much a miracle as an audience with the "long ghosts" who walk his halls (*U* 804). Jeff tells him about a miracle in the Bronx—the "apparition" of Esmeralda, to which I'll return later—but Nick wonders if the real miracle is the web itself, where "everybody is everywhere at once, and he is there among them, unseen" (*U* 808). On the web everything is connected, and yet nobody is truly there. In contrast, Nick yearns for the "days of disarray when I walked real streets and did things slap-bang and felt angry and ready all the time" (*U* 810). His nostalgia is nothing less than the desire for desire itself (Stewart, *On Longing* 23).

Just as in his profession he has come to accept the "intractability of waste," at the end of the novel Nick may have reached an accommodation with his personal waste (*U* 805). But though the elegiac tones of these passages are moving, his sadness is also oppressive, because he remains as much a "mystery" to himself as he was at seventeen (*U* 810). By now even the ball offers little comfort—he takes it out from time to time, but forgets why he bought it (*U* 809). And when he muses that "we feel a reverence for waste, for the redemptive qualities of the things we use and discard. Look how they come back to us, alight with a kind of brave aging," this recognition implicitly judges his melancholy self-pity (*U* 809). He remains, like Milton's Satan, in a self-made hell, tormented by "the thought / Both of lost happiness and lasting pain" (*Paradise Lost* 1.54–55). The closed landfill across the road, with its invisible methane emanations, thus represents both his self-containment and the radiant life from which he seems forever exiled. What remains is not light, but darkness visible.

The Fraternity of Missing Men

Nick is far from the only alienated character in *Underworld*. Indeed, DeLillo has suggested that the novel explores a "mystery of loss" much more general than Nick's personal pain ("Window" 4). This social theme is portrayed partly through a motif of male absence and failure most emphatically displayed in Part 2, "Elegy for Left Hand Alone." Here Brian Glassic visits the tomblike home of Marvin Lundy, an eccentric baseball memorabilist and owner of the Thomson baseball, which Marvin has traced back to the day after the game. Lundy has received many visitors in search of lost time; he dubs them "the fraternity of missing men" (*U* 182). Nick Shay, who ends up purchasing the ball, is one of these men, but the novel unearths several others as well, depicting their absence synedochically as both cause and effect of America's fall from grace. Each of these men is in some sense a counterfeit, a dodger—a living exemplum of the bad faith and inauthenticity that characterizes the Cold War period—and most of them are associated with the Thomson baseball, which enables us to compose with them "the song of loss that goes unwritten in the records" (*U* 309). Like Nick Shay, these men are victimized and ruled by what they hide from, by the waste that always returns.

In Part 2 DeLillo also first adopts the quasi-montage technique that he again uses to stunning effect in Part 5. We move cinematically, first watching the unnamed Matt Shay view and comment on the videotape of Judson Rauch's murder by the Texas Highway Killer, then switching to Marian Shay's first meeting with Brian Glassic, who will be her lover. We then accompany Brian on his visit with Marvin and hear Nick's phone call to him, follow Nick's visit with Matt, and then walk with Matt's former chess teacher, Albert Bronzini, through the derelict neighborhood. We meet another elderly denizen, Sister Edgar, as she hands out food to the poor; cut back to Marian and Brian; and finally are introduced to Richard Henry Gilkey, the Texas Highway Killer himself. As in montage, meaning accrues through juxtaposition. For example, Matt's observation of automotive murder gives way to Marian's observation of Brian looking at old cars as prelude to their adulterous affair. The suggestion is that their encounter is a kind of murder, too. Similarly, after Brian leaves Marvin's basement he drives to Fresh Kills, as if to draw an analogy between the landfill and Marvin's landfill of male longing. If this technique establishes the characters' connections, it also indicates the opposite: as in *Players* and *Libra*, narrative dispossessions represent the characters' disconnection from others. Thus in challenging the reader to discover links, DeLillo's method encourages us to read actively and thereby regenerate the collective sense that the characters have lost. Not only do we thereby understand that everything is connected; we ourselves connect things.

The character who gets the ball moving is Cotter Martin's father Manx, who stands outside of this circle of connection and whose role even Marvin, that obsessive chronicler of counterhistory, never discovers. Both he and Cotter are lost men of history. Manx's internal exile further represents not only the fragmentation of families and community, but also the specific economic and social trauma of African-American men and their erasure from official records.[13] Irregularly employed, often drunk, always in search of a score, Manx is missing even from his own family's life, and so his resemblance to Jimmy Costanza makes Nick's final ownership of the ball even more appropriate. After pilfering the ball from his son, Manx hitches a ride toward the Polo Grounds in the garbage-filled car of his friend, Antoine, and then finally makes his way toward Yankee Stadium, where people are lined up in the middle of the night for World Series tickets. As Manx walks toward the crowd, the ball momentarily makes him feel at one with the others (*U* 366; this scene also reiterates Cotter's walk into the crowd the previous day and Nick's lonely walk in the preceding section). More importantly, the ball reminds Manx of baseball's myth of father/son atonement, and so he realizes that his best bet is to persuade a father to buy the ball for his son (*U* 643). The son, he thinks, will believe in baseball, even if the father doesn't. But the opposite turns out to be true: Charles Wainwright buys the ball because *he* wants to believe in the possibility of redemption, because he desires to win back his insolent son Chuckie (*U* 648). At first both buyer and seller are temporarily elated, but soon Manx feels cheated and depressed: the ball now signifies his ineffectuality within his family and his invisibility in society. A fake fan and bad father, Manx will always be a dodger.

Wainwright pays $32.45 for the ball, which thus appreciates more than a thousandfold by the time Nick Shay buys it. This monetary surplus is the trace of a deeper semiotic overdetermination, as each possessor of the ball adds to it private meanings that accumulate like the scars on its surface. The ball is certainly a commodity; but to each owner it becomes what Annette Weiner terms an "inalienable possession" that "acts as a stabilizing force against change because its presence authenticates . . . origins, kinship and political histories" (9). Each owner then imbues it with his own personality. Thus Wainwright (*Underworld*'s counterpart to *Americana*'s Clinton Bell), whom we visit in his advertising office (in the Fred F. French Building: cf. *U* 374, 398) ten years later, creates a shrine to the Thomson ball, which he treasures as the one thing in his life that marks him as a "regular guy" (*U* 530). Yet it also symbolizes his disconnection from Chuckie, who has become an "aimless wayward aging kid, a displaced person in his own life" (*U* 531). Now he intends to give the ball to Chuckie as a sign of his "trust, a gift, a peace offering, a form of desperate love and a spiritual hand-me-down" (*U* 611)—a stand-in for the fatherly guidance he has failed to provide. But Chuckie, whom we meet as a navigator on the B-52 named Long Tall Sally (which Klara Sax repaints and turns into an artwork in 1992), eventually loses the ball. Rather than ensuring origin and kinship, then, the ball signifies the loss of those qualities, as well as the limitations of baseball's myth of filial atonement. As Chuckie guides the bomber, he exemplifies how baseball has been supplanted by bombs, how longing on a large scale has mutated into the triumph of death.

It is Chuckie, later a crewman on a tramp steamer, whom Marvin Lundy pursues in San Francisco in 1978. Chuckie is Marvin's "key to the chain of possession" running back to October 3, 1951 (*U* 306). But a cloud of unknowing hovers over that day. Marvin needs Chuckie to complete the story, because "what good is a story without an ending? Although I suppose in this case it's not the ending we need but the beginning" (*U* 314). In Europe when Thomson hit his homer, Marvin wants the ball to complete his personal narrative of absence, but also desires not to find it so that he may continue the pursuit. He needs the ball to locate himself within time, but is also enticed by the lure of addiction, which involves "losing yourself to time" (*U* 319). A believer in conspiracy theories and the theology of secrets on which they depend, Marvin envisions the ball as a talisman that will allow him to match "the enormousness of the known forces in the world with something powerful in [his] own life" (*U* 323).

But not only *his* life: the ball whispers the tales of those he meets during his quest for it. Like a magic charm, it inspires "people to tell him things, to entrust family secrets and unbreathable personal tales." He becomes a postmodern confessor, and the ball his holy icon or communion host. After he finally buys the ball (a transaction never dramatized), Marvin's radiance grows, and he welcomes other missing men to his underworld. Like Virgil with Dante—or perhaps like Pluto himself—he voices their needs with deadpan black humor: "you think you're missing something and you don't know what it is. You're lonely inside your life . . . you're a lost speck" (*U* 170). During his meeting with Brian, Marvin also points out that the radioactive core of an atomic bomb is the same size as a baseball (*U* 172); the Thomson ball indeed seems radioactive, causing fission or infection in whomever it touches—the troubled Martins, the dysfunctional Wainwrights, the "bone cancer kid from Utah" (*U* 317), Judson Rauch (murdered by the Texas Highway Killer), the haunted Nick Shay, and even Marvin himself, who carries a "fungating mass" (a mushroom-shaped tumor) in his stomach (*U* 192). Mixing magic and dread, the ball fuses the streams of history started on the day of the two "blasts." Like the atomic bomb, it emits a "radiant amaze" (*U* 176) that spawns an endless series of photos, documents, stories, and secondary symbols (scoreboard, clock) that multiply its mystery.

Susan Stewart observes that the objects in a collection no longer tell of their origins, but tell the story of "the collector himself," and particularly the tale of the object's acquisition (*On Longing* 156). This baseball doesn't just restore time; it also makes all time synchronous (*On Longing* 151). In other words, Marvin's collection is also about containment—the attempt to regain lost time. A work of "Talmudic refinement" (*U* 177), it functions like Nick Shay's priestlike profession: both are designed both to incorporate history and master it, but in fact prove that it can never be recovered. Likewise, the ball represents both the desire to emerge fully into history and the truth that these missing men will always remain partly invisible. Hence, Marvin can own the ball, but he can never really possess it, because it represents precisely those things that can never be regained. Marvin interprets this phenomenon in personal terms: as he talks on the phone to Nick Shay about selling the ball, he finally realizes that the death of his wife, Eleanor, has become a "terror working deep beneath the skin that made him gather up things, amass possessions and effects against the dark shape of some unshoulderable loss" (*U* 191–92). Like the pianist to whom Marvin listens obsessively, the ball bespeaks missing parts; it plays an elegy for one hand alone.

The Bronx neighborhood where Marvin buys his favorite cheesecake is also a domain of missing men—the homeless, drug-addicted, and impoverished families fractured by absent fathers and dying children. One of the few remaining men is Albert Bronzini, who continues his habitual walks through a much-changed environment, and listens to a Saint-Saens piano work that echoes Marvin's soundtrack of loss. A philosopher of time, Albert seemed elderly even in his thirties, and saw the future as far back as 1952, when people whom his less tolerant friends described as "tizzoons" — from *tizzone d'inferno*, those who have been burnt black (*U* 768) — began to move into the neighborhood. Like Joyce's Leopold Bloom, with whom he shares many features, Bronzini is sociable and alert, but lacking ambition.[14] Bronzini, "too rooted" to leave the Bronx (*U* 214), also seeks the roots of all phenomena, including the atom (see *U* 736). But like the atom, and like the Highway Killer videotape that runs in the background, Bronzini engages in an eternal round of repetition, repeatedly reviewing the same places and reliving the same circumstances; for example, in 1951 he tended his dying mother, and now nurses his dying sister. His warmth and humanity notwithstanding, Bronzini embodies a spirit of loss that emanates not just from the emptying of his community, but also from the opportunities he has missed. He is, of course, the missing man in the relationship between Klara and Nick, and as with Marvin's and Nick's, all his losses are shadows of a single great absence: "Klara's departure" (*U* 233). When she left, she took Albert's spirit with her.

In contrast, his former chess student, Matt Shay, seems solidly grounded. And yet his initial appearance in the novel as an anonymous "you" describing the Texas Highway Killer video suggests an emptiness in his heart as well. Three missing men orbit this scene: Matt Shay, whose rage the video vicariously expresses; Judson Rauch, the victim, shot as he drives his Dodge; and the killer himself, Richard Gilkey, physically absent from the video but present as a violent cause and symbol of alienation and despair. The murder was accidentally videotaped by an anonymous girl, so that the video's immediacy comes from a "jostled" quality that makes it seem "more real, truer-to-life than anything around you. . . . The tape is superreal, or maybe underreal" (*U* 157). That is, it seems real because it is on tape. The video re-presents the "real" in a packaged form that makes "reality" more palatable both for its viewers and for its "performers," who are simultaneously absent and present, all of them hovering like "spirits living apart from their bodies . . . out there somewhere at the edges of perception" (*U* 159).

DeLillo uses this scene to limn a more profound waste — as in "empty, void, vanish" (*U* 120) — in American life that is exacerbated by the very acts of violence designed to fill it. Matt wonders whether "this kind of crime became more possible when the means of taping an event and playing it immediately . . . became widely available," and suggests that viewing it "dangles a need to do it again" (*U* 159). Not only does the act of taping inure us to the violence; it also encourages reruns, "copycat" crimes—but of course even the first murder is already in some sense a copy of all the cinematic and televised murders previously shown. This crime, then, takes place on three levels: the murder, the taping of the murder (a violation of that most private moment, the instant of death), and the repeated viewing, in which that primal violation is reenacted and eventually robbed of meaning. Each crime reflects and encourages the sociopathic blankness that caused the original crime. As DeLillo writes in "The Power of History," "If you view the tape often enough, it tends to transform *you*, to make you a passive variation of the [criminal] in his warped act of consumption" (63). Safely stationed outside the circle of observation, we seem able to dodge responsibility. However, as I noted in regard to *Running Dog*, our reading about the crime adds a fourth layer of outrage and implicates those of us who watch the watchers. DeLillo captures this condition of mutual responsibility and alienation by using the second person, so that when Matt says that "you look because this is the nature of the footage, to make a channeled path through time," he is simultaneously accusing us of his crime, insinuating that we're all alike, and hiding his own identity in the pronoun (*U* 157). TV's "channeled path" cuts through us all, and the pronoun at once indicts us and frees the accuser from sole blame: we are all here and yet nobody is here, nobody is responsible. In our "freedom" and emptiness, we are victims and perpetrators at once. Behind it is the ubiquity of video, which reduces us all to dodgers, to throwaway subjects of consumption.

Appropriately, the killer himself first appears—or rather, fails to appear (only his disguised voice is heard, talking to anchorwoman Sue Ann Corcoran)—on Matt's TV, defending himself from accusations of abnormality. His descriptions of his technique—left hand alone, always while moving—are fittingly given in second person (*U* 217, 266). Most tellingly, like *Libra*'s Lee Oswald, Gilkey commits his crimes as a way of coming into being: "Richard had to take everything outside, share it with others, become part of the history of others, because this was the only way to escape, to get out from under the pissant details of who he was" (*U* 266). Killing alone is not enough; he must talk to Sue Ann on TV because only by making eye contact with the TV set can he "take shape as himself" (*U* 269). He commits the crimes in order to be on television, which is the only way he exists at all; his murders permit him to assume radiant form and thereby become one with the other viewers. Similarly, he studies the names and stories of his victims so that he can survive "in the memories of the family . . . twinned, quadrupled" (*U* 270). Everything is connected in television's universal second person: here you can be a star. Ironically, then, Gilkey commits his murders not to take revenge, but to take shape, to create the social life that he otherwise lacks. But despite his efforts, he remains unfulfilled, ghostly, ineffectual, absent; meaning dodges him. In Gilkey, DeLillo dramatizes a deeper void at the heart of postmodern America. In him we see that waste is not only in our garbage, but in our souls. Even our attempts to contain waste—in commodities, in secrets, in baseballs, in videotape— only allow it to consume us. We no longer contain waste; it contains us.

WEAPONS

Fission: The Mushroom

If Nick Shay has always been attracted to the underworld, his younger brother Matt is instead afflicted with "a curse of innocence" and wears his "meek freedom from guilt" like a badge (*U* 221). The contrast between Nick (the satanic) and Matt (the righteous) embodies some of the novel's most important dyads, especially waste versus weapons. Thus, whereas Nick works for Waste Containment, Matt works on nuclear weapons. DeLillo presents them as counterparts in other ways as well: Nick quits school while Matty studies diligently; Nick's mentor is a heroin addict while Matt's is a nun; Nick steals cars while Matty plays chess. Each of them, however, has undergone a psychic fission that is partly the result of paternal abandonment and partly the consequence of larger social forces. Matt is as filled with rage as Nick. But whereas Nick expresses his anger over his father's disappearance by killing George Manza, Matt, under the tutelage of Bronzini, channels his into chess, a game "of enormous hostility" in which "You crush your opponent" (*U* 212). At first Matt thrives under Bronzini's guidance, but when he begins to lose regularly, the game can no longer "contain all his rage" (*U* 715).

The word "contain" not only implies his similarity to his brother, but also invokes the historical and political meaning of "containment" noted above. Thus DeLillo juxtaposes Matt's education in dread with Nick's introduction to George's heroin addiction, tracing the "twin streams" of weapons and waste in these private lives and implying their fusion in each boy's need for authority. Matt's yearning to be a perfectly "contained" subject is depicted during atomic war drills, during which the "overbrained boy of the thirty-two pieces and the million trillion combinations liked to nestle in his designated slot" (*U* 728). He becomes a chess piece. Unlike Nick, who exorcises his anger through impulsive action, Matt sublimates his into Sister Edgar's terrifying Catholic nuclearism. Under Sister Edgar's direction, Matt learns to worship "the cloud of all-power," the mushroom that mixes magic and dread.

Like her namesake, J. Edgar Hoover, Sister Edgar reveres secret power. And like her other namesake, Edgar Allan Poe, she is half in love with death, learning his ominous poem, "The Raven," in order to teach her children fear, which is the "secret heart of her curriculum" (*U* 776).[15] Sister Edgar also shares Hoover's fear of microbial invasion and his fetish for cleanliness, as if she can scour away the sins which, in her raven's heart, she knows she has committed. In her latex gloves she feels "masculinized, . . . condomed ten times over," all threats contained, but she is never completely at ease, and her elaborate containment mechanisms only make the menace seem more powerful (*U* 241). Hence she both fears and loves The Bomb, imagining that a nuclear war would be "thrilling," and gloatingly picturing the "dead who will come out of the earth to lash and cudgel the living, . . . death, yes, triumphant" (*U* 245, 249). Thus even though Sister Edgar performs corporal works of mercy in a neighborhood abandoned by adult men, she has replaced much of her Christian faith with the belief in "radioactivity, the power of alpha particles and the all-knowing systems that shape them, the endless fitted links" (*U* 251). The other Edgar projects his psychic fission outward, perceiving the world as an ongoing battle "between the state and secret groups of insurgents" who try to bring about "apocalyptic change." With the advent of the "mushroom cloud," the "godhead of Annihilation and Ruin," the state owns "the means of apocalypse" (*U* 563). Both Edgars are true believers in the religion of nuclearism, because of which the United States has become a "universal container" for the contradictions of nuclear power (Nadel 14).

This indoctrination in terror and containment helps explain Matt Shay's fascination with the Texas Highway Killer, and his brutal insistence that his wife Janet watch the video again and again suggests his identification with the murderer. It seems only appropriate that by 1974 Matt is working on safing mechanisms for nuclear weapons. Like Nick's, his job involves containment—ensuring that the weapons detonate only where they're supposed to. Whereas Nick's underworld is internal, Matt works physically underground, in "the Pocket," a secret installation in New Mexico, where those "awed by the inner music of bomb technology" can redefine the "limits of human perception and dread" (*U* 404, 422). It is secret in more ways than one: not only is the installation protected from public knowledge, but many of those who work here don't even know if their job involves weapons. Both workers and citizens are kept in a cloud of unknowing, permitted only the faith that "Everything connected at some undisclosed point down the systems line" (*U* 408). Another of DeLillo's would-be mystics, Matt has accepted this vocation with the goal of knowing himself better, of "fixing. . . willful limits" (*U* 413), of probing his own secret desires to "see a fireball" or "one of the monster shots that vapored an atoll" (*U* 402–3). Talking about weapons to Janet, he makes The Bomb "sound like God," a "critical mass that will call down the Hindu heavens" (*U* 458). Like Gary Harkness, Matt is drawn to the "mystery" and "wonder" of the weapons and to the awesome power they give him (*U* 408).

But he entertains doubts about the morality of his profession, doubts reinforced by one of his co-workers, Eric Deming. Divulging horrific rumors about the effects of nuclear testing and manufacture, Deming utters the secret history that the state has tried to contain: that of the downwinders, residents of Nevada and Utah on whom radioactive dust from aboveground tests fell. He tells of their teeth dropping out, of multiple myelomas, leukemias, and kidney failures; he relates the experiences of atomic veterans who were marched through ground zero immediately after tests, or who were forced to fly through mushroom clouds during blasts (*U* 405–6, 414, 417). This underhistory partakes, like that mystical "third line" described in *Libra* (*L* 339), of the supernatural. As Perrine notes, one reason that radiation is so terrifying and has been so often sublimated in artistic treatments is that it "somehow connects to mystical processes and magical powers" (84). Similarly, the invisibility of radiation makes Eric's stories hard to believe, and even he claims to disbelieve them. But they are true.[16] These cases reveal how, rather than reinforcing citizens' faith in the government, the pursuit of perfect security bred a paranoia that Deming articulates when he warns Matt, with a Dr. Strangelovean accent, "never underestimate the willingness of the state to act out its own massive fantasies" (*U* 422). Most chillingly, because of the bombs' large yield and the prevailing wind patterns, the physical consequences of those "fantasies" were not limited to thinly populated areas of the desert Southwest. Everything is connected; as Col. Langdon Harrison says, "we're all downwinders" (quoted in Gallagher 89). Because of these tests, by the end of the 1950s people were applying words such as "contamination, poison, impurity, pollution, obscenity" to fallout (Weart 214). Weapons became linked with waste, and with the very fear of invasion they were designed to thwart. Forced to choose between patriotism and horrible disease, Americans experienced an unhealable psychic and emotional fission.

Matt comes to believe Deming's tales, partly because his experiences in the Vietnam War taught him that "everything he'd ever disbelieved or failed to imagine turned out, in the end, to be true" (*U* 418). Matt's service in Vietnam was also related to his father's disappearance: he went because he refused to "slip away, . . . dodge, desert, resist, chicken out, turn tail, . . . as his old man had done" (*U* 463). Instead of a dodger, Matt wanted to be a giant, and during his service attained a giant's point of view by poring over airborne surveillance charts to discover enemy encampments. Also in Vietnam is Long Tall Sally's navigator, Chuckie Wainwright, an equally angry young man who gets a "sado-sort of grudge pleasure" from dropping bombs on the Vietnamese (*U* 612). On Chuckie's crew is a black man named Louis Bakey, whose experiences verify Deming's rumors. He tells of flying directly through a fifty-kiloton atomic blast that seemed to bring alive Bruegel's "Triumph of Death." Amidst the "boiling and talking and crackling" mushroom cloud, he saw his own bones through closed eyes, as if the plane were filled with "skeleton men" (*U* 613–14). The physical effects—loss of coordination, urinary tract damage, neurological problems—have stayed with Louis, who carries death inside him more palpably than does Matt Shay. The psychological effects are just as deep. Louis feels no qualms about acting out the state's massive fantasies, which the airmen shrewdly describe as a brand of deviant sexuality that equates bombing with penetration: "first we fuck them. Then we bomb them" (*U* 616). They act out the safely condomed sexual aggression of Matt and the two Edgars.

Filled with an unexpressed anger that fights with his essential goodness, Matt too is undergoing psychic fission, betraying the same "contradictions of being" depicted in *Unterwelt*, the film about radiation that Klara Sax watches during the same summer, 1974 (*U* 444; I'll return to Eisenstein later). Torn by the competing demands of magic and dread, he cannot decide whether or not to quit his job; he loves The Bomb too much. Driven by Edgar-instilled impulses, he undertakes a journey into a weapons testing range to purge himself of this uncleanness. The previous night he has accidentally ingested a mind-altering substance, perhaps one of those "mushroom caps that implode your brain," and now he hurtles with Janet toward a white space on the map where he can become "undone" (*U* 446). Matt taps into the "supernatural side of the arms race. Miracles and visions," on the missile range, a place where one mushroom illuminates the meaning of the other (*U* 452).[17]

In Matt's heightened state, everything seems connected: the photo he saw in Vietnam of Nixon flanked by Thomson and Branca could just as easily be "Oppenheimer and Teller" (*U* 466). "All technology refers to the bomb" (*U* 467). So does nature: Matt associates the fungus, the "fleshy cap that might be poisonous or magical," with the "cloud shaped like a mushroom" (*U* 466). Their identity lies in the collective unconscious. Psilocybin allows you to perceive the underworld of images previously "known only to tribal priests" who may in times past have "popped magic mushrooms and s[een] a fiery cloud"; these mushrooms "can turn your soul into fissionable material" (*U* 466; cf. Weart 403). As Weart shows, one reason that the popular imagination fixed on the mushroom as the preferred metaphor for atomic blasts (instead of a dome, parasol, cauliflower, or funnel) is that fungi have long been associated with rot, poison and death (402). But they are also associated with uncontrolled growth and supernatural powers. As Matt thinks, "Death and magic, that's the mushroom. Or death and immortal life" (*U* 466–67). The mushroom embodies the fusion of magic and dread, of death and life, of weapons and waste. Inspired by both kinds of magic mushroom, Matt achieves a radiant, frightening glimpse of the novel's underlying theme: that binaries are not opposed, but partake of each other, and that "everything connects in the end, or seems to, or seems to only because it does" (*U* 465).

Fusion: The Orange

In the bunker Matt remembers that the drums of Agent Orange he saw in Vietnam resembled "cans of frozen Minute Maid," and asks, "how can you tell the difference between orange juice and agent orange if the same massive system connects them at levels outside your comprehension?" (*U* 465). As I noted in the introduction to this chapter, Matt's question reaches beyond drug-induced paranoia, as the workings of that massive system are gradually unmasked in the novel, partly by means of the motif of oranges. The fruit is suitable for such a metaphorical task. First, as an omnipresent fixture in American households, oranges are an obvious image of consumption and of the global capitalism that allows tropical fruit to become commonplace in the northern United States. Second, oranges consist of individual sections that can be eaten separately or at once, and thus serve well as a trope of fission or of fusion. In *Underworld* oranges and the color orange come to represent a capitalism so pervasive that it reaches from oranges, to toxic defoliants, to a solvent employed to clean graffiti from subway trains. But ultimately orangeness not only represents capitalism's range and the fragmentation of individuals such as Matt Shay, but also reveals the linkages between small- and large-scale events, indicates the fusion of weapons and waste, and outlines modes of regeneration. This fusion of theme and figure is also reflected in DeLillo's technique. Part 5, entitled "Better Things for Better Living Through Chemistry,"[18] employs the montage technique I mentioned earlier, juxtaposing different scenes that invite readers to generate thematic links and make everything connect. The operations of the "massive system" that Matt recognizes is thus embodied in the novel's fragmentary structure, which dramatizes alienation and helplessness and forges a relationship among consumerism, war, and waste. Upon recognizing these links, the reader is asked to do what society has failed to do: perform fusion, execute a salvage operation.

Chapter 2 of Part 5 provides a prime example of the convergence of form and content. Its second section, set in Mississippi during the civil rights era, features Cotter Martin's sister Rosie, and displays how authorities used the products of chemical companies such as DuPont to contain internal dissent. In this scene African-American demonstrators become downwinders as they are gassed by police who, stalking through the "cloud" of gas, resemble giant mutated insects in 1950s SF films, the chemicals giving them a "radiance, a night glow" (*U* 526). This scene of forcible dispossession, of "living through chemistry," immediately precedes our visit with Charles Wainwright, whose ad campaigns similarly involve "sublimated forms of destruction" (*U* 529). Capitalism needs ad-men like Wainwright who will indiscriminately market anything from gasoline to toxic gas, and for whom nuclear weapons are just another useful image for selling products. Thus although Wainwright "killed" the "Bomb Your Lawn" campaign for a giant chemical company (which exploited the knowledge that fertilizer plus oil could produce a bomb [*U* 528]), he proudly recalls an equally cynical commercial he created for Equinox Oil, in which two cars—one black (Soviet), one white (American)—were to race across the Jornada del Muerto desert, site of the Trinity test (*U* 529–30). The first to reach ground zero (the white car, of course, fueled by Equinox) was to win. Although African-American organizations scuttled this campaign, it nonetheless epitomizes the way the advertising exploits technological anxiety to sell products. Once again DeLillo, who has criticized the collusion of corporations, advertising, and government ever since *Americana*, dramatizes how consumer capitalism underwrites—and undermines—American dreams by turning commodities into containers for dread. "Whoever controls your eyeballs runs the world," declares Wainwright (*U* 530). He is thinking of the way that packaging uses "psychic data" to entice consumers, but his words also describe how Cold War institutions manipulated the "eyeballs" of citizens, hiding unpleasant facts and highlighting positive ones to ensure profits and retain power.

Wainwright's greatest professional pride is the Minute Maid orange juice campaign, which made bright orange cans "orgasmically visual" to millions of (mostly female) consumers. By tapping into undercurrents of desire, Wainwright "connects millions of people across a continental landmass, compelling them to buy a certain product" (*U* 533–34): ads make everything connect in the universal third person—or rather, the universal second person, since, like Matt's description of the Texas Highway Killer video, Wainwright's recollection is narrated by and to "you." The ideal examples of this second person appear in the first section of the same chapter, where we meet the Demings, who have purchased not only Wainwright's products but also the belief in better living through chemistry. In their suburban home a "benevolent gleam, of eyeball surprise" at the bounty of consumer products bathes everything in radiance (*U* 517). Erica Deming is the stereotypical 1950s housewife, with her delight in new appliances, her words to live by ("crisper," "breezeway," "Fruit juicer" [*U* 520]) and her recipes for Jell-O, perhaps the quintessential twentieth-century grocery item. Indeed, DeLillo has elsewhere implied that Jell-O is a perfect image of the capacity of consumerism to "absorb social disruptions and dangers into the molded jell of mass-brand production" ("American Blood" 27): its gelatinous consistency embodies the congealing force of consumerism.

Yet Erica senses something "faintly unnerving," a "throb" or flow beneath the happiness (*U* 518).[19] The date of this vignette, October 8, 1957, points to a possible source of that unease: it is just after the Soviets have successfully launched Sputnik, and one day after the last of the "Plumbob" series of American atomic tests (Ball 76, 81). Sputnik generated enormous discomfort in Americans. Were we behind the Russians? Were there "other surprises coming, things we haven't been told about them?" (*U* 518–19). Perhaps this anxiety explains why Erica declines to use the Jell-O mold that looks "guided missile-like" (*U* 515). The Plumbob tests also seem to permeate the very atmosphere, causing products like the "strontium white" loaf of bread on the table to radiate unseen menace (*U* 516). DeLillo indicates this undercurrent of fear by inserting between Erica's thoughts product warnings such as "Don't puncture or incinerate," and "If swallowed, induce vomiting at once" (*U* 519, 515). By this time even Jell-O had lost its innocence: convicted spy Julius Rosenberg allegedly signaled Soviet agents with a cut-up Jell-O box, which became a prime piece of evidence in the government's case against him (Garber 11–12). Erica may be asking herself, along with the Jell-O ad of a decade earlier, "Is there a Party hiding in your Ice-box?" (Garber 18, 20). Containment is never perfect; suppressed fear eventually needs an outlet. "Danger. Contents Under Pressure" (*U* 516).

Her son Eric Deming, who sits in his room masturbating into a condom, has found an outlet. The future bombhead uses a condom because it reminds him of his favorite weapons system, "Honest John," which carries warheads with a yield of up to forty kilotons (*U* 514). Worshipping the missile's "saintly and sun-tipped" length, he jacks off to "Atomic Jayne" Mansfield (*U* 484), whose breasts jut out like missiles or bullets. As in Chuckie Wainwright's B-52, so in the Deming household the repressed desires underneath Cold War containment ooze out as a sterile, violent sexuality in which the iconic Jayne, like Long Tall Sally, becomes both penetrator and penetrated. And just as Eric's condom contains his semen and prevents contamination of the house, and just as he later wears gloves to handle plutonium (U 419), so Erica wears rubberoid gloves to protect herself from organic murk and invisible invaders—and from Eric. This condomology caps the chapter's formal and thematic links between chemistry and capital, Jell-O and oranges, bombs and breezeways: all of them are, as Lenny Bruce declares during the Cuban Missile Crisis, "what the twentieth century feels like" (U 584).

Marian Bowman (later Shay), whom we encounter on a brief visit home to Madison, Wisconsin, also seeks "hygiened perfection" (U 604), but cannot prevent troubling social forces from seeping in via the radio broadcasting student protests on Dow Day. It is so called because recruiters are on campus from Dow Chemical, one of whose new products is Jell-O's dark twin, an "improved form of napalm with a polystyrene additive that made jellied matter cling more firmly to human flesh" (U 599). Just as the real and the simulated riot blend and collide in an "audio montage of gunfire, screams, sirens, klaxons and intermittent bulletins real and possibly not" (U 599), so DeLillo employs textual montage to represent the links between Marian's private life and the era's political unrest. Everything is connected: as the protesters and announcers tauntingly chant the slogans of Dow and DuPont, the police deploy tear gas manufactured by those same companies. Meanwhile, the radio reminds listeners that bomb material can be made from ammonium nitrate and fuel oil—ANFO: "We are talking about waste, we are talking about fertilizer, we are talking about waste and weapons, we are talking about ANFO, the bomb that begins in the asshole of a barnyard pig" (U 600). Jell-O mutates into ANFO; weapons and waste converge. Placed just before the Vietnam scene in which Chuckie Wainwright and Louis Bakey bomb the Vietnamese, this section implies a causal as well as a chronological connection: Jell-O and napalm jelly, orange juice and Agent Orange emerge from the same "massive system," just as Chuckie's anger and the protesters' rage are comparable responses to a shared feeling of dispossession.

What unites these disparate events and strands is capitalism, which by the mid-1990s, when we meet up with Nick Shay again, seems to have subsumed even nationalism. As Nick remarks in *Das Kapital*, the novel's epilogue, capital "burns off the nuance in a culture," because it "customcater[s] to cultural and personal needs, not to cold war ideologies of massive conformity. . . . But even as desire tends to specialize . . . the force of converging markets produces an instantaneous capital that shoots across horizons at the speed of light, making for a certain furtive sameness" (U 785–86). Capital permits the illusion of individual preference, but only as part of a larger jellified mass. Yet things have changed since the Cold War, when each superpower's weapons reflected the (desired or imagined) national character, and the desires of governments and the fears they promoted seemed clear; now a more nebulous dread is at work. The end of the Cold War has also clarified the convergence of weapons and waste so that we can see what we have wrought.

Nick is in the former Soviet Union to witness how radioactive waste can be destroyed with nuclear explosions. The irony is that the weapons themselves are also unnecessary leftovers from the past, so that the explosions eliminate two different kinds of waste at once. As bombs fueled by plutonium blow up plutonium waste, engineers fuse two streams of history, attempting to "kill the devil" they have brought into being (*U* 791). Indeed, plutonium is itself a byproduct—a kind of waste—created by atomic power plants. However, the association of atomic energy and waste is not new; it goes back to the very inception of the atomic age. Early in the novel, for example, Klara Sax quotes J. Robert Oppenheimer, who told his colleague Leo Szilard that "The atomic bomb is shit" (quoted in Weart 298; cf. *U* 76): it is waste material because it is beyond words, like the feces that stop Gary Harkness short in *End Zone*. In the same vein, nuclear industry workers describe radioactively contaminated articles as "crapped up" (quoted in Weart 298). This crap, the "dark multiplying byproduct" of atomic energy (*U* 791), has until now been contained—not physically, as any downwinder can attest, but at least informationally. Now it has emerged from the underworld, and we need waste managers like Maltsev—whose company's name, "Chaika" or seagull, is named after a waste-eating bird—to store it, hide it, or blow it up so that what we have been excreting does not continue to consume us.

Nick experiences two explosions in Russia. First, he ends his personal containment by punching Brian Glassic, whose affair with Marian he has discovered. Afterward he feels briefly relieved of his "phony role as husband and father" (*U* 796). But nothing significant happens. The nuclear explosion is equally anticlimactic: because nuclear tests are now executed underground, there is no "ascending cloudmass . . . or rolling waves of sound" (*U* 799), but only a muffled rumble. The blast remains contained, unlike the earlier atmospheric tests that irradiated nearby citizens, or the underground tests that leaked radiation into the air. These tests were not, of course, limited to the United States, as Nick is reminded when Maltsev takes him to the Museum of Misshapens, which displays the human "byproducts" of the arms race. Here are the Russian downwinders, the victims not only of atomic radiation but also of the secrets and lies purveyed by Soviet authorities. Yet the cyclops, the two-headed fetuses, the misplaced heads here seem less pitiful than the living victims: the retarded dwarf girl, the bald-headed boys with radiation-induced cancer, the cheer-

ful cretins, the children without left arms, the blind people whose impair-
ment embodies the blindness of the citizens and governments who brought
about their suffering. Here the underhistory, the suppressed and contained
facts, the buried aggression, rise to the surface like toxic waste. "Everything is true": the "secrets kept in whitewashed vaults, the half-forgotten
plots—they're all out here now, seeping invisibly into the land and air,
into the marrowed folds of the bones" (*U* 801–3). Everything is connected:
although not everyone has suffered physically from atomic weapons, we
all share the guilt, the loss of faith, the psychic fission. The most dreadful
legacy of the Cold War may be this: we are all spiritual downwinders.

Yet even this despair may foster hope, as when a Ukrainian woman
claims to be a second Christ (*U* 802), or when a miracle may happen in
the burnt-out Bronx. Although we may be skeptical about these particular
manifestations, DeLillo suggests that it is possible—indeed, necessary—to
salvage something from the wreckage. Whereas Nick Shay is content merely
to recycle and wallow in the waste of the past, the artists depicted in *Underworld* perform more valuable recycling, transforming the very physical debris left by weapons and waste into objects that testify to the uncontain-
ability of human aspiration. These works save meaning from the triumph
of death. Although works of art alone do not alter the facts of history, and
although DeLillo's ultimate stance about the possibility of peace is ambiguous, he suggests that artists can begin the process of salvage by writing a
new, underground history from the waste of the past.

SALVAGE

The Contradictions of Being

Each of these artworks is motivated by what Klara Sax calls a "graffiti
instinct—to trespass and declare ourselves," to decorate or deface hege-
monic edifices (*U* 77). Each of the artists employs bricolage—a spontaneous method, a patchwork style—with whatever materials come to hand.
The methods are therefore political, in that these artists use waste to contest "massive systems," to express and celebrate the "idiosyncratic self" that
DeLillo describes as the source of art and of political resistance ("Power"
62). Each one springs from the underworld to lay bare the secrets of Cold
War culture and criticize the excesses of capitalist society, but, more importantly, to redeem its artifacts and transmute them into lasting testaments
to eccentricity and community. If each of them also embodies irresolvable
contradictions, the most successful of them nonetheless construct a vision
of healthy community in which "everything is connected." Ultimately, I

submit, DeLillo has designed *Underworld* as a similar act of artistic resistance and redemption, using the same techniques of montage and bricolage to generate artistic grace.

J. Edgar Hoover represents the powers who strive to contain these eccentric energies. As I have noted, because of his position Hoover is able to translate his personal pathologies—lust for power, repressed homosexuality, a fetish for secrecy, phobic fear of invasion—into public policy, so that his personal rejection of "unacceptable impulses" drives him to quash whatever he deems "unacceptable" in society as well.[20] However, he is forced to acknowledge that he is "half a gangster" himself. "Conflict"—internal contradictions analogous to those of his alter egos, Sergei Eisenstein and Ismael Muñoz—is the tiny fission charge that drives Hoover's inner power plant (*U* 573). Despite his efforts, however, the Director knows that he will never totally silence the "undervoice" (*U* 563) welling up from the psychic and social underground. That undervoice speaks during the Black-and-White Ball scene (set in 1966), when Hoover learns that garbage guerrillas are planning to ransack his garbage, analyze it, have sex with it, write poems about it, and finally eat and excrete it (*U* 558). These terrorists will astutely use Hoover's own methods of surveillance to violate him and bring into the open what he most fears: that he himself *is* garbage. Wallowing in his waste, they will enact his deepest desire: to be penetrated by filth. But the scene reveals that his evil lies less in his relentless surveillance than in his essential falseness; his flimsy mask fails to camouflage the petty appetites on which his power his based.

One of the masked protesters is costumed as a nun. If to us she foreshadows Sister Edgar, to Clyde Tolson she brings to mind Lenny Bruce, recently dead from a drug overdose. Tolson recalls a police photo of the bloated body and muses that it could be titled *The Triumph of Death* (*U* 574). As Hoover's alter ego, Bruce is motivated on the one hand by his love of "shit" (heroin), and on the other by a corrosive honesty about his own fears and America's repressions. He therefore also embodies what Klara, describing Eisenstein, calls "the contradictions of being" (*U* 444). Bruce plays the same role as *Libra*'s Weird Beard: the "undervoice" who articulates the fear and alienation of the voiceless listeners. The real-life Bruce rubbed noses in the dirty truths that Americans pretended not to see, fighting censorship and risking imprisonment to make Americans confront what freedom of speech really means. His performances—executed in a kind of verbal bebop antithetical to Hoover's fascistic organization—are interspersed throughout Part 5, as he comments on the most dangerous moment in the Cold War: the Cuban Missile Crisis of October 1962, when the United States and the Soviet Union nearly went to war.

Early in the crisis, the audience need Bruce to help them "make a transition" from a feeling of false safety to one of near panic; they must become "accustomed to a different level of dread" than ever before (*U* 504). He cynically charges that certain powerful men whose very names—McGeorge, Roswell, and Averell—bespeak their sense of entitlement and prestige (*U* 592) "roll out a periodic crisis" to "remind us of our basic state" of powerlessness (*U* 507). But he also acknowledges that life on the brink is "a rush" (*U* 505), the rush of containment breaking apart. By October 24 Bruce is making the strange claim that it is all about "Instant mashed potatoes. The whole technology, man, of instant and quick, because we don't have the attention span for normal wars anymore" (*U* 544–45).[21] He means that the crisis has evolved from consumer culture run amok, and conjures up a perfect consumer named DeeAnn who confuses the president's speech about the crisis with "a pitch for insect repellent or throat spray," and mistakes the missile buildup in Cuba for the grease buildup in her oven (*U* 508). Bruce is not just mocking the Erica Demings of the world; he's also shrewdly noting the complicity between capitalism and technologies of mass destruction. As we have seen, they are also the same for people like Charles Wainwright, for whom atomic weapons are a "scary ad campaign that had gotten out of hand" (*U* 546). Bruce is likewise suggesting that nuclear bombs are just another of Wainwright's radiant products—the most monstrously fetishized commodity of all.

In a later performance he pulls out a condom and begins to play with it, reminding his listeners that Dow Chemical, which manufactures Saran Wrap and prophylactics, is also a major weapons producer (*U* 582), and then sardonically announces that the whole point of the crisis is "the sexual opportunity it offers" (*U* 586). In other words, "First we bomb them, then we fuck them," or vice versa. Bruce is exposing the macho posturing that underpins deterrence and "containment," as well as the craving for power and possession that motivates it. What is most thrilling, however, is not Bruce's analysis, which is too scattershot to be entirely coherent, but his frank articulation of his audience's deepest fears: "*We're all gonna die.*" Hearing in his lament "the obliteration of the idea of uniqueness and free choice," his listeners are forced to envision the "replacement of human isolation by massive and unvaried ruin" (*U* 507). As he moves across the country, repeating the cry, he feels his own fear purified and made public, and hears his voice echoing the unworded speech, the "idlike wail," from the "desperate buried place" in his audience's souls (*U* 547).

Crusader, philosopher, drug addict, hustler, lounge lizard, "self-styled lawyer, . . . self-critical Jew," moralist and race commentator (*U* 627), Lenny Bruce is one of *Underworld*'s primary spokespersons for the "secret history that never appears in the written accounts" (*U* 594). His audience, those "wastelings of the . . . lost country that exists right here in America" (*U* 628), are not just the homeless, the disenfranchised, the beatnik poets; rather, DeLillo implies, they are all who feel alienated, helpless, enraged, frightened—everybody. Once the crisis is over, however, Bruce runs out of fuel and disappointedly reverts to old routines. Further, despite performing important acts of resistance, he cannot defeat the systems against which he rails. Instead he becomes a martyr, not just to the bluenoses who finally limit him to performing only in San Francisco, but to another commodity, the underworld equivalent of Ipana and aspirin: heroin, also known as shit. Waste consumes him too.

The other resistant art works in the novel circulate around Klara Sax, who herself contains a number of internal conflicts. She long ago left Albert Bronzini, and by the summer of 1974 she is a distinguished member of the New York art scene who is still seeking a workable aesthetic and a new audience. Her main section, entitled "Cocksucker Blues" after Robert Frank's long-unreleased documentary about the Rolling Stones, intercuts her activities with those of Matt Shay and Ismael Muñoz, a bisexual graffiti writer. The title thus encompasses not only Klara's seduction by and of the avant-garde art world, but also Matt's subjection to the phallocentric culture of the bombheads and Ismael's secret sexual practices. As a garbage strike in New York exposes the waste that everyone has previously agreed to ignore, the Watergate hearings reveal the underworld activities of the Nixon administration. It is a moment on the cusp, seemingly ripe for subversive stirrings, but also marking the end of the 1960s, a decade of such stirrings that have failed to bloom. During the course of the summer Klara watches three underground films—*Cocksucker Blues*, Eisenstein's *Unterwelt*, and the famous Zapruder home movie of JFK's assassination—that affect her powerfully and help her to forge a new set of artistic practices and philosophies. She also pursues Ismael, comments on his work, and visits Watts Towers. These latter works of cultural destruction and salvage fuel her project of rehabilitating junk and saving it for art (*U* 393), eventually culminating in restored B-52s such as Long Tall Sally.

Cocksucker Blues (named after a blues song about a gay hustler) follows the Rolling Stones on their 1972 American tour. The film was withheld because of its unflattering portrayal of its decadent protagonists and their entourage. Ironically, the Rolling Stones' squeamishness contradicts the very image they so long cultivated of a rough, "subversive" band of malcontents playing raw, blues-influenced music with blatantly sexual lyrics.[22] The fans in the film who follow the group around, propelled by uncontainable impulses welling up from underground, seek transcendence through the group's music (which, despite the drugs and backstage chaos, is terrific), and yearn to identify with Mick Jagger, the self-proclaimed "Lucifer of Rock." With its numerous shots of tunnels, its "corruptive and ruinous" atmosphere, and its frequent use of morgue-like blue light that radiates the "nimbus of higher dying," the film lures us into the group's morbid aura (*U* 384).

However, the more authentically underground art here is not that of the Rolling Stones but that of filmmakers Robert Frank and Daniel Seymour, who capture a moment when, in the wake of Altamont, the idealism of the 1960s was turning rancid. They sharply display the contradictions between the Rolling Stones' "revolutionary" image and their decadent lifestyle in a scene on the tour plane. A voiceover from a radio program discusses the banning of their song, "Street Fighting Man," which allegedly "advocated revolution"; meanwhile the Stones and their entourage encourage a roadie to strip and nearly rape a female traveler. The plane is not a political vehicle but a "jerk-off monotonic airborne erotikon" (*U* 384). The portentous radio voice declares that these are "young people who care about the world around them." But in fact, the film shows a group devoted mostly to hedonism, one whose "revolutionary" activities consist of tossing TV sets from hotel balconies and indulging in all varieties of illegal drugs. One could argue that the TV-set prank is a protest against consumer culture—epitomized by the commercial we hear for Excedrin ("significantly more effective than common aspirin" [*U* 384])—which is, after all, as much a drug culture as the rock world. But there is no sense that Keith Richards's TV tossing contains an anti-establishment message. Indeed, when asked why he originally formed a rock band, he answers, "to make a lot of money."

Perhaps rampant hedonism is a response to the threat of atomic annihilation. The radio voice implies as much when it claims that the group appeals to youth inured by the "reality of destruction"—we're all gonna die, so what the fuck? But the film makes clear that, even if the Rolling Stones began as underground artists, by 1972 they were nothing more or less than a successful corporation. *Cocksucker Blues* exposes how the "graffiti instinct" is recontained by capitalism. As Klara recognizes, Andy Warhol's famous lips insignia has become "the corporate logo of the Western world" (*U* 382), perfectly portraying not only Jagger's androgynous sexuality, but the voracity of consumerism itself: these lips want to devour everything from ice cream cones to cocaine. The film dramatizes how the subversive energy of rock 'n' roll has been deflected into wasteful addictions, devolving into just another form of consumerism. In this sense, the title alludes to capitalism's capacity to consume its own opposition, to seduce and subdue threatening impulses and render them harmlessly submissive. At the same time, *Cocksucker Blues* betrays the filmmakers' conflicting aims: although one might see in it a commentary on consumerism, the filmmakers seem too fascinated with these "emaciated millionaire pricks" to demystify them entirely (*U* 385). In depicting their drug use, boredom, and sexual hijinks in lurid hues, the film reinforces the group's aura as glamorous bad boys. *Cocksucker Blues* thus embodies irresolvable contradictions, at once exposing the rock world as a branch of capitalism and retaining reverence for its debauched beauty.

At one point Jagger faces the camera and disgustedly tells the filmmakers that they are "a bunch of voyeurs." But Mick and the boys love the camera, as proven by the numerous times they are shown filming themselves and the things they see—including the filmmakers. And while the incoherent dialogue, unrehearsed activities, and amateurish camera work give the appearance of unvarnished reality, the subjects always know they are being filmed. Hence the "real" life shown here is as much a performance as the concerts; the film depicts a staged reality that still eludes the control of the subjects, who are both diminished and glorified by the filming.

The presentation of the Zapruder film also comments on the relationship between film and reality. It seems to have arisen from the collective unconscious as "streamy debris of the deep mind" (*U* 496), bringing with it a dread of chaos exemplified both by the death it depicts and the very fact of its depiction. DeLillo suggests that the Zapruder film and the Texas Highway Killer video are counterparts: both depict the murder, in Texas, of a fortyish man in a car (see *U* 156, 496); both have that "jostled" quality (*U* 156, 495) that earmark them as chance documents. More importantly, the novel implies that the Zapruder film and the assassination it captures have encouraged the proliferation of such phenomena as the Texas Highway Killer video. Many critics argue that the television era truly began with the news stories of the Kennedy assassination, which ushered in the time when any event could be—even had to be—filmed or taped. The Zapruder film, then, advances an "argument about the nature of film" (*U* 495): that film does not just capture reality but constitutes it, and that the possibility of filming or taping certain actions makes similar actions more likely.

The Zapruder film both inaugurates an era and marks the end of one. Those who gather to watch it feel a "floating fear" that is confirmed by the film, which testifies to "forces in the culture that could outimagine them, make their druggiest terrors seem futile and cheap" (*U* 488, 495). Yet the film also possesses an elegiac feeling, its very artlessness conveying an innocence and faith demolished by the event that it depicts. The juxtaposition of the historical moment when it was filmed and the moment when it is screened in the novel introduces a large irony: Klara watches the end of the "innocent" 1950s from the end of the rebellious '60s, and views the death of one president just as another (his former opponent) is forced to resign for criminal activities. If the latter event means that those destructive forces in the culture issue from above as well as from below, both events prove that our icons are only flesh and blood. In this sense, the Zapruder film also serves a subversive function, its starkness inducing a "startle reaction" similar to the one depicted in the Texas Highway Killer video. And yet, as the film's recent video release proves, shock has a short shelf life: what was once upsetting is now just another piece of merchandise. Like the Hitler film in *Running Dog*, the Zapruder film exemplifies how history can become a commodity. Both *Cocksucker Blues* and the Zapruder film, then, embody the paradox displayed in *Great Jones Street* and *Mao II*: the very "underground" quality that once made them dangerous eventually enhances their commodity value.

Unlike the first two films, the third one in this section, Soviet director Sergei Eisenstein's fabled lost work *Unterwelt*, exists only in the novel. Yet it carries as much personal and political weight as the other two, not only inspiring Klara's later work, but also standing as a metaphor for DeLillo's own art (LeClair, "Underhistory" 116). Klara has always been struck by the "contradictions" in Eisenstein's cinema, where the "comically overwrought" alternates with breathtaking juxtapositions (*U* 425). Similar contradictions extend to the environment: the film is presented at Radio City Music Hall, where the Rockettes perform prior to the screening, in seemingly gross violation of the film's seriousness. But Eisenstein advocated similar theatrical effects in his early "montage of attractions" theory, which aimed to blend theater and cinema to produce emotional shocks in the spectator that would in turn evoke a specific ideological message (Goodwin 28). Similarly, Klara senses how the audience is "reconfigured" by this prelude and prepared for the bizarre film to come (*U* 428).

For his films Eisenstein developed an immensely powerful technique of montage and "rhythmic contradiction" (*U* 429); his films are constructed almost entirely of juxtaposed static shots with very little camera movement. He also created an elaborate set of theories about this method, the most famous of which is that of "dialectical montage." In this technique "the camera angle [creates] a kind of dialectic" (*U* 429): the collision of antithetical images generates a synthesis in the viewer's mind that in turn directs him or her toward a desired political conclusion (Eisenstein 161). For example, in *October* (1928) Eisenstein intercuts shots of Alexander Kerensky, despised head of the provisional government, with shots of a mechanical peacock unfurling its tail fathers; we are to conclude not only that Kerensky is vain but that the bourgeois government he represents is artificial and empty (Bordwell 45).[23]

As I have been suggesting, *Underworld* is similarly built of juxtaposed fragments (or "cells," as Eisenstein called them) that create thematic associations, although without Eisenstein's dogmatism. The similarities between *Underworld* and *Unterwelt* involve content as well as form. Allegedly shot in the mid-1930s, when most of Eisenstein's work was suppressed or lost, *Unterwelt* depicts a mad scientist with an atomic ray gun and generally deals, as does DeLillo's novel, with "people living in the shadows" (*U* 424).[24] The description of the film is intercut with Matt Shay's experiences in "The Pocket," thereby linking the film with the themes of secrecy and nuclear power explored in Matt's sections. Musing on one "silly, off-kilter and technically impressive" scene, Klara wonders whether Eisenstein was prescient about the nuclear menace or only about Japanese cinema — '50s mutation flicks like *Godzilla* — in which the monsters "not only come from the bomb but displace it" (*U* 429–30). Klara is right: *Unterwelt*, like those later films, both is about containment and embodies it. Hence it is silent because "silence suited the development of his themes": here the scientist controlling atomic power represents the Soviet state, which muzzled idiosyncratic artists and forced them to choose between losing their livelihood — and possibly their lives — or becoming "disciplined and sovietized" (*U* 431, 443). Eisenstein's film, dramatizing the conflict between eccentric individuals and oppressive institutions, "contains" the theme of DeLillo's novel.

But there is something else, something in the "glances that get exchanged," in the way the scientist touches his victims (*U* 432): *Unterwelt* is also an allegory of the closet, a cloaked parable of the homosexual underworld. As DeLillo has noted, "sexual self-repression" links Eisenstein (a lifelong bachelor who may have been gay) and J. Edgar Hoover, both of whom may have shared the desires of the hustler in "Cocksucker Blues" ("American Strangeness" 14). The committed communist and the arch-anticommunist are also connected via the musical accompaniment for the film: Prokofiev's *Love for Three Oranges*, which includes a movement entitled "Scene Infernal" and which was used as theme music for a well-known radio program about the FBI. The motif of oranges again fuses force and counterforce, just as the music blends farce and seriousness.

The music's shift to a lighter mood also suits the second half of the film, in which the once-imprisoned figures move "upward through gouged tunnels," first to a dark, rainy night, and then to a "landscaped shocked by light" (*U* 441–42). Like the brutalized workers in *Strike*, or the desperate revolutionaries in *October* who emerge from cellars to invade the Winter Palace, the protagonists in *Unterwelt* represent forces—sexual, artistic, political—that defy containment. If Hoover and Eisenstein share the belief that the world is divided into "Us and Them," Eisenstein utters the "under-voice" that Hoover devoted his life to silencing (*U* 444). As Klara sees the same cyclopes and people with missing organs that Nick Shay later sees in the Russian Museum of Misshapens (*U* 443), *Unterwelt* brings to light Hoover's deepest fears: the appearance of those "inconvenient secret[s] of the society" whose mutilated faces embody the psychic and political de-formations wrought by official power. Everything is connected: opposites merge in the shared contradictions of Hoover and Eisenstein. In the film's final image, Eisenstein uses a reverse time-lapse effect (like that in *Under-world* itself) to undo the damage done by the state: the artist has the final say, but can overcome institutional oppression only through a trick.

In "The Dramaturgy of Film Form," Eisenstein writes: "ART IS ALWAYS CONFLICT. . . . it is the task of art to reveal the contradictions of being" (161). *Unterwelt* surely does. It also impresses itself on Klara, who feels that she is "wearing the film instead of a skirt and blouse" (*U* 445), weaving itself into her identity, capturing her own conflicts and inspiring her future work. For a moment she "becomes" Eisenstein, (unintention-ally?) quoting him when she recognizes that the film depicts "the contra-dictions of being. You look at the faces on the screen and you see the muti-lated yearning, the inner divisions of people and systems, and how forces will clash and fasten, compelling the swerve from evenness that marks a thing lastingly" (*U* 444). Another "sneak attack on the dominant culture" (*U* 444), *Unterwelt* incorporates its creator's self-contradictions as a com-mitted Communist who makes a film criticizing the state that provides his living. But its contradictions transcend the merely personal; like the work of Lenny Bruce and Robert Frank, it both opposes and embodies the nuclear age and its contradictions. DeLillo's Eisensteinian technique similarly reveals the "inner divisions" of his own society, the "mutilations" of yearning generated by weapons and waste. Unlike *Cocksucker Blues* or the Zapruder film, however, both *Unterwelt* and *Underworld* salvage dig-nity from the wreckage; they move beyond pity and terror to embrace the underworld as a source of renewal.

Economies of Grace

At the intermission of *Unterwelt*, DeLillo cuts to a train carrying sixteen-year-old graffiti writer Ismael Muñoz, another gay artist seeking to sub-vert daylight institutions. Ismael—known as Moonman 157 (add the digits and you get 13)—literally works underground, spraypainting his name on subway trains. His work, like Eisenstein's, celebrates the marginalized, the backstreet life of those invisible people who live in the shadows; when the subway trains emerge into the light, Ismael's figures repeat the trajectory of Eisenstein's victims. According to the authorities who try to erase them with orange juice compound (*U* 433), his graffiti are just dirt, waste that threatens the "system of meanings by which such surfaces acquire value, integrity, and significance" (Stewart, *Crimes* 216). Indeed, Ismael's work is multiply subversive: in writing his name with stolen materials, he ironically appropriates the consumer society's fixation on brand names and transforms it into an attack on private property (Stewart, *Crimes* 227).

Ismael believes his work tells those in power that "you can't *not* see us anymore, you can't *not* know who we are" (*U* 440). Hence, to display his work in galleries, as Klara and her friend Esther aim to do, would be to obliterate its essential nature, to repeat the Rolling Stones' progression from tunnel to spotlight, from subversive force to corporation. Fortunately, Ismael remains uncaptured, and his economies of time and means remain separate from capitalism. Here the "graffiti instinct" not only preserves the otherness of the underworld but also recycles it into statements of individual freedom and perhaps even of communal strength. *Underworld*'s hope for renewal lies in the work of artists like Ismael and in the collective faith of the disenfranchised communities for which he speaks. In the efforts of Ismael, Sabato Rodia, and Klara Sax, and in the ambiguous transformation of a dead girl into an angel, DeLillo offers the potential for phoenixlike resurrection out of the ashes of capital, holding out the bare possibility of a new kind of connection, one that replaces massive, dehumanizing systems with "the argument of binding touch" (*U* 827). In these scenes, *Underworld* moves from criticism to celebration, championing those who forge economies of grace from the dead matter of weapons and waste.

At the end of the "Cocksucker Blues" section Klara visits Watts Towers, which Nick had seen earlier in the novel (Nick's scene is later chronologically). Whereas Nick interprets the structures as an emblem of his father, Klara immerses herself in the work with an artist's awareness of texture and emotion. For Klara and for DeLillo, Watts Towers, constructed out of the detritus of consumer society without using a drill, bolts, welding torch, or even a nail (Goldstone and Goldstone 59), exemplifies how art may act as an economic and moral agent of redemption. Its creator, Sabato Rodia, used the "leftovers from his daily bread"—which was no doubt meager—to create a "sculptural garden" (Gio Pomodoro, quoted in Goldstone and Goldstone 13) that nourished both himself and his community. Rodia's technique—taking whatever was at hand and making a kind of jazz composition in mortar—epitomizes bricolage. Both beautiful and bizarre, Watts Towers incarnate Rodia's "idiosyncratic self," not only because he built it alone, but because the towers, constructed without scaffolding, were scaled to his diminutive size so that he could construct each part by standing on what he had already made. The size of the work was thus determined by his "innate capacity to lift so much, stretch so far, climb so high, to create at the extreme limits of his being" (Goldstone and Goldstone 20); that is, Watts Towers *is* Sabato Rodia, even bearing (like Ismael's graffiti) his initials on its front arch (*U* 277). Embodying his identity, the towers manifest his contradictions as a small, nearly illiterate man with an outsized vision, but also represent his achievement in transcending them.

The bright colors of Watts Towers come from the tiles, but also from the Fiesta and Harlequin tableware, the 7-Up, Phillips' Milk of Magnesia, Canada Dry Ginger Ale, Clorox, beer and wine bottles that cover its surfaces (Goldstone and Goldstone 70). By bonding them to the mortar, Rodia demonstrates the "redemptive qualities of the things we use and discard" (*U* 809). Thus Watts Towers are not only, as Klara acknowledges, an "amusement park, a temple complex" and an "Italian street feast (*U* 492), but also a giant landfill, an archaeological find, and a counterhistory of mid-century American consumer culture. This history, created by ordinary people, arises from the underworld to decorate the towers like the "gang graffiti" in the streets around them (*U* 277). What is Rodia but an exemplum of the American dream, one of the "wretched refuse" welcomed in Emma Lazarus's poem, "The New Colossus," graven into the Statue of Liberty? From refuse as well Rodia fashioned a mélange of materials that functions as a synecdoche of the community, capturing the multicultural mix—like that of Nick Shay's Bronx—that characterized Watts from the 1920s through the 1950s. Advertising this function, the words "Nuestro Pueblo"—Our Town—are written with tiles on the entrance to the West Tower (Goldstone and Goldstone 48–49). Watts Towers not only embody one man's singular identity and vision, but also express an idea of history and community based upon the synthesis of disparate forces and created through an economy of recycling. Growing from Rodia's poverty and immense labor, Watts Towers represent how "graffiti" can turn waste into wealth and bind the private to the public. Perhaps most importantly, in their transformation of refuse the towers function as what LeClair calls an "internal metaphor" for *Underworld* ("Underhistory" 115), also constructed out of fragments that combine public and private worlds. Watts Towers thus epitomize how art can become an "agent of redemption," reconstructing hope and beauty out of the wreckage of history; as such it offers a model for all post-Cold War artists.

Klara is as elated and moved by Watts Towers as she was by *Unterwelt,* and leaves the Towers filled with a "delectation" that approaches helplessness (*U* 492). Rodia's achievement fuels her own work, as is clear early in the novel when Nick visits the desert where she and her helpers are crafting her latest project, spraypainting worn-out B-52 bombers. Klara has been working with "castoffs" for years, but this enterprise marks a new stage because it operates on the very symbols of the Cold War, transforming the waste that was weapons into works of singular beauty. Scarred as it is by craters and signs, visible emblems of the secret war that took place on American soil, the desert is the perfect setting for her project. Just as the girl named Long Tall Sally, painted on the nose of Chuckie Wainwright's former bomber, acted as a "charm against death," Klara wants to conjure another such charm in her name (*U* 77).[25] With the end of the nonwar that held "the world together" in terror, it is the duty of artists, she believes, to forge new connections, to "unrepeat," to write a new history (*U* 77). In redeeming wasted weapons, Klara, in her orange T-shirt, seeks to rediscover the "ordinary life behind the thing" (*U* 77), the radiance in dailiness that DeLillo has cited as the goal of his own work. Klara's "crisis art" again represents DeLillo's own response to the Triumph of Death: just as she saves discarded planes, so he recollects shots heard round the world, Sputniks, Sallys, and Minute Maids, not merely to document the waste wrought by weapons but also to offer a charm against death that radiates from the very things we have wasted and that have wasted us. From within the heart of war and capitalism DeLillo discovers an economy of grace.

In contrast, Sister Edgar, who reappears in the novel's epilogue, "Das Kapital," seeks grace by following a prudent spiritual economy in which "Prayer is a practical strategy, the gaining of temporal advantage in the capital markets of Sin and Remission" (*U* 237). She and her colleague Sister Grace distribute food and medicine to the homeless, addicted, and addled in the Bronx, hoping to rescue assets from this human landfill, this "squander of burnt-out buildings and unclaimed souls" (*U* 238). The sisters' ministry is paired with the operations of the older Ismael Muñoz and his crew, who salvage wrecked autos for parts, creating a "junkworld sculpture park" of cratered and crippled cars in a once-vacant lot (*U* 241). Ismael also rescues "runaways and throwaways," giving them jobs, responsibility, self-worth, and some money (*U* 813). His earlier, subversive labor has matured into a communal project that more explicitly tells of backstreet life: whenever a child dies in the neighborhood, his crew spraypaints a memorial "angel" on a wall, inscribing the child's name, cause of death, and personal comments. The "angels" rescue dignity from death, and remind those driving by of the human leftovers of capital's bounty.

Saddened by the deaths, Sister Edgar is heartened by the angels, which prove to her that her mission lies here. She is particularly intrigued by an elusive twelve-year-old girl named Esmeralda, who appears "unwashed but completely clean somehow," and who bears a "charmed quality," a "radiant grace" that restores the old nun's faith (*U* 244, 811). When Esmeralda is raped and thrown from a roof, Sister Edgar is shaken, finding no comfort in the poignant commemorative "angel" in Nike Air Jordans (because she was a running girl) that Ismael's crew paints. Already unsettled when the "great Terror" of the Cold War was removed, Edgar feels even more "weak and lost" after Esmeralda's horrifying death (*U* 816). She feels herself falling into a crisis of nihilism that conceives creation as a "spurt of blank matter" filled with stars and "random waste in between" (*U* 817).

Edgar is rescued by an event that is either a genuine irruption of the spiritual world or a group hallucination. Either way, hope wells up from below, fed by the secret desires of a poor community and filled out by rumor. Here again is the "longing on a large scale" that makes history. When the lights from passing trains light up a certain billboard, the lost Esmeralda's face seems to appear on the ad. Rejecting Sister Grace's skeptical claim that it's just "tabloid superstition" (*U* 819) and desperate for a sign to ward off the creeping void, Sister Edgar goes to see it. While a "madder orange moon" hangs in the sky, the huddled masses stare at the Minute Maid billboard, on which an affluent-looking white woman pours "a vast cascade of orange juice . . . diagonally from top right into a goblet" (*U* 820). Incarnating Charles Wainwright's credo about controlling "eyeballs," each fleck is embellished with the "finicky rigor of some precisionist painting," yielding an awe like that in "medieval church architecture" (*U* 820). At first blush these personified cans seem to epitomize Karl Marx's description of commodity fetishism in volume 1 of *Das Kapital*, where he analyzes how products acquire "mystical" properties, thereby reducing human relations to "the fantastic form of a relation between things" (Marx and Engels 320–21). And certainly the critique of consumer capitalism that DeLillo has been pursuing in *Underworld*—and throughout his career—partly underwrites this scene: consumerism again seems a dream that invokes the "universal third person" we all want to be (*A* 270). But if the billboard (which also consummates the motif of oranges) can be read as another example of the inauthenticity of postmodern culture, it also suggests that the same forces and conditions that create bad faith and rampant waste may also germinate effective counterfaiths: the juice cans cannot contain all the large-scale longings that seep from them.

Thus, when the train passes, the crowd "brings things to single consciousness," and gives forth a "holler of unstoppered belief," as behind the billboard's misty lake, the murdered girl's face seems to appear (*U* 821). Sister Grace claims that her visage is merely the "undersheet" showing, and in a sense she is right: the apparition embodies the "undersheet" of hope and desire hidden beneath the capitalism that largely bypasses the Bronx like the trains heading for the suburbs (*U* 822). But Edgar is not troubled by doubt. Under the "rainbow of bounteous juice" she feels "someone living in the image, an animating spirit" that bathes her with joy and hope (*U* 822). For the first time, she yanks off her latex gloves, embraces Ismael, whom she suspects to have AIDS, and becomes "nameless . . . lost to the details of personal history, a disembodied fact in liquid form, pouring into the crowd" (*U* 823): Sister Edgar is transubstantiated into the "living juice," the blood of a new covenant that promises universal connection and even redemption (*U* 824).

Yet doubt soon leaches in to taint this moment of rapture. The apparition becomes commercialized and turns into an occasion for phony sentimentality. Finally the ad is taken down, leaving the lonely words *Space Available* to represent the void left in the hearts of believers. Was this a genuine spiritual manifestation? As in *White Noise*, DeLillo remains studiously neutral; his narrator refrains from spoonfeeding us either irony or credulousness, instead just posing questions in the second person that invite our active participation: "Is the memory thin and bitter and does it shame you with its fundamental untruth . . . ? Or does the power of transcendence linger, . . . something holy that throbs on the hot horizon, the vision that you crave because you need a sign to stand against your doubt?" (*U* 824). Again the second-person voice draws the reader inexorably into the dialogue, as if to say, "the cure is here for those who wish to drink it." Sister Edgar does, cleaving in her mind and soul to the sight of "the virgin twin who is also her daughter" and the "fellowship of deep belief" her image has evoked (*U* 824). Ultimately, however, what matters is not whether the apparition is "real" (it resides in a fiction, after all), but that each reader be forced to decide if such things are possible, and what they mean if they are. What is irrefutable is DeLillo's continued fascination, even celebration, of the ways that hope emerges out of large-scale ruin (*WN* 147), how in *Underworld*, as in *The Names, White Noise* and *Mao II*, you find transcendence in unlikely places, as the very emblems of capital are transmuted into an economy of grace. This passage dramatizes most forcefully how counterhistory is scripted on the undersheet of waste, and how uncontainable yearnings emerge from within and below to challenge and redeem the devastations wrought by the makers of official history. The true makers, he suggests, are not the Hoovers of the world, but the Ismael Muñozes, Sabato Rodias, and Klara Saxes who transform those Minute

Maid cans, Canada Dry bottles, and B-52s—waste and weapons—into weapons *against* waste.

EPILOGUE: THE ARGUMENT OF BINDING TOUCH

All that remains for Sister Edgar is to die, and in a passage that alludes subtly to the end of Joyce's "The Dead," DeLillo portrays her demise amidst softly falling snow—or fallout (*U* 824). Her death represents the end of the era of containment, but may signal the dawn of a new faith, for her soul goes not to heaven but to cyberspace, where "Everything is connected," where, indeed, there are "only connections" (*U* 825). However, while people on the Internet create links, they remain disembodied, sterile. Thus if we are not exactly in DeLillo's *Inferno*, we are clearly far from Paradise. Now the "you" speaker takes control of the text, as if becoming its Deus Otiosus, and sends Edgar to that other hidden god who electronically inhabits the H-bomb home page. All connections culminate here, all the data gathered from every nuclear explosion, and Sister is right in it, merging with the god of atoms, its "dripping christblood colors, solar golds and reds" (*U* 825), when The Bomb, that twentieth-century Alpha and Omega, that transcendental signifier of the numinous (Chernus 26; Weart 396), explodes. As the mushroom cloud spreads around her, Edgar feels the "power of false faith." Perhaps she understands that she has worshipped a bogus deity, or how technology has made downwinders of us all, how, unlike the divinity limned in *The Cloud of Unknowing*, which draws our love up through the cloud, this god only pulls us apart, "leaving us vague, drained, docile . . . willing to be shaped" like Erica Deming and young Matty Shay (*U* 826). Atomic fusion now generates a synthetic fusion that brings together Edgar and J. Edgar, Church and State, the dexter and sinister sides of the Cold War. Death triumphs over them too.

However, unlike many of DeLillo's works, *Underworld* ends not with a sardonic twist but with a tentative hope. In its embrace of the human yearning for transcendence and community, it follows *The Names*, and in its movement outward toward a cosmic or collective perspective, it recapitulates the denouement of *Ratner's Star*. The conclusion of *Underworld* reveals an author cautiously uncovering a belief in renewal. On the book's last pages a word appears to the narrator from the "lunar milk of the data stream" to replace the airbursts, inspiring him or her to trace its "tunneled underworld" of roots and meanings (*U* 826). Once again magic rises from below, and we learn that this word has evolved from earlier words meaning to "[f]asten, fit closely, bind together," as shown by cognates such as "pact" — to agree, to make a concord, to come together in harmony. The word not only denotes that everything is connected, but in its branching, intricately looping history, embodies it (*U* 827). This is DeLillo's rendering of that powerful, one-syllabled word invoked in *The Cloud of Unknowing*, the word that the supplicant is told to "fasten[ ] to you," the better to beat upon the cloud and the "darkness above you" (*Cloud* 134). It is not to be "unfastened" but kept whole to provide strength and cohesion. As the word appears, the text's "you" — now encompassing us as well as the writer — looks out of the window and hears the voices of children playing a game. It's "your voice," again, American (*U* 827): the sound and the game fasten us back to the opening paragraph of the novel (see *U* 11). The narrator invites us to join this community, to make everything connect, not in cyberspace or in the fevered minds of paranoids and bombheads, but in works of imagination that we collaborate in making. Only by salvaging artifacts of history, by transmuting waste and weapons through artistic grace, DeLillo implies, can we avoid the despair of Lenny Bruce and the sick fetishes of J. Edgar Hoover. Only art, it seems, can translate imaginary "serenities and contentments . . . its whisper of reconciliation" out into the streets, and there pit against fission, secrecies, and violations the "argument of binding touch" (*U* 827). Only art can link the writer's desire and our own to engender that large-scale longing that remakes history. Only art that both demonstrates how everything is connected and promotes such connection can materialize what the word signifies. Although you remain skeptical that the word can move from behind the screen to the world outside it, you allow the word its own resting place in the final paragraph. This is your hopeful benediction.

Peace.

Notes

Chapter 1

1. These shifts are not jump cuts, as Douglas Keesey claims (205): jump cuts excise sections of continuous scenes to create temporal disjunctions but do not generally operate between discrete scenes. Of course, Godard is famous for popularizing the use of the jump cut in *Breathless*.

2. Unless otherwise noted, all citations from *Americana* are taken from the 1989 reprint rather than from the 1973 paperback edition. Although the Pocket paperback contains the full text of the novel as originally published, only the 1989 version is now in print. This later version also incorporates DeLillo's corrections.

3. Caroline prefigures *Underworld*'s Klara Sax, who makes art from discarded B-52s and other waste.

4. Protests against Dow Chemical play a minor role in the early life of Marian Bowman Shay in *Underworld* (*U* 598–604).

5. Hirsch (296–300) and Buckley (17) provide helpful summaries of *Bildungsroman* plot conventions.

6. I have borrowed these terms from Ian Reid, who also furnishes useful definitions and examples of these and other kinds of textual frames (44–58).

7. Even Bell's brief marriage (presented in flashback in Part 1) seemed "arranged for the whim of a camera" (*A* 30): most of their evenings out were devoted to attending films, always wearing "certain clothes for certain movies" (*A* 35), and their sexual encounters "took their inspiration from cinema" (*A* 35). A "blend of jump-cuts and soft-focus tenderness" (*A* 37), it was "all there but the soundtrack" (*A* 36).

8. In *Ulysses* Stephen envisions his mother, dead from cancer, returning from

the grave, "her wasted body within its loose brown graveclothes giving off an odour of wax and rosewood, her breath . . . a faint odour of wetted ashes" (5). Similarly, David recalls "the vast white silence of my mother's deathbed, candlewax and linen, her enormous eyes . . . her body . . . little more than ash, crumbs of bone; her hands . . . dry kindling" (A 97).

9. The Barthesian/Derridean version of intertextuality argues that "every sign can be *cited*, put between quotation marks" (Derrida 320); looking for specific allusions is pointless. Other theorists, most notably Michael Riffaterre, claim that intertextuality is meaningful only insofar as specific intertexts can be found and juxtaposed with the text under consideration (see Riffaterre, "Syllepsis" 620 and "Compulsory" 76). The "infinite citationality" thesis, though undoubtedly true in some sense, leaves little for the practical critic to do. I am claiming that identifying specific precursors is crucial for an adequate interpretation of DeLillo's novel. For a more detailed discussion of these competing versions of intertextuality, see Osteen 228–32.

10. This technique corresponds to *mu*, a Zen concept in which the spaces between materials are conceived as an integral part of the work (D. A. Cook 795–96). Indeed, even watching an Ozu movie is a kind of Zen exercise, as one must shift expectations away from the mobile camera, quick cutting and plot-oriented scripts of most American films and cultivate the patience needed to accept meaningful absence.

11. DeLillo himself seems fascinated with "the interview technique," using it repeatedly in his novels and plays: *Great Jones Street* contains a mock transcript of a chaotic interview with Bucky Wunderlick (*GJS* 102–7); Billy Twillig is questioned, interview-style, throughout *Ratner's Star*; Brita Nilsson's photography session with *Mao II*'s Bill Gray is a kind of pictorial interview; and almost all of DeLillo's most recent play, *Valparaiso*, consists of a round of interviews. The interview technique provides a ready-made format for dialogue and creates a stagy ambience that combines authenticity and unreality.

12. LeClair and Keesey briefly mention Bell's and DeLillo's debts to Godard's unconventional plots and use of interviews and monologues (LeClair, *Loop* 56; Keesey 26). Neither, however, analyzes this intertextual relationship in detail, and both misquote the phrase from *Masculin féminin* as "Marxism and Coca-Cola" (*Loop* 56; Keesey 24).

13. For a treatment of DeLillo's subversion of generic expectations, see Johnston, "Generic."

14. This self-reflexive strategy (which Godard also uses in *Le mépris* [*Contempt*]) is employed in David's segment 14, as Simmons St. Jean, David's college film instructor, offers a set of similarly pompous pronouncements (A 315).

15. Cf. the words of advertising executive Jerry Goodis, who declares that "Advertising doesn't always mirror how people are acting, but how they're dreaming" (quoted in Leiss et al. 200).

16. After filming his first segment, David phones Simmons St. Jean to ask questions about the scene in *Ikiru*: "One: did Kurosawa shoot up at the old man? Two: did he shoot the whole scene without cutting? Three: did the old man swing on the swing or did he remain stationary?" (A 248). St. Jean admits that he has never seen Kurosawa's masterpiece. For the record, the answers are (1) he shoots

from just below eye level; (2) Kurosawa cuts once, when moving from a side-angle to a frontal shot of Watanabe; (3) the old man swings almost imperceptibly as he sings.

17. Cowart astutely suggests that DeLillo and Kurosawa both realize "that personal and national corruption are coextensive." Unlike Bell, Cowart observes, but "like Kurosawa . . . (or for that matter, St. Augustine), DeLillo understands that *ikiru*, living, can never be pursued outside the process of dying" ("For Whom" 613).

18. In the original version of the novel (Pocket edition, 273–74), this passage of self-recognition is considerably longer, and contains additional allusions to Eisenstein's *Alexander Nevsky*, *The Agony and the Ecstasy* (with Kirk Douglas), *Bonnie and Clyde*, Sydney Greenstreet (misspelled) in John Huston's 1942 *Across the Pacific*, Richard Lester's *The Knack and How to Get It*, and the opening scene of *Citizen Kane*, among others. The edited version sharpens the thematic point of these allusions.

Chapter 2

1. Michael Oriard has pointed out the ascetic tendency in DeLillo's novels, but argues (I think, mistakenly) that DeLillo uncritically endorses this simplifying impulse.

2. LeClair (*Loop*) notes the prevalence of the looping patterns in DeLillo's novels.

3. DeLillo's novels often end in deserts or motels: David Bell ends his quest for origins in a circular race track in the Texas desert; Selvy returns to the Texas desert and there sacrifices himself; Lyle Wynant, in *Players*, is suspended at the end of that novel in a motel room, which he contemplates as a place "to be afraid on a regular basis" (*P* 209–10); Gladney consummates his quest to kill death in a motel room. Gary Harkness's end zone—a desert motel—combines these terminal sites.

4. For a discussion of the theological foundations of the apocalyptic mentality in American fiction, see Robinson.

5. *End Zone*'s emphasis on the dire consequences of all-out nuclear war is somewhat less pertinent after the demise of the Cold War, and Schell's apocalyptic forecasts are less likely to come true. Nevertheless, the belief in the Bomb's power to save national prestige and bring about a redemptive cleansing lies partly behind such recent phenomena as the 1998 exchange of nuclear tests by India and Pakistan.

6. DeLillo returns to the theme of nuclear theology in the Matt Shay and Sister Edgar sections of *Underworld* (discussed in Chapter 8). Bearing out Lifton's assertion about the affiliation between nuclearism and asceticism, DeLillo connects Sister Edgar's pathological fear of infection to her desire for apocalyptic purification.

7. Although the conflict in "Human Moments in World War III" is nonnuclear, the soldiers who fight it are nonetheless shielded by distance and technology from its dirty consequences. With their lives "governed by specific rules, by patterns, codes, controls" (581), war seems to reveal the "hidden simplicity of

some powerful mathematical truth" (574). But "human moments" seep in, and with them come "upwelling awe and dread" (579).

8. DeLillo fleshes out this association between nuclear weapons and waste in *Underworld*, where Klara Sax cites J. Robert Oppenheimer's description of the first atomic weapon as "merde," because "something that eludes naming is automatically relegated . . . to the status of shit" (*U* 77).

9. The most influential discussion of the relationship between fictional endings and apocalyptic fiction is Kermode's *The Sense of an Ending*. For an illuminating examination of similar experimental techniques in several novels about nuclear holocaust, see Schwenger.

10. See Oriard (3) for a contrasting view of DeLillo's Thoreauvian themes.

11. Only three detailed treatments of *Great Jones Street* exist: DeCurtis's "The Product," Chapter 4 of LeClair's *In the Loop* (87–110), and a chapter in Keesey's study. The other critics who mention the novel either dismiss it (for example, Nadeau calls it "DeLillo's least impressive, most transparent narrative" [168]), or find it uninteresting (e.g., Oriard 9, 15).

12. LeClair (*Loop* 91) observes that the "generic model for *Great Jones Street* is theatrical" and that the characters are little more than voices or "wearers of costumes." Aaron similarly likens all of DeLillo's characters to "actors in a traveling theatrical company, ready at any moment to harangue, comment, speculate, improvise" (74). See also Johnston ("Generic" 262–63), who remarks that the characters constantly seem to be "facing the camera."

13. Two of Ben Jonson's masques seem particularly pertinent to *Great Jones Street*. His *Masque of Blackness*, which praises the daughters of Niger for having beauty despite their blackness (Meagher 108), is echoed in Azarian's fixation on the meaning of "blackness" (*GJS* 123, 183). Jonson also wrote the *Masque of Queens*, which, like DeLillo's novel, examines the nature of fame (Meagher 152). After an introductory "false masque" consisting of twelve hags representing Suspicion, Ignorance, Cruelty, etc., this masque "makes it clear that in the House of Fame, heroism is a secondary virtue . . . [to] the enduring and transforming power of poetry" (Orgel 61, 65). Bucky Wunderlick's House of Fame is also peopled by hags and sycophants; like Jonson's masque, DeLillo's ultimately presents literature as the real hero. As Meagher comments, the masque implies that "fame needs its supervisors and custodians" (156), a message not far removed from that of DeLillo's novel.

14. Mottram (63) briefly points out the relevance of Bataille's concept of excess for *Great Jones Street*. It is worth noting that the Renaissance masque also involved an economy of excess: the extravagance of these performances were designed to display the monarch's largesse and thereby enhance his or her status (Fletcher 59). Bucky seeks a similar final glorification, and the masque he views (and writes) is a necessary preparation.

15. Here I agree with LeClair: DeLillo shares Jameson's belief that "the profound vocation of the work of art in a commodity society [is] not to be a commodity, not to be consumed, to be unpleasurable in the commodity sense" (Jameson, *Marxism* 395; see *Loop* 15).

1. DeLillo has stated that he also wrote a "shadow book" with the "same story, same main character, but a small book . . . the size of a children's book, maybe it *was* a children's book" ("Art of Fiction" 288–89). The children's book briefly peers from the shadows in the picture-book headlines—"I Take a Scary Ride," "I Don't Feel So Good"—that demarcate the sections of "Reflections."

2. LeClair (*Loop* 125) provides a useful chart of the major figures in this history, and I have followed his lead in my remarks, which expand upon his outline.

3. Among these conventions are parodies of Socratic dialogues (virtually all of Part 1); independence from realistic plausibility (the star message); the use of "slum naturalism" (Billy's childhood memories of the Bronx); an "extraordinary philosophical universalism" and willingness to confront ultimate questions (*Ratner's Star* addresses human evolution and cosmology); a construction on three levels, Olympian, earthly, and underworld (stars, earth and a number of holes and caves), and so on. For a complete list, see Bakhtin, *Problems* 114–18; see also Relihan 6–7, and Kharpertian 32.

4. Keesey (74) also notes the resemblance between DeLillo's scientists and Swift's Laputians, who are so wrapped up in "Cogitation" that they constantly fall down, and who are thrown into a panic by the possibility of an eclipse (Swift 146–47, 151).

5. DeLillo acknowledges only similarities of "format, not characters or themes or story except in the loosest sense" (Interview with LeClair 27). LeClair (*Loop* 112, 117) and Keesey (68–69) cursorily note a few parallels.

6. Verifiable reality is said to be "pebble-rubbed" (hence "*khalix, calculus*") because the Pythagoreans represented numbers by placing pebbles in sand (Hollingdale 16).

7. "Directions for knowing all dark things" is the title of the famous mathematical text written by the Egyptian sage Ahmes the Scribe (see Kline, *Western Culture* 21).

8. The emphasis on growth in Chapter 4, "Expansion," obviously parallels the changes in size that Alice undergoes in chapter 4 of *Alice*. Billy also recalls the growth of his father's black dog, generically named "puppy," an allusion to the giant puppy who threatens Alice at the end of chapter 4 (Carroll 64).

9. Thales of Miletus, the earliest of the Greek scientist-philosophers, claimed that the first principle of all things was water (Wheelwright 44; his theory is incarnated by hydrologist Una Braun). Thales also predicted the solar eclipse of 585 B.C., which occurred during a battle and threw both armies into confusion (Wheelwright 44; cf. Hollingdale 15). Thales allegedly brought geometry to Europe after figuring out how to measure the Egyptian pyramids by the length of their shadows (Serres 84–85). Serres (93n) offers a fanciful etymology of Thales' name that links it to the Greek words for "sprout" or "grow"; if Serres is right, Billy is a new Thales, a "sprout" who gains maturity through an encounter with an eclipse.

10. Kepler's first book, *Cosmographicum Mysterium* (1597), attempted to prove that the orbits of the planets are determinable by using only the five "regular" solid polyhedrons (Kline, *Western Culture* 113–14). He later retracted this theory after discovering that their orbits were elliptical.

11. As I noted above, Kepler's book has many similarities to DeLillo's (and

Carroll's): all three texts frame the action as a dream, and depict a cave-dwelling civilization (Lear 154–55). DeLillo's and Kepler's also incorporate a disquisition on eclipses (Lear 144–50) and an imaginary extraterrestrial race (Lear 155). The entire text of *Somnium* may be found in Lear, 79–163; the passage quoted in *Ratner's Star* is found on pages 103–4.

12. For a discussion of Pascal's work on the cycloid, see Hollingdale 159–64.

13. The key also alludes to the first chapter of *Alice*, when Alice, after her long fall down the rabbit-hole, discovers a "tiny golden key" that opens a door leading to a garden (Carroll 29). To get through the door, she must drink the liquid that shrinks her.

14. For Newton's less mystical description of gravitation, see Kline, *Western Culture* 206–7.

15. Several critics have cited this passage as an example of the way that De-Lillo "aestheticizes mathematics" (Mendelsohn 145) throughout Billy's sections. But the passage must be read in terms of the historical narrative that underlies "Adventures." Indeed, Billy's words echo the meditations of distinguished scientists such as Albert Einstein, who writes in "The Temple of Science" that through science, "Man seeks to . . . overcome the world of experience by striving to replace it to some extent by his own image" (quoted in Hayles, *Chaos Bound* 99).

16. This symbol refers to the constant limit (approximately 0.5772 . . .) that the harmonic series—a divergent infinite series—of fractions ($1+ 1/2 +1/3 + 1/4 . . . + 1/n - \ln n$) approaches but never reaches (Hollingdale 284–86). An example of a convergent series is $.3 +.03 + .003. + .0003 . . .$, which "converges" to 1/3. See also Motz and Weaver 195–96.

17. Thus, for example, Riemann's work on *n*-sheeted surfaces emerged from that of Gauss and Euler; Gauss's student Richard Dedekind formulated the Dedekind cut (a method of partitioning points on a line that permits the discovery of one-to-one correspondences with real numbers) only because of Gauss; Dedekind's theorem became an axiom only when later formalized by Georg Cantor (Hollingdale 356). The Dedekind cut later appears in Billy's thoughts: "Given a straight line and any point not on this line, it is possible to draw through this point only one line that is parallel to the given line" (*RS* 130).

18. The title of chapter 9 alludes to chapter 9 of *Alice*, which is populated by composite figures like the Gryphon and Mock Turtle (Carroll 125–27).

19. The tape refers to several Renaissance Italian mathematicians, including Del Ferro, Cardano (who wrote on ghosts as well as on *The Art of Solving Algebraic Equations* (*Ars Magna*), Fior, and Fontana, and to Sylvester and Cayley, two English mathematicians who were so closely associated that, as LeClair notes, they enter most histories of mathematics as a "composite figure" like *Ratner's Star*'s Melcher-Speidell (LeClair, *Loop* 130). Sylvester and Cayley's work on vector analysis and matrix theory provided an important foundation for Einsteinian relativity (Hollingdale 350; Motz and Weaver 284).

20. Ratner's mystical ideas about opposites echo Pythagorean metaphysics, in which the universe is constructed by ten sets of opposites (e.g., odd vs. even, male vs. female, light vs. darkness, etc.; Gorman 141). His views about the body also resemble Pythagorean doctrine, which holds that the body is "held together by the tensive relation" between opposites, while the soul is "a blending and attunement of those same elements" (Wheelwright 211).

21. At this point Softly alludes to Frege's work on the logical foundations of mathematics, noting that it was published the same year as a book on non-Euclidean geometry by Dodgson/ Lewis Carroll (*RS* 273). Although Softly doesn't tell us, the year was 1879, 100 years before *Ratner's Star* takes place.

22. Although chaos theory (a misleading name, it seems) restores the notion that reality exists independently of observation (Rice 85), it also implies that this order cannot be measured or fully calculated. For more on fractals, see Hayles, *Chaos Bound* 164–69.

23. The "golden-thighed" Pythagoras lived in a cave near Samos with his followers (Gorman 76–77); his "golden thigh" was probably a birthmark similar to Jean Venable's star-shaped mark on her left buttock.

24. Her notion of the writer as gamemaster and logician echoes Carroll's own Humpty-Dumptyian views on language: "I maintain that any writer of a book is fully authorised in attaching any meaning he likes to any word or phrase he intends to use" (*Symbolic Logic* 166).

25. The Logicon project inverts the aims of Swift's Professors in the School of Language, who seek to eliminate contamination by carrying all the objects they wish to discuss (Swift 174–75). While Logicon is a metalanguage, Swift's is an anti-language; both share the notion that language is filth.

26. Gödel's thesis is usually referred to as the "Incompleteness Theorem." For fuller accounts of this principle, see Civello 116–19 and Hayles, *Cosmic* 33–35 and *Chaos Bound* 267ff. Molesworth (147) also notes the importance of this theorem for *Ratner's Star*.

27. "Googol" is a number invented in the 1930s that designates 1 followed by 100 zeros, or 10^{100}. Googolplex is an almost unimaginably large number: 1 followed by a googol of zeros, or 10^{googol}. "Glossolalia" refers to the ritual of speaking in tongues, which plays an important role in *The Names*.

28. Another intriguing parallel to Lewis Carroll's works arises here. Chapter 23 of Carroll's *Sylvie and Bruno* (1889) depicts an "Outlandish watch" that functions as a time machine. Setting its hands back also sets events back to the time indicated; pressing a reversal peg starts events moving in reverse. Endor's clock similarly indicates the moment when cosmic and human time will "go the other way." Also, in chapter 5 of *Through the Looking Glass*, the White Queen tells Alice about the problems of living in reverse: for example, the Queen bleeds, but only later cuts her finger. As LeClair has noted (*Loop* 116), the same reversal happens to Billy, who wears a bandage on his finger in Chapter 1 (*RS* 8), but doesn't cut his finger until the end of the novel (*RS* 423). DeLillo makes "things go the other way" again in *Underworld*, which contains a similar philosophy of history as does *Ratner's Star*.

29. According to my informant, Dr. Neng Liang of Loyola College, the word can, depending upon context, mean family history, the root or stem of a tree, a foundation, essence, or book.

30. At the end of *Through the Looking Glass* Alice cries that she "can't stand this any longer"; candles go up, bottles fly away, and she shakes the Red Queen, who then turns back into her cat (Carroll 335–36). Kelly notes that this scene is "tantamount to a sexual orgasm," a connection also indicated by her "mating" of the King on the book's chessboard (105).

31. The conclusion has been read as primarily negative by Mendelsohn, who

nonetheless asserts that the value-dark dimension offers "myriad possibilities" (176), and especially by Nadeau, who interprets the ending as signifying how "closed systems of abstraction . . . provide a virtual guarantee that the entire human experiment will come to an abrupt halt in nuclear war" (173). Other critics, notably Molesworth (149) and Allen (paragraph 2) recognize signs of rebirth in the oxymoronic dust.

Chapter 4

1. For discussions of *Running Dog* in relation to generic expectations, see Frow, *Marxism* 147, Johnston, "Generic" 271–72, and LeClair, *Loop* 174.

2. DeLillo uses second-person for similar thematic ends in the "Texas Highway Killer" section of *Underworld* (155–60).

3. In Wolfram von Eschenbach's *Parsival*, the hero is forced to wear the queen's mantle when entering the Fisher King's castle (Brown 181). In the earliest extant Grail story, an unknown knight is met on his quest by Guinevere and Sir Gawain; they agree to accompany him, but before they reach camp he is killed by a dart cast from an invisible hand (Weston 33). Thus in Ludecke, DeLillo conflates Christ, Sir Percival, and the anonymous knight who inspires the Grail quest.

4. Narrative "dispossession" is a "textual strategy for preempting or usurping interest as to whose side of the story will be heard," carried out through a "wresting or arresting of control over the relative positions of the parties" (Reid 27).

5. In his essay "Silhouette City," DeLillo remarks on how "Nazi lore and notation represent a rich source of material to be consulted in the service of fantasy and self-fulfillment," and goes on to note how Nazism addresses us individually, because "each of us spins on a life-axis of power and submission" (29, 30).

6. Selvy exemplifies Sontag's argument that the rise of porn is related to "the traumatic failure of modern capitalistic society to provide authentic outlets for the perennial human . . . need for exalted self-transcending modes of concentration and seriousness" ("Pornographic" 231).

7. Actually, "fascism" derives from the Latin *fasces*, referring to a bundle of rods with a projecting blade used by ancient Roman magistrates as a symbol of authority. Thus fascism seeks to unite the many under a single dictatorial authority that relies upon the everpresent possibility of violence—hence the projecting blade.

8. Perhaps for this reason several critics have rightly observed that the novel is largely " 'about' representation" (Frow, *Marxism* 145; cf. Johnson 75). O'Donnell even terms it a "parody of representation" (70–71).

9. As Johnson notes, Selvy is merely an "extreme example of what DeLillo often gives us: a site at which various lines and pressures converge, rather than a 'character' " (76).

10. His bladework harks back to classical Grail legends, which usually feature an enchanted sword that must be pieced together or pulled out. For example, one of the strange sights that Sir Percival (in some versions, Sir Gawain) encounters is a Bleeding Lance, a sword from which blood flows (Chrétien 88; l. 3197; cf. Weston 35). Mudger approximates such a blade when he nicks his thumb to test his weapon's sharpness (*RD* 120).

11. Numerous observers remarked upon Hitler's devotion to dogs, particularly Blondi (see Bullock 717). One of the dictator's final acts was to euthanize his pet.

12. This pattern again fits Grail Romance tales. For example, the conclusion of the early English quest romance *Sir Percyvelle* finds Percival reunited with his mother (Weston 46).

13. This gruesome fate may also have a medieval intertext. In the thirteenth-century Welsh romance *Peredur*, the young knight is presented, along with the grail, a "platter containing a severed head swimming in blood" (Cline, "Introduction" to Chrétien xx).

14. Many critics have found this final exhortation jarring, because it abruptly shifts the film's tone and fails even to resolve the Hynkel/Barber mistaken identity plot. For several years afterward, nonetheless, Chaplin delivered the speech to public audiences. For a summary of the critical reception of the film and speech, see Maland 176–86.

15. This adjustment need not be as radical as one might think. Certainly the atmosphere in the bunker was scarcely conducive to shooting cute home movies. The bunker's remaining denizens—Hitler and Eva, the Goebbels family, their servants and aides, and a few remaining military advisors—were traumatized and desperate. In the final days of the bombing of Berlin, electrical power was intermittent, and so it would have been extremely difficult to operate a movie camera. But there were two occasions when making such a film would have been possible: April 20 and April 23, 1945. The first date is that of Hitler's fifty-sixth birthday; the second marks the point when, finally recognizing that the German army was defeated, Hitler assumed an "unnatural state of calm" (Trevor-Roper 136–37), and thus could have been ready to engage in some frivolity.

16. Goebbels had six children, whose names all began with "H." As Lightborne comments, all six were poisoned after Hitler's death, and died along with their parents.

17. Hitler's medical conditions—perhaps Parkinson's disease, or a small stroke—have been amply documented. See, for example, Galante and Silianoff 7 and Trevor-Roper 127.

18. Both Bryant (26) and Morris (118) mention the significance of Ob and note its connection to Owen, but neither develops its structural and thematic role in the novel.

19. The concurrent emergence of alphabetic writing and engraved money has been analyzed in detail by Shell (*Economy*, 11–62) and Goux, who argues that the prevalent mode of writing in a society is "congruent to the status of the dominant form of economic exchange" (69; see also 71, 84). Many extant epigraphs indeed record contracts and monetary accounts; for examples, see Cook 32, 36, 43. As Weinstein notes, Axton's "business" is just a more sophisticated version of such accounting (293), except that his contracts are designed to be anonymous and impermanent.

20. DeLillo has also spoken of his delight in "the way the words and letters look when they come off the [typewriter] hammers onto the page—finished, printed, beautifully formed" ("Art of Fiction" 283); cf. the Nadotti interview (95).

21. Recent Minoan digs have turned up signs of human sacrifice. Since the novel is set in 1979–80, DeLillo may be referring to an actual 1979 dig at Anemo-

spilia in Crete that found evidence of human sacrifice (see Hughes 13–17). The Names cult—whose first victim is discovered at this point in the novel—may be reenacting such Minoan rituals.

22. Goux describes this stage as the "Asiatic mode of production," because of its use of ideographs (80). Although his model is useful, its mappings of economic, linguistic, and historical modes elide important differences. It also veers dangerously close at times to the kind of ethnic essentialism that *The Names* implicitly condemns.

23. As Foster further notes, their work is not really "preverbal" but "prelinguistic" (159). Similarly, Sontag comments on how a "discontent with language" inevitably develops when thought "reaches a certain high, *excruciating* order of complexity and spiritual seriousness," and prompts purifying movements ("Aesthetics of Silence" 195). Harvey Cox points out that such a revolt also underlay the rise of modern Pentecostalism (93).

24. The preacher quotes 1 Corinthians 13:1, where Paul writes that "men can speak with the tongues of angels" (*N* 306). In this passage Paul lists the "gifts of the Holy Spirit," but concludes that their greatest value is communal: as Morris points out (118), the passage actually implies that "glossolalia . . . is worthless when isolated from human concerns." It ends with the famous verse, "When I was a child, I spake as a child, I understood as a child, I thought as a child; but when I became a man, I put away childish things" (1 Cor. 13:11). In other words, Paul is arguing that childlike innocence is insufficient for finding the Kingdom of Heaven.

25. Ong notes the close historical relationship between oral language and the sacred, whereby the spoken word is used more often than the written word in religious rituals. This insight is exemplified by the emphatically oral form of worship depicted in the excerpt from Tap's novel that closes the book.

26. As Marshall Sahlins argues, gift exchanges are associated with the "solidarity extreme" normally identified with a household and family. That is, the gift economy is founded upon the notion that human beings are kin; moreover, the exchanges of gifts creates a feeling of kinship in producers (Sahlins 194; cf. Hyde 56–60, 74–94).

27. Clearly, then, I disagree with John McClure, who claims that DeLillo's Acropolis looks "dangerously like a Western rallying point, the anxiously constructed and agonistic alternative to his Mecca, a place where Muslims are seen to exchange sober individuality for intoxicating fanaticism" ("Post-Secular" 155). In critiquing the objectifying perceptions of both Westerners and the cult, DeLillo warns against all forms of exploitation that fail to see the Other as Other. Indeed, formulated in *The Names* as an offering or gift, speech extends the boundaries of the household, potentially turning Others into brothers.

28. The Kansas setting for the excerpt is also appropriate, since many historians trace modern Pentecostalism to Charles Parham's Bible college in Topeka, Kansas (Dayton 16).

29. Both glossolalists and scholars of the practice claim that tongue-speaking is a "child-like form of language" (Kildahl 31) in which speakers are delivered from "the iron cage of grammar" (Cox 87). Although Maltby is certainly right that DeLillo's work sometimes celebrates childhood and purity in a way that resembles the Romantics, he also betrays a deep mistrust of such nostalgia, because, as he shows repeatedly, it is so easily converted into authoritarianism.

30. Pentecostal worship is called "charismatic" because tongue-speaking is considered a gift — "charism" — of grace, but also, as Kildahl shows, because most tongue-speakers are able to do so only when under the influence of a charismatic authority-figure (Dayton 24; Kildahl 40). In this respect the worshippers' loss of ego comes uncomfortably close to those forms of group-think that DeLillo repeatedly criticizes in his other novels.

Chapter 5

1. For a more detailed definition of the dynamics of secrecy, see Calinescu 227–28.

2. O'Donnell persuasively analyzes the secrecy process in *Running Dog*.

3. As Keesey notes (92), carrying on a love affair "requires many of the same practices as an espionage mission: secret communications, hidden rendezvous," and so on. Lyle's relationship with Kinnear also seems latently sexual, and when Kinnear's surrogate, secretary Rosemary Moore, appears at the end of the novel wearing a plastic phallus, it is as if she were bearing out Lyle's and Kinnear's secret desire for a homosexual relationship like the one depicted in Pammy's chapters.

4. In his survey of approaches to secrecy, Tefft describes two that apply to *Players*. One is the "dramaturgical model," in which the social world is structured in terms of the interactions of individuals, scripts and other players (40). Another comes from exchange theory, which presents social interactions as (balanced) exchanges of goods and services. Both, Tefft argues, are inadequate. Dramaturgy cannot account for ways that "team" or "cast" members keep secrets from one another (Tefft 41–42); exchange theory is based upon a rationalist, economistic model of human motives that fails to encompass the risks and benefits of secrecy, particularly when it involves large groups (see Tefft 42–45). Still, both metaphors shed light on the Wynants' secret lives.

5. This affiliation between secret money and sacred mystery is not surprising since, as Goux points out, in ancient times "Temples . . . also served as mints and as public treasuries. Monetary capital partakes of the same social logic as divine centralization: religious centers are fulcrums of capital" (91). Thus in his ambitious schema of symbolic economies, Goux places gold in the same position as the Godhead (in religion) and the phallus (in psychoanalysis). See Goux 54.

6. There is obviously some overlap between forms: certainly the plotters are concealing attributes that may bring harm, and their secrecy is also "protective." Moreover, private-life secrecy can certainly become aggressive, as Oswald's own trajectory proves. While the distinction may be too schematic, nonetheless it helps to clarify the differences and similarities between the two plots and their characters.

7. See also "Art of Fiction" (303): "the intelligence agencies represent old mysteries and fascinations, ineffable things. . . . They're like churches that hold the final secrets."

8. Mackey's words strikingly echo those of Simmel, who writes that "the attractions of secrecy are related to those of its logical opposite, betrayal" (333); indeed, by its nature, the secret is "surrounded by the possibility and temptation of betrayal" (334).

9. In a striking coincidence that seems to bear out Oswald's belief in destiny, *Suddenly* was produced by Richard Bassler, for Libra Productions.

10. Simmel argues that secret organizations most often proliferate in societies either in their infancy or, as DeLillo seems to be implying here, in decay (347). The America of *Libra*, Millard notes, is one "immunized against community, unified in acceptance of fragmentation" (22).

Chapter 6

1. See Conroy for a treatment of *White Noise* as evidence of the "crisis of authority" in postmodern culture (98).

2. The *Ancient Egyptian Book of the Dead* contains numerous spells to protect dead souls from snakes as the departed pass to the Field of Reeds. See the "chapters" or "spells" in the *Egyptian Book of the Dead* numbered 33, 34, 37, 39, etc.

3. This episode has acquired its own aura as the "most cited scene in *White Noise*," probably because it so perfectly exemplifies certain (Fredric Jameson's as well as Baudrillard's) theories of postmodernism. See, for example, Frow ("Last Things" 180–81), Keesey (136), and especially Wilcox.

4. Murray was excited by kitsch in his previous incarnation in *Amazons*, where he became sexually aroused by Cleo Birdwell's recitations of her childhood in the village of Badger, with its "flying red horse in the Socony Mobil station" (*Amazons* 290). Apparently Murray's enthusiasm is shared by real-life professors at a certain large midwestern American university which, I discovered in a conversation with some of its undergraduates, offers a major in Packaging.

5. The original dust jacket of *White Noise* itself resembles a generic package, as if simultaneously to declare and denounce its condition as packaged commodity.

6. On patina see McCracken 31–43.

7. Frow argues that the insertions evolve from "apparently impersonal enunciation to more localized points of origin" ("Last Things" 188). That is, in the latter parts of the novel the commodity mantras issue more often from other characters than from Gladney; cf. White 14–15.

8. For a fuller discussion of parataxis in *White Noise*, see Hayles, "Parataxis," 408–13.

9. Maltby analyzes this scene as a prime instance of DeLillo's "romantic metaphysics": a belief in the heightened spiritual capacity and wisdom of children that recalls Romantic writers such as Wordsworth (267–68). What Maltby doesn't acknowledge is the similarity between Wordsworth's neo-Platonism and religious practices such as those in *The Tibetan Book of the Dead*. For Wordsworth and believers in transmigration, children are wise because they haven't yet forgotten their past lives, which they can "channel" by recollection.

10. As I noted in Chapter 2 (and as Messmer also points out), the toxic cloud stands in for an atomic mushroom cloud—the most powerful source of dread for Cold War-era Americans (Messmer 407).

11. Like Nyodene D, these products are designed to defeat the natural process of decay: Krylon is a brand of paint; Rust-Oleum is a rust-inhibiting enamel; Red Devil removes black soot. If the list functions as what Patti White calls a "nar-

rative toxin" that interrupts the flow of language (14), here the products themselves are toxic.

12. The documentary *Tabloid Frenzy* estimates, for example, that the *National Enquirer* reaped $100 million in profit in a recent year.

13. This scene has prompted as much critical comment as the "most photographed barn" scene. The two critical extremes are exemplified by Paul Maltby, who adduces the scene as evidence of DeLillo's tendency to "seek out transcendent moments in our postmodern lives that hint at possibilities for cultural regeneration" (261), and by Arthur Saltzman, for whom Steffie's words are toxic, "at once as synthetic and as deadly as Nyodene D" ("Figure" 811).

14. The gasoline references point back to the moment of Jack's exposure, when not he but "death entered."

15. The trash compactor foreshadows a scene in *Underworld* in which waste analyst Nick Shay describes how he and his wife Marian see "products as garbage even when they sat gleaming on store shelves, yet unbought. . . . We asked whether it is responsible to eat a certain item if the package the item comes in will live a million years" (*U* 121).

16. The debate between Winnie and Murray derives, as LeClair notes (*Loop* 213), from Becker's *The Denial of Death*. Murray advocates what Becker calls the "healthy-minded argument" that the fear of death isn't natural; Winnie espouses the "morbidly-minded argument" that such fear is naturally present in everyone (Becker 13–15). While Becker agrees with Winnie that "the fear of death must be present behind all our normal functioning, in order for the organism to be armed toward self-preservation" (16), he also seems to be the source of Murray's claim that repression is necessary for us to function (Becker 17, 265; LeClair *Loop* 213).

17. Keesey (147) shrewdly observes that the acronyms also designate what Jack wants to destroy: the violence (RAM), unhelpfulness (AIDS) and insanity (MAD) of modern technology; cf. White 18.

18. Although later displaced by Osiris, Ra is supreme in the earliest texts. The introductory hymn praises Ra upon rising and asks for his protection (see Faulkner trans. 27; Budge trans. 7–10). Many other spells laud Ra, particularly Chapter or "Spells" 130 (already cited in the text) and and 131. In these spells the dying person takes on the qualities of Ra, and is blessed so that "his soul will live forever and he will not die again."

19. Conroy argues that the preceding events have merely taught Jack "the exhaustion of previous narrative promises of immortality, not any bright new hope" (108). On the other hand, Bonca finds the conclusion to be "generous-spirited," in that DeLillo has "attempted to complicate the stiff categories of ideological or cultural critique" (40). Maltby takes a middle ground, asserting that DeLillo's moments of radiance "provide a standard by which to judge the spiritually atrophied culture of late capitalism" (274).

Chapter 7

1. For a critical response to DeLillo's argument, see Edmundson 122.

2. Wicke uses the term to refer to P. T. Barnum's method of "writing" spectacular advertisements about the spectacles that he produced. See Wicke 54–85

for an astute discussion of the interrelationships between nineteenth-century advertising and American authorship.

3. I have borrowed these phrases from Kevin McLaughlin, who argues that in *Capital* Marx imitates the language of commodities in order to submit it to a "lethal" reading (17).

4. The word "aura," which derives from the Latin word for money and later became associated with halos or coronas in medieval painting (Shell, *Art* 38), indicates the combined economic and religious appeal of Moon's theology of images.

5. Similar metaphors of disease recur throughout the novel. Moon himself employed disease metaphors in his keynote speech, "God's Hope for America," given at Yankee Stadium on June 1, 1976. He predicted that "America will become mortally ill because the cells of its body are decaying," but reassured followers that "God has sent me . . . in the role of doctor" (Moon 7).

6. McClure points out how many new American spiritualities are "inflected with the rhetoric and values of consumer capitalism" ("Post-Secular" 142). Of course, American preachers and religious leaders have long been good at using spectacle. For an illuminating historical analysis of the intersection of public relations and religion in the United States, see Moore, especially 41ff, and 263–64.

7. Bill's understanding of the relationship between the author's identity and his words echoes DeLillo, who states that a writer "can begin to know himself through his language," and even "shapes himself as a human being" through that language (Interview with LeClair 23).

8. For reproductions of this series, see MacShine 333–39. Actually, the Warhol work entitled *Mao II* is not one of these serial silkscreens, but a single pencil drawing (see MacShine 340).

9. As Simmons points out (55; 204n11), DeLillo and Benjamin use the term "aura" in nearly opposite ways: for DeLillo the word refers to the enhanced emotional or spiritual messages, or radiance, of a photographic icon; for Benjamin "aura" is the trace left by the aesthetic, "mythic" value of originality.

10. For reproductions of the "Self-Portrait" series (1964–67), and his later variations on it, see MacShine 83–99. In the 1967 "Self-Portrait" series, Warhol's image is altered and smeared with colors as Mao's is in that series. For a persuasive description of the "three" Warhols, see Henry Geldzahler's remarks in MacShine 427.

11. See, for example, Winogrand's photo of Norman Mailer's fiftieth birthday party, reproduced in Szarkowski 164.

12. DeLillo has stated that he was inspired to write *Mao II* in part by Khomeini's *fatwa* against Salman Rushdie. As Margaret Scanlan points out, the ayatollah's death sentence "has all the marks of a media event; had [he] simply wanted Rushdie dead he could have dispatched a hit squad months earlier" (234).

13. "Terrorism" is a highly charged word ideologically, and until the Oklahoma City bombing, it was used by Americans to refer almost exclusively to acts of foreigners, particularly Middle Easterners. Thus Harold Bush claims that, because DeLillo's terrorists in this novel are Asian, he is guilty of an ethnocentric contrast between "enlightened West" and "philistine and tyrant-laden East" (2). One might counter that DeLillo is merely documenting real conditions: as Weimann and Winn show, "Palestinian groups [have been] the source of more than one-

third of all terrorist acts" (46). Moreover, as we have seen, in earlier novels DeLillo has depicted terrorists of all nationalities and walks of life, from the European and American "revolutionaries" in "The Uniforms," to the ex-Jesuits and former stock-brokers of *Players*.

14. It is perhaps no accident that political terrorism and the Romantic idea of individual genius emerged at almost the same time and place: late eighteenth-century Europe. Foucault, in fact, suggests that books began to have authors in the modern sense at the moment when they "became subject to punishment, that is, to the extent that discourses could be transgressive" ("Author" 148). Perhaps, then, the Romantic notion of individual authorship is inextricably linked with the possibility of violating the system of property—that is, with crime.

15. In a phrase that seems suitable for *Mao II*, Laqueur dubs this tendency for the media to become apologists for terrorists "the Beirut syndrome" (125). Wei-mann and Winn also quote one terrorist who recalls how all the participants in one such action raced home to watch it on TV, as if to confirm that it had really happened (59). Thus Baudrillard's insight that all such crimes are now "simula-tions," prescripted according to the images and stories we have all seen on TV and in movies ("Simulations" 179), seems as apt for *Mao II* as it does for DeLillo's early fiction.

16. Here my reading jibes with that of Baker (paragraph 34). For a com-parable though quite different fictional consideration of the relationship between novelists and terrorists, see Paul Auster's *Leviathan*, which is dedicated to DeLillo.

17. If DeLillo's self-reflexive strategy blends all three writers—DeLillo, Gray, and Julien—(Tabbi 205), it also unveils DeLillo's Dedalian use of his authority, for not only is Jean-Claude thereby reduced to one of Bill's "symptoms" (Scanlan 245–46), but DeLillo himself seems to be capriciously exerting authorial control in a way that violates the characterological freedom Gray has just celebrated.

18. Baker (paragraphs 28–29) argues that the novel's failure is DeLillo's in-ability to create a "satisfactory counterpart to the Western novelist in the figure of the terrorist leader." But Abu Rashid's one-dimensionality is part of DeLillo's point: the terrorist has been consumed by own image.

19. My discussion here is indebted to Michaels's analysis of photography (236–39).

Chapter 8

1. In fact, nuclear weapons capacity is largely a matter of engineering and ma-terials, and the "secret" of atomic energy had been known for decades. See Gold-berg 51–52 on the myth of the "big secret." This Soviet bomb, actually set off on September 25, had a yield of approximately forty kilotons. For a list of Soviet nuclear tests in the 1950s see Holloway 322.

2. The general contractor for the weapons plant was DuPont, apparently hard at work bringing about "Better Things for Better Living through Chemistry."

3. These were the so-called "Buster-Jangle" tests (Ball 64–65). Although never acknowledged by the AEC, these tests lit up the night sky over Los Ange-les and San Francisco, hundreds of miles away (Boyer 304). For a complete list of American aboveground nuclear tests in the 1950s, see Ball 61–83.

4. Duvall ("Baseball" 303) argues that Hodges "still performs the same order of simulation in his broadcast . . . even when he is present."

5. These subterranean racial tensions surface when Cotter obtains the Thomson home run ball after struggling with Waterson, and reemerge throughout *Underworld* in the relationship between Nick Shay and Simeon Biggs. Between the earlier version in *Harper's Magazine* and this episode's appearance in *Underworld*, however, DeLillo excised some of Waterson's more blatantly racist comments (cf. *U* 56 and "Pafko" 68).

6. The AEC was aware the effects of radiation because of the Hiroshima and Nagasaki bombs and the Bikini tests. The government also knew as early as 1953 that animals were dying of radiation from aboveground atomic testing but suppressed the information (Schneider xvii).

7. The presence of dying parents is a recurrent motif in the novel: Richard Gilkey, the Texas Highway Killer, takes care of his ailing father; just before Klara's liaison with Nick, Bronzini's mother, whom he had tenderly nursed, dies after a long illness; Nick brings his mother to Phoenix where she passes her final days in an air-conditioned mausoleum.

8. Aeneas is described similarly as *inscius*, or "not knowing," when he asks the spirit of his father what certain heroes are doing in the underworld. See *Aeneid* 6.937 [p. 162], and Macdonald 33.

9. This motif is manifest not only in Nick's pseudo-mysticism, but also in Hoover's germ phobia, and in Marvin Lundy's and Sister Edgar's compulsive wearing of latex gloves.

10. Waste has its own mythology, as exemplified by the legendary ship full of waste that cannot find a place to dock. Nick and Simeon Biggs argue over whether it is loaded with sewage or with CIA heroin — with "shit" or shit (see *U* 278, 329–30). This ship, which also figures into Marvin Lundy's search for the Thomson baseball in the other chapter of "The Cloud of Unknowing" (see *U* 309–12), is probably based upon the *Mobro 4000*, a barge filled with New York City garbage that spent fifty-five days looking for a place to dump (Rathje and Murphy 28).

11. Detwiler is likely based on A. J. Weberman, the infamous "peeping-tom garbologist" of the early 1970s (see Rathje and Murphy 17). Detwiler's theory that civilization sprang up in response to waste was first advanced in real life in the 1940s by archaeologist Gordon Willey (Rathje and Murphy 33).

12. The statistics he quotes about the landfill's size and volume — that it's twenty-five times the size of the Great Pyramid, and that it constitutes the highest point on the Eastern seaboard — are verified by Rathje and Murphy (4, 1–2). However, Fresh Kills is not a sanitary landfill, and the chemicals in it slowly seep into New York Harbor. Its waste is not really contained.

13. Manx is one of those missing persons to whom Simeon Biggs refers when he tells Nick that blacks are undercounted in the census (*U* 335–36). Rathje and Murphy note that "missing minority men" have long been a problem in census records, and the undercount of black men in 1990 has been estimated at 6 percent (although how the government arrived at this number seems mysterious. See Rathje and Murphy 139, 143).

14. Bronzini is DeLillo's latest tribute to Joyce's great character. Like Bloom, Bronzini is thirty-eight years old during his most detailed scenes (taking place in 1952). Like Bloom, he enjoys walks around the city, and both knows and sup-

presses the knowledge that his wife is cuckolding him. Bronzini also resembles Bloom in his voracious interest and astute observation of people and material conditions.

15. Ravens are carrion-eating birds who live off the waste of industrial society. DeLillo uses birds similarly throughout *Underworld* both to suggest the ecological effects of human activity, and to draw from the mythological associations of avians as symbols of death and rebirth.

16. Their truth has now been amply documented. Deming's rumor about being able to see one's bones through clothes (repeated later in Louis Bakey's experience as an atomic veteran) is verified by the accounts of actual atomic veterans, and his tales of multiple myelomas and a woman's hair falling out are verified by (indeed, they seem to have been taken directly from) Carole Gallagher's *American Ground Zero* (99, 124). See also Proctor, and the disturbing ABC news special "Cover-up at Ground Zero." For a survey of the scientific evidence about leukemia rates and other diseases of the downwinders, see Ball 70. Ball (39) also provides strong evidence that the government knew the tests were not safe.

17. As if to bear out the mystical connections at work, while Matt and Janet drive to the weapons range they listen to Wolfman Jack talking about Little Richard — composer of "Long Tall Sally" (*U* 454).

18. The title refers, of course, to the slogan of the DuPont Corporation, a chemical company that has long been involved in both manufacturing weapons and producing toxic waste.

19. The throb may issue from the television set: as Nelson notes (37), until the mid-1960s, television sets emitted detectable low-level radiation from three different sources.

20. Hoover was probably a closeted homosexual, although some recent biographies suggest that he emerged from time to time. According to Anthony Summers, he sometimes attended parties in drag, and allowed young men to perform fellatio on him — all the while wearing rubber gloves (quoted in Dumm 87).

21. DeLillo has altered the actual chronology here. He has Bruce performing in San Francisco on October 24, but in fact on October 24, 1962 the real Lenny Bruce was arrested for obscenity at the Troubador in Hollywood (Cohen 305).

22. One of their most crudely sexual lyrics comes from the song that gives the film its title, which the Stones recorded for a proposed "party tape" but never released. The speaker is a gay hustler who shouts, "Where can I get my cock sucked? / Where can I get my ass fucked?" But the Stones' roughneck image was otherwise largely a fabrication, since, except for Keith Richards, they came from more affluent backgrounds than most other 1960s British rock icons.

23. For a full discussion of the varieties of Eisensteinian montage, see Bordwell 125–33.

24. There is no evidence of an Eisenstein film called *Unterwelt*, and there was little opportunity for him to have created it. During the 1930s Eisenstein traveled to Germany and throughout Europe, and then went to the United States, where he developed three films for Paramount, all of which were scuttled by the studio (Bordwell 17–18). After spending months filming in Mexico, he had to abandon that project when he was summoned back to the Soviet Union in late 1931. Upon his return, Eisenstein was out of favor with the authorities for his "formalism," and his film *Bezhin Meadow* was turned down and later lost. DeLillo has invented

a plausible Eisenstein film: the director once said that he'd like to make a modern *Götterdammerung*, and once proposed a film set in the "medieval plague . . . based in the graphic idea of a society engulfed in blackness" (Goodwin 126, 155). In addition, like *Unterwelt*, Eisenstein's actual late work is dominated by a graphic environment of "shadows and darkness" (Goodwin 138).

25. Similarly, the first atomic bomb tested at Bikini in 1946 was named Gilda, after the "bombshell" character played by Rita Hayworth in the film of that name (*Radio Bikini*).

Works Cited

Works by Don DeLillo

"American Blood: A Journey Through the Labyrinth of Dallas and JFK." *Rolling Stone*, December 8, 1983: 21–28, 74.
"The American Strangeness: An Interview with Don DeLillo." With Gerald Howard. *Hungry Mind Review* 43 (Fall 1997): 13–16. Online, http://www. bookwire.com/hmr/hmrinterviews.article$2563
Americana. 1971. New York: Penguin. 1989. [*A*]
Americana. 1971. New York: Pocket, 1973.
Appendix ["The Uniforms"]. *Cutting Edges: Young American Fiction for the '70s.* Ed. Jack Hicks. New York: Holt, 1973. 532–33.
"The Art of Fiction CXXXV." An Interview with Adam Begley. *Paris Review* 128 (1993): 274–306.
"Baghdad Towers West." *Epoch* 17 (1967–68): 195–217.
"Coming Sun. Mon. Tues." *Kenyon Review* 28 (1966): 391–94.
The Day Room. New York: Penguin, 1986.
End Zone. Boston: Houghton Mifflin, 1972. [*EZ*]
"The Engineer of Moonlight." *Cornell Review* 1 (1979): 21–47.
Great Jones Street. Boston: Houghton Mifflin, 1973. [GJS]
"Human Moments in World War III." *Great Esquire Fiction: The Finest Stories from the First Fifty Years*, ed. L. Rust Hills. New York: Penguin, 1983. 572–86.
"An Interview with Don DeLillo." With Thomas LeClair. *Contemporary Literature* 23 (1982): 19–31.
"An Interview with Don DeLillo." With Maria Nadotti. *Salmagundi* 100 (Fall, 1993): 86–97.

Libra. New York: Viking, 1988. [*L*]

Mao II. New York: Viking, 1991. [*M*]

The Names. New York: Knopf, 1982. [*N*]

"'An Outsider in This Society': An Interview with Don DeLillo." With Anthony DeCurtis. Lentricchia, *Introducing Don DeLillo*. 43–66.

"Pafko at the Wall." *Harper's*, October 1992: 35–70.

Players. New York: Knopf, 1977. [*P*]

"The Power of History." *New York Times Magazine*, September 7, 1997: 60–63.

Ratner's Star. New York: Knopf, 1976. [*RS*]

Running Dog. New York: Knopf, 1978. [*RD*]

"Seven Seconds [Interview with Don DeLillo]." With Ann Arensberg. *Vogue*, August 1988: 337–9, 390.

"Silhouette City: Hitler, Manson, and the Millennium." *Dimensions* 4, 3 (1989): 29–34.

"Take the 'A' Train." *Epoch* 12, 1 (Spring 1962): 9–25. Reprinted in *Stories from Epoch*, ed. Baxter Hathaway. Ithaca, N.Y.: Cornell University Press, 1966. 22–39.

"A Talk with Don DeLillo." With Robert R. Harris. *New York Times Book Review*, October 10, 1982: 26.

Underworld. New York: Scribner, 1997. [*U*]

"The Uniforms." 1970. *Cutting Edges: Young American Fiction for the '70s*, ed. Jack Hicks. New York: Holt, 1973. 451–59.

Valparaiso: A Play in Two Acts. New York: Scribner, 1999.

White Noise. New York: Viking, 1985. [*WN*]

"Window on a Writing Life: A Conversation with National Book Award Winner Don DeLillo." With Diane Osen. The BOMC Reading Room. Book of the Month Club. Online. <www.bomc.com/ows-bin/owa/rr_authorinterviews_sub?intid=50>.

Secondary Sources

"A. E. C. Head Doubts 'Atomic Peace' Now." *New York Times*, October 4, 1951: 7.

Aaron, Daniel. "How to Read Don DeLillo." Lentricchia, *Introducing Don DeLillo*. 67–81.

Allen, Glen Scott. "Raids on the Conscious: Pynchon's Legacy of Paranoia and the Terrorism of Uncertainty in Don DeLillo's *Ratner's Star*." *Postmodern Culture* 4, 2 (January 1994). n.p.

The Ancient Egyptian Book of the Dead. Ed. Carol A. R. Andrews, trans. Raymond O. Faulkner. Austin: University of Texas Press, 1990.

Arendt, Hannah. *The Origins of Totalitarianism*. Part 3, *Totalitarianism*. New York: Harcourt, Brace, World, 1966.

Auster, Paul. *Leviathan*. New York: Viking, 1992.

Baker, Peter. "The Terrorist as Interpreter: *Mao II* in Postmodern Context." *Postmodern Culture* 4, 2 (Spring 1994): n.p.

Bakhtin, Mikhail M. "Discourse in the Novel." *The Dialogic Imagination*. Ed. Michael Holquist, trans. Caryl Emerson and Michael Holquist. Austin: University of Texas Press, 1981. 259–422.

———. *Problems of Dostoevsky's Poetics.* Ed. and trans. Caryl Emerson. Minneapolis: University of Minnesota Press, 1984.

Ball, Howard. *Justice Downwind: America's Atomic Testing Program in the 1950s.* New York: Oxford University Press, 1986.

Barthes, Roland. *Camera Lucida: Reflections on Photography.* Trans. Richard Howard. New York: Hill and Wang, 1981.

———. *S/Z.* Trans. Richard Miller. New York: Hill and Wang, 1974.

"Baruch Sees Hope for Atom Control." *New York Times*, October 4, 1951: 6.

Bataille, Georges. *The Accursed Share.* Trans. Robert Hurley. New York: Zone, 1988.

Baudrillard, Jean. "Consumer Society." Trans. Jacques Mourrain. *Selected Writings.* Ed. Mark Poster. Stanford, Calif.: Stanford University Press, 1988. 29–56.

———. "Simulacra and Simulations." Trans. Paul Foss, Paul Patton, and Philip Beitchman. *Selected Writings.* 166–84.

———. "Symbolic Exchange and Death." Trans. Jacques Mourrain. *Selected Writings.* Ed. 119–48.

Bawer, Bruce. "Don DeLillo's America." *New Criterion*, April 1985. 34–42.

Becker, Ernest. *The Denial of Death.* New York: Free Press, 1973.

Beckett, Samuel. *Endgame.* New York: Grove, 1959.

Benjamin, Walter. "The Work of Art in the Age of Mechanical Reproduction." *Illuminations.* Trans. Harry Zohn. New York: Schocken, 1968. 217–51.

Bernstein, Stephen. "*Libra* and the Historical Sublime." *Postmodern Culture* 4, 2 (January, 1994): n.p.

Birdwell, Cleo [Don DeLillo]. *Amazons.* New York: Holt, 1980.

Bok, Sissela. *Secrets: On the Ethics of Concealment and Revelation.* New York: Pantheon, 1982.

Bolle, Kees W. "Secrecy in Religion." *Secrecy in Religions*, ed. Kees W. Bolle. Leiden: Brill, 1987. 1–24.

Bonca, Cornel. "Don DeLillo's *White Noise*: The Natural Language of the Species." *College Literature* 23, 2 (June 1996): 25–44.

The Book of the Dead. Trans. E. A. Wallis Budge. New York: Arkana/Penguin, 1989.

Bordwell, David. *The Cinema of Eisenstein.* Cambridge, Mass.: Harvard University Press, 1993.

Bourdon, David. *Warhol.* New York: Abrams, 1989.

Boyer, Paul. *By The Bomb's Early Light: American Thought and Culture at the Dawn of the Atomic Age.* 2nd ed. Chapel Hill: University of North Carolina Press, 1994.

Brown, Arthur C. L. *The Origin of the Grail Legend.* Cambridge, Mass.: Harvard University Press, 1943.

Brown, Michael F. *The Channeling Zone: American Spirituality in an Anxious Age.* Cambridge, Mass.: Harvard University Press, 1997.

Bruno, Vincent J., ed. *The Parthenon.* New York: Norton, 1974.

Bryant, Paula. "Discussing the Untellable: Don DeLillo's *The Names*." *Critique* 29 (1987): 16–29.

Buckley, Jerome. *Season of Youth: The Bildungsroman from Dickens to Golding.* Cambridge, Mass.: Harvard University Press, 1974.

Budge, E. A. Wallis. "Introduction." *The Book of the Dead.* New York: Arkana/Penguin, 1989. xxv–ccxii.

Bullock, Alan. *Hitler: A Study in Tyranny*. London: Odhams, 1952.

Burch, G. B. "The Counter-Earth." *Osiris* 11 (1954): 267–94.

Bush, Harold K., Jr. " 'The Future Belongs to Crowds': Cultural Conservatism in Don DeLillo's *Mao II*." Paper delivered at the Midwest Modern Language Association Conference, St. Louis, November 3, 1995.

Calinescu, Matei. *Rereading*. New Haven, Conn.: Yale University Press, 1993.

Cantor, Paul. " 'Adolf, We Hardly Knew You.' " Lentricchia, *New Essays*. 39–62.

Carmichael, Thomas. "Lee Harvey Oswald and the Postmodern Subject: History and Intertextuality in Don DeLillo's *Libra*, *The Names*, and *Mao II*." *Contemporary Literature* 34 (1993): 204–18.

Carrier, James G. *Gifts and Commodities: Exchange and Western Capitalism Since 1700*. London and New York: Routledge, 1995.

Carroll, Lewis. *The Annotated Alice. Alice's Adventures in Wonderland and Through the Looking Glass*. Ed. Martin Gardner. New York: World, 1960.

———. *Mathematical Recreations of Lewis Carroll: Symbolic Logic and the Game of Logic*. 1887, 1896. Reprint New York: Dover, 1958.

Chernus, Ira. *Dr. Strangegod: On the Symbolic Meaning of Nuclear Weapons*. Columbia: University of South Carolina Press, 1986.

Chrétien de Troyes. *Perceval, or, The Story of the Grail*. Trans. Ruth Harwood Cline. New York: Pergamon, 1983.

Civello, Paul. *American Literary Naturalism and Its Twentieth-Century Transformations: Frank Norris, Ernest Hemingway, Don DeLillo*. Athens: University of Georgia Press, 1994.

Clifford, James. "Traveling Cultures." *Cultural Studies*, ed. Lawrence Grossberg, Cary Nelson and Paula A. Treichler. New York and London: Routledge, 1992. 96–112.

The Cloud of Unknowing. Ed. and intro. James Walsh, S.J. New York: Paulist Press, 1981.

Cohen, John, ed. *The Essential Lenny Bruce*. New York: Ballantine, 1967.

Connor, Steven. *Postmodernist Culture: An Introduction to Theories of the Contemporary*. Oxford: Blackwell, 1989.

Conroy, Mark. "From Tombstone to Tabloid: Authority Figured in *White Noise*." *Critique* 35 (Winter 1994): 97–110.

Cook, B. F. *Greek Inscriptions*. Berkeley: University of California Press/British Museum, 1987.

Cook, David A. *A History of Narrative Film*. 2nd ed. New York: W. W. Norton, 1990.

Cornford, F. M. *From Religion to Philosophy: A Study in the Origins of Western Speculation*. 1912. Reprint New York: Harper, 1957.

Cowart, David. "For Whom Bell Tolls: Don DeLillo's *Americana*." *Contemporary Literature* 37 (1996): 602–19.

———. *Literary Symbiosis: The Reconfigured Text in Twentieth-Century Writing*. Athens: University of Georgia Press, 1993.

Cox, Harvey. *Fire from Heaven: The Rise of Pentecostal Spirituality and the Reshaping of Religion in the Twenty-First Century*. Reading, Mass.: Addison-Wesley, 1995.

Dante Alighieri. *The Inferno*. Trans. John Ciardi. New York: Mentor/NAL, 1954.

Danto, Arthur C. *Beyond the Brillo Box: The Visual Arts in Post-Historical Perspective.* New York: Farrar, Straus and Giroux, 1992.

Dayton, Donald W. *The Theological Roots of Pentecostalism.* Metuchen, N.J.: Scarecrow, 1987.

Debord, Guy. *Comments on the Society of the Spectacle.* Trans. Malcolm Imrie. New York: Verso, 1990.

———. *Society of the Spectacle.* Trans. Donald Nicholson-Smith. New York: Zone, 1994.

DeCurtis, Anthony. "The Product: Bucky Wunderlick, Rock 'n Roll, and Don DeLillo's *Great Jones Street.*" Lentricchia, *Introducing Don DeLillo.* 131–41.

Derrida, Jacques. *Margins of Philosophy.* Trans. Alan Bass. Chicago: University of Chicago Press, 1982.

Dewey, Joseph. *In a Dark Time: The Apocalyptic Temper in the American Novel of the Nuclear Age.* West Lafayette, Ind.: Purdue University Press, 1990.

Docherty, Thomas. "Postmodern Characterization: The Ethics of Alterity." *Postmodernism and Contemporary Fiction,* ed. Edmund J. Smyth. London: Batsford, 1991. 169–88.

Drebinger, John. "Giants Capture Pennant, Beating Dodgers 5–4 in 9th on Thomson's 3-Run Homer." *New York Times,* October 4, 1951. 1, 42.

Dumm, Thomas L. "The Trial of J. Edgar Hoover." Garber and Walkowitz, *Secret Agents.* 76–92.

Duvall, John N. "Baseball as Aesthetic Ideology: Cold War History, Race, and DeLillo's 'Pafko at the Wall.'" *Modern Fiction Studies* 42 (1995): 285–313.

———. "The (Super)Marketplace of Images: Television as Unmediated Mediation in DeLillo's *White Noise.*" *Arizona Quarterly* 50, 3 (Autumn 1994): 127–53.

Edmundson, Mark. "Not Flat, Not Round, Not There: Don DeLillo's Novel Characters." *Yale Review* 83, 2 (April, 1995): 107–24.

Eisenstein, Sergei M. "The Dramaturgy of Film Form." *Selected Works,* vol. 1. *Writings, 1922–34.* Ed. Richard Taylor. Bloomington: Indiana University Press; London: British Film Institute, 1988. 161–80.

Ewen, Stuart, and Elizabeth Ewen. *Channels of Desire: Mass Images and the Shaping of American Consciousness.* 2nd ed. Minneapolis: University of Minnesota Press, 1992.

Ferguson, Harvie. "Watching the World Go Round: Atrium Culture and the Psychology of Shopping." Shields, *Lifestyle Shopping.* 21–39.

Ferraro, Thomas J. "Whole Families Shopping at Night!" Lentricchia, *New Essays.* 15–38.

Fidel, Kenneth. "The Dynamics of Military Secrecy." Tefft, *Secrecy.* 178–97.

Fletcher, Angus. *The Transcendental Masque: An Essay on Milton's Comus.* Ithaca, N.Y.: Cornell University Press, 1971.

Fornari, Franco. *The Psychoanalysis of War.* Trans. Alenka Pfeifer. Bloomington: Indiana University Press, 1975.

Foster, Dennis A. "Alphabetic Pleasures: *The Names.*" Lentricchia, *Introducing Don DeLillo.* 157–73.

Foucault, Michel. *Discipline and Punish: The Birth of the Prison.* Trans. Alan Sheridan. New York: Vintage, 1979.

———. "What Is an Author?" *Textual Strategies: Perspectives in Post-Structuralist Criticism*, ed. Josué V. Harari. Ithaca, N.Y.: Cornell University Press, 1979. 141–60.

Freeman, Ira Henry. "15,000 in Carolina Speed Atom Plant." *New York Times*, October 3, 1951: 1, 22.

———. "Atom Plant 'D.P.'s' Escape Unscathed." *New York Times*, October 4, 1951: 7.

Frow, John. "The Last Things Before the Last: Notes on *White Noise*." Lentricchia, *Introducing Don DeLillo*. 175–91.

———. *Marxism and Literary History*. Cambridge, Mass.: Harvard University Press, 1986.

Galante, Pierre and Eugene Silianoff. *Voices from the Bunker: Hitler's Personal Staff Tells the Story of the Führer's Last Days*. Trans. Jan Dalley. New York: Anchor, 1990.

Gallagher, Carole. *American Ground Zero: The Secret Nuclear War*. New York: Random House, 1993.

Garber, Marjorie. "Jell-O." Garber and Walkowitz, *Secret Agents*. 10–22.

Garber, Marjorie and Rebecca L. Walkowitz, eds. *Secret Agents: The Rosenberg Case, McCarthyism, and Fifties America*. New York: Routledge, 1995.

Giannetti, Louis D. "Godard's *Masculine-Feminine* [sic]: The Cinematic Essay." *Godard and Others: Essays on Film Form*. Rutherford, N. J.: Fairleigh Dickinson University Press, 1975. 19–59.

Godard, Jean-Luc. "Marginal Notes While Filming: August 1959-August 1967." *Godard on Godard*, ed. Jean Narboni and Tom Milne. New York: Da Capo, 1986. 161–243.

Goldberg, Stanley. "The Secret About Secrets." Garber and Walkowitz, *Secret Agents*. 47–58.

Goldstone, Bud and Arloa Paquin Goldstone. *The Los Angeles Watts Towers*. Los Angeles: Getty Conservation Institute and the J. Paul Getty Museum, 1997.

Goodwin, James. *Eisenstein, Cinema, and History*. Urbana and Chicago: University of Illinois, 1993.

Gorman, Peter. *Pythagoras: A Life*. London: Routledge, 1979.

Goux, Jean-Joseph. *Symbolic Economies: After Marx and Freud*. Trans. Jennifer Curtiss Gage. Ithaca, N.Y.: Cornell University Press, 1990.

Gregory, Chris. "Kula Gift Exchange and Capitalist Commodity Exchange: A Comparison." *The Kula: New Perspectives on Massim Exchange*, ed. Jerry W. Leach and Edmund Leach. Cambridge: Cambridge University Press, 1983. 103–117.

Hayles, N. Katherine. *Chaos Bound: Orderly Disorder in Contemporary Literature and Science*. Ithaca, N.Y.: Cornell University Press, 1990

———. *The Cosmic Web: Scientific Field Models and Literary Strategies in the Twentieth Century*. Ithaca, N.Y.: Cornell University Press, 1984.

———. "Introduction: Complex Dynamics in Literature and Science." *Chaos and Order: Complex Dynamics in Literature and Science*, ed. N. Katherine Hayles. Chicago: University of Chicago Press, 1991. 1–33.

———. "Postmodern Parataxis: Embodied Texts, Weightless Information." *American Literary History* 2 (1990): 394–421.

Heffernan, Teresa. "Can Apocalypse Be Post?" *Postmodern Apocalypse: Theory and Cultural Practice at the End*, ed. Richard Dellamora. Philadelphia: University of Pennsylvania Press, 1995. 171–81.

Hilgartner, Stephen, Richard C. Bell, and Rory O'Connor. *Nukespeak: The Selling of Nuclear Technology in America*. New York: Penguin, 1983.

Hine, Thomas. *The Total Package: The Evolution and Secret Meaning of Boxes, Bottles, Cans and Tubes*. Boston: Little, Brown, 1995.

Hirsch, Marianne. "The Novel of Formation as Genre: Between Great Expectations and Lost Illusions." *Genre* 12 (1979): 293–311.

Hollingdale, Stuart. *Makers of Mathematics*. New York: Penguin, 1989.

Holloway, David. *Stalin and the Bomb: The Soviet Union and Atomic Energy, 1939–1956*. New Haven and London: Yale University Press, 1994.

Holman, C. Hugh. *A Handbook to Literature*. 3rd ed. Indianapolis: Odyssey, 1972.

Horowitz, Irving Louis. "Sun Myung Moon: Missionary to Western Civilization." *Science, Sin and Sponsorship: The Politics of Reverend Moon and the Unification Church*, ed. Irving Louis Horowitz. Cambridge, Mass.: MIT Press, 1978. xiii–xviii.

Hughes, Dennis D. *Human Sacrifice in Ancient Greece*. New York and London: Routledge, 1991.

Hyde, Lewis. *The Gift: Imagination and the Erotic Life of Property*. New York: Random House, 1983.

James, Caryn. " 'I Never Set Out to Write an Apocalyptic Novel.' " *New York Times Book Review*, January 13, 1985: 31.

Jameson, Fredric. *Marxism and Form: Twentieth-Century Dialectical Theories of Literature*. Princeton, N.J.: Princeton University Press, 1971.

———. "Seriality in Modern Literature." *Bucknell Review* 18 (1970): 63–80.

Johnson, Stuart. "Extraphilosophical Instigations in Don DeLillo's *Running Dog*." *Contemporary Literature* 26 (1985): 74–90.

Johnston, John. "Generic Difficulties in the Novels of Don DeLillo." *Critique* 30 (1989): 261–75.

———. "Post-Cinematic Fiction: Film in the Novels of Pynchon, McElroy and DeLillo." *New Orleans Review* 17, 2 (1990): 90–97.

Joyce, James. *A Portrait of the Artist as a Young Man: Text, Criticism, and Notes*. Ed. Chester G. Anderson. New York: Viking, 1968.

———. *Ulysses*. Ed. Hans Walter Gabler et al. New York: Random House, 1986.

Kahn, Herman. *On Escalation: Metaphors and Scenarios*. New York: Praeger, 1965.

Keesey, Douglas. *Don DeLillo*. New York: Twayne, 1993.

Kelly, Richard. *Lewis Carroll: Revised Edition*. Boston: Twayne, 1990.

Kermode, Frank. *The Sense of an Ending*. New York: Oxford University Press, 1966.

Kharpertian, Theodore D. *A Hand to Turn the Time: The Menippean Satires of Thomas Pynchon*. Rutherford, N.J.: Fairleigh Dickinson University Press, 1990.

Kildahl, John P. *The Psychology of Speaking in Tongues*. New York: Harper and Row, 1972.

Kline, Morris. *Mathematics in Western Culture*. New York: Oxford University Press, 1953.

———. *Mathematics: The Loss of Certainty*. New York: Oxford University Press, 1980.

Langman, Lauren. "Neon Cages: Shopping for Subjectivity." Shields, *Lifestyle Shopping*. 40–82.

Laqueur, Walter. *The Age of Terrorism*. Boston: Little, Brown, 1987.

Lawrence, W. H. "Soviet's Second Atom Blast in 2 Years Revealed by U. S.; Details Are Kept a Secret." *New York Times*, October 4, 1951: 1, 6.

Lazarus, Emma. "The New Colossus." *The Norton Introduction to Poetry*. 7th ed. Ed. J. Paul Hunter. New York: W. W. Norton, 1999. 262.

Lear, John. *Kepler's Dream. With the Full Text and Notes of* Somnium, Sive Astronomia Lunaris, *Joannis Kepleri*. Berkeley: University of California Press, 1965.

LeClair, Tom. *In the Loop: Don DeLillo and the Systems Novel*. Urbana: University of Illinois Press, 1987.

———. "Post-Modern Mastery." *Representation and Performance in Postmodern Fiction*, ed. Maurice Couturier. Nice: Delta, 1982. 99–111.

———. "An Underhistory of Mid-Century America." *Atlantic Monthly*, October 1997. 113–16.

Leiss, William, Stephen Kline, and Sut Jhally. *Social Communication in Advertising: Persons, Products & Images of Well-Being*. 2nd ed. New York: Routledge, 1990.

Lentricchia, Frank, ed. *Introducing Don DeLillo*. Durham, N. C.: Duke University Press, 1991.

———. "*Libra* as Postmodern Critique." Lentricchia, *Introducing Don DeLillo*. 193–215.

———., ed. *New Essays on* White Noise. Cambridge: Cambridge University Press, 1991.

———. "Tales of the Electronic Tribe." Lentricchia, *New Essays*. 87–113.

Lifton, Robert Jay. *The Broken Connection: On Death and the Continuity of Life*. New York: Basic Books, 1983.

Lyotard, Jean-François. "The Sublime and the Avant-Garde." *Postmodernism: A Reader*, ed. Thomas Docherty. New York: Columbia University Press, 1993. 244–56.

Macdonald, Ronald R. *The Burial-Places of Memory: Epic Underworlds in Vergil, Dante, and Milton*. Amherst: University of Massachusetts Press, 1987.

MacShine, Kynaston, ed. *Andy Warhol: A Retrospective*. New York: Museum of Modern Art; Boston: Little, Brown, 1989.

———. "Introduction." MacShine, *Andy Warhol*. 13–23.

Maland, Charles J. *Chaplin and American Culture: The Evolution of a Star Image*. Princeton, N.J.: Princeton University Press, 1989.

Maltby, Paul. "The Romantic Metaphysics of Don DeLillo." *Contemporary Literature* 37 (1996): 258–77.

Mao Zedong. "Talks at the Yenan Forum on Literature and Art." *Selected Readings from the Works of Mao Tsetung* [sic]. Peking: Foreign Languages, 1971. 250–86.

Marijnissen, R. H. and Max Seidel. *Bruegel*. New York: Harrison, 1984.

Marx, Karl and Friedrich Engels. *The Marx-Engels Reader*. Ed. Robert C. Tucker. 2nd ed. New York: W. W. Norton, 1978.

McClure, John A. "Postmodern/Post-Secular: Contemporary Fiction and Spirituality." *Modern Fiction Studies* 41 (1995): 141–63.

————. "Postmodern Romance: Don DeLillo and the Age of Conspiracy." Lentricchia, *Introducing Don DeLillo*. 99–115.

McCracken, Grant. *Culture and Consumption: New Approaches to the Symbolic Character of Consumer Goods and Activities*. Bloomington: Indiana University Press, 1988.

McLaughlin, Kevin. *Writing in Parts: Imitation and Exchange in Nineteenth-Century Literature*. Stanford, Calif.: Stanford University Press, 1995.

Meagher, John C. *Method and Meaning in Jonson's Masques*. Notre Dame, Ind.: University of Notre Dame Press, 1966.

Mendelsohn, James Robert. *The Brute Fact: The Cultural Authority of Science in Twentieth-Century American Literature*. PhD Diss. Washington University, 1992.

Messmer, Michael W. " 'Thinking It Through Completely': The Critique of Nuclear Culture." *Centennial Review* 23, 4 (Fall 1988): 397–413.

Michaels, Walter Benn. *The Gold Standard and the Logic of Naturalism: American Literature at the Turn of the Century*. Berkeley: University of California Press, 1987.

Millard, Bill. "The Fable of the Ants: Myopic Interactions in DeLillo's *Libra*." *Postmodern Culture* 4, 2 (January, 1994). n.p.

Miller, D. A. *The Novel and the Police*. Berkeley: University of California Press, 1988.

Milton, John. *Paradise Lost and Selected Poetry and Prose*. Ed. Northrop Frye. San Francisco: Rinehart, 1951.

Molesworth, Charles. "Don DeLillo's Perfect Starry Night." Lentricchia, *Introducing Don DeLillo*. 143–56.

Moon, Sun Myung. "God's Hope for America. Keynote Speech at Yankee Stadium, June 1, 1976." Horowitz, *Science, Sin, and Sponsorship*. 2–11.

Moore, R. Laurence. *Selling God: American Religion in the Marketplace of Culture*. New York: Oxford University Press, 1994.

Morris, Matthew J. "Murdering Words: Language in Action in Don DeLillo's *The Names*." *Contemporary Literature* 30 (1989): 113–27.

Moses, Michael Valdez. "Lust Removed from Nature." Lentricchia, *New Essays*. 63–86.

Mottram, Eric. "The Real Needs of Man: Don DeLillo's Novels." *The New American Writing: Essays on American Literature Since 1970*, ed. Graham Clarke. New York: St. Martin's, 1990. 51–98.

Motz, Lloyd, and Jefferson Hane Weaver. *The Story of Mathematics*. New York: Plenum, 1993.

Nadel, Alan. *Containment Culture: American Narratives, Postmodernism, and the Atomic Age*. Durham, N.C.: Duke University Press, 1995.

Nadeau, Robert. *Readings from the New Book on Nature: Physics and Metaphysics in the Modern Novel*. Amherst: University of Massachusetts Press, 1981.

Nelson, Joyce. "TV, the Bomb, and the Body: Other Cold War Secrets." Garber and Walkowitz, *Secret Agents*. 31–45.

Nietzsche, Friedrich. *The Birth of Tragedy and the Genealogy of Morals*. Trans. Francis Golffing Garden City, N.Y.: Doubleday, 1956.

O'Donnell, Patrick. "Obvious Paranoia: The Politics of Don DeLillo's *Running Dog*." *Centennial Review* 34, 1 (Winter 1990): 56–72.

O'Donoghue, Jacqueline Zubeck. "Reading Literally: The Parody of the Postmodern in Don DeLillo's *The Names.*" Unpublished essay.

Ong, Walter J. *Orality and Literacy: The Technologizing of the Word.* London and New York: Methuen, 1982.

Orgel, Stephen. *The Illusion of Power: Political Theater in the English Renaissance.* Berkeley: University of California Press, 1975.

Oriard, Michael. "Don DeLillo's Search for Walden Pond." *Critique* 20 (1978): 5–24.

Osteen, Mark. *The Economy of Ulysses: Making Both Ends Meet.* Syracuse, N. Y.: Syracuse University Press, 1995.

Passaro, Vince. "Dangerous Don DeLillo." *New York Times Magazine,* May 19, 1991: 34–38, 76–77.

Perrine, Toni A. *Film and the Nuclear Age: Representing Cultural Anxiety.* New York: Garland, 1998.

Powers, Richard Gid. *Secrecy and Power: The Life of J. Edgar Hoover.* New York: Free Press, 1987.

Pratt, Mary Louise. "Arts of the Contact Zone." *Profession 91,* ed. Phyllis Franklin. New York: MLA, 1991. 33–40.

Proctor, Robert N. "Censorship of American Uranium Mine Epidemiology in the 1950s." Garber and Walkowitz, *Secret Agents.* 59–75.

Rathje, William and Cullen Murphy. *Rubbish! The Archaeology of Garbage.* New York: HarperCollins, 1992.

Reeve, N. H. and Richard Kerridge. "Toxic Events: Postmodernism and DeLillo's *White Noise.*" *Cambridge Quarterly* 23 (1994): 303–23.

Reid, Ian. *Narrative Exchanges.* London: Routledge, 1992.

Relihan, Joel C. *Ancient Menippean Satire.* Baltimore: Johns Hopkins University Press, 1993.

Rice, Thomas Jackson. *Joyce, Chaos, and Complexity.* Urbana and Chicago: University of Illinois Press, 1997.

Riffaterre, Michael. "Compulsory Reader Response: The Intertextual Drive." *Intertextuality: Theories and Practices,* ed. Michael Worton and Judith Still. Manchester: Manchester University Press, 1990. 56–78.

———. "Syllepsis." *Critical Inquiry* 6 (1979–80): 625–38.

Robinson, Douglas. *American Apocalypses: The Image of the End of the World in American Literature.* Baltimore: Johns Hopkins University Press, 1985.

Rosenblum, Robert. "Warhol as Art History." MacShine, *Andy Warhol.* 25–37.

Roud, Richard. *Jean-Luc Godard.* Bloomington: Indiana University Press, 1970.

Sahlins, Marshall. *Stone Age Economics.* Chicago: Aldine, 1972.

Said, Edward W. *Orientalism.* New York: Random House, 1978.

Saltzman, Arthur M. *Designs of Darkness in Contemporary American Fiction.* Philadelphia: University of Pennsylvania Press, 1990.

———. "The Figure in the Static: *White Noise.*" *Modern Fiction Studies* 40 (1994): 807–26.

Scanlan, Margaret. "Writers Among Terrorists: Don DeLillo's *Mao II* and the Rushdie Affair." *Modern Fiction Studies* 40 (1994): 229–52.

Schell, Jonathan. *The Fate of the Earth.* New York: Avon, 1982.

Schneider, Keith. Foreword to Carole Gallagher, *American Ground Zero: The Secret Nuclear War.* New York: Random House, 1993. xv–xix.

Schudson, Michael. *Advertising, the Uneasy Persuasion: Its Dubious Impact on American Society*. New York: Basic Books, 1984.

Schwenger, Peter. "Writing the Unthinkable." *Critical Inquiry* 13 (1986): 33–48.

"Secrecy to Blanket Coming Atom Games." *New York Times*, October 4, 1951: 6.

Serres, Michel. *Hermes: Literature, Science, Philosophy*, ed. Josué V. Harari and David F. Bell. Baltimore: Johns Hopkins University Press, 1982.

Shell, Marc. *Art & Money*. Chicago: University of Chicago Press, 1995.

———. *The Economy of Literature*. Baltimore: Johns Hopkins University Press, 1978.

Shields, Rob, ed. *Lifestyle Shopping: The Subject of Consumption*. New York and London: Routledge, 1992.

Shields, Rob. "Spaces for the Subject of Consumption." Shields, *Lifestyle Shopping*. 1–20.

Simmel, Georg. "Secrecy." *The Sociology of Georg Simmel*. Ed., trans. and intro. Kurt H. Wolff. New York: Free Press, 1950.

Simmons, Philip E. *Deep Surfaces: Mass Culture & History in Contemporary American Fiction*. Athens: University of Georgia Press, 1997.

Sontag, Susan. "The Aesthetics of Silence." *A Susan Sontag Reader*. Intro. Elizabeth Hardwick. New York: Vintage, 1983. 181–204.

———. "Fascinating Fascism." *A Susan Sontag Reader*. 305–25.

———. "Godard." *A Susan Sontag Reader*. 235–64.

———. "The Image-World." *A Susan Sontag Reader*. 350–67.

———. "The Pornographic Imagination." *A Susan Sontag Reader*. 205–33.

Stam, Robert. *Reflexivity in Film and Literature: From Don Quixote to Jean-Luc Godard*. Ann Arbor: UMI Research Press, 1985.

Stewart, Susan. *Crimes of Writing: Problems in the Containment of Representation*. New York: Oxford University Press, 1991.

———. *On Longing: Narratives of the Miniature, the Gigantic, the Souvenir, the Collection*. Baltimore: Johns Hopkins University Press, 1984.

Swift, Jonathan. *The Annotated Gulliver's Travels*. Ed. Isaac Asimov. New York: Potter, 1980.

Szarkowski, John. *Winogrand: Fragments from the Real World*. New York: Museum of Modern Art, 1988.

Tabbi, Joseph. *Postmodern Sublime: Technology and American Writing from Mailer to Cyberpunk*. Ithaca, N.Y.: Cornell University Press, 1995.

Tefft, Stanton K., ed. *Secrecy: A Cross-Cultural Perspective*. New York: Human Sciences, 1980

———. "Secrecy, Disclosure and Social Theory." Tefft, *Secrecy*. 35–74.

Thomson, Bobby. "Rode 'on a Cloud' on Tour of Bases." *New York Times*, October 4, 1951. 45.

Thoreau, Henry David. *Walden and Civil Disobedience*. New York: Penguin, 1986.

The Tibetan Book of the Dead: The Great Liberation Through Hearing in the Bardo. By Guru Rinpoche according to Karma Lingpa. Trans. with commentary by Francesca Fremantle and Chögyam Trungpa. Boston: Shambala, 1975.

Tololyan, Khachig. "Cultural Narrative and the Motivation of the Terrorist." *Inside Terrorist Organizations*, ed. David Rapoport. New York: Columbia University Press, 1988. 217–33.

Torgovnick, Marianna. *Closure in the Novel*. Princeton, N.J.: Princeton University Press, 1981.

Trevor-Roper, Hugh R. *The Last Days of Hitler*. New York: Macmillan, 1947.

Virgil. *The Aeneid*. Trans. Allen Mandelbaum. With Thirteen Drawings by Barry Moser. Berkeley: University of California Press, 1971.

Warren, Carol and Barbara Laslett. "Privacy and Secrecy: A Conceptual Comparison." Tefft, *Secrecy*. 25–34.

Weart, Spencer R. *Nuclear Fear: A History of Images*. Cambridge, Mass.: Harvard University Press, 1988.

Webb, Stephen H. *Blessed Excess: Religion and the Hyperbolic Imagination*. Albany: State University of New York Press, 1991.

Weimann, Gabriel and Conrad Winn. *The Theater of Terror: Mass Media and International Terrorism*. New York and London: Longman, 1994.

Weiner, Annette B. *Inalienable Possessions: The Paradox of Keeping-While-Giving*. Berkeley: University of California Press, 1992.

Weinstein, Arnold. *Nobody's Home: Speech, Self, and Place in American Fiction from Hawthorne to DeLillo*. Oxford: Oxford University Press, 1993.

Westbrook, Deeanne. *Ground Rules: Baseball and Myth*. Urbana and Chicago: University of Illinois Press, 1996.

Weston, Jessie L. *The Quest of the Holy Grail*. New York: Haskell, 1965.

Wheelwright, Philip, ed. *The Presocratics*. Indianapolis: Odyssey, 1966

White, Patti. *Gatsby's Party: The System and the List in Contemporary Narrative*. West Lafayette, Ind.: Purdue University Press, 1992.

Wicke, Jennifer. *Advertising Fictions: Literature, Advertisement, and Social Reading*. New York: Columbia University Press, 1988.

Wilcox, Leonard. "Baudrillard, DeLillo's *White Noise*, and the End of Heroic Narrative." *Contemporary Literature* 32 (1991): 346–65.

Williams, Raymond. "Advertising: the Magic System." *Problems in Materialism and Culture: Selected Essays*. London: Verso, 1980. 170–95.

Williams, William Carlos. *Selected Poems*. New York: New Directions, 1968.

Williamson, Judith. *Decoding Advertisements: Ideology and Meaning in Advertising*. London: Boyars, 1978.

Young, Robert. *White Mythologies: Writing History and the West*. London and New York: Routledge, 1990.

Film, Television, Music

À bout de souffle [Breathless]. Dir. Jean-Luc Godard. Perf. Jean-Paul Belmondo and Jean Seberg. Georges de Beauregard, Societé Nouvelle de Cinema, 1959.

Cocksucker Blues. Dir. Robert Frank and Daniel Seymour. 1972.

"Cover-up at Ground Zero." Dir. Roger Goodman. Wr: Peter Jennings and Elena Mannes. *Turning Point*. ABC, 1994.

The Connection. Dir. Shirley Clarke. Connection, 1961.

From Here to Eternity. Dir. Fred Zinnemann. Perf. Burt Lancaster, Montgomery Clift. Columbia, 1953.

The Great Dictator. Dir. Charles Chaplin. United Artists, 1940.

Ikiru. Dir. Akira Kurosawa. Perf. Takashi Shimura. Toho, 1952.

The Man in the Gray Flannel Suit. Dir. Nunnally Johnson. Perf. Gregory Peck and Jennifer Jones. 20th Century Fox, 1956.

Masculin féminin. Dir. Jean-Luc Godard. Anouchka-Argos Films, 1966.

Le mépris [Contempt]. Dir. Jean-Luc Godard. Rome-Paris Films, Films Concordia, Compagnia Cinematografica Champion, 1963.

October. Dir. Sergei Eisenstein and Grigory Alexandrov. Sovkino, 1928.

Persona. Dir. Ingmar Bergman. Perf. Bibi Andersson, Liv Ullmann. Svensk, 1966.

Pierrot le fou. Dir. Jean-Luc Godard. Perf. Jean-Paul Belmondo. Rome-Paris Films, 1965.

Prokofiev, Sergei. *Love For Three Oranges Suite,* op. 33A. Orch. Nationale de France. Cond. Lorin Maazel. CBS, 1985.

Radio Bikini. Dir. Robert Stone. *The American Experience.* PBS, 1987.

Strike. Dir. Sergei Eisenstein. Sovkino, 1924.

Suddenly. Dir. Lewis Allen. Perf. Frank Sinatra, Sterling Hayden. United Artists, 1954.

Tabloid Frenzy. Dir. Desmond Smith. Wr: Desmond Smith, Fred Langan. Newsco, in coproduction with CBS Newsworld, 1994.

Weekend. Dir. Jean-Luc Godard. Films Copernic, 1967.

Index

Acknowledgments

Any book is in some sense a collaborative undertaking. In that spirit I would like to thank the following people who read all or part of the manuscript, and whose comments helped me to improve upon it: Glen Scott Allen, David Cowart, John N. Duvall, Jacqueline O'Donoghue, and an anonymous reader for the University of Pennsylvania Press. Others who have offered encouragement or constructive criticism include Tom LeClair, Frank Lentricchia, and Phil Nel. Jerome Singerman, acquisitions editor at Penn Press, also furnished invaluable guidance and advice as I was preparing the final version of the book.

A sabbatical leave and summer research grants funded by Loyola College were indispensable in providing time for me to devote to this book. I would also like to thank Dean John Hollwitz of the College of Arts and Sciences at Loyola for providing a generous grant to defray publication costs.

An earlier version of Chapter 1 was published in *Contemporary Literature*; somewhat different versions of the two parts of Chapter 2 were published in *Papers on Language and Literature* and *Critique* respectively. A slightly different version of Chapter 7 was published in *Modern Fiction Studies*. I gratefully acknowledge these journals' permission to reprint these chapters.

Finally, the most important contributions have, as always, been those of my wife, Leslie Gilden, and my son, Cameron, both of whom provided constant inspiration, listening ears, and a sense of balance.